China, the United Nations, and Human Rights

Pennsylvania Studies in Human Rights

Bert B. Lockwood, Jr., Series Editor

A complete list of books in the series is available from the publisher.

China, the United Nations, and Human Rights

The Limits of Compliance

Ann Kent

PENN

University of Pennsylvania Press

Philadelphia

10 9 8 7 6 5 4 3 2 1

Published by
University of Pennsylvania Press
Philadelphia, Pennsylvania 19104-4011

Library of Congress Cataloging-in-Publication Data
Kent, A. E. (Ann E.)
    China, the United Nations, and human rights : the limits of
compliance / Ann Kent.
        p.   cm. — (Pennsylvania studies in human rights)
    Includes bibliographical references and index.
    ISBN 0-8122-3478-2 (alk. paper). —
ISBN 0-8122-1681-4 (pbk. : alk. paper)
    1. Human rights — China.   2. United Nations — China.   I. Title.
II. Series.
JC599.C6K48   1999
323′.0951 — dc21   99-12228
                                                        CIP

For Bruce,
wise and gentle scholar

The Chinese Government has always abided by the principles and purposes of the UN Charter, committed itself to the respect and protection of human rights and fundamental freedoms, and [been] actively involved in and supported the United Nations in its work in the field of human rights. China has consistently sent factual replies and information, including those concerning the "June 4th incident," in a responsible manner, to the relevant UN bodies as well as to the Special Rapporteurs of the Commission on Human Rights on torture, religion, summary or arbitrary executions and forced or involuntary disappearances. China has also regularly submitted periodic reports to the monitoring bodies established by international instruments to which China is a State Party.

— China's delegate, UN Commission on Human Rights, February 1990

To the extent that the Chinese government must live within the confines of an ongoing multistate world, it has gradually come to adjust itself on a day-to-day basis to this world. . . . The government appeals to international law wherever it finds it to its advantage to do so. It often employs conventional national power politics. It has accepted the whole machinery of international diplomacy often in a highly literal and extremely formalistic way. The . . . leadership may regard all this as in some ultimate sense provisional. If the world continues to be a multistate world for some time to come . . . the provisional may easily slip over into the category of the normal.

— Benjamin Schwartz, 1968

The contrast between the precepts of law and the realities of politics [is] sufficiently greater in the international realm than in the domestic realm to make one want to shift from the normative to the empirical, if only in order to understand better the plight of the normative.

— Stanley Hoffmann, 1977

Contents

Acknowledgments

This book has been the beneficiary of globalization. Since 1996 it has gained from the critiques and comments of scholars in many different fields and locations. It has been read by R. Randle Edwards, Director of the Chinese Legal Studies Center, Law School, Columbia University; Jack Donnelly of the Department of International Relations, University of Denver; Theo van Boven of the Law Faculty, University of Limburg, the Netherlands; Philip Alston of the Law Faculty, European University Institute, Italy; and Samuel Kim of the East Asian Institute, Columbia University. In Australia, I am indebted to James Richardson, Department of International Relations, Australian National University; James Cotton, Department of Political Science, Australian Defence Force Academy, University of NSW; John Braithwaite, Law Program, Australian National University; Joseph Camilleri, Department of Politics, Latrobe University; and Ian Wilson, formerly of the Political Science Department, Australian National University.

A fruitful period as Visiting Scholar at the East Asian Institute of Columbia University in the 1996 Fall Semester was made possible by the kind invitation of Andrew Nathan. The Woodrow Wilson School at Princeton was also hospitable, allowing me some productive months in the Firestone Library. The Carnegie Council on Ethics and International Affairs enabled a brief return to Harvard to discuss concepts of human rights in East Asia. The work was completed in the congenial environment of a Visiting Fellowship, then an Australian Research Council Fellowship, in the Law Program, Research School of Social Sciences, Australian National University.

Apart from friendly critics of my work, I am deeply indebted to a host of people acknowledged in my notes, both interviewees and authors of secondary sources. In particular, grateful thanks are extended to those officials of the UN and the ILO and of different governments, for obvious reasons wishing to remain anonymous, who gave generously of their time, memories, experience and judgment to provide the crucial background, historical context and human dimension of the events played out in documentary sources. In particular, Douglas Poulter, former Chairman of the Governing Body of the International Labor Organization (ILO), Lee Swepston, Chief, Equality and Human Rights Coordination Branch, ILO, and Bent Sørensen, of the International Rehabilitation Council for Torture Victims in Denmark, have been the source of many insights.

I thank former Australian Ambassador to China, Garry Woodard, for his invitation to join the delegation to China of the Australian Institute of International Affairs in late 1992 as human rights spokesperson; and the Chinese People's Institute of Foreign Affairs for arranging discussions on human rights at the State Council and other foreign policy and human rights venues. I am indebted to the Ludwig Boltzmann Institute, Vienna, for its invitation to attend the NGO Conference at the UN World Human Rights Conference in June 1993; to the *Canberra Times* for enabling my attendance at the formal UN Conference; and to the Law School, Hong Kong University, for facilitating my research there in early 1995.

I pay tribute to the magnificent work of the NGOs, Human Rights in China, Human Rights Watch/Asia, Amnesty International, International Service for Human Rights, Lawyers' Committee for Human Rights, International League for Human Rights, June 4th China Support Group, *China Labour Bulletin*, Asia Monitor Resource Centre, the ICFTU, Tibetan Information Network, Australian Council for Overseas Aid and Human Rights International. Their work has informed my own. In particular, I thank Sophia Woodman, Robin Munro, Xiao Qiang, Adrien-Claude Zoller, Bill Barker, Sidney Jones, Philip Baker, Lau Bing, Trini Leung, Li Lu, Beatrice Laroche, Apo Leung, Ma Weipin, Chhime Chhoekyapa, Michael Van Walt, and notable others preferring anonymity, mostly Chinese, who gave the unsung heroes a voice. I salute one of those heroes, Wei Jingsheng, for his courageous and unremitting struggle for human rights, whether as dissident in China from 1979 to 1997, or in his present role as roving Ambassador of China's human rights to the world. And, from a distance, I watch with awe the continuing work of Han Dongfang.

Bert Lockwood, under his two hats as series editor of the Pennsylvania Studies in Human Rights and editor-in-chief of *Human Rights Quarterly*, has been an indispensable part of my scholarly life for eight years, even though we have never met. Nancy Ent, recipient of many an e-mail, has been a good companion. I thank all at University of Pennsylvania Press, for their assistance, efficiency, and support. I am particularly grateful to the Director, Eric Halpern, and to Noreen O'Connor, Frances Hwang, Kim Hastings, and Pamela Hansell.

I have also received generous assistance from the librarians of the United Nations Library, Geneva, and in particular, UN Law Librarian, Werner Simon; the International Labor Organization Library, Geneva; the Law Library, University of Hong Kong; the Universities Service Center, Chinese University of Hong Kong; the Asian Collections and Petherick Room of the

Australian National Library, Canberra; and the Menzies and Law Libraries, the Australian National University, Canberra. I am grateful to Andrew Chin, of the Parliamentary Library, Commonwealth Parliament, Canberra; Darrell Dorrington of the Menzies Library; and Frances Cushing of the Edward A. Clark Center for Australian Studies, University of Texas.

I am indebted to Greg Fry, Liz Gardiner, Jacinta O'Hagan, Johanna Sutherland, Lynne Payne, and Amy Chen, of the Department of International Relations, Australian National University; to Igor de Rachewiltz, of the Department of Far Eastern History, Australian National University; and to Hilary Charlesworth, Carol Heimer, Carol Jones, Robert McCorquodale, Jane Stapleton, Leslie Zines, and all my colleagues in the Law Program, Australian National University. Warm thanks are extended in particular to Peter Cane, Head of the Law Program, to Chris Treadwell, for her help and thoughtfulness, and to John Braithwaite, for his enthusiasm, support and inspiration. Finally, this book would not have been possible without Bruce Kent's continuing support, and our children's remarkable patience.

February 1999

Introduction

In the turbulence of the post–Cold War era, scholarly interest has begun to focus on three issues in the fields of international law, international relations, and human rights. The first is the general question of states' compliance with international treaty obligations. The second is the specific matter of China's compliance with these obligations, its gradual socialization through interaction with treaty bodies, and its preparedness to moderate its urge to independence in response to the contemporary pressures for political and economic interdependence. The third is the question of the effectiveness of the United Nations human rights system in monitoring the implementation of treaty obligations by states and, particularly, by China.[1]

In this book I address these three issues — compliance, socialization, and effectiveness — within the context of China's interaction with the UN human rights regime. I study the vexed question of China's readiness, or ability, to comply with international norms by focusing on its relationship with the multilateral human rights bodies of the United Nations and, to a lesser extent, with the nongovernmental organizations (NGOs) that participate in their deliberations. Where compliance is manifested, I ask the basic questions of China's socialization and learning — to what extent it absorbs the norms of the regime and to what extent it merely adapts itself instrumentally. Where compliance is not indicated, I ask to what extent China is seeking to reshape existing international norms and to what extent it is seeking to bypass or even negate them. Finally, I attempt to evaluate the effectiveness of UN bodies in monitoring China. In so doing I join the current move in regime analysis away from preoccupation with regime formation to understanding how regimes affect state behavior and collective outcomes in international society.[2]

China's attitude toward global interdependence has been a source of controversy since the beginning of the Cold War, particularly during the period of the Cultural Revolution (1965–76), when its failure to respect international standards of behavior was cited as a principal reason for voting against its entry into the United Nations. The issue of international socialization is given new urgency by China's emergence as a major economic force, a military power, and an important global actor. Its enhanced status raises the age-old problem of how the international community adjusts to the ambitions of a newly powerful state and, conversely, how such a state adjusts to the international community. This problematic coincides with a new age in which states not thoroughly imbued with Judeo-Christian and natural law traditions are "in the first rank."[3]

More than a quarter century after China's entry into the United Nations in 1971, one of the main arguments against its exclusion — that only membership in international organizations could promote its international socialization — may be put to the test. China's compliance or noncompliance with the norms of the human rights regime constitutes the most rigorous test of international citizenship, for human rights present an immediate challenge to the principle of state sovereignty. Unlike the international political economy regime, it is a moral regime whose norms currently conform not to the goals of the Chinese state, but rather to the ideals of a politically conscious stratum of its domestic population.

For a number of reasons, China represents a "least likely case study" that provides the human rights regime with its most rigorous test.[4] Because of its ascribed superpower status, its economic and strategic muscle, and particularly its position as a Permanent Member of the Security Council, China is a very special case: the difficulties experienced by the UN Commission on Human Rights over a series of sessions in adopting a resolution on China — a resolution that might not have been a problem in the case of other target states — are testimony to this fact. China is also a special case because it has signed the International Covenant on Civil and Political Rights (ICCPR) and the International Covenant on Economic, Social and Cultural Rights (ICESCR) but has not ratified either of them. This means that it is not yet subject to the jurisdiction of the two UN human rights bodies monitoring compliance with these treaties, the UN Human Rights Committee and the UN Committee on Economic, Social and Cultural Rights, except insofar as it has indicated a preparedness to continue reporting to these bodies on the condition of human rights in Hong Kong.[5]

However, precisely for these reasons, the subject of human rights in China is of importance, both from the point of view of China and from the perspective of the regime. The nature of China's participation in the international human rights regime offers evidence in a most sensitive area of its preparedness or lack thereof to accept political interdependence. The very brief history of Chinese involvement with international organizations and international regimes gives it a special place in any attempt to measure the impact on states of the application of regime norms. And China's status in the world community, as well as its crucial role in international organizations, makes the issue of intrinsic significance.

Apart from the use of the human rights regime as a test of international socialization, the issue of human rights in China is of vital importance in itself, not only to China but to the world. The right of 1.2 billion people to live free from fear and hunger does not need to be argued. The ability of the United Nations to influence this outcome, however, requires investigation, for the stability of the region and of the global community depends on its impact. The return of Hong Kong to China in July 1997, and the question of the territory's subsequent fate, has only heightened a global interest in China's human rights that was kindled by the shocking events in and around Tiananmen Square in June 1989.

Since Tiananmen, there have been numerous specific and descriptive studies of China and human rights in the international arena, including books and articles on the overall China–U.S. relationship, some of which also address most-favored nation status (MFN) and U.S. policy on China's human rights.[6] Apart from the work of Andrew Nathan and a few others, this literature combines description and prescription and generally falls into one of two genres: that which argues the efficacy of continuing pressure on China, and the "business as usual" approach, which emphasizes the trickle-down effect of market forces on China's human rights.[7] The work published on the impact of international sanctions on China is also, for the most part, descriptive.[8] A number of monographs address the relationship between human rights and Chinese values and the question of universal standards and values in Asia.[9] Others address the issue of China and human rights in the international community in general and the UN in particular,[10] as well as China and international law.[11] One article has analyzed China's human rights diplomacy in Asia and two very broadly address the question of China and international regimes.[12] However, in this literature, regime theory, if alluded to, has not been fully explored.

The most significant of these writings have been published since 1989. In his excellent article on human rights in Chinese foreign policy, Andrew Nathan states from the outset that "the domestic politics of human rights have influenced China's human rights abroad, and in an example of 'the second image reversed,' international affairs have rebounded to reshape domestic affairs."[13] Nathan concludes that Beijing's policies have been successful in achieving a gradual return to mainstream diplomacy, but that China's leaders fail to understand the stubborn cultural roots of Western human rights policy. They lack an antidote to the appeal of human rights in China and have been forced into a defensive posture. Nathan predicts that China will be a "taker and not a shaper" of emerging world norms and institutions in the rights field and that the effects of human rights pressure show how an international regime can influence a domestic one.[14] Similarly, James Seymour's essay "Human Rights in Chinese Foreign Relations" describes and analyzes the broad thrust of China's international human rights policy and the international response. It concludes that the human rights question has changed China's international relations by causing it to lose control of its own foreign policy battles; that Tiananmen changed foreigners' predisposition to deal with the People's Republic of China as a unitary international actor; and that the issue of human rights in China will be determined by the course of internal political events, with "international standards and foreign involvement playing a secondary role."[15]

In another significant essay, James Feinerman analyzes China's growing international legal consciousness and the influence on its policy of international law in a number of discrete areas. In his section on human rights, he summarizes the difference between Western and Chinese human rights concepts and the Chinese attitude toward international human rights treaties. Unlike the previous writers, he does not attempt to assess the relative importance of international and domestic pressures, but concludes broadly that although China's future participation in the international legal order is certain, its acceptance of existing standards with respect to "certain subjects" is "less predictable."[16] Finally, Feinerman and Donald Clarke look at the relationship between international human rights law and China's criminal law and conclude that criminal law has "proved resistant to the forces of change affecting the rest of the society" and remains closely tied to politics and the Party.[17]

Thus, the current literature consists of broad overviews of China's attitude toward human rights and interdependence. However, as yet there has been no rigorous study of the actual process of China's interaction with the discrete facets of the international human rights regime. Andrew Nathan has set the parameters of the problem: a more detailed examination is now required to determine whether China is more a "taker" than a "shaper" of human rights norms. New theoretical work at the detailed, disaggregated level is being done on the domestic, cognitive sources of Chinese foreign policy, but only now is there beginning to emerge disaggregated, regime-based research that could throw light on the external dimensions of the socialization process.[18] This is important since, as Samuel Kim has pointed out, "the virtually unexplored notion of circular feedback may be crucial in determining whether the Chinese foreign policy system is adaptive or maladaptive."[19] However, the existing research still fails to exploit the extensive, detailed data now available on China's interaction with international organizations.

The human rights regime, with its well-established norms, principles, and institutions, falls under the rubric of regime theory, particularly of the neorealist or liberal institutionalist variety espoused by Stephen Krasner and other scholars.[20] Krasner defines regimes as "sets of implicit or explicit principles, norms, rules and decision-making procedures around which actors' expectations converge in a given area of international relations."[21] The definition is a valuable one, despite the overlapping nature of principles (beliefs of fact and causation), norms ("standards of behavior defined in

terms of rights and obligations"), and rules ("specific prescriptions or pro-
scriptions for action").[22]

Krasner also asserts that regimes alter "not just calculations of interest
and the weight of power but also the interests and capabilities that underlie
the calculations and weights."[23] This gives the principles, norms, rules, and
decision-making procedures an indirect causal role. Regimes can modify
state behavior in their capacity as utility modifiers, enhancers of cooperation, bestowers of authority, learning facilitators, role definers, and agents
of internal realignments.[24] A regime's effectiveness may be judged according to its capacity to meet these six criteria, as well as by its persistence and
robustness.

The liberal institutionalist model of regimes adopted here is neither exclusive nor static: it is adapted to take into account both cognition and
behavior as well as process and structure. This is because the international
human rights regime is an organic social institution that must evolve in
accordance with social and political change if it is to survive. As Adorno has
put it, "closed systems are bound to be finished."[25] A regime must be seen as
an "ordering logic" that is both "a foundation of authority and an arena of
struggle."[26]

The model must also be adapted to counter the critique that regime
analysis excludes domestic politics, and actors apart from the state; that it
lacks a historical dimension; and that it fails to take account of the dynamic
between actions and existing world order.[27] Regime theory is not an exclusive analytical tool, but one that should be used in conjunction with other
theories. As Jack Donnelly has pointed out, it should be seen not so much as
a theory but rather as a very broad perspective, approach, or typology, with
heuristic and organizational rather than explanatory value.[28] I therefore
treat a regime as a framework to which a number of theories or models are
applicable. Regime analysis asks the "what" questions — what are the norms
governing cooperation and conflict in the issue areas, what decision-making
procedures bolster interdependence, to what degree do states comply with a
regime's norms, and what is the effect when they do not. In answering the
more wide-ranging "why" questions, a number of other models, theoretical
fragments, or secondary theories, can be deployed (640). These include
socialization and learning theory, or the assumption that states can reassess
their interests through experience and — in Gilpin's words, that they "can
learn to be more enlightened in their definitions of their interests and can
learn to be more cooperative in their behavior."[29] The variation in patterns
of regime compliance is explained with the aid of the notion of "transnational agenda setting," according to which changes in domestic politics
caused by a new national mood, a new leadership, and interest group activity can alter the degree to which "learning" can be either facilitated or
obstructed.[30] Just as foreign policy has domestic effects, so domestic political issues affect international politics.[31] Individual learning is necessary, but

not sufficient, for organizational or governmental learning, since the learning process may be circumvented by a number of conflicting causal variables impacting on government.

Compliance

Any judgment about the extent to which China complies with its treaty obligations and with the norms and procedures of UN human rights bodies depends, in the first place, on the standards against which compliance is measured. Universalists, cultural relativists, and essentialists clearly have different views about such standards.[32] This book uses the normative assumptions current within international human rights bodies, replete as they are with contradictions. Likewise, it assesses compliance with reference to the way in which norms are currently operationalized in monitoring procedures. It deals not with prescriptions but with empirical reality. China is adjudged to learn as it adapts to, and internalizes, prevailing rules, norms, and procedures of UN human rights bodies and their treaties.

Within these assumptions, three caveats must be entered. First, the Universal Declaration and human rights treaties provide an abstract and ideal standard of compliance with the regime, but in practice there is a level of "overall compliance" that is judged "acceptable" in the light of the provisions of each treaty or human rights body.[33] Moreover, this acceptable level is subject to variation across different parts of the regime, and according to different periods and situations (201). Second, in the human rights regime there is considered to be "an extreme case of time lag between undertaking and performance" (197). The time factor is therefore important. Third, although according to the concept of *pacta sunt servanda* (treaties are to be obeyed) human rights treaties are acknowledged to be legally binding on the states that ratify them, unless they are self-executing they do not automatically become a part of the law of the land. It is sometimes assumed that, by virtue of China's membership in the United Nations and its accession to treaties, international human rights law should automatically prevail over its national laws. Indeed, the Chinese themselves built up this expectation in their statement before the Committee against Torture (CAT) that for China, "international instruments took precedence over domestic law."[34] However, even some Western states which, unlike China, have ratified the ICCPR and the ICESCR and the Optional Protocols, do not automatically allow the provisions of international human rights treaties to prevail over, or be implemented in, their domestic law. In Australia, for instance, ratified international treaties do not change the domestic law until Parliament enacts them into law. According to one view, international bodies like the UN Human Rights Committee should have no role in influencing Australian law or policy and Australia is not accountable to them for implementing its international obligations.[35] Even in the United States, there is evidence that courts are not always attentive to defensive assertions based on treaty provisions.[36] This book should, therefore, be read with an important reservation in mind: to what extent can the international community expect a state not steeped in Western traditions and the rule of law, and which has not ratified the major international human rights covenants, to comply with international human rights norms? Moreover, since China has ratified more international human rights treaties than the United States, does its failure to harmonize its domestic law with its treaty obligations render it less compliant than the U.S.? These caveats are not entered as an apology for China, but merely to place this issue in comparative international perspective.

There is a further problem about how to measure compliance. It has been suggested that "the general level of compliance with international agreements cannot be empirically verified."[37] Yet in the case of the human rights regime, it is possible to distinguish five stages of international and domestic compliance.[38] At the international level, the continuum consists of (1) accession to human rights treaties, the acceptance of the norms that this entails, and acceptance by the target state of the right of UN bodies to monitor conditions and of its obligation to respond; (2) procedural compliance with reporting and other requirements; and (3) substantive compliance with the requests of the UN body, exhibited in international or domestic behavior. At the domestic level, the continuum extends into (4) *de jure* compliance, or the implementation of international norms in domestic legislative provisions; and (5) *de facto* compliance, or compliance at the level of domestic practice.

Because this is a study of international behavior and its effects rather than of the domestic wellsprings of foreign policy, it does not seek to disaggregate and map the domestic source of every Chinese policy decision on international human rights. Rather, it identifies broad changes in national mood and leadership as a background to its major effort to understand how China's participation in the international human rights regime affects its international behavior and its domestic human rights conditions. Thus, as well as delineating the politics of China's interaction with UN human rights bodies, and to a lesser extent, other states, it also analyzes the degree to which China has implemented international human rights norms in its domestic laws and practice, and considers the evaluations of its compliance by UN bodies and other authoritative organizations.

International Socialization and Learning

Although all states' policies evolve with experience, or reflect a process of learning, whether positive or negative, the function of the concept here is to throw light on China's attitude toward interdependence and its international socialization. Consequently, manifestations of international "learning" are defined in a positive sense as any constructive effort to maintain or redefine the international human rights regime in ways that respect, promote, and expand, rather than destroy, the norms embodied in international treaties or in customary procedures adopted by UN bodies. Compliance, in contrast, should be understood in a more limited sense as referring to acceptance of the norms as currently in operation.

Learning occurs at different levels.[39] Cognitive/normative learning, or the internalization of norms, is here differentiated from instrumental or adaptive learning, but both forms represent learning.[40] The question is whether a change of behavior and outcomes, as a result of a state's participation in the international political process, feeds back into the domestic policy-making process to alter fundamental beliefs, strategic policy, or only tactical preferences. The first level of change represents cognitive learning, whereas the latter two represent instrumental or adaptive learning.

With regard to the differentiation between cognitive and instrumental learning in the levels of compliance outlined above, international levels (1) and (2), that is, acceptance by the state of the right of UN bodies to monitor its human rights and procedural compliance with the requirements of the monitoring body, represent instrumental or adaptive learning (although cognitive learning is also implicit in the act of accession to a treaty), whereas international level (3), substantive compliance with the regime, and domestic levels (4) and (5), *de jure* and *de facto* compliance, represent different forms and degrees of cognitive learning. The most negative possibility is that change and learning at the international level are blocked at the domestic level and do not produce change and indications of positive learning in subsequent policy.[41]

As Charles Ziegler observes, learning tends to be more difficult in an authoritarian than in a democratic political system. Closed systems attempt to limit the flow of information from outside and to compartmentalize its dissemination. The parameters of intellectual debate are constrained, while a comprehensive belief or authority system will inhibit innovation and reward the status quo. A controlled press, secrecy, and a lack of interest-group participation inhibits the learning process.[42]

This is particularly true of learning in an international regime where the values and beliefs do not accord with those of the state being monitored. In China's case, there are additional obstacles presented by its political culture to acceptance of the norms and constraining influences of international law. A culture reliant on ethics rather than law, moral consensus rather than judicial procedure, benevolent government rather than checks and balances, and a preference for solving conflict through bilateral state relations rather than multilateral intervention, contrasts with the Western preference for formal contractual agreements to resolve differences, and for reliance on the constraints of international law.[43] So, too, does its preeminently realist attitude to international relations. As a result, rather than adopting a rational actor model, China's responses should be understood as fitting into a pattern of "bounded rationality that reacts to problems as they arise and searches for solutions within a familiar and accustomed repertoire."[44]

At the same time, learning is not a one-way process. A living, organic regime, it has already been argued, changes and adapts in response to the input of its member states. To the extent that China has sought to introduce new priorities of rights and to influence existing UN norms and procedures, the UN human rights regime has been under continual challenge. How it has maintained the balance between its dual functions as a "foundation of authority and an arena of struggle," how it has adapted itself to constructive change, and how it has sought to maintain core standards, are part of the story in the analysis that follows.

Effectiveness

Any attempt to assess the effectiveness of UN human rights bodies must grapple with two questions. First, to what extent can the effectiveness of the UN regime be tested separately from the effects of the human rights regime as a whole? Second, how can the effectiveness of the international regime be tested separately from the impact of human rights pressures within China?

It has been observed that UN activities with respect to human rights are only one of numerous facets of the international human rights regime, all of which may reinforce each other:

The many factors at work include, first and foremost, an awareness of their dignity by the persons concerned, under the influence of national human rights defence groups; international pressure exerted by NGOs; bilateral inter-state deterrence, in varying forms and degrees; diplomatic representations, measures of cultural and political isolation, withdrawal of economic and technical assistance, commercial boycott; the positions adopted by churches and religious groups; the implementation of complaints procedures at regional level Council of Europe, the Organisation of American States (OAS) and within the sectoral framework of the specialized agencies of the United Nations, in particular ILO; and lastly, the activities of the United Nations.[45]

The role of the United Nations and its specialized agencies in setting standards of human rights and in promoting and monitoring their implementation is vital not only to the regime but to the international socialization process. In the absence of intergovernmental organizations that could provide a credible mechanism to monitor China's human rights at a regional level, UN bodies are the principal mechanism of multilateral monitoring. Multilateral monitoring is crucial because it enjoys collective, consensual, historical, and institutionally based moral authority, which bilateral mechanisms lack. It pits the sovereignty of a single state against a community of sovereign and formally equal states and thus requires a diplomatic process of cooperation and coalition building. The collective and authoritative nature of UN resolutions and procedures makes it difficult for target states to invoke the principle of state sovereignty and to inflame nationalistic sentiments in an effort to deflect the human rights critique. Multilateral monitoring also provides a protective umbrella under which states may pursue their collective or separate normative goals. Moreover, the custom of consensus seeking in UN forums and the habitual adoption of thematic human rights resolutions without a vote require states to accept the normative content of the international human rights regime, even though they may at the same time challenge its right to apply these same norms in the censure of a specific state.

Some critics point out that the UN human rights regime is composed of widely accepted substantive norms and standard-setting procedures and institutions, but has a limited degree of international implementation and no international enforcement.[46] For instance, the most recent authoritative source of international human rights standards, the 1993 Vienna Declaration, failed to address the problem of the enforcement of human rights, confining itself to the general statement that "every state should provide an effective framework of remedies to redress human rights grievances and violations."[47] This statement places the emphasis on state agency, on recommendation rather than requirement, and on cure rather than prevention. Thus, despite recent UN progress toward enforcement in limited areas, such as the multilateral monitoring of elections and increased discussion of the advisability of UN humanitarian intervention, the strength of the UN human rights regime lies chiefly in its monitoring powers, with its strongest "enforcement" power being a critical public resolution or reports.[48] "Exposure" is the main instrument at the United Nations' disposal for the protection of human rights.[49]

International human rights monitoring has as its premise the right of international organizations, states, and groups of individuals to supervise the relationship between selected states and their citizens, but it stops short of the "coercive external interference" involved in the notion of "humanitarian intervention."[50] It pursues the civil rights of the citizen only to the point where pursuit is seen to conflict with the rights of the state, and thus in its very conception demonstrates the limits of its jurisdiction.[51] Implementation therefore relies very much on the conventions accepted by states, on publicity of abuses through the UN resolutions, reports, and investigative missions, on systematic review and assessments of individual members' performance in relation to treaty obligations, and on different forms of international persuasion or shaming.[52] Above all, it relies on states' political will to comply. For this reason, in his framework for the evaluation of the effectiveness of UN human rights organs, Philip Alston has preferred the heading "establishing accountability," covering actions ranging from monitoring to mild forms of preventive diplomacy and economic sanctions, to the usual UN term, "enforcement."[53] Despite the fact that these procedures are generally noncoercive, they have been judged to exert strong pressure on parties to comply with their obligations, specifically through "the process of jawboning."[54]

A second category of human rights mechanisms relevant to this study are NGOs. Although for analytical purposes the formal and informal processes of monitoring are differentiated, monitoring agencies include not only the formal regime of international organizations, institutions, and charters of norms, but also NGOs and even individuals, the transnational actors, or "epistemic communities," that often assume the burden of responsibility for the monitoring and implementation of norms when the formal institutions fail or when they need external support. As Foucault has observed, "it is essential that we refuse the arbitrary division of tasks that assigns thought and action to governing bodies and indignation to the individual."[55] Non-state actors are increasingly influential, as the following chapters will demonstrate, in promoting human rights issues for inclusion on international agendas, providing crucial information not otherwise accessible to multilateral human rights bodies, and focusing international attention on abuses that might otherwise be ignored.[56] Although not all UN human rights bodies have official procedures for receiving information from NGOs, they will usually accept informal submissions pointing out inadequacies in the states parties reports.[57] However, in the case of an authoritarian state like China, which does not normally respond to international NGO critiques directly and which has not allowed the establishment of genuine nonofficial domestic human rights organizations, the impact of NGOs is mainly indirect, even though their influence in increasing the efficacy of the monitoring bodies is incalculable.[58] The activities of the NGOs and concerned individuals are therefore woven into the case studies, rather than receiving separate treatment.

A third category of mechanisms within the international human rights regime is bilateral interstate deterrence or bilateral (also conceived as unilateral) monitoring. This opposes the sovereignty of two sovereign but effectively unequal states, and is thus peculiarly susceptible to sovereignty issues. It depends for its effectiveness both on the size of the resources that can be channeled into it and on the superior power of the monitoring state. In cases where the monitoring state has fewer resources and less power than the target state, the moral authority exerted must be demonstrably superior. The monitoring state must lead by example or by participating in collective sanctions rather than by imposing unilateral sanctions.[59] By definition, bilateral monitoring lacks the collective, historical and institutionally based authority of multilateral mechanisms. It also lacks consistency, both in application and in standards. Yet bilateral monitoring is more easily imposed, less vulnerable to collective opposition, and more accessible to NGO pressures.

The main weakness of bilateral monitoring is that it is not based on any formal agreement or specifically agreed standard.[60] Different states may invoke many different values in their monitoring procedures, not all of them derived from international instruments. As a mechanism it therefore lacks international authority and legitimation. Its usefulness in measuring international socialization is therefore less apparent than in the case of multilateral mechanisms. In this book, the effect of bilateral monitoring — and in particular that imposed by the U.S. through the MFN mechanism — in securing specific goals such as the release of Chinese political prisoners is seen as significant. Moreover, bilateral monitoring not only provides an instrument against which to compare the effectiveness of the multilateral regime, but has also influenced that effectiveness, since certain multilateral mechanisms affecting China are discovered to have gained or diminished in force in direct proportion to the changing strength of U.S. bilateral monitoring. However, because it lacks internationally validated standards, in general bilateral monitoring should be seen as only an indirect or, at the very most, a supplementary agent of change. For this reason, the story of MFN is subsumed here into the account of the multilateral pressure applied collectively by the U.S. and other states in their capacity as members of the United Nations.

How to separate out the effects of external pressure from domestic pressures raises difficult issues of causality. The issue is whether regimes, in influencing state behavior, constitute autonomous causal variables or merely intervening variables. Abram and Antonia Chayes acknowledge that there is no way of proving either assumption, but they tend to assume that noncompliance with regimes represents "a deviant rather than an expected behaviour."[61] While this is possibly true for most states, it is argued here that for a least likely case study such as China, an international regime is more realistically viewed as an intervening, rather than autonomous, variable. Autonomous variables include, in China's case, issues relating to power and self-interest such as economic imperatives, changes in leadership, domestic constituency interests, ad hoc interests, the need for internal stability, the preservation of territorial integrity, and concerns about independence and sovereignty. However, precisely because China also views participation in international organizations as an expression of its sovereignty, autonomous variables include its need for legitimacy and moral leadership in international forums, its concern about status and reputation, its sensitivity to external pressures for consensus, and its wish to be considered a reliable participant in international organizations. The pressure from such conflicting causal variables, rather than from the norms of the regime, brings compliance or noncompliance, depending on the strength of the particular pressure, with the rules and procedures of the regime. Like the learning process, these variables may be broadly grouped into categories of belief/theory, strategy, and tactics.

Yet the precise causal variables accounting for compliance with a regime are hard to isolate. First, as Levy and others have pointed out, most problems serious enough to cause the formation of a regime also motivate actors to pursue solutions through a variety of means, not only through the regime.[62] Second, particularly in the case of a "moral" regime like human rights, which does not rest directly on the perceived material interest of a state, forces tend to be mobilized and norms created or strengthened as the result of both domestic political events and international moral reaction.[63] Conversely, norms are complied with, challenged, or negated in response to both domestic and international developments. This is because, even in the case of a partially closed state like China, the boundaries dividing the inside of the state from the outside have been subtly eroded in the technocratic age. The effective linkage of external and internal pressures on China to comply with human rights norms or not is one practical indication of the fragility of the formal, legalistic interpretation of state sovereignty. This linkage creates obvious obstacles to identifying the precise causal variables in each case of compliance or noncompliance with regime norms. As a result, attempts to isolate the precise causal variables leading to compliance with a regime are not fruitful. What can be measured, however, is, first, the intermittent correlation between the pressures and norms of the regime and related behavior and outcomes, and, second, the degree to which subsequent policy decisions, behavior, or statements of values suggest a learned response to those outcomes. This is achieved through what Levy and others call "natural or quasi-experiments," involving comparisons across different issue areas over time within a single evolving regime.[64]

Hence, the first purpose of this study is to document the impact of the different issue areas, or case studies, of the UN regime on Chinese behavior, and, conversely, the impact of Chinese behavior on the UN regime. The second purpose is to document the feedback effect of related behavior and outcomes of the regime process on subsequent Chinese policy.

The Monitoring Process and China's Response

Having discussed the notions of compliance, international socialization, and effectiveness, we must now define the terminology of different aspects of the United Nations monitoring process. Philip Alston's general taxonomy is helpful in distinguishing the principal categories of regime activity — standard setting, promotion, and the establishment of accountability (monitoring).[65] The word "monitoring" is used in this study in two senses: (1) as a loose, generic term, with a general meaning of "establishing accountability" and (2) in a narrower, more technical sense, qualified by the terms "active" and "passive."[66] Hence the overall application of the regime not only may be strong or weak but its specific application and implementation through each constituent human rights body may also be active or passive. The International Labor Organization (ILO), a UN specialized agency, uses the term "supervision" rather than "monitoring," but the meaning is similar.[67]

UN human rights bodies operate a strong promotional regime and monitor both actively and passively. Apart from the UN role in setting standards and promoting human rights, its monitoring powers are considerable.[68] Monitoring moves along a continuum across which human rights bodies and states range at will: enforcement through sanctions (only through the Security Council); effective fact-finding (active monitoring); and monitoring by regular reviews and examination of progress made (passive monitoring).

Different techniques are used for obtaining results, ranging from cooperation and dialogue, reporting, observations by special rapporteurs, recommendations by committees, and remonstrances and shaming through resolutions at plenary sessions of the UN General Assembly and other human rights bodies. The policy-making organs of the United Nations, the Commission on Human Rights, its Sub-Commission, and the General Assembly have established special procedures to monitor country situations; and thematic working groups and special rapporteurs, such as the Special Rapporteur on Torture, have been set up by the UN Commission on Human Rights to monitor thematic issues. The UN Committee Against Torture (CAT) and the ILO Governing Body Committee on Freedom of Association (CFA) have a regular supervisory system which is noncontentious and based on dialogue.

The strongest form of censure applicable to China, the adoption of country-specific resolutions in plenary debate by the UN Commission on Human Rights and its Sub-Commission, relies heavily on what might be called a process of "reintegrative shaming."[69] Although the adoption of resolutions does not fall into the category of monitoring in the strict, technical sense, its function as a constraint on state behavior places it in the category of monitoring in the broad, generic sense. A less adversarial position is taken by the treaty and thematic bodies, whose main supervisory mechanism is the system of reporting, and which therefore depend to a large extent on the continuing cooperation of the state involved.

The reporting system is the supervisory procedure most commonly applied and accepted in the United Nations.[70] It has been described as "a kind of examination of conscience demanded by the international community."[71] It has four main aims: to make states accountable for their human rights to the international community; to encourage them to review measures to bring national law and policy into line with the conventions; to monitor states' progress made in the *de jure* and *de facto* implementation of rights; and to facilitate public scrutiny of government policies and NGO participation.[72] Its benefits are that "in some cases the exercise has approached an ideal learning experience: the members of the treaty body have come to bettter understand the situation in the country and the governments to realize that their problems are not unique and that they stand to gain from the experience of experts."[73]

The result has been

the emergence of a comprehensive reporting system applicable in varying degrees (depending upon the number of treaties acceded to or ratified), to the great majority of States in the world today. It is characterized by: the voluntary undertaking of reporting obligations by States; the spelling out of those obligations in treaty provisions; the creation of independent expert committees to examine the reports; and the assumption that the primary aim is to assist governments rather than just to criticise their performance. . . .

Reporting is not something that is imposed upon an unwilling state, nor is it something designed as an adversarial process. Rather, it is premised on the assumptions first that every State is an actual or potential violator of human rights (no matter how good its intentions might be) and second, that a degree of routinized international accountability is in the best interests of the State itself, of its citizens, and of the international community.[74]

The time frame adopted in this book is designed to test the weak and strong applications of the multilateral human rights regime. Although it was only in 1989 that China's human rights became the subject of strong and sustained monitoring by UN human rights bodies, it is also important to compare the post-1989 period with the weaker application of the regime before that time. There have been three main phases of China's interaction with the international human rights regime in the United Nations. The first phase of involvement, characterized by little attention to human rights issues, began when the People's Republic of China replaced Taiwan as China's representative in the UN in 1971 and became subject to the norms and the constraints that the regime imposed. The second phase (1979–89) occurred mainly within the UN system and was inaugurated when China began participating in the UN Human Rights Commission, thus formally abandoning its earlier policy of avoidance and noninvolvement in human rights matters. In this phase, China was subject to the routine, socializing, if still weak, pressures of the regime.

The third phase, precipitated by the Chinese government crackdown on the Democracy Movement in June 1989, began an extraordinarily strong application of the regime, in which China was subjected to extensive monitoring as well as to rigorous, overt, and sustained multilateral and bilateral pressures. In this period, as has been noted, China did not ratify the major international covenants of human rights, although in late 1997 it signed the ICESCR and a year later signed the ICCPR. China was, however, a party to the four other core human rights treaties: the Convention on the Elimination of All Forms of Racial Discrimination, the Convention Against Torture and Other Cruel, Inhuman or Degrading Treatment or Punishment, the Convention on the Elimination of All Forms of Discrimination Against Women, and the Convention on the Rights of the Child. It was also a member of the UN Commission on Human Rights and the UN Sub-Commission on Prevention of Discrimination and Protection of Minorities and, like other UN Member states, was subject to the jurisdiction of the thematic working groups and special rapporteurs. An understanding of the differences in China's response to these distinct phases yields some conclusions about the results of the regime's different applications.

The book is also designed to demonstrate China's response to the different forms of UN monitoring. Chapter 1 describes the UN human rights regime and its weak application to China from 1971 to 1989. It also provides a historical analysis of China's human rights theory and practice and its concepts of international law and state sovereignty. Chapters 2 to 7 deal with the strong application of the regime between 1989 and 1998. Chapters 2 to 4 contain five case studies of China's interaction with multilateral human rights bodies. Chapter 2 focuses on the Charter-based bodies, the UN Human Rights Commission and the UN Human Rights Sub-Commission; Chapter 3 examines the Committee Against Torture, with accompanying reference to other treaty bodies, and the Special Rapporteur on Torture, as well as other special rapporteurs and working groups involved with China; and Chapter 4 analyzes China's interaction with the International Labor Organization. These three chapters scrutinize different forms of monitoring within the UN system. The Human Rights Sub-Commission is important as the first UN human rights organ to censure a permanent member of the Security Council: the Human Rights Commission assumes significance later in the period under review. Both bodies have a more political character than the treaty bodies or the UN specialized agencies. CAT has been chosen as a treaty-based body that is one of the UN human rights organs with jurisdiction over aspects of China's individual civil rights. The Special Rapporteur on Torture was established by the UN Human Rights Commission. Both institutions, with their complementary roles, are at the cutting edge of the debate on human rights between China and the West. The ILO is a UN specialized agency whose underlying norms, the rights of workers and freedom of association, not only lie at the heart of the now muted East-West debate but are still central to the North-South debate and to the legitimacy of the current Chinese regime. Like that of the treaty bodies, its monitoring is carried out mainly through the reporting system: but as an autonomous organization, it exerts a variety of other organizational pressures not at the disposal of bodies within the UN proper.

Chapters 5 and 6 describe the wider themes of China's theoretical and diplomatic responses to the international human rights regime. Chapter 5 includes a study of China's developing human rights theories after 1989 and an analysis of China's human rights diplomacy in the years leading up to the UN World Human Rights Conference in Vienna in June 1993. Chapter 6 is an account of China's participation in the Vienna Conference that compares its contribution with its role in the prior Preparatory Meeting of Asian Governments in Bangkok and in the Preparatory Committees. Chapter 7 provides detailed analysis of China's international and domestic implementation of human rights norms since 1993, and assesses the depth of its compliance with its human rights obligations. The Conclusion summarizes the different Chinese responses and analyzes the nature of China's learning experience, and conversely, its influence on the changing character of the international human rights regime. It also assesses the overall impact of the different phases and facets of the UN human rights regime on China's international and domestic human rights policy, thereby evaluating the effectiveness of the regime and the extent, and limits, of China's compliance.

Chapter 1
The UN Human Rights Regime and China's Participation Before 1989

> The exclusion of one fifth of the world's population from the international system of human rights protection is self-evidently a major continuing limitation on the ambition of universal acceptance of common human rights norms.
> — Kevin Boyle, 1995

The emergence of the human rights regime as a focus of international politics in the late 1980s and the early 1990s originally arose from pressures on and in Eastern Europe and the former Soviet Union to move away from the socialist system. It was further encouraged by the trend to democratization and liberalization in parts of the Third World and the apparent dawn of a new world order in which international law and international institutions would assume increasing importance. The new prominence of human rights norms was also a product of globalization, which brought the individual into contact with international trends, and an outcome of the technological revolution, where "instantaneous communication has extended the basis for symbolic, and perhaps physical, interventions into domestic processes in which gross violations of international norms are occurring."[1] Thus, former UN Secretary-General Perez de Cuellar observed in April 1991, "We are clearly witnessing what is probably an irresistible shift in public attitudes towards the belief that the defence of the oppressed in the name of morality should prevail over frontiers and legal documents."[2] At the same time, this new emphasis on human rights was indicative of the darker side of the new world disorder, of the need to project and strengthen international standards of state behavior as a bulwark against conditions of regional anarchy, of ethnic and tribal violence, and of national disintegration and reconstruction. It became the focus of an era in which states were searching for new national identities to replace the loss of ideological certainties, and for the norms on which a changing global order should be based. Thus, the post–Cold War period is one in which human rights have assumed greater importance and are more at risk.

Despite this fragility, events since 1989 have resulted in a clear alteration in the political discourse between states, from a situation dominated by ideological struggle to one in which many states in their relations increasingly make human rights their "discourse of choice."[3] Within that discourse new priorities of rights are emerging that reflect these changes. The United Nations has become the principal forum of this interaction.[4] From the 1993 Vienna World Human Rights Conference convened under its auspices emerged a rearticulation of human rights norms at a strategic point in the global transition of power. At the same time, increased intervention by major industrialized powers, particularly the United States, is being encouraged by many Western NGOs to compensate for perceived gaps or inadequacies in UN enforcement mechanisms.[5]

The international human rights regime is thus an agent of change that is itself undergoing transformation. Many countervailing trends in international human rights discourse revolve around questions about the priority of individual versus collective rights, and of the civil and political rights, embodied in the ICCPR, versus the economic and social rights incorporated in the ICESCR.[6] Within Asian states, both collective and individualistic strands of human rights values coexist uneasily, with the governing elites favoring communitarian interpretations, and individual citizens, particularly members of the middle class and domestic NGOs, adopting more individualistic positions. However, even though Asian cultures are being promoted as a shield against the penetration of Western values, in many cases they are also being invoked to expand the human rights discourse rather than to negate it. Asian elites now more readily accept the nexus between human rights and democracy articulated in formal human rights forums, even if they resent the political implications of Western human rights rhetoric tied to conditionality. The increasingly cosmopolitan nature of the discourse is evidenced by the fact that, whether defending their practices by resort to the principles of sovereignty and noninterference, or, as is often the case, with reference to the actual norms of the regime itself, non-Western states like China often invoke Western human rights standards and conventions of international law.

For their part, some Western states enlarge their own conceptual horizons by accepting collective rights like the right to development, while at the UN Human Rights Conference in Vienna, under pressure from the South, the U.S. administration expressed its readiness to move toward signature and ratification of the ICESCR. However, this internationalism has not eliminated cultural differences in human rights values, and the urge for pluralism appears to be as strong as the urge for globalization. On one hand, a trend to globalization is suggested by the U.S. role as the only remaining superpower in a multipolar world capable of projecting its own priorities in human rights monitoring independently of the UN system. And although human rights concepts have replaced the ideological rhetoric of the past, they are still articulated in the familiar Cold War language of "freedom" and "democracy." The political vacuum left by the collapse of the former Soviet Union has provided, moreover, a favorable international environment for such hegemonic logic. On the other hand, pluralism has been encouraged by the spectacular economic growth in the Asian region between 1989 and 1997 which correspondingly diminished Asian vulnerability to the conditionality and sanctions that encourage compliance with it, leading them rather to advocate what has been called "the Pacific way."[7] More recently, the spectacular downturn in the regional financial situation has tempered this confidence in "Asian values," but to what degree is still unclear.[8]

In other words, the puzzle is hard to assemble, because "both the pieces and the picture are in a constant state of flux."[9] The question of China's socialization or learning process in relation to the international human rights regime therefore involves larger questions about tensions within the norms of the regime and in the current dynamic of world order.

Underlying this continuing tension between North and South are two related issues: (1) the tension between the universality of human rights norms and the claims of cultural relativism, or the claim that a culture is a self-contained, static entity whose values do and should remain independent of international norms and influences; and (2) the tension between state sovereignty, which projects the notion of human rights primarily as rights of the state, and human rights as a set of norms empowering the individual in his or her relationship with the state and the international community.

Universality, Cultural Relativism, and Selectivity

A major source of contention is the universality of the international human rights regime, in the sense of a universal acceptance of its norms and principles, the scope of its monitoring, and the impartiality of its application.[10] Although there is no doubt that the regime exists and that it is both formally accepted by, and applies to, all states, it is not clear that it holds the same meaning for all. Obstacles to universality of interpretation include (a) a lack of consensus about norms; (b) the need for norms to be processed and put in operation through institutions; and (c) the fact that the carriers of ideas in institutions are states.

Bilahari Kausikan has distinguished between a "pretentious and unrealistic universalism" and a "paralysing cultural relativism" currently pervading human rights discourse.[11] This analysis creates a false dichotomy: it misconstrues both the function of universalism and its relation to relativism. More incisive is the analysis of Martti Koskenniemi, who has referred to the enduring impact of modernity in appearing to globalize internal culture. Citing Jean Baudrillard, he draws a distinction between the once true, authentic artifacts that conveyed a sense of, and ultimately helped constitute, community and the current proliferation of the "simulacra" of these artifacts.[12] These simulacra in the international arena include both global institutions and rhetoric. Thus, "our rhetoric — mere simulacra but the vessels of our meaning nonetheless — is not powerful enough to realise our express commitments" (404).

Koskenniemi shares Stanley Hoffmann's belief that a community of vocabulary is not the same as a community of values.[13] His metaphor helps explain the disjuncture between formal vocabulary and its informal meaning. Thus, states may use identical terms like "self-determination," "sovereignty" and "human rights," but these terms are ascribed different meanings. As Hedley Bull earlier demonstrated, rights of sovereignty have often been asserted by non-Western states in such an extreme form that they seemed incompatible with the idea of an international society that also has rights over its members; racial equality is related to equality of rights of white and nonwhite peoples within the international state system rather than to the rights of ethnic populations within states; and economic rights, including the right to development, are related to the rights of poor states rather than to the crucial issue of distribution within states.[14] Moreover, the principle of the right to self-determination has been narrowly interpreted by non-Western states in accordance with its "external," rather than its "internal," implication. Its meaning as the right of peoples within states to choose their form of government has been correspondingly neglected.[15] Yet these simulacra that disguise cultural heterogeneity must not be dismissed as sheer hypocrisy. They have the constructive function of providing a buffer between states' needs to interpret culturally how the norms in international treaties should be implemented domestically and their simultaneous wish not to dismantle the regime.

Such culturally specific interpretation is not, moreover, a problem limited to non-Western states. David Forsythe has convincingly demonstrated that, despite the belief in the U.S. that its human rights values represent *the* Western position, its homegrown norms are in fact different from most Second and Third World countries, "where communal values rank more highly than individualism and skepticism of unregulated economies is widespread."[16] Here again, part of the problem lies in the continuing debate within Western culture itself as to the proper hierarchy of civil, political, economic, social, and cultural rights.

Thus, the terms utilized in human rights discourse may have their origins in Western philosophy, but their ascribed meanings may have a cultural and political difference that relates to the specific political culture of individual states, whether Western or non-Western.[17] The globalization of the vocabulary disguises the culturally based content of meaning. In addition, norms have been added to the corpus of internationally recognized rights that unambiguously reflect the collective priorities of many socialist and developing states. The historical evolution of the Universal Declaration of Human Rights, and the inability of the international community to agree to a single enabling instrument incorporating civil, political, economic, and social rights demonstrates the inherent dualism of civil/political and economic/social and cultural rights during the ideological cleavage of the Cold War era. The early political debates that determined the bifurcation of these norms into two separate instruments, the ICCPR and the ICESCR, both containing individual and group rights, simply foreshadowed continuing differences.

In a vast oversimplification of a complex reality, during the post-War decades civil, political, and individual rights were seen as inherently Western whereas economic, social, cultural, and collective rights were viewed as the province of the socialist and developing world. Scholars have recognized a less reductionist tripartite distinction, detecting differences in interpretation between developed, developing, and socialist states, or between First, Second, and Third World states.[18] Whatever the subtle shadings of difference, the core of these distinctions lies in the developed world's tendency to emphasize civil and political rights, while socialist states, although sharing the collectivist, developmental, anti-imperialist and anti-colonial emphasis of the developing states, have further differentiated themselves by placing priority on economic, social, and cultural rights.

At the same time, pressures for convergence have been at work. Together with the Universal Declaration of Human Rights, both civil/political and economic/social rights were integrated into what is now known as the International Bill of Rights. Socialist and Third World states prevailed over Western preferences in achieving in both Covenants an acceptance of the importance of collective rights, in particular the right of self-determination and the right to development. Disagreement over the inclusion of the right to self-determination, which was finally incorporated into both Covenants, was one of the reasons their drafting was not completed until 1966. In addition, the Western value of the right to property was excluded as a result of non-Western intervention, since it was not now considered by the majority of states to be worthy of protection on a universal level. Socialist and some Third World states also contributed to weakening the system of international control over the application of the two Covenants proposed by the West, and in making the most important part of it voluntary (supervision of the observance of the ICCPR, exercisable on individual request, is foreseen in an Optional Protocol, and not in the Covenant itself). A third generation of collective and developmental or "solidarity" rights, including the 1986 Right to Development, was later added in response to the requirements of socialist and developing states, although such rights were not given equal status to the Covenants. In addition, the non-West influenced the West to take economic, social, and cultural rights more seriously, so that in 1985 the Committee on Economic, Social and Cultural Rights was set up to monitor observance of the ICESCR. The doctrinal distinctions between the different generations of rights were papered over in the subsequent recognition of the indivisibility and interdependence of all human rights. The result has been not the Westernization of human rights norms, but rather their universalization. Supporters of "Asian values" often overlook this important recent history of the development of current human rights norms, which in itself reflects the institutionalization of an ongoing "dialogue."[19] Norms have been globalized in a cosmopolitan discourse that transcends and comprehends, but does not reconcile, cultural differences.

If norms have been globalized but not reconciled, how has this contradiction been resolved in practice? Only in the operationalization of norms may one discover the effective cultural meaning given to them. And here lies the rub. Although human rights theoretically constitute a source of authenticity outside the system of sovereign states, they must be interpreted, enumerated, prioritized and put into operation by institutions based on the principle of the sovereign equality of those states.[20] Koskenniemi rightly observes that although the concept of state sovereignty is often invoked to justify an abuse of human rights, the existence of international human rights instruments means that states may not claim that statehood justifies any internal activities (398). On the other hand, states, to be distinguished from their citizens, still disagree about human rights priorities, and yet remain the vehicle whereby substantive disagreement is directed into institutionalized debate.

In terms of operationalized policy, this debate within the United Nations had very little impact until the late 1960s. In 1970, however, the UN Commission on Human Rights was authorized to conduct confidential investigations of systematic human rights violations, and over the next two decades reviewed the situation in nearly forty countries. It also set up "largely depoliticized" monitoring programs, each headed by a special rapporteur, on disappearances, torture and arbitrary and summary executions. These programs followed the setting up of human rights treaties which required parties to submit periodic reports to independent monitoring committees.[21] In spite of such progress, mainly in the area of civil rights, and in spite of the setting up of the Committee on Economic, Social and Cultural Rights in 1985, its first chairman, Philip Alston, has complained that the effort of the UN Commission on Human Rights to deepen the conceptual foundations of the package of rights contained in the Universal Declaration and its Covenants is still being "played out within a largely theoretical context." Although the concept of peoples' rights is beginning to take root, and a greater effort has been made to give content to political participation rights, "both cultural and economic rights remain late starters."[22] In other words, although human rights norms are recognized as universal, the way in which they have been put into operation has been mainly to monitor civil rights.

It is one thing to recognize the Western bias in the operationalization of international human rights norms, and another to explain it. Apart from the political, institutional, and administrative problems raised above, it is clear that one historical reason lies in the impact of U.S. power to channel discourse and build coalitions within the UN system, at least until the 1970s.[23] Explanations since that time, and particularly since the establishment of the Economic, Social and Cultural Rights Committee, prove to be more complex.

In this regard, the debate over the role of culture in international relations assumes relevance. In considering the well-worn thesis that in the post–Cold War era, "the clash of civilizations will dominate global politics," one must make a distinction between the culture that legitimately expresses an "interpersonally shared system of meanings, perceptions and values" and the constructed, instrumental "culture" that is projected by states as an arm of power in international relations.[24] Such a distinction allows clarification of the nature of the international human rights debate, which has seen the manifold cultures or civilizations of the Asian, African, and Latin American regions coalesced together in the name of cultural difference as a banner against Western civilization and U.S. hegemony. Rather than "a clash of civilizations," different cultures and civilizations are being manipulated as a political weapon against a specifically "Western" civilization; global politics are being clad in the garb of culture, replacing the ideological clothing of the Cold War. By this means, non-Western states use the banner of cultural difference to attempt to restore a greater degree of operational equity to the human rights monitoring process, not in favor of their own particular civilization but in the interests of the non-Western world generally, by emphasizing collective and developmental rights. They are also defending their legitimate right to interpret, in the process of specific domestic implementation, the meaning of the abstract norms incorporated in international treaties.[25] However, in pursuing this particular form of debate, human rights values are not being pluralized but reduced to a self-protective dualism differentiating simply between Western and non-Western rights preferences. This instrumental use of culture is rendered dubious by the clear differences within, and between, Asian states themselves in their interpretations of human rights, not the least being those between states sharing a common Confucian culture: China, Taiwan, and Korea.[26]

Thus, one question that has not been asked is the extent to which Third World states have actually been complicit in supporting the Westernized operationalization of human rights. Contrary to their declaratory policy, many non-Western states do not in fact wish in their operational policy to focus on individual economic and social rights, since such rights involve sensitive political, economic and social issues of redistribution. The collective right of self-determination is also becoming problematic for them. Developmental rights, being collective rights of the state, are preferred as a focus. Where the focus is on individual rights, however, such states may in fact prove to be complicit with the current Western bias in primarily monitoring civil rights.

The universality of the international human rights regime is also brought into question by the selectivity of its targets. Within the strict context of the UN human rights system, however, a simple West versus non-West dichotomy does not explain this selectivity. It stems rather from the strategic interests of the great powers. As Philip Alston demonstrates in his study of the monitoring activity of the UN Commission on Human Rights, the United States, the former Soviet Union, the United Kingdom, France, and, until 1989, China have all enjoyed a degree of immunity from scrutiny. Regional solidarity has been effective in preventing scrutiny of African and Arab nations, but less effective as regards Asia and Latin America. No Western European state and only two former East European states have been targeted. Even the "disproportionately strong focus" of UN human rights bodies on Latin America may be attributed to the strength of the democratic/rights tradition in that region, the brutality of the violations, the special concern of activist American NGOs and the Inter-American Commission, as well as the role of the Catholic Church.[27] Similarly, with respect to bilateral monitoring, American preoccupation in the 1970s and 1980s with the condition of civil rights in the former Soviet Union contrasted with its and the world's indifference to an arguably worse condition in China's civil rights, a selective myopia that accorded with U.S. strategic, if not ideological, priorities.

The Principle of State Sovereignty

The international human rights regime differs from other regimes such as the political economy regime and the arms control regime in that its norms, with the exception of collective norms like the right to development, do not conform with the material or strategic interests of the state but rather with the ideals of its citizens. In international forums it lacks the bargaining chip of reciprocity that may be invoked in trade and arms control regimes. It differs even from the environment regime in that — except in the basic sense of the right to life — global survival and thus long-term national interest, does not depend on its enforcement. The human rights regime is also different in that its norms as embedded in the Universal Declaration are not legally binding, although they are regarded by some as part of customary law. They are formally binding only on those states that have ratified the international covenants, or, in a more limited sense, that have ratified treaties protecting specific rights like the Convention Against Torture, or regional treaties. Domestically, as we have seen, the paradox is that a citizen's civil and political rights are exercised against the state but depend on the state for legal and practical implementation.[28] For that reason, debates within the regime are peculiarly preoccupied with the principle of sovereignty, with respect to both international and domestic jurisdictions.

Sovereignty and human rights are given equal weight in the UN Charter. Thus, under Chapter 1 on "Purposes and Principles," Article 1, Paragraph 3 aims "to achieve international cooperation . . . in promoting and encouraging respect for human rights and for fundamental freedoms for all without distinction as to race, sex, language or religion," whereas Article 2, Paragraph 7 declares that "nothing contained in the present Charter shall authorize the United Nations to intervene in matters which are essentially within the domestic jurisdiction of any state or shall require the Members to submit such matters to settlement under the present Charter."[29] The UN Charter therefore allows selective choice by each member state as to which principles to invoke as legal authority for its position on human rights. Given the state's central role in enforcement, and the conflict between states' rights and individual rights that human rights entails, it is clear that its particular concept of sovereignty is crucial in determining its acceptance of international human rights norms. An absolute and exclusive interpretation becomes incompatible with the observance of human rights. As former UN Secretary-General Boutros Boutros-Ghali has observed: "While respect for the fundamental sovereignty and integrity of the state remains central, it is undeniable that the centuries-old doctrine of absolute and exclusive sovereignty no longer stands, and was in fact never so absolute as it was conceived to be in theory. A major intellectual requirement of our time is to rethink the question of sovereignty—not to weaken its essence, which is crucial to international security and cooperation, but to recognise that it may take more than one form and perform more than one function."[30]

Thus, although the doctrine of state sovereignty, as defined by the Permanent Court of International Justice, meant that the state was "subject to no other state, and ha[d] full and exclusive powers within its jurisdiction," as early as 1923 the Court also noted that sovereignty was "an essentially relative question"—dependent on whatever law there was to curtail it.[31] Legal sovereignty does not admit of degrees, nor of redefinition: "The narrow standard of traditional sovereignty forms a threshold: once nations achieve a kind of critical mass, they are catapulted to a transcendent status through recognition by other members of the states' club."[32] It constitutes what has been termed "pristine sovereignty in the form of lawlessness."[33] A more political interpretation of sovereignty, however, claims that it is possible to be "more or less sovereign": the strict legal interpretation of sovereignty has been redefined to include challenges, so that sovereignty "is not seen as incompatible with individual rights, non-state actors, or permeable boundaries."[34] John Vincent goes further, arguing that where once international legitimacy was based almost wholly on the principle of sovereignty, it is now also coming to rest on the way a state treats its citizens.[35]

Even if this is not yet the case, it is clear that in the context of membership of international organizations and regimes, the question of sovereignty is a highly complex matter. For although, as is often emphasized, membership may limit sovereignty, it also constitutes an important dimension of a state's sovereignty. As a former President of the UN General Assembly, H. V. Evatt, once pointed out: "A treaty is . . . in one sense a surrender of sovereignty. But in another sense it is an exercise of sovereignty. It is the supreme mark of the sovereign independence of a state to be able to undertake obligations or to exact undertakings from other states."[36]

There is thus no simple solution to managing the problem of sovereignty. For each state it is a complicated matter of steering between the benefits for sovereignty that membership of international organizations and regimes entails, and the potential threat to sovereignty that it implies. For China, whose dramatic improvement in international status coincided with its entry into the United Nations and other international organizations after 1971, the dilemma is relatively recent. Although it recognizes that the problems arising from participation are substantial, it also acknowledges that the benefits are significant.

Adopting the general analytical dualism of legal and political interpretations of sovereignty, but preferring the notion of a continuum operating globally between the two conceptual extremes, this study seeks to trace the extent to which China has been moving away from formal legalistic interpretations of sovereignty in either stated or enacted policy, to more political, relative, and contextual interpretations. The preparedness to adopt a more relative view of sovereignty is seen as a key indicator of China's international socialization. Its preparedness is also indicated behaviorally, in the record of the ongoing dialectic between its theories, its declaratory policy, and the actual process of its diplomacy in the human rights field. In addition, the study identifies Chinese concessions made to the regime through deliberate initiatives or as the unintended consequence of related actions or of decisions made for ad hoc reasons. For the implementation of norms not only may be a result of an incremental learning process through the application of pressures, but is often the outcome of arbitrary, erratic, and circumstantial developments.

China and the UN Before 1989

The People's Republic of China replaced Taiwan as China's representative in the United Nations in 1971, toward the end of the Cultural Revolution. The worst excesses of the movement had subsided, but the abuse of citizens' civil rights and the rigid control of their thoughts and actions by the Party and state continued unabated. China's interest in breaking out of its global isolation, reflected in its overtures to the U.S. and its establishment of diplomatic relations with an increasing number of states, was the initial impetus behind its entry: thoughts of the corresponding duties of membership, which included an acceptance of the international community's right to monitor its human rights, were not in the forefront of its considerations. At the time, China's economic and social rights were regarded by many development experts as a model for other developing states.[37] However, China did not receive credit for this achievement in human rights bodies, since during this period the actual monitoring mechanisms and the attention of the world community focused solely on civil and political rights: the UN Committee on Economic, Social and Cultural Rights, which monitored implementation of the International Covenant on Economic, Social and Cultural Rights by states parties, and which arguably conferred a higher status on economic and social rights within the United Nations, had not yet been set up. In contrast, the condition of China's civil and political rights was clearly inconsistent with the norms encapsulated in the Universal Declaration of Human Rights and the human rights treaties.[38]

How this gap could be minimized through the intervention of the international community depended in part on the will, and watchfulness, of that community. At the time of China's entry, however, a preparedness to exempt China from its human rights responsibilities was apparent in the world at large, which concentrated first on "bringing China in."[39] Preparedness to exempt China was also partly a deferential response to China's different conception of human rights, international law, state sovereignty, and the international protection of human rights.

China's Human Rights Before 1989: Theory and Practice

Neither China's imperial past nor its communist phase were conducive to Western ideas of natural rights.[40] The unquestioned duty of the community and the individual to the state in both periods was accompanied by an implicit sense of the state's responsibility to the people to maintain stability and guarantee basic subsistence rights. The notion of human, or civil, rights, in the sense of the individual's right to protection from the incursions of the state, did not exist. Under the post-1949 communist government, national goals were articulated not in terms of human rights, which were associated with the civil or "natural" rights advocated in Western liberal thought, but with Marxist goals of equal distribution and socialist ownership of the means of production. The basic content of economic and social rights was encompassed in the form of a more equal distribution of resources and the guarantee of the right to work through which citizens had access to social welfare and social security, as well as of the universal right to education. As a socialist state, China now conformed with the views of other socialist and Third World countries that emphasized the collective aspirations of national self-determination, anti-colonialism, development, opposition to discrimination, and, in a domestic context, the economic and social aspects of human rights. Consequently, the aspirations of its people were seen as realizable mainly through collective political, social, and economic action.

Internationally, Marxist principles supporting the liberation of peoples were supported not in the name of human rights but in the name of socialism or "Marxism-Leninism and Mao Zedong thought." However, from the 1950s to the 1970s, Chinese critiques of Western violations of the rights of Third World states sometimes appealed not just to the principle of state sovereignty, but also to the need for respect for fundamental human rights.[41] This form of self-defense drew its strength from its resonance with the values in Western thought; it was also in keeping with the principle expressed in the 1955 Bandung Communiqué, endorsed by China, of "respect for fundamental human rights and for the purposes and principles of the Charter of the United Nations."[42]

The view of human rights as primarily collective and economic arose from a complex mix of socialist and Maoist ideas, and of traditional thought and practices, as well as of the historical experience of the Chinese revolution. Yet China, if not itself a member of the United Nations, was now operating as a sovereign state within an international system. The new post World War II environment, still reverberating from the human and material devastation of the conflict, and from the appalling revelations of the Holocaust, manifested a new awareness and concern about the principles of human rights, and particularly civil and political rights. Following the precedent of the majority of other states established in the postwar era, and influenced by the Soviet Constitution, China therefore incorporated in its first Constitution of 1954 the majority of the human rights principles identified in the Universal Declaration of Human Rights. In spite of their changing character, all four of China's post-1949 constitutions provided guarantees not only of economic, social, and cultural rights, but of civil and political rights. Over time, some rights were added and some subtracted, but they all included guarantees for the freedoms of speech, correspondence, press, assembly, association, procession and demonstration, and for freedom of person, freedom of religious belief, the right of appeal against state functionaries, and the autonomy of national minorities. Political rights were guaranteed under the Chinese constitutions to all citizens aged eighteen and over as "the right to vote and stand for election."[43] On the other hand, civil rights not contained in the constitutions included rights laid down in the Universal Declaration and the International Covenant on Civil and Political Rights, such as freedom of residence or movement, the right to choose one's work, freedom from forced labor, freedom from torture, and the right to the presumption of innocence, though there was a right of defense and of a public trial.[44] Under the current 1982 Constitution, the right to strike contained in the 1975 and 1978 Constitutions was also eliminated.

Moreover, those civil and political rights formally guaranteed were subject to a number of crucial limitations that effectively undermined the guarantee. First, like other communist countries, China was a state operating according to concepts of civil law that saw law itself as based on the will of the state and the legislative provisions made by it.[45] Since the Constitution was not judicially actionable, the state was not obliged to put the guaranteed rights into action. Second, the socialist emphasis on the supremacy of the state over the individual strengthened the existing historical bias toward the dependence of the individual on the state for rights, the view of law as an instrument of the state, the emphasis on a citizen's responsibility to the state rather than on his rights, and the view of human rights as a matter of domestic jurisdiction as well as a potential threat to state sovereignty.

As in the earlier part of the century, a Chinese citizen's duty to the state took priority over his rights. Every right conceded the Chinese citizen had a corresponding duty, and in the event of that duty being threatened, it took precedence over the right. The view of law as an instrument of the state also meant that there was no promise of remedies to ensure the citizens' enjoyment of their rights, and that the rights themselves could be cancelled (or expanded) by state laws. In addition, state laws could be overruled by Party fiat. This flexibility was not simply a function of the state's will: under Mao, legality was governed, much as it had been in imperial China, both by legal codification and by extralegal norms, such as ideology, prevailing state and Party policies, and the continuing *Gemeinschaft* tendency to resort to mediation and conciliation rather than judicial action. The Party's influence was felt through a system of political-legal committees composed of Party and government legal figures, which operated at all levels of the Party independent of the court system. In important criminal cases these committees enforced Party and state interests. A culture of the "ceremonial use of rules," in which existing rules bore little relation to their implementation, grew up.[46] Superimposed on this historical and political legal structure was the fledgling development of a *Gesellschaft* system of law, based on individualism and competition and drawing its provisions from Anglo-American and continental civil law.[47] Finally, the state's predominance over the individual and his or her rights was expressed in the Chinese emphasis on the principle of state sovereignty in relation to human rights issues and in its insistence that only states could be subjects of international law, whereas individuals were subjects only of municipal law.

Even this fragile legal culture was not sacrosanct. During the Cultural Revolution, which was launched in 1966 to rekindle revolutionary fervor among the masses and to weed out members of the elite who represented a challenge to Mao, the judiciary was dismantled, the Public Security organs were attacked, and summary people's justice was dispensed through revolutionary tribunals. During "struggle meetings," many leading cadres and intellectuals accused of right-wing deviation were humiliated, summarily tortured, killed, or driven to commit suicide. Not until the early 1970s did military control over law enforcement give way to more normal legal practice, and not until 1978 was the Procuratorate reinstituted.

This condition of civil and political rights, in which the *de jure* theory of rights protection contrasted with the *de facto* practice of abuse, began to change in the late 1970s after Mao's death. The modernization process initiated in late 1978 by Deng Xiaoping gave rise to a complex chain of restructuring in the economic, social, and political systems, which had unintended consequences for human rights. Its emphasis on competition over egalitarianism placed new importance on the individual, and on the benefits to the community of tapping the individual's resources. The economic role of the state also diminished.[48] Modernization harnessed China to the system of global communications, introducing sophisticated technology that transcended the national barriers that had hitherto filtered the content of material and the type of information which could be imported and purveyed within the country. And it brought a creeping liberalization to the political system—for a degree of democracy was seen by the Chinese government both as the prerequisite and as the inevitable outcome of the economic liberalization process.[49] Civil freedoms at an informal level expanded in the gap that began to emerge between state and society. Finally, the integration with the world economy increased pressures on Chinese leaders to regularize the marketing process, and to replace the existing flexibility in the system of social control with a degree of predictability and dependability, thereby necessitating the development of a coherent legal system.[50]

However, as of 1989, the informal condition of liberalization did not have any corresponding support in the existing constitutional, legal, and institutional framework. The increased exercise by citizens of freedoms of speech, thought, press, and association was not underpinned by enabling legislation, apart from those nominal constitutional provisions that were already overridden by other laws or constitutional provisions. Liberalization could not therefore be interpreted as the equivalent of official support for formal "rights." As in the past, freedoms were still granted, or rescinded, at the whim of the state.

Moreover, rights of due process, as distinct from freedom of expression, showed no improvement in this period, despite the increasing amount of new criminal legislation.[51] The Criminal Law and the Criminal Procedure Law of 1979 gave insufficient protection against arbitrary arrest and failed to guarantee a fair trial; they did not allow for preparation of the defense, nor did they guarantee the right to be presumed innocent.[52] There were altogether fifty-five capital offenses in China, among which were fourteen counterrevolutionary offences. To the twenty-one offenses listed in the Criminal Law, thirty-four had been added by subsequent legislation. Many less serious offenses were subject to administrative sanctions, which bypassed the judicial system altogether.

As informal freedoms of expression — speech, press, assembly — and of movement expanded, the freedoms of immunity that were not guaranteed — such as due process and freedom from torture, arbitrary arrest, and execution — were increasingly at risk. Periodic law and order campaigns attempted to control the increasing incidence of criminal behavior, and the number of death sentences rose. In the 1983 Anti-Crime Campaign, for instance, between August and October 1983, 600 death sentences were reportedly carried out, whereas in 1990 Amnesty International recorded some 960 death sentences, of which 750 were carried out.[53] This constituted one-third of the world's reported executions for that year. Similarly, the practice of torture, widely exercised during the Cultural Revolution, re-emerged as a problem during the Anti-Crime Campaign of 1983. Between 1985 and 1989, Chinese authorities took steps to reduce the high incidence of torture in Chinese prisons. However, according to Chinese authorities' own published statistics, the campaign was not effective and the volume of torture cases increased over this period.[54] Four key factors were identified as obstructing these efforts: inadequate legal safeguards for the rights of detainees; emphasis by the police on obtaining confessions in order to facilitate prompt convictions by the courts; failure by the authorities to investigate and prosecute police officers who used torture; and the widespread use of administrative (extrajudicial) forms of detention to handle the spiraling crime rate (2).

Besides contributing to crime rates, economic restructuring had important implications for civil, industrial and economic rights. The problem of growing unemployment and the movement of tens of millions of job seekers throughout China was exacerbated by the fact that social insurance was located in the workplace (*danwei*) and therefore inaccessible to the unemployed. In the industrial workplace, although the "iron rice bowl" was not smashed, its surface became marked with hairline cracks in the shape of redundancy, unemployment, large wage differentials, and inflation. Protection of workers' interests was undermined by prohibitions on freedom of association and on the right to strike, and the lack of a right of collective bargaining or of the right to form and join the trade union of one's choice, without previous authorization. The functions of the single government-run trade union, the All-China Federation of Trade Unions (ACFTU), did not comply with International Labor Organization (ILO) standards. Apart from ensuring the maintenance of social services and decent housing, it was mainly a mechanism to exhort workers to increase production. The worker was expected to obey the rules of the enterprise and accept the guidance of the Party and of management.

If the formal structure and provision of rights in China was slow to change, the popular impulse for change was increasingly expressed in official and unofficial writings. A developing interest in human rights led to its broader conceptualization. Apart from China's formal activities and pronouncements with respect to human rights in international organizations, this new attitude was reflected in the writings of individual Chinese scholars publishing in such formal and semiformal media as *Hongqi* ("Red Flag"), *Renmin ribao* ("People's Daily"), *Xuexi yu tansuo* ("Study and Exploration"), and the *Beijing Review*, as well as in citizens' handbooks, encyclopedias, and legal textbooks.

The era of the first post-1949 democracy movement, the Democracy Wall Movement, was a period of extensive intellectual ferment. Between 1978 and 1980, a wide range of issues, discussion of which had been forbidden in the Maoist era, were freely debated in the press and in society at large. Most of these were found in underground publications, but some also surfaced in legal journals and in the major official newspapers.[55] Conservative official articles continued to rehearse the old arguments on human rights. By contrast, the outer limits of the human rights debate in this period were established in an article entitled "Human Rights and the Legal System," which declared the relevance of the struggle for civil rights in the period of socialism, since China still suffered the influence of feudalism. The article prescribed bold remedies to the abuse of human rights in China: to develop socialist democracy and the socialist legal system; to implement the right to vote, using it as a mechanism to put arbitrary dictatorship to the vote; to protect the people's right of supervision and recall of cadres; to change the situation whereby basic-level cadres had the power of life and death over the people; to guarantee that the rights of the person were not violated; and to truly implement the principle of equality before the law (20). These were arguments similar to those adopted during the Democracy Wall Movement by Chinese dissidents like Wei Jingsheng, Wang Xizhe and Xu Wenli in their underground newspapers and *dazibao* (big character posters). They were also echoed in more open publications: in March 1979, *Gongren ribao* (the "Workers' Daily") emphasized that human rights were not respected in socialist society and that a campaign should be launched to defend human rights and seek help from abroad.

Even after the suppression of the Democracy Wall Movement in 1981, scholarly interest in human rights continued. Over the decade, human rights were seen in an increasingly positive light. It was claimed that the human rights doctrine itself had changed, from its narrow, bourgeois, individual-based origins in civil and political rights to broader and internationally consensual principles emphasizing the second and third generation of rights; it had expanded to encompass economic and social rights, and collective rights of the self-determination of peoples and developmental rights, as well as civil and political rights. A generally consistent case was made that under bourgeois rule civil and political rights had disguised effective inequality and unequal access to material goods and opportunity, and led to exploitation. Nevertheless, the historical revolutionary contribution made by human rights in the period of bourgeois ascendancy was increasingly acknowledged.[56]

Thus, although the traditional priority of economic and social rights and of the collective rights of self-determination and development was formally preserved in the constitutions, the parameters of discussion of civil and political rights were broadened. Human rights, in the general scholarly view, were neither abstract nor natural: they were contingent and cumulative. But civil and political rights were accepted by scholars, and implicitly by the officials who permitted their publications, as legitimate items on the human rights agenda and as a necessary corollary (along with their associated duties) to the Four Modernizations.

Although the 1978–80 period was the high point for discussion of China's human rights, in the late 1980s debate was resumed. Many of the writings reflected an advance on the earlier period, which, for all its radical character, had generally maintained consistency with the official line that human rights were citizens' rights, were concrete, and had a class character. In contrast, post-1980s theorists argued that human rights had an aspect beyond class and that "human rights should include both the rights of the individual and the rights of the collective and that a citizen's political right is as important as his economic, social and cultural rights."[57]

Whatever the areas of difference in the interpretation of human rights during the 1979–89 period, Chinese scholars were generally unanimous about the need to support human rights in the international arena. In 1982, an article entitled "On the Question of Human Rights in the International Arena" argued that despite the politicization of the issue of human rights, it was the Third World's duty to support them; moreover, it claimed, "socialism and human rights are one (*shi yizhi de*)."[58] Another article gave qualified support to the notion of international involvement in human rights situations.[59] As early as the late 1970s and early 1980s, official journals stressed the importance of incorporating human rights into Chinese foreign policy. An article in the official journal *Hongqi* stated that: "in today's international activities, human rights occupies a secure position. One aspect of UN activities is to discuss and deliberate on (*shenyi*) human rights questions. . . . We must seriously analyse and study the complex struggle around the question of human rights in the current international [system] and make an effort to insist on our principled stand in order to maintain world peace and safeguard the right to self-determination and the fundamental human rights of the people of every country."[60]

In his article in the official *Beijing Review* on China's view of human rights, Ma Jun distinguished between cases of legitimate interference and cases where interference was not acceptable: "China has no objection to the

United Nations expressing concern in a proper way over consistent and large-scale human rights violations in a given country, but it opposes the interference in other countries' internal affairs under the pretext of defending human rights."[61]

Chinese Theories of International Law, State Sovereignty, and the International Protection of Human Rights

From its entry into the United Nations in 1971 until the late 1970s, China was still clearly operating on the assumptions of an earlier period.[62] The onset of the Cultural Revolution in late 1965 and the suspended publication of legal journals had prevented further conceptualization of Chinese theories in the late 1960s and 1970s. Prior to 1979, therefore, China's official attitude to international law, the principle of state sovereignty, and the question of international jurisdiction over human rights was elucidated in the official statements and scholarly debates of the late 1950s and 1960s, which clearly set out the parameters of the issues. On the whole, Chinese authorities avoided elaborating an official position on legal issues, but revealed China's policy in reaction to specific events. Although there was no evidence that Chinese authorities regarded scholarship as a formal, if subsidiary, source of law, it was clear that, like their Soviet counterparts, they recognized that in practice scholars had an important influence on the interpretation and application of international law.[63] Thus, official Chinese statements would even cite bourgeois scholars, such as Oppenheim, to argue a point of international law.[64]

China's attitude to international law issued from the complex intertwining of a number of interrelated variables: China's history of protecting itself from foreign incursions, its political culture and Marxist ideology, and its position within the international community (335). By the early and mid-1970s, the main change in those variables was China's increasing voice in international organizations, especially the United Nations, which softened the sharpness of its rhetoric and its calls for UN reform, and further institutionalized its role as leader of the developing world. China's underlying political culture, however, with its stress on hierarchical relationships, on ethics rather than law, informal consensus rather than formal adversarial procedures, and moral principles rather than international law, remained a barrier to the internalization of the customary and historically evolved norms and procedures governing relations in the international state system.[65]

The Western concept of international law first came to China in the early years of the Qing dynasty (1644–1911), but was adopted by the Qing and the subsequent Republic of China only after foreign incursions threatened the survival of the Chinese state. Although there were instances in both Imperial and pre-Imperial China when governments dealt with each other on the basis of equality, such instances were the exception, indicating merely that

China was "capable of accommodating its hierarchical theory and practice to political necessities."[66] Otherwise, China's concept of "world order" was reflected in the hierarchically based tributary system, according to which on occasions China intervened in the affairs of other states where it judged necessary, because, as one scholar has observed, "the Chinese emperor was responsible for all peoples under heaven and . . . their rulers were viewed as his appointed representatives."[67] By the early 1860s, however, international law, in the instrumental sense of a weapon of self-defense respected by Western powers, was systematically introduced: the Qing court recognized many independent states and acknowledged the need to rule its foreign relations by international law.[68]

By the collapse of the Qing dynasty in 1911, China had become a formal participant in the Western state system and was attuned to its institutions and values even if it did not internalize them. It was even claimed that, during the period of the Republican government, Chinese authorities took part in the progressive development of international law (12–13). The advent of the communist government in 1949, however, posed a dilemma for Chinese leaders and scholars. According to Marxist theory, law was part of the super-structure of a state developing from its economic base and representing the interests of the ruling elite of that state. The dilemma was how to reconcile this notion with a legal system claiming to govern the relations between states of different social systems (47). This problem was first faced by the Soviet government, which recognized the need for a universal international law that would protect its interests, and those of small and developing states, against capitalist states, but which at the same time could be reconciled with Marxist principles. This debate was resolved by the formation of consensus within the Soviet Union in the late 1950s that contemporary international law consisted of general international law and socialist internationalism (48). In China, however, the debate continued as to whether there were two discrete forms of international law, socialist and capitalist, or whether the "inheritability" of international law made it a law without a class basis apply-ing equally to all states.[69]

In contrast to the lack of congruence between the Chinese traditional view of world order and the Westphalian principles of international order, the Western concept of sovereignty, in the broad sense of a belief in every state's right to manage its own affairs, had its resonances in China's pre-Imperial past and was invoked, if ineffectually, by the Manchu emperors as a means of protection against the incursions of Western powers.

From 1949, the concept of state sovereignty (*guojia zhuquan*) was at the core of China's concerns in its involvement in all issues of international law. It was defined as the principle that "a state has the power, in accordance with its own will, to decide its own form of state, political system, and social-economic system, and intervention by other states in those matters is abso-lutely not permissible."[70] According to the Chinese view, the rights of international organizations and individuals only began where states' sovereign rights ended, since international law was a law among states, not above them (76). However, sovereignty was not seen as the exercise of government power without external limitations. China's perspective was close to that of classical Western international law, since it espoused the notion neither of absolute sovereignty, which allowed no limitations on the sovereignty of the state, nor of the relative sovereignty put forward by Lauterpacht and others. It was equally critical of theories of "absolute sovereignty, restrictive sovereignty and denial of sovereignty," and called instead for "mutual" sovereignty, or "the principle that other states respect our sovereignty and we respect the sovereignty of other states."[71] It was thus an essentially protective rather than offensive concept of sovereignty, reflecting "the immense weight of past grievances."[72] In diplomatic practice China claimed its right to exercise its sovereign right to protect its nationals abroad, since "no one can deny this minimum standard of international law."[73] China also criticized the Soviet invasion of Czechoslovakia as an attack on Czech sovereignty.[74]

The Marxist requirement that international power relationships be changed, however, required the traditional concept of state sovereignty to be modified in Chinese thinking to allow for secession and the emergence of new revolutionary states. It was even argued that national liberation movements should be given the rights of states under international law, so that "national sovereignty" became synonymous with the right to self-determination.[75] China considered it an internationalist duty to support the "revolutionary struggles of the oppressed peoples." In the 1950s Guo Qun pointed out that "acts of suppressing national liberation movements basically are not a question of a state's internal affairs [because] such acts violate the fundamental United Nations Charter principles of national self-determination and respect for human rights and also threaten the peace and security of the world . . . both the General Assembly and the Security Council have the duty and authority to handle this matter."[76]

A clear line was drawn, however, between China's support for self-determination in the case of oppressed people under foreign slavery and colonial rule and the case of a nation within a state (such as Tibet) demanding independence or self-government. Such people were viewed as minority nationalities, and not as indigenous peoples, since the latter were understood to be essentially products of European colonial settlement.[77] The position of minority nationalities in China was still considered a matter for the jurisdiction of the state and the principle of national self-determination did not apply.[78] This distinction made it difficult for China to justify its intervention, in the name of socialist internationalism, in support of communist movements or insurgencies in other independent, or newly independent, sovereign states.

Accordingly, by the post-colonial era, the principle of the right to self-determination was being used by China, like other socialist and developing states, to justify the "statist" argument against the international jurisdiction of human rights law with respect to individual and peoples' human rights. In keeping with its statist position, subjects of international law were seen not to include international organizations or individuals. China's view of international organizations was reflected in an early description of the United Nations:

the United Nations Organization is one form of international organization of sovereign states. Its resolutions in general have only the character of a recommendation (with the exception of Security Council decisions to maintain peace, taken under Chapter VII of the Charter). Such resolutions cannot *ipso facto* bind member countries. Even the legal drafts prepared by the International Law Commission and adopted by the General Assembly must still go through the procedure of an international conference and the conclusion of a treaty before they acquire binding force . . . the United Nations is an international organization among sovereign states, not a "world government" above them.[79]

Consistent with its strong views on sovereignty, China was a signatory to the UN Charter but not to either of the International Covenants, despite Taiwan's earlier signature of both. The articles of the Charter most often cited by China to bolster its arguments on sovereignty and noninterference were, and continued to be, Article 2, Paragraphs 4 and 7, which enunciated the United Nations role as upholder of the sovereignty of the state. Articles 1 and 55, which stated the concomitant UN obligation to encourage respect for human rights and "fundamental freedoms," were, on the other hand, rarely cited. China's position on the Charter was that "the prohibition of intervention in internal affairs provided for in Article 2, paragraph 7, of the Charter is listed in the beginning of the Charter as one of the principles of the United Nations. Article 2, paragraph 7, is related to Article 1, paragraph 1, which stresses the principle of sovereign equality. This means that nonintervention in internal affairs is a fundamental principle of the United Nations Charter which must be strictly observed. It is impermissible to invoke other Charter provisions to cancel or weaken this principle . . . to use Articles 10 and 55 of the Charter to resist Article 2, paragraph 7, is obviously a distorted interpretation of the Charter."[80] The principle of noninterference, already incorporated in the Five Principles of Peaceful Coexistence agreed to in the Joint Communiqué of the 1955 Bandung Conference, was seen as an extension of the principle of state sovereignty, and as another central foreign policy doctrine.[81]

Even in the early days of its UN membership, the People's Republic did not formally oppose the international protection of human rights as such.[82] However, it argued that protection was required only in the case of matters affecting global peace and security. The individual was not seen as a subject of international law and China was concerned about the uses of "human rights" as a pretext for interference in the internal affairs of socialist states. As Kong Meng had stated in the late 1950s:

As to the protection of "fundamental human rights" (Preamble) and respect for "fundamental freedoms" (Article 62) emphasized in the United Nations Charter, the fact that the United Nations General Assembly has adopted the "Declaration of Human Rights" and "Draft Covenant of Human Rights" does not mean, as described by certain bourgeois jurists (such as Lauterpacht and Jessup), that the United Nations Organisation, its Economic and Social Council, or its Commission on Human Rights can bypass states to protect the "human rights" of individuals in the various states and thus make individuals subjects of international law. As a matter of fact, the principle concerning fundamental human rights prescribed in the United Nations Charter is that the various member states are obliged to guarantee that individuals under their rule enjoy certain rights. But the fundamental human rights enjoyed by individuals are not conferred on them by an international organisation, but rather by the municipal law of the various member states which undertake such obligations. . . . All individuals, whether citizens within a state or aliens, are under the sovereignty of the state and are not subjects of international law.[83]

In contrast, just as China had expanded its concept of sovereignty to exempt the right to self-determination from its confining jurisdiction, so it exempted from this general prohibition some collective rights whose abuse was seen as having the potential to undermine world peace and security. The collective rights of peoples not to be discriminated against on the basis of race and sex were also rights endorsed in the two International Covenants that converged with Chinese socialist foreign policy principles, as did opposition to genocide, slavery, and terrorism.

This position was maintained by China in the post-1979 modernization era. A 1981 legal textbook listed the preservation of the right to self-determination, the prevention of discrimination, the prevention and punishment of genocide, the prohibition against slavery and similar systems and customs, and the prevention and punishment of terrorism as international obligations, and pointed out that "necessary measures taken by all states and international organisations to suppress these behaviours [were] consistent with generally recognized principles of international law and should not be considered as intervening in the internal affairs of a state."[84] However, in this same textbook, the list of rights within the scope of international protection was also expanded to include questions relating to the status of refugees, migrant workers, political rights of women, rights of children, and freedom of the press and of association (266). By the beginning of the modernization era, the idea of international protection of human rights had therefore broadened in the minds of leading Chinese legal scholars to encompass not only standard collective rights but civil rights impacting on individual and industrial rights.

After the suppression of the Democracy Movement in June 1989, however, this more liberal interpretation reverted back in official policy to the collective rights supported in Maoist China. China continued to maintain that the international community had a legitimate role to play in upholding the protection of these collective human rights, but not in supporting individual rights. The 1991 White Paper on human rights stated that the international community "should interfere with and stop acts that endanger world peace and security, such as gross human violations caused by colonialism, racism, foreign aggression and occupation, as well as by apartheid, racial discrimination, genocide, slave trade and serious violation of human rights by international terrorist organizations."[85] All other rights were judged to be internal matters.

Weak Application of the International Human Rights Regime, 1971–89

In theory, China became part of the international human rights regime in 1971 when it joined the United Nations.[86] Chinese Communist Party representative Dong Biwu had been a member of the Chinese United Front delegation to the founding San Francisco Conference in 1945 and had signed the Charter. However, it was not until 1971 that the People's Republic of China replaced Taiwan in the official "China" seat. As has been noted, the PRC did not accept the obligation to continue to respect the ICCPR and ICESCR which Taiwan had signed in October 1967 in the name of China. However, as a UN member, the PRC was required to respect the principles in the Universal Declaration of Human Rights and, as a signatory to the Charter, became party to the basic human rights principles embodied in it.[87] It became subject to the general principle accepted by UN members and incorporated in Articles 55 and 56 of the UN Charter, that members should "take joint and separate action in cooperation with the Organization for the achievement of . . . universal respect for, and observance of, human rights and fundamental freedoms for all without distinction as to race, sex, language or religion." During the entire 1971–89 period, China was thus open to the passive, routinizing processes of the human rights regime. However, not until 1979, when China began to actively participate in the UN human rights organs, was the socializing effect of the regime reflected in its policy. In the first phase, 1971–79, China experienced regime influence mainly by default; in the second phase, 1979–89, it submitted voluntarily to its influence. In this second phase, China also became more responsive to governmental and nongovernmental pressures. Whatever its immediate perceptions and understanding of the significance of that move in the late 1970s, China's decision to participate actively proved crucial, given that in theory it was now submitting itself to formal international scrutiny.

Phase One: 1971–79

In the early years of its UN membership China limited its involvement to issues of collective human rights that it had supported since 1949 in its international relations, such as the right to self-determination and opposition to apartheid.[88] This position reflected its more general "system reforming" attitude to international organizations in the 1970s, in which it "treat[ed] the UN and other global IGOs as a legitimizing dispenser of normative claims for the underdogs rather than a vehicle for promoting Chinese national interests, and as an arena for anti-hegemonic [anti-Soviet] struggle rather than a functional actor in the service of China's development."[89] In this spirit, China refused to participate in the work of the UN Commission on Human Rights but took part in another Economic and Social Council (ECOSOC) functional committee, the Commission on the Status of Women. As a member of ECOSOC and the Social, Humanitarian and Cultural Committee of the General Assembly, as well as of the Assembly itself, it also had to respond to various human rights proposals that came before these bodies. On 30 May 1972, China made its most comprehensive statement on human rights questions. Its representative, Wang Junsheng, stated that "the question of human rights was an important issue for the Economic and Social Council. China was ready to work together with all the countries and peoples who loved peace and upheld justice in supporting the struggles of the peoples of the world against imperialism, colonialism and racism and for the attainment and defence of national independence, national sovereignty and fundamental human rights in accordance with the spirit of the Charter."[90]

In line with its strict focus on collectivist and state-based Maoist norms, however, China maintained a cautious approach to the Universal Declaration and the two International Covenants, emphasizing as they did the rights of the individual as well as of the collective:

the Universal Declaration of Human Rights . . . had been adopted at the third session of the General Assembly, prior to the founding of the People's Republic of China. It was therefore necessary for [the Chinese] Government to examine its contents . . . The International Covenant on Economic, Social and Cultural Rights had been adopted at a time when the People's Republic of China had been deprived of its lawful rights in the United Nations. It had been illegal for the Chiang Kai-shek clique to sign that Covenant in the name of China and the Chinese Government assumed no obligation thereunder. As in the case of the Universal Declaration of Human Rights, the Chinese Government had to examine and study the Covenant and reserved the right to comment on the two documents. (486)

In this period China did not become party to any of the conventions relating to human rights: it thus was not subject to the monitoring of these bodies. It appeared to be feeling its way, wishing neither to offend UN conventions nor to conform to any identifiable position on human rights, adopting in preference an "evasive position of non-commital" (485). Yet, the very process of involvement in ECOSOC, the Social, Humanitarian and Cultural Committee of the General Assembly, and the deliberations of the General Assembly obliged it to expand its working concept of human rights. Until 1980, in line with its socialist policy, China supported United Nations General Assembly resolutions on self-determination, on the granting of independence to colonial countries and on opposition to apartheid, racial discrimination and discrimination against women; it absented itself from resolutions on human rights in Chile and El Salvador, as well as on questions of drugs and the elimination of religious intolerance. China supported UN peacekeeping and UN sanctions against South Africa, if not against Cuba and Libya.[91] Its support for human rights was articulated in terms of its support for the UN Charter rather than for the Universal Declaration of Human Rights.

Although apart from these issues it sought to abstain from voting or to absent itself, it voted for Assembly resolutions condemning torture based on the Universal Declaration and the ICCPR, and did not object to the Assembly's adoption by acclamation of the Declaration on the Protection of All Persons from Being Subjected to Torture and Other Cruel, Inhuman or Degrading Treatment or Punishment.[92] It also advocated stronger sanctions against Southern Rhodesia and South Africa under Chapter VII of the Charter. With respect to China's neighbors, it attacked Taiwan for the suppression of democracy advocates and criticized human rights in the Soviet Union: "Moscow pretended to have a clear conscience and boasted about the right to work, education, social welfare, vote . . . in the Soviet Union, to make itself out to be the champion of 'human rights.' But as the Soviet Union today has become a land of KGB agents, bristling with prisons full of its citizens while many others have been exiled, what 'human rights' can it talk about?"[93]

In such ways, the actual process of UN diplomacy, and the dictates of its foreign policy, led China imperceptibly to cross the theoretical divide between external inquiries into matters involving specific collective rights that China regarded as legitimate, and international inquiry into matters of domestic civil rights, which in theory it proscribed. This impact of diplomatic process on its theory and policy of human rights, gradual at best, became more pronounced in the second pre-1989 phase once China itself chose to participate actively in the regime.

Phase Two: 1979–89

The real beginning of its voluntary, as opposed to involuntary, participation in the human rights regime coincided with the commencement of China's modernization and with its formal repudiation of the excesses of the Cultural Revolution. China's active involvement in the international human rights regime from 1979 also coincided with the beginning of its "system-maintaining and system-exploiting" approach to international organizations, as it began to "ask more and more what international organizations could do for China and less and less what China itself could do to reform or transform the existing world order."[94] The actual date first reflecting this new attitude has been confirmed by the account of Chinese diplomat Pang

Sen, who has identified the year in which China began to participate voluntarily in the regime by sending observer delegates to the Human Rights Commission as 1979.[95] As it grew in confidence in its UN status and as the benefits of organizational involvement were seen to outweigh its disadvantages, China began to assume the more assertive role befitting a Permanent Member of the UN Security Council and an increasingly influential power. In its official pronouncements and activities in international forums, it was more responsive to making formal adjustments to the international law of human rights than its domestic legislation would suggest. It also began to participate cautiously in human rights activities in international bodies. In doing so, it heightened the likelihood of conflict between its formal adherence to the principles of state sovereignty and noninterference and its activities within the United Nations.

Although China initially adopted a passive role with respect to the regime, spending time learning the procedures, its speed and efficiency in catching up was facilitated by the energy it put into its "human rights diplomacy" (*renquan waijiao*). In general, China's diplomats working within the human rights regime specialized in the area of international organizations and attended session after session of both the UN Commission on Human Rights and its Sub-Commission. They were therefore engaged in an uninterrupted learning curve. Some had been attached to China's delegations since China entered the United Nations in 1971 and, as one diplomat pointed out in 1993, "knew everything about human rights, from A to Z." This specialization was different from the case of other Asian states, where diplomats normally only worked on human rights for the duration of UN sessions. It was also different from the practice of many Western states, whose departmental policies tended to discourage such intense specialization over a long period. Within the International Organizations Department in the Chinese Foreign Ministry, a Human Rights Division of ten people testified to the importance given the issue by the early 1990s in China's foreign policy.

At first China attended as observer at the Human Rights Commission's sessions in 1979, 1980, and 1981. However, in 1981 China was elected by ECOSOC as a member of the Commission and in 1982 sent an official delegation (210). By 1981, China had changed its approach from being absent for votes in the General Assembly on human rights in Chile, El Salvador, and Guatemala to abstaining, thus at least indicating a preparedness to be involved in the consideration of civil and political rights issues. In 1984, China supported the appointment of a rapporteur to examine the human rights situation in Afghanistan, despite Soviet and Eastern European protests that this would constitute interference in internal affairs; and in 1985, China supported a Human Rights Commission resolution for an investigation into the human rights situation in Chile, although not in El Salvador and Iran.[96]

In the same year, China voted for a UN General Assembly resolution,

"The Indivisibility and Interdependence of Economic, Social, Cultural, Civil and Political Rights." Although meant to redress the imbalance between the rights in favor of economic and social rights, this resolution suggested at the same time the need for full realization of civil and political rights.[97] In the Human Rights Commission, resolutions adopted without a vote in March 1989, following preliminary amendments contributed to by China, included decisions and resolutions on human rights in Burma and Chile and on a host of civil and political rights issues.[98]

The sensitivity of China's position in these forums and the difficulty faced when practical issues of sovereignty conflicted with human rights was indicated in one Chinese analysis:

> In its activities in the UN in the field of human rights China lays stress on expounding the Chinese government's position on human rights and its attitude to each human rights issue. As to the issue of UN human rights bodies monitoring each state's ongoing, serious violations of human rights, the Chinese government, in accordance with the strictures and principles of the UN Charter, distinguishes right from wrong, and according to different circumstances, decides its position and voting attitude . . . China believes that . . . the UN should take appropriate methods to show its concern and carry out prevention [of abuses], but it should prevent the great powers from using the pretext of interfering in a state's internal affairs.[99]

At the same time, a change occurred in China's attitude to the Universal Declaration and the Covenants. In a speech to the forty-first session of the UN General Assembly in 1986, the Chinese Foreign Minister, referring to the twentieth anniversary of the ICCPR and the ICESCR pointed out that "the two Covenants have played a positive role in realising the purposes and principles of the UN Charter concerning respect for human rights. The Chinese Government has consistently supported these purposes and principles."[100] In September 1988, at the forty-third session of the General Assembly, the Chinese Foreign Minister reevaluated the Universal Declaration of Human Rights, describing it as "the first international instrument which systematically sets forth the specific contents regarding respect for and protection of fundamental human rights. Despite its historical limitations, the Declaration has exerted a far-reaching influence on the development of the post-war international human rights activities and played a positive role in this regard."[101]

Besides membership in the Human Rights Commission, in 1984 China joined the Sub-Commission on Prevention of Discrimination and Protection of Minorities (the Sub-Commission on Human Rights), the panel of human rights experts.[102] From 1980 to 1989 it successively signed, or signed and ratified seven human rights conventions and one protocol:[103] China participated in working groups to draft and formulate international legal human rights instruments such as the Convention Against Torture and Other Cruel, Inhuman or Degrading Treatment or Punishment, and the Declaration on the Protection of Rights of Persons Belonging to National,

Ethnic, Religious and Linguistic Minorities.[104] Under the Racial Discrimination Convention, China was obliged to report on, and receive criticisms of, its treatment of national or ethnic minorities to an international committee of eighteen states.

Paradoxically, the period from 1988 to early 1989 represented a high point in China's international human rights activities. At the forty-fifth session of the UN Commission on Human Rights in early 1989, Qian Jiadong was elected Vice-Chairman. Having ratified the Convention Against Torture on 4 October 1988, China was obliged to report to the UN Committee Against Torture. It also took part in the working groups drafting the Conventions on the Rights of the Child and the Rights of Migrant Workers.[105] For the first time, the Foreign Ministry's survey of China's international relations, *Zhongguo waijiao gailan*, carried a separate section on China's international human rights activities (459–462). In the same year, China responded to the United Nations call and took a further step in the direction of human rights by commemorating the fortieth anniversary of the Universal Declaration of Human Rights. This activity, in the form of a symposium in Beijing and publication of some commemorative articles, lasted one week, from 4–10 December 1988, and was regarded by China as highly significant.[106]

As of 1989, there were even indications that China might be considering signing and ratifying the ICCPR and the ICESCR.[107] This was partly because the Sino-British Joint Declaration of 1984 on the Question of Hong Kong (Annex 1, Art. 13, Para. 4) had stated that "the provisions of the International Covenant on Civil and Political Rights and the International Covenant on Economic, Social and Cultural Rights as applied to Hong Kong shall remain in force," under the general agreement that, from 1 July 1997, when Hong Kong was restored to China, "Hong Kong's previous capitalist system and lifestyle shall remain unchanged for fifty years," and that the rights and freedom of Hong Kong citizens would be ensured by law.[108]

Whether expressed in terms of acquiescence or merely passive involvement, China's active participation in the international human rights regime from 1979 increased its vulnerability to similar investigations into its own activities. Although it was not subject to the jurisdiction of the UN Human Rights Committee or the Economic, Social, and Cultural Rights Committee, it was subject to those bodies supervising the treaties to which China was now a party. It was an active member of the UN Commission on Human Rights and its Sub-Commission. Its participation in the International Labor Organization (ILO) brought China under the scrutiny of the Committee on Freedom of Association (CFA); it had also begun co-operation with the International Committee of the Red Cross, and had extended permission to the World Food Programme to visit poor areas in China.[109]

Yet, China was still only subject to the weak influence of the international human rights regime. Not until 1989 did UN human rights bodies single out

China for sustained criticism of its human rights abuses. In the 1986 and 1989 Human Rights Commission sessions, China was taken to task for acts of racial discrimination and violation of human rights in Tibet.[110] However, cosponsors of a draft resolution on the human rights situation in Tibet during the fortieth session of the Sub-Commission in August 1988 withdrew the resolution as a result of political pressures applied by China. China's representatives were alleged to have complained in a meeting with the UN Secretary-General that the proposed draft resolution on Tibet constituted interference in China's internal affairs.[111] They also invoked the principle of state sovereignty to counter aspects of the Special Rapporteur's report on the Implementation of the Declaration on the Elimination of All Forms of Intolerance and of Discrimination Based on Religion or Belief. In response to its claim that bishops of the Catholic Church in China were appointed by Chinese secular authorities, China insisted that the Church in China would not accept external jurisdiction.[112] However, in none of these cases was international attention focused on China in any thorough-going, systematic way. In his 1985 report, in response to Amnesty International information, the Special Rapporteur on Summary and Arbitrary Executions drew attention to "executions" in a certain country "for a wide range of criminal offenses not normally punishable by death." However, his report did not mention China by name.[113]

At the same time, during the 1980s China became more responsive to occasional criticisms of its human rights by governments and NGOs. On a few occasions from the late 1970s, Chinese officials showed a willingness to make concessions to U.S. officials on human rights, especially when economic and political benefits would result (530). In 1978 and 1981, at the height of the Democracy Wall Movement, French officials intervened successfully to obtain the release of four political prisoners. In 1983 Amnesty International submitted to the Chinese government a list of prisoners of conscience and detainees, two of whom, Ren Wanding and Chen Lu, were subsequently released by Chinese authorities (531). And, although for some years the Chinese had been refusing to participate in meetings with Amnesty representatives, from 1982 Chinese officials began meeting with them at the United Nations in Geneva and New York (532).

Conclusion

From 1949 to 1989, despite peripheral adjustments to the human rights provisions in its four constitutions, the formal constitutional, legal, and institutional framework of China's human rights conformed with the socialist view of individual civil and political rights as subordinate to state sovereignty and the rights of the state. This view was projected into the manner in which China responded to the mechanisms of the international human rights regime after it joined the United Nations in 1971. The turmoil of the

Cultural Revolution in which it was then embroiled and a period of intense domestic introspection impeded any effective response to the weak application of the human rights regime, despite the simultaneous expansion of its foreign relations. Nevertheless, China embarked on a learning process, and showed selective compliance with the values and procedures of some UN human rights bodies, including the UN General Assembly.

The end of the Cultural Revolution in 1976 and the opening of Chinese society to the outside world in 1979 had three main repercussions: it brought an informal liberalization in the civil and political freedoms allowed its people, and a burgeoning of popular expectations; it generated the environment for the development of a rule of law and provided the conditions for an expansion in the scholarly and official conceptualization of human rights; and it saw a development in China's interaction with the international regime, and China's voluntary decision to participate in UN human rights activities. The initial impetus for change was domestic and economic, and born of a need to interact with the international community. It represented a shift away from sovereignty as exercised through autonomy of action toward sovereignty as expressed through participation in international organizations. The process of international interaction, whether intended or unintended, widened the ambit of China's involvement in international human rights activities and began to erode the firm line drawn by China between its formal interpretation of state sovereignty and the areas in which it was prepared in practice to accept international involvement in a state's human rights conditions.

By 1989, China had become absorbed in numerous ways into a web of involvement and obligation in the international human rights arena. China continued to stress the principles of state sovereignty and noninterference in relation to the international protection of human rights. It had not signed or ratified the two major International Covenants, the ICCPR and the ICESCR, or the Optional Protocol, and was not subject to the jurisdiction of their treaty bodies. Moreover, its support in the United Nations for issues of civil and political rights was selective and erratic. Nevertheless, China had modified its position on human rights over the years since entry into the United Nations and, in that forum at least, had come closer to accepting a basic core of universally accepted human rights. It had shown adaptive learning in adjusting to the human rights regime. Indeed, by 1988 it had begun to show in its declaratory policy, and some of its activities, evidence of cognitive learning. It had accepted the weak application of the regime, complied with some of its procedures, and shown acceptance of some of its norms. It had also responded, if again in a highly selective way, to some governmental and nongovernmental pressures. By commencing formal participation in the UN human rights regime, China had already sacrificed a measure of sovereignty and independence. It was, in effect, agreeing to be assessed by the international community according to human rights standards that were very different in concept and practice from those it had experienced in its long history. The challenge for the international community was to encourage a closer convergence between China's formal international position on human rights and its more inflexible domestic constitutional, legal, and institutional framework, and to break through the compartmentalization existing between them.

Chapter 2
China, the UN Commission on Human Rights, and the UN Sub-Commission on Human Rights

This is the seventh time that certain Western countries [have] tabled an anti-China draft resolution in the Commission on Human Rights. They have asserted time and again that they do so because China's human rights record is deplorable. This is an outrageous distortion of China's reality. . . . The Commission on Human Rights has already paid a high enough price for confrontation. I therefore urge once again those Western countries bent on confrontation to abandon this approach and return to the path of dialogue and cooperation.

—Ambassador Wu Jianmin before the UN Commission on Human Rights, Geneva, 15 April 1997

This is a fitting time to pay tribute to the members of this organ which throughout its history has seen enormous efforts and great achievements but also moments of deep despair.

—UN Commission on Human Rights, February 1997, on the occasion of its fiftieth anniversary

China's crackdown on its Democracy Movement in June 1989 had a profound impact on its relations with the international community and with the international human rights regime. In emphasizing state sovereignty at the expense of popular sovereignty, it marked the end of its immunity from international criticism. Widespread international sanctions were initiated, with states cooperating in multilateral forums to provide a collective response. Foremost among the multilateral bodies were the European Community, the Group of Seven, and the World Bank, under pressure from the U.S.[1] Under the umbrella of this response, individual states also applied sanctions. These sanctions, designed more as a temporary expedient to punish China for Tiananmen than to provide a continuing deterrent for future abuses, drew a negative response from China, and a withdrawal back to a position where it denied the applicability of regime norms to it, even though it did not deny the validity of the norms themselves.[2] This defensive reaction was partly due to the fact that, as a result of collective international action, China had now lost control over the nature of its participation in the human rights regime.

Within the United Nations, the application of the regime to China strengthened and became more widespread and consistent, with repercussions throughout the UN human rights system, from the Secretary-General, the UN General Assembly, the UN Commission on Human Rights, and the Sub-Commission on Prevention of Discrimination and Protection of Minorities, to the treaty bodies and the thematic special rapporteurs and working groups. Although there were many types of possible multilateral response, in China's case it mainly took the forms of the country-specific draft resolutions moved in the Commission and Sub-Commission, and the reporting activities required by the treaty bodies and the thematic special rapporteurs and working groups. In the former case, the changing fortunes of the draft resolution, "Situation of Human Rights in China," reflected the changes in international world order that quickly followed on the dismantling of the Berlin Wall in 1989. Its fate was also influenced by the marked alterations in China's status in the global community.

A rough coincidence between the events of Tiananmen, the strong application of the human rights regime to China, and the collapse of the communist system in European states in late 1989 served to highlight the role of human rights in China's foreign policy. China was obliged not only to deal with the negative impact of its human rights abuses on its foreign relations, but to confront the wider uncertainty of power shifts in the international system. The end of the Cold War brought a fluidity to world affairs that neither China nor the rest of the world community had anticipated, or could initially comprehend.[3] The confidence with which China had moved within the "strategic triangle" created by itself, the Soviet Union, and the United States was replaced by uncertainty as it also sought to cope with international criticism of its domestic actions.[4]

Initially, in a period coinciding with its rejection of foreign sanctions, China was unwilling to take on board notions of "multipolarity," seeing a lurking hegemon behind the concept of the new world order. Before 1989 China had perceived the external environment as generally peaceful, despite being suspicious of the West's motives in advocating the "peaceful evolution" (*heping yanbian*) of communist states. In the post-Cold War era, however, and particularly after the failure of the August 1991 coup in the Soviet Union, China's leaders viewed the international environment as potentially more threatening. A sense of external vulnerability was matched by internal insecurity. The Tiananmen crackdown had revealed the emptiness of the regime's claims to popular support and had intensified its sensitivity to

how does Humro situation affect China's sense of external vulnerability and insecurity?

any sources of instability on China's borders, whether issuing from minority problems in the far western provinces or from the political liberalization occurring to the east in Hong Kong and Taiwan. The leaders' solution to these manifold pressures and uncertainties was to resurrect the Five Principles of Peaceful Coexistence issuing from the 1955 Bandung Conference, with their strong basis in respect for state sovereignty and the principle of noninterference. A dualism developed within Chinese foreign policy, marked by the simultaneous invocation of a formal, legalistic interpretation of state sovereignty in order to protect the legitimacy of its domestic regime, and a more liberal interpretation of sovereignty in its practical diplomacy in response to the imperatives of the economic reform program and its extensive participation in international organizations.[5] At first, the interdependence/sovereignty dualism led to a new readiness to entertain the idea of multipolarity, and to adopt an "omnidirectional" (or "be nice to everyone") diplomacy, due in part to China's need to counter foreign criticism of its human rights and to improve its international reputation.[6] However, the need to counter in the short term the pressures of the U.S. "hegemon" and to resist international interference in its human rights policies impelled China to reiterate its strong "pristine" position on sovereignty.

From 1990 to 1993, the interdependent side of this dualism generally prevailed, with sovereignty being relegated to a lesser role. An expansion in China's regional and international relations, and in its economic and military power, coincided with the period of its active human rights diplomacy (*renquan waijiao*). At a lesser level of intensity, the power of the United States and the power balance between the U.S. and China were tested through the metaphor, and reality, of human rights. The U.S. threat to remove China's MFN trading status was the most conspicuous outward sign of the West's continuing will to influence changes in China's human rights conditions. It resulted in some clear successes, achieving the release of well-known political prisoners. The political nature of this bilateral monitoring mechanism, however, meant that it was also inextricably entwined in the power play between the two great states.

From April 1993, the balance struck between political interdependence and sovereignty shifted. As China's economic and military power expanded, domestic instability increased, as a function of both social unrest and the leadership struggle induced by Deng Xiaoping's failing health. China's position on sovereignty became nonnegotiable, both in theory and practice, as conservative senior military figures increasingly dominated the policymaking process. From this time, it challenged U.S. power and authority, once again through the language, and concrete reality, of human rights.

During the same period, monitoring by the UN human rights bodies was consistent, continuous, and discreet, and more reflective of global power shifts than bilateral, hegemonic challenge. This was partly because the United Nations, by virtue of its multilateral character and institutionalized norms, was, at least until 1997, more immune to China's sovereignty claims and the constraining impact of national interests. Monitoring by UN human rights bodies was based on legal documents containing internationally accepted standards and spelling out monitoring functions that China, by virtue of its membership of the United Nations, its decision to join UN human rights bodies, and its accession to UN treaties and ILO Conventions, had already accepted.

The most dramatic public response within the United Nations to the crackdown on the Democracy Movement came with the passage of a resolution by the UN Sub-Commission on Prevention of Discrimination and Protection of Minorities (known informally as the UN Sub-Commission on Human Rights) in August 1989. By targeting a Permanent Member of the Security Council for the wide-scale abuse of human rights within its territory, this UN human rights body achieved an international "first."[7] Its action appeared to symbolize the winding down of the Cold War and the inauguration of a new era in which human rights would assume their proper place in the discourse between states. The most effective supervisory body initially was the Sub-Commission and, in the latter part of the period under study, its parent body, the Commission on Human Rights. China's fear of censure by these two bodies was palpable, and was the source of extensive lobbying and diplomatic activity. As has been pointed out, monitoring in these more political, Charter-based bodies was carried out primarily through a reintegrative shaming process of country-specific resolutions, which placed pressure on states members to bring their domestic human rights conditions into conformity with international human rights standards, and yet credited them for reform efforts.[8]

The following analysis of the diplomatic activity and coalition building undertaken by China to avoid becoming the subject of a resolution in either of these bodies is made against a background of the larger changes in the global balance of power in the post-Cold War world and the bilateral monitoring undertaken by the U.S. It highlights the distinctively political character of the two bodies and the reintegrative shaming procedures to which they had recourse. It involves careful consideration of the way in which the Commission and Sub-Commission dealt with China between 1989 and 1997, analyzing in particular detail both the forty-first and the forty-fifth sessions of the Sub-Commission. The extent of China's compliance with procedural requirements, and its substantive compliance with the norms of the regime, is thereby revealed. Norms may be assessed not only from the content of reports and resolutions, but from the character of the institutions and relationships comprising the Sub-Commission and Commission, which reflect their democratic structure. China's responses and impact may be measured not only in terms of its voting patterns, but in its attitudes toward NGOs, toward the principle of the independence of experts, and toward the relationship between the Commission, Sub-Commission, other human rights organs, NGOs, and observer governments.

Attention to such issues highlights the extent to which China has complied with the norms and customary procedures of these bodies, sought to reshape the operationalization of norms, and challenged those norms and procedures. It thereby illuminates the effectiveness of this monitoring route.

Institutional and Historical Context

The main body dealing with human rights issues in the United Nations is the Commission on Human Rights, established by ECOSOC (Economic and Social Council) in 1946.[9] Its role, albeit not totally or consistently discharged, has been defined as that of a catalyst in the preparation and dissemination of human rights information all over the world; a manager of human rights activity; a coordinator of the United Nations human rights program; a generator and legitimator of norms; and a protector of individuals and groups.[10] Its importance is indicated by the fact that the level of general participation in its activities, including by governments and NGOs, is greater than in virtually any other UN area (209).

Initially, the Commission had mainly a standard-setting role of drafting international human rights instruments (139). Indeed, it responded to the initial opportunity to define some protective role by concluding that it had none.[11] This situation changed in 1967 with the introduction of two facilitating procedures. ECOSOC Resolution 1235 of 6 June 1967 established the principle that violations by individual states could be examined and responded to. ECOSOC Resolution 1503 provided for confidential procedures in which "a consistent pattern of gross and reliably attested violations of human rights" could be pursued with the governments concerned.[12] Thus, the United Nations passed from a situation where, to justify action, it had to find that human rights violations constituted threats to peace and security, to one where wide-scale and persistent abuse of human rights was itself seen as justifying international involvement. This power was increasingly exercised after 1979.

As part of its response to violations, the Commission set up subsidiary bodies such as the Sub-Commission, and bodies to investigate human rights problems in specific countries, as well as thematic working groups and special rapporteurs that reported back to it. After 1979, it took a number of country-specific actions under the 1235 procedure that included appointments of special rapporteurs, independent experts, working groups, and a Commission delegate; reviews of information by a Sub-Commission member; and reports to the Commission by the Secretary-General. It also adopted country-specific resolutions and decisions that stopped short of introducing a special procedure (160–61). The Commission promoted four different types of activity: consultation among regional groupings; the search for co-operative solutions to problems; the canvassing of new issues; and the provision of a forum for the resolution of conflict. These constituted "an important socialization process by which competing conceptions are not just communicated but explained and justified" (205). Unlike the Sub-Commission, the Commission on Human Rights is composed of government representatives. It has grown from eighteen members at its first session in 1947 to fifty-three members in 1992. It is a political body whose decisions are nevertheless based on international legal standards and an attempt to be consistent and fair (193). Yet its controversial nature has been acknowledged in one appraisal of "the effort so many governments have made to restrain the [Commission's] forward progress and to evade its primitive machinery for enforcement. By their acts they have acknowledged the influence the idea of human rights has acquired over the minds of their subjects. Hypocrisy continues to offer credible evidence of the possibility of virtue."[13]

The Commission's more political character has enhanced the Sub-Commission's contribution, especially in relation to the violation of human rights by particular states. Within its generalized mandate, the use of the Sub-Commission as a mechanism "to circumvent or conceal deep conflicts within the Commission" has led to an expansion of its role.[14] The Sub-Commission has brought particular situations of abuse to the attention of the Commission through resolutions and decisions. It has thus sometimes compelled the Commission to act on situations that political pressures from its member states might otherwise have impeded. Such was the Sub-Commission's intention when it adopted its 1989 resolution on China.[15]

The Sub-Commission has been described as "among the finest institutions of the United Nations in the field of human rights."[16] It has been seen by experts as the most effective human rights forum linking official governmental bodies and policy with the general public through the intervention of NGOs. The NGOs have viewed it as "the best hope for a non-selective application of human rights standards."[17] This perception persists, despite the fact that even in its case political considerations have often influenced the selection of the nominally independent experts serving in an individual capacity and despite the growing tensions between NGOs and governmental observers participating in the Sub-Commission sessions.

The Sub-Commission currently consists of twenty-six experts whose members are elected on a regional basis to ensure adequate representation of different regions, legal systems and cultures. Seven are from African states; five from Asia; six from the West European and Others Group (WEOG); five from Latin American and Caribbean states; and three from Eastern European states. Although there is no formal criterion for assessing the qualifications of nominees, there is a requirement that members should be "independent experts."[18] The annual four-week session every August is also attended by a large number of observers, representing NGOs, intergovernmental organizations, the Secretariat, and an increasing number of governments.

The functions of the Sub-Commission, like those of other human rights organs, have been described as standard setting, promotion and implementation.[19] Methods for responding to alleged violations of human rights developed by the United Nations have included Sub-Commission activities under procedure 1503.[20] The advantages of the 1503 procedure are that governments initially have the protection of confidentiality and so are less threatened by it. According to the 1235 procedure, however, under Agenda Item 6 the Sub-Commission allows public debate on violations of human rights in all countries; under Item 12 the Commission does likewise. This allows allegations of violations to be presented by NGOs, by Sub-Commission members, and even by government observers who may accuse other governments of violations, often in response to allegations about their own.

China and the Human Rights Commission and Sub-Commission Before 1989

China's interest in the UN human rights bodies coincided with a period in which it began to play a full role in the United Nations as a whole. After sending Observers to the Human Rights Commission for three years, in 1981 China was elected a member of the Commission and the following year formally took part in its thirty-eighth session; it has been a continuous member ever since.[21] In 1984, Gu Yijie was elected a member of the Human Rights Sub-Commission. She was replaced in 1987 by Tian Jin, China's former Ambassador to Bern, who, after two terms in office, was replaced in 1994 by former Ambassador to the United Nations, Fan Guoxiang.[22] Before 1989, China's main interventions in the Commission and the Sub-Commission related to the right to self-determination and the right to development.[23]

According to Pang Sen, a Chinese diplomat who for some years has represented his country in both the Human Rights Commission and Sub-Commission, the Commission is seen by China as the main organ responsible for human rights questions, and in particular is judged to have an important function in censuring the large-scale violations of human rights, as well as in promoting the implementation of the right to development. Particular cases where the Commission is seen to have been effective are its resolutions on South Africa, Cambodia, Afghanistan, and the U.S. and Panama.[24] The Sub-Commission, Pang observes, has the virtue of requiring states to examine their policies and of providing a supervisory mechanism (138). Yet it allows states to attack each other and is seen as imposing the values of the West on the Third World (148). Finally, Pang has criticized the failure to limit the activities of NGOs that have been allowed to attack sovereign states (152–53).

From the forty-first session of the Sub-Commission in August 1989, following the suppression of the Democracy Movement, China became the focus of sustained UN attention. Before that time, its role in the Commission and Sub-Commission had been ambiguous. In 1987, for instance, the issue of torture in China, raised by Amnesty International at the Sub-Commission, had provoked a strong retort from the observer for China, Wu Shanxiu.[25] Yet there were indications that China was assuming a more important role in the Commission. At its session in early 1989, Qian Jiadong's election as a vice-chairman broke an understanding that representatives of the permanent members of the UN Security Council would not sit on the bureau of the Human Rights Commission or other functional commissions of ECOSOC. It was even anticipated that China might assume the chair at the 1990 Commission.[26] Ironically, this possibility was raised only a month before China's declaration of martial law in Tibet. The 1989 Commission session was therefore a stormy one, with many lengthy interventions from China's diplomats on the subject of Tibet, and an embarrassing revelation about racist attitudes and treatment encountered by African students in China.[27] Numerous NGOs intervened on the subject of Tibet. On 7 March, Chinese delegate Li Zuomin embarked on a long history of the China-Tibet relationship, in which he regretted the fact that riots had been provoked in Lhasa "by a few separatists," just when democracy and the rule of law were being consolidated.[28] Not until 9 March did he refer to the riots of 5–7 March, which had ended with the official declaration of a state of emergency. As if to blame external forces, Li observed that "it was significant that the events had occurred during the Commission's session."[29]

The Forty-first Session of the Sub-Commission, August 1989

The forty-first session of the Sub-Commission in August 1989 was an important occasion in the history of multilateral human rights monitoring for a number of reasons, apart from the unprecedented censuring of a Permanent Member of the Security Council.[30] It was the first time that the pressure of the UN human rights regime had been actively brought to bear on China, a pressure applied by both developed and developing states. It was at this session that the forum itself developed protective procedural mechanisms facilitating the censure of powerful states. The session demonstrated the crucial role of NGOs and the importance of individual agency in bringing pressure to bear on a large state in a human rights crisis.

Already the events in China had created such international concern that the Central American and Caribbean states that did not usually make an issue of human rights had met with others in the General Assembly to discuss them, and the UN Secretary-General had expressed concern to the Chinese Ambassador.[31] For this reason, and as a result of the continuing worldwide condemnation of the internationally televised massacre, the

China issue dominated the Sub-Commission session. China not only suffered the indignity of the world community's censure, but its diplomatic skills in dealing with an active human rights regime, as yet reasonably unhoned, were put to a severe and public test. The onus was on the Chinese expert, Tian Jin, and the members of China's observer delegation to avoid the threatened outcome, and to that end they employed heavy-handed tactics. These tactics were, however, ably countered by both Western and Third World experts. In response to NGO urging, Agenda Item 6, under which specific country issues were debated, was moved to an earlier position, and the China question was discussed first.[32]

Early in the debate on 15 August, a dramatic intervention was made by Li Lu, spokesman for the International Federation for Human Rights, and one of the twenty-one Chinese students wanted by the Chinese Public Security Bureau for involvement in the Tiananmen demonstrations. China's observer Mr. Zhang deplored the fact that a "criminal" on the list of persons most wanted by China's police had been allowed to address the Sub-Commission.[33] He was also reported by an academic observer to have called Li Lu a "liar" who "spread rumours" and was "one of the major organisers of counterrevolution."[34]

Zhang was rebuked the following day by the French expert, Louis Joinet, a central figure in the proceedings over the next two weeks. Joinet stated that Zhang's "allegation was slanderous and might even be a matter for the Geneva courts." He added that although "he respected the principle whereby it was for a State to determine under its national laws who was a criminal and who was not within its own frontiers, he did not believe that international law permitted a State to impose the laws on everyone outside its own frontiers. If such a line of reasoning had been followed, Mr. Arafat would never have come to the United Nations and Mr. Mandela would never be able to come."[35]

The main defense used by the Chinese expert and observer delegates during their four major interventions to persuade experts not to support the draft resolution were the principles of noninterference and state sovereignty. This hard-line position drew sharp retorts from Western experts and remonstrances from their Third World colleagues. Observer Yu Zhizhong, on the intervention of Miguel Alfonso Martinez (Cuba), was allowed extended time to explain the Chinese government position on the massacre in Beijing. He claimed that the government had acted on 3–4 June because the whole country was in a state of crisis, and that the disturbances had to be ended "precisely to safeguard the human rights and fundamental freedoms of the vast majority of the Chinese people." He insisted that "not a single person had been killed by the army or run over by a military vehicle and to assert that there had been a bloodbath on the square was a sheer fabrication."[36] Finally, he stated that "the putting down of riots and rebellions so as to maintain State order was a domestic affair of the State concerned alone and no foreign country or international organization had a right to intervene on any pretext whatsoever" (at 7).

Yu's statement drew a firm reply later that afternoon from Fatma Zohra Ksentini (Algeria), normally a strong spokeswoman for the developing world: "On the principle of noninterference, no State could claim any longer to be a special preserve, and the concept had gradually given way to that of international interest in the field of human rights. A balance had thus to be found between domestic law and the right to intervene in certain situations when domestic remedies had been exhausted. . . . A liberal approach to human rights, with emphasis on individual and political rights, had long been followed" (at 13).

In spite of this statement, on 22 August expert Tian Jin again invoked the principles of sovereignty and noninterference. In response, Joinet concluded that "if the Sub-Commission adopted the opinion of those advocating application of the principle of noninterference in the field of human rights, together with the views of those who were opposed to the resolution on specific countries and those who are in favour of deleting Item 6 or curtailing Item 9, its work would be totally paralyzed" (at 16–17).

A week later, in a final appeal against the draft resolution "Situation in China," Tian took a notably more moderate line on the principle of noninterference.[37] His Ambassador, Fan Guoxiang, was, however, less amenable to the persuasion of the body of experts, and his concluding words were that draft resolution L. 31 "in effect constituted interference in China's internal affairs and an attempt to exert pressure on China. The draft was moreover incompatible with the purposes and principles of the Charter of the United Nations and contravened the rules that regulated international relations" (at 6).

In the ensuing secret ballot, Draft Resolution E/CN.4/Sub.2/1989/L.31, as amended, was adopted on 31 August by 15 votes to 9, as Resolution 1989/5. It was a mild document with significant implications:

The Sub-Commission on Prevention of Discrimination and Protection of Minorities,
Concerned about the events which took place recently in China and about their consequences in the field of human rights,
1. *Requests* the Secretary-General to transmit to the Commission on Human Rights information provided by the Government of China and by other reliable sources;
2. *Makes an appeal* for clemency, in particular in favor of persons deprived of their liberty as a result of the above-mentioned events.

The Chinese representative immediately exercised his right of reply: "The Chinese government categorically rejects this resolution. It is null and void and has no binding force on China whatsoever."[38]

The forty-first session was unique for the amount of Chinese pressure applied outside the conference room. Interviewees have all remarked on this strategy, which extended to sending a diplomat from China expressly to pressure one of the Western diplomats with threats of trade sanctions against his country, and reports of African delegates being approached in their hotel rooms.[39] As the debate on Item 6 had continued, informal counts had begun to show that a resolution critical of China would succeed by a margin of several votes. Four or five Latin American states were willing to join the six Western members, together with enough African and Asian members to carry the resolution. The result remained unclear, however, because of the enormous Chinese pressure on the experts and the governments. Allegedly, there were also pressures on ambassadors of the experts' countries in Beijing, including cautions that their votes would affect bilateral economic relations.[40] One observer wrote: "Old hands at the UN . . . commented on the unprecedented Chinese invasion. At times it seemed as if every table on the delegates' lounge had been commandeered by the Chinese mission, and there appeared no way in which a member of the Sub-Commission in need of a tea-break could escape the diplomatic offensive. One of Hong Kong's group found herself cornered by a Chinese First Secretary with the unnerving opening gambit: "What passport do you hold?"[41]

The proceedings also highlighted the crucial role of NGOs: the final outcome was the result of unprecedented cooperation between them.[42] NGO interventions covered the events of 3–4 June and their aftermath, the situation of students, trade unions, the legal system, and the press. In a display of NGO unity, on 17 August, Niall McDermot, Secretary-General of the International Commission of Jurists, made a statement on behalf of eleven other NGOs, as well as his own.[43] However, Asian and European ambassadors anticipated that a great deal of heat would be generated by the China debate but, like the NGOs, they reportedly did not expect a resolution on China to be successful.[44]

One of the most important, and unintended, effects of the focus on China in the forty-first session was that it brought about procedural changes that had not only a significant role in shaping the 1989 session but a lasting impact on facilitating the monitoring of human rights by the Sub-Commission.[45] In order to circumvent the enormous diplomatic pressure being exerted on members concerning the "Situation in China" draft resolution, and following the successful vote on the use of secret ballot for the 1503 procedure, Louis Joinet proposed a secret ballot for the consideration of all country-specific resolutions to be addressed in public session under Agenda Item 6.[46] The secret ballot issue precipitated protracted debate and convoluted diplomatic manoeuvring, as it required the deferral of voting on Item 6. Tian Jin vigorously opposed it as "not tenable." He observed that experts were independent, but were "not living in a vacuum."[47] If the rules of procedure were suspended for "short-term purposes," he warned, the supporters of the proposal might one day find themselves in "a difficult position" as a result of this precedent.[48] Nevertheless, the motion passed with 14 in favour, 6 against (Cuba, India, the Soviet Union, Romania, Somalia, China), 3 abstentions, and 3 not present.[49]

The forty-first Sub-Commission session represented a leap forward in the international human rights regime's capacity to monitor the great powers. It demonstrated considerable unanimity between the Western powers and the majority of Third World experts over the ways in which human rights abuses should be monitored. It provided evidence of the effectiveness of a united front between the NGOs. And it indicated the regime's surprising resilience in enabling the introduction of procedural mechanisms to circumvent heavy diplomatic pressures exerted by a powerful target country, at least in the context of what was internationally regarded as a human rights crisis. The session also exemplified the crucial importance of human agency, in this case the expert from France, Louis Joinet, in achieving these procedural adjustments.

For China the resolution's success was a heavy, even incredible blow, representing inter alia a rejection of its aggressive tactics and its defence on the basis of noninterference and state sovereignty. As a target state, China was obliged to take a negative, defensive position but, as Joinet pointed out, pursuit of such hard-line tactics called into question not just the norms of the human rights regime but the regime itself. And events, as Ksentini noted, had already moved far beyond debate over such principles. Whatever China's response to the experts' opinions, fears were expressed by observers that China might retaliate in the future by leading a move at the Commission to limit the role of the Sub-Commission (306). These fears were echoed in a newspaper report that China had raised the possibility of such measures at the Conference of Non-Aligned States in Djakarta.[50]

The Sessions of the Human Rights Commission and Sub-Commission, March 1990–March 1993: China's Evolving Human Rights Diplomacy

The three-and-a-half year period following the 1989 Sub-Commission was marked by complicated political manoeuvring, the outcome of which was partly determined by the changing balance of global power. Changing political coalitions within the Commission and Sub-Commission reflected the collape of communism in the former Soviet Union and Eastern Europe, while the effects of that change were partly counterbalanced by global economic forces that saw China's emergence as a power to be reckoned with both regionally and internationally. In the first few years, the results of this larger political change militated against China's expectation of support from states of the South. However, by 1992, as its economy began to boom, and as its defensive diplomacy in human rights forums became more effective, China began to find the support it had been anticipating from the countries of the South, and began to exploit the divisions within the

West/North. Two sessions in particular exemplified this trend, the August 1991 Sub-Commission and the February–March 1992 Commission. The former demonstrated, on one hand, the strength of the Sub-Commission as a body of experts in which individual agency still had an important role, and the latter indicated, on the other, the political weakness of the Commission as a forum representing governments.

China's delegates went into the autumn 1989 UN General Assembly session in a defensive mood. In an angry protest, which they circulated as an official document under Item 12 of the agenda, they asserted that the Sub-Commission's China resolution had "brazenly interfered in China's affairs" and violated the UN Charter and international relations norms; they declared it "null and void."[51]

At the forty-sixth session of the UN Commission on Human Rights in February–March 1990, a large Chinese delegation of more than forty diplomats lobbied "in not always courteous ways."[52] They anticipated an increase in Third World support, particularly in view of the trend towards a united front of all countries of the South (6). Both the lead up to the vote and the subsequent successful outcome of the vote for China, however, undermined these expectations. As in the case of the earlier Sub-Commission proceedings, events were to indicate that the Third World bloc was not an undifferentiated mass. The draft resolution had solid Western cosponsorship and the European Community also lobbied. The text of the draft resolution was written by Australia, Canada and Sweden. However, in a meeting organized by Australia and cosponsored by the United States, the Japanese deputy also took an interest and removed any items the Chinese government might have found objectionable. When the Chinese representatives lobbied states parties of the Commission, including Australia, to have the Secretary-General's report struck out, the Filipino Chairman would not allow it. Other tactics further undermined China's standing, as its representatives tried to prevent delegates from speaking and were overruled.

The final form of the draft resolution was a mildly worded document.[53] Voting on the draft took place a day before it was expected, and Western lobbying was weak. China called for a "no" motion, and a procedural no-action vote was proposed by Pakistan, which succeeded by a narrow margin of 17 in favour, 15 against, and 11 abstentions. China's response was to condemn the Western attempt "to equate the action of a government to stop a handful of people from violating the law and order with 'violation of human rights'." It claimed that

The Chinese Government has always abided by the principles and purposes of the UN Charter, committed itself to the respect and protection of human rights and fundamental freedoms, and [has been]actively involved in and supported the United Nations in its work in the field of human rights. China has consistently sent factual replies and information, including those concerning the "June 4th incident," in a responsible manner, to the relevant UN bodies as well as to the Special Rapporteurs of the Commission on Human Rights on torture, religion, summary or arbitrary executions and forced or involuntary disappearances. China has also regularly submitted periodic reports to the monitoring bodies established by international instruments to which China is a State Party. It is, therefore, entirely unnecessary to solicit information from China through any additional procedures.[54]

In the vote, success of the no-action motion was determined by the Soviet and Ukraine vote, a fact demonstrating the fragility of a support base in the process of erosion. Moreover, the support China was anticipating from the Third World had not been forthcoming. It was clear that some Third World states which had supported the no-action motion would probably have abstained had the issue been subjected to a substantive vote. The coalition of Western, former Eastern European, and Latin American states that had been evolving as the Cold War eased and Latin American states became liberalized was not disturbed. In addition, a Cuban resolution at the end of the session, which attempted to invoke Article 2, Paragraph 7 of the Charter to claim the application of the principle of noninterference to human rights, was defeated as the result of two and a half pages of amendments. Although it had not overtly taken the lead in this effort, China was generally believed to have been the prime mover behind it. This defeat, in combination with the very narrow margin of success on the no-action motion, appears to have broken Chinese resistance to the notion of human rights as a legitimate part of the international agenda. Such acceptance, however, did not betoken a new attitude of passive compliance, but heralded the adoption of new defensive mechanisms.

The following August, at the forty-second session of the Sub-Commission, an anticipated resolution on Tibet failed to materialize. Session members agreed not to introduce a resolution on Tibet, a move that was possibly in response to China's indication that it would consider behaving in a less cooperative manner in the UN Security Council and block certain Western initiatives in the Gulf.[55] A resolution which was "in the pocket" was therefore withdrawn. Furthermore, China continued its offensive against the secret ballot. Tian Jin joined Miguel Alfonso Martinez in dissenting on a resolution proposing that ECOSOC add a footnote to the rules of procedure that would permit the Sub-Commission in future sessions to vote on violations of human rights under Item 6 by secret ballot. This resolution passed by 20 votes, with only 2 dissenting votes and 2 abstentions.[56] Tian gave as his reason for dissent the fact that "the independence of experts was a matter of principle that did not have to be guaranteed by a vote by secret ballot."[57]

At the next Commission session (February–March 1991), China was mentioned during the general discussion on human rights violations under Item 12, but no resolution was introduced. Perhaps the most significant of China's interventions was an attack on the Sub-Commission, anticipated since the Sub-Commission's forty-first session, by China's observer delegation. Somewhat surprisingly, Zhang Yishan identified the essential characteristic of the Sub-Commission as its composition by experts, and its primary concern "to concentrate its limited human and financial resources and its time on the study of major and practical subjects concerning the promotion and enjoyment of human rights, to draft valuable studies and to put forward feasible suggestions to the Commission." For this reason, he objected to the Sub-Commission's tendency to become politicized and overlap with the responsibilities of the Commission, to engage in political debate, and "to make wanton attacks on the domestic affairs of sovereign states."[58] He attacked its failure to make sufficient time to discuss other matters like the right to development. He complained of the procedural alteration at the forty-first and forty-second sessions to allow a secret ballot for passing draft resolutions. He charged that the Sub-Commission had failed to improve its working methods and efficiency as required by the Commission. Moreover, "no effective control was exercised over the participation of Non-Governmental Organizations." He insisted that "the Commission must seriously consider the desirability of reaffirming the nature of the Sub-Commission's work and mandate" and called upon it "strictly to abide by and implement the provisions in relation to its agenda items" (at 25).

At the forty-third Sub-Commission session in August 1991, China's human rights conditions were the subject of a second resolution. By this point, NGOs had reached an informal arrangement whereby the China issue would alternate every second year with the Tibet issue. The resulting resolution on the human rights situation in Tibet was regarded as the most notable of the session, as well as the closest vote. It was also regarded by some as more significant than the 1989 resolution, since it related to long-standing Chinese policy in Tibet rather than to a single incident.[59] It expressed concern at the "continuing reports of violations of fundamental human rights and freedoms which threaten the distinct cultural, religious and national identity of the Tibetan people" and requested the Chinese government to "fully respect the fundamental rights and freedoms of the Tibetan people."

The Tibet resolution was achieved against considerable procedural and diplomatic odds, and again owed its success to individual agency. Resolutions on both China and Tibet were pending, cosponsored by Theo van Boven (Netherlands), on the eve of his departure from the Sub-Commission, and UN Rapporteur Bautista (Philippines). At the time of the vote, however, Bautista was away, Louis Joinet was in the Chair and thus unable to vote, and Erica-Irene Daes (Greece), in her function as member of the Joint Inspection Unit, declined to vote.[60] In addition, the Chinese Mission in Geneva hosted a big reception at the beginning of the session, at which it showed a lengthy film on Tibet. Such diplomatic activities, however, reportedly had an effect on experts contrary to that intended, and may well have facilitated the passage of the resolution. Another factor in the decision was apparently the impressive nature of the Tibetan delegation. Finally, China's case was not strengthened by Tian Jin's intervention just before the vote. He claimed that for more than seven hundred years Tibet had been an integral part of China, and that Tibetan conditions of life, culture, and religion were flourishing as never before. He admitted that human rights in Tibet, as elsewhere, could be improved. However, "only those who were nostalgic for colonialism and wished to dismember China denied that Tibet was an integral part of the country . . . those who distorted the facts, who clamoured for the independence of Tibet, who talked about alleged violations of human rights pursued only one objective, to foment disorders in China and to split the country."[61] In reply, van Boven stated that he and Bautista had prepared the draft resolution on the basis of disquieting reports of human rights abuses in Tibet. He insisted that "the sole purpose of the draft resolution was to defend the human rights and cultural identity of the Tibetan people and it had been drafted in very measured terms intentionally" (at 8).

Draft Resolution E/CN.4/Sub.2/1991/L.19 was then adopted by secret ballot by 9 votes to 7, with 4 abstentions. Ambassador Fan Guoxiang rejected the resolution unequivocally and asserted that it was "null and void" (at 8). Although this formula was identical to China's response to the 1989 resolution, an observer at the session has commented that, unlike the case in 1989, in 1991 China's delegates within the Sub-Commission took their defeat "on the chin."[62] Nevertheless, from Beijing, a spokesman for the Chinese Foreign Ministry issued a sharp protest, claiming that the resolution violated the principles of state sovereignty and noninterference respected in the UN Charter and in international law.[63]

The 1992 Human Rights Commission session exemplified the difficulties faced by an inherently political organization whose voting members were all government representatives. It also demonstrated the increasing difficulties facing any claim to the self-determination of peoples, in view of the problems it was causing in Bosnia-Herzegovina. In contrast to the general progress made at the Commission, and to the achievements of the preceding Sub-Commission, China proved its thorniest problem. Its failure on China has been called "the primary example of the traditional limitations of the Commission."[64] It has been widely described as a product of bungling and ineptitude, both deliberate and unintended. It has also been described as the turning point on the China issue in the two UN human rights organs.

At this session, the Chinese delegation found the support from the South it had been seeking earlier.[65] It was the first working session for the newly expanded membership, which had been increased from forty-three to fifty-three members, most of whom were from the South. China had also found a new form of self-defense that it had already hinted at in the 1991 Commission session and which had a broader base of support from the South than the principle of noninterference. Cultural relativism as articulated by China's Ambassador, Fan Guoxiang, meant that "measures aimed at protecting human rights should be decided by each individual country in the light of its history, tradition and level of economic development."[66] The significance of the 1992 Commission was that from henceforth, some observers believed, barring any new developments within China, another motion against it was unlikely to be successful. At the same time, China now realized that it would not be able to negate the UN human rights program.

The China issue demonstrated the newly unified South position on human rights in this session, as well as the divisions within the North/West. Before the Commission was a weighty note from the Secretary-General based on the request of the earlier Sub-Commission resolution to gather information on the situation in Tibet. However, a majority of African states had reportedly arrived in Geneva with instructions not to support the China resolution.[67] In the subsequent vote, almost all African countries supported the Pakistani no-action motion, with only Senegal and Gabon abstaining. Among the Latin American delegations, only Costa Rica voted against the motion. In contrast, Western states were divided. Paradoxically, this was partly because it was also the first opportunity for the European Community to exercise the coordinated approach implicit in the Treaty of Maastricht.[68] Depending heavily on the approach suggested by the Tibetan lobby, which made the draft resolution "politically problematic," the European Community, led by Germany, sponsored a resolution that had not been coordinated with other WEOG (Western Europe and Others Group) states. The U.S., Australian, and Japanese delegations expressed unhappiness with this resolution, particularly because it conflicted with the "one China" policy. The U.S. delegation thus suggested a general China resolution that also encompassed Tibet. For the next few weeks there were acrimonious exchanges within the Western group, but at the last minute the European Community gave in to U.S. demands.

Having lobbied hard to obtain a modification of the draft, the U.S. delegation appeared to lose interest when it came to getting the results of its efforts adopted. It was widely believed that this ambiguous behavior served the purposes of the then Bush administration in providing an indication of continuing U.S. concern for the human rights situation in China, despite the President's veto of Congressional legislation setting conditions for the renewal of China's MFN, invoked on 2 March 1992.[69] The resultant resolution was entitled "Situation in China/Tibet," and the original preamble and operative paragraphs were broadened to refer more generally to China.[70]

For a resolution to succeed within the UN framework, time to lobby is essential. When voting began on the hastily conceived resolution, China invoked the argument that the resolution's aim was to undermine its sovereignty and give support to Tibetan separatists. Using a similar argument, Pakistan submitted a procedural motion proposing that the Commission should not make any decision on the draft. After a long debate, the Commission adopted this motion by 27 votes to 15 with 10 abstentions.[71] Observers have commented on the open and noisy self-congratulation indulged in by

China and some of its supporters in the conference room at the expense of the WEOG states when the result of the vote was made known.

The prophecy of observers from the 1992 Commission proved self-fulfilling. In the 1992 Sub-Commission session, the Tibetan NGO coalition had prepared several oral statements and provided experts with a dossier covering all events. However, in deference to the informal agreement, priority was given to China in this session. Although the China issue was not, like the Tibetan issue, complicated by the difficult issue of self-determination, attempts by the NGO coalition to persuade the experts to table a resolution on China were not successful.[72] At this session, China's expert, Tian Jin, went on the offensive, targeting the recent Los Angeles riots and arguing the need for rethinking human rights in ways which did not marginalize the Third World.[73]

As a result, the EC Twelve took the initiative in the 1993 Commission to push for a resolution on human rights in China. However, they faced a newly confident opponent. From the end of 1991, China's economy had begun to boom, wiping out the economic downturn created in part by Tiananmen and combined multilateral and bilateral sanctions. This development coincided with a more assertive Chinese strategy on human rights which began with the publication of the State Council's first White Paper on human rights in October 1991.[74] This paper had already been identified by Zhang Yishan in the 1992 Commission as China's response to the US State Department's "blue book" on human rights.[75] It introduced a new right, the right to subsistence, which, together with the right to development and the claims of cultural relativism, was to be given priority in China's human rights policy.[76] At this Commission, China's delegates took a positive position of emphasizing China's support for the reoperationalization of human rights norms, specifically by placing a priority on economic, social and cultural rights and the right to development. Chinese diplomat Zhan Daode did attack the "practice of distorting human rights standards, exerting political pressure through the abuse of monitoring mechanisms, engaging in selectivity and applying double standards . . . infringing the sovereignty and offending the dignity of many developing countries."[77] However, he also supported the right to development as "an important basis for democracy and human rights." His new Ambassador, Jin Yongjian, admitted that "civil and political rights and economic, social and cultural rights deserve[d] equal attention," but observed that "the right to independence, subsistence and development [were] of paramount importance to the overwhelming majority of the developing countries."[78] He also reflected China's new sense of achievement, charging that the support for this resolution by the U.S. and other Western states demonstrated their unhappiness with China's goals and progress.[79]

The draft resolution, "The Situation of Human Rights in China," expressed concern over the continuing reports of violations of human rights and fundamental freedoms in China, called upon the Chinese government to take measures to ensure the observance of human rights and improve the administration of justice, invited the government to continue to cooperate with the special rapporteurs and working groups and requested the Secretary-General to bring the resolution to the attention of the Chinese government and prepare a report for the Commission on Human Rights on the basis of available information.[80]

Shortly before the vote, and as an indication of its new assertiveness, the Chinese delegation took the initiative, launched an attack on its opponents, and introduced a procedural motion requesting the Commission to take no decision on the draft resolution. The motion was adopted by a narrow margin of five, with 22 votes in favor, 17 against, and 12 abstentions. Abstentions were mostly from Latin American countries, whereas Bulgaria, the Czech Republic, Japan, Poland, Romania and the Russian Federation were among those who joined the Western states voting against.

The 1993 vote saw the defection of Chile, Gambia, and Lesotho from a vote in favor in 1992 to an abstention in 1993. Six states that had voted in favor in 1992 were not in the 1993 Commission, as against the addition of four new states voting in favor in 1993. Two other new countries, Bulgaria and Poland, voted against in the 1993 vote. This accounted for the contrast between the margin of China's success of five in the 1993 vote as against the margin of twelve in the 1992 vote. Observing this positive comparison, the NGO adviser, Adrien-Claude Zoller of the International Service for Human Rights, commented that the Chinese had "lost considerable ground."[81] It was thus in a spirit of restrained optimism that NGOs contemplated the forthcoming 1993 Sub-Commission session.

The Forty-fifth Session of the Sub-Commission, August 1993: After Vienna

The forty-fifth session of the Sub-Commission on Prevention of Discrimination and Protection of Minorities, which followed the UN Vienna Human Rights Conference in June 1993, represented the turning point in the comparative effectiveness of the Sub-Commission in its impact on China, and the transfer of the high moral ground to the Commission. The Sub-Commission's strength as a body of experts accessible to individual and NGO intervention, which had earlier allowed it to maintain the monitoring initiative, was now marred by intense political pressures. Its forty-fifth session has been described as one of the most politicized in the memory of longtime NGO participants.[82] The tension between principles, personality, and politics that is latent in the Sub-Commission's activities surfaced in an extreme form as a palpable threat to the harmony and viability of future sessions, as well as to the cherished notion of the "independence" of its experts. The uncertainty of the new international order and the concern of developing states (from which the majority of experts were drawn) that, with the breakup of the power of the former Soviet Union, only China could act as a bulwark against the encroaching hegemony of the United States were given as the two major reasons for this development.[83] Added to these international political reasons was the heavy, if shorter term, pressure placed by China on its diplomats not to allow any resolution to be adopted critical of China's human rights prior to the decision of the International Olympic Committee on the choice of venue for the year 2000 Olympic Games.

In interviews during the session, Chinese diplomats expressed a sense of siege and beleaguerment as the result of outside criticism. Yet, unlike other governments under attack for their human rights policies, such as Sri Lanka, Iran, and even Japan, they did not in this session seek the floor for the right of reply after an attack on China's policies. During the forty-fifth session, NGO pressure was maintained fairly consistently on the issue of Tibet.[84]

Despite the infrequency of China's formal diplomatic interventions and the restraint of its expert, Tian Jin, China's power within the Sub-Commission was both manifest and implicit. It lay in the physical presence of Chinese diplomats within the hall and in the increasing subtlety, and force, with which the Ambassador and the members of his Mission were able in their lobbying to harness a variety of diplomatic techniques and arguments, of both carrot and stick variety, all resting on the unspoken, and sometimes heavily emphasized, premise of China's great power status combined with the characteristics of a developing state. The impact of this implicit and explicit power was all the more formidable in that it was both held in check by the Chinese government observers and at the same time given formal expression in the interventions of Cuban expert Miguel Alfonso Martinez. With his long Sub-Commission experience and his unparalleled command of procedural intricacies, Martinez continued to assume the mantle as overt leader and protector of the interests within the Sub-Commission of the "group of seventeen" representing developing states. Indeed, it could be argued that it was partly Martinez' skilful maneuvering which enabled the Chinese Observers to maintain their diplomatic composure in the face of strong NGO criticism.[85]

During the voting on Item 6 of the Agenda, which dealt with human rights violations in specific countries, the tension in the Sub-Commission erupted. The debate that followed the introduction of the draft resolution on Tibet was a study in clumsy tactics and personality differences that only marginally disguised serious political undercurrents. The failure of the majority of experts speaking in favor of the resolution to supply, or even attempt to supply, persuasive policy vindications for their positions only further emphasized the political nature of the arguments.

Immediately after the introduction of Item L.26 on 20 August, British expert Claire Palley declared that there had been "intolerable" diplomatic pressures put on the Sub-Commission not to refer to human rights in the People's Republic of China. She stated that the current Chinese Ambassador had threatened to break off all dialogue with Tibet if she moved the current resolution. He had also threatened that China's dialogue with the Sub-Commission would be broken off. Although he accepted that the experts were independent, it was China's position that if a secret ballot were taken on the draft resolution, China would hold the government of each expert responsible for the outcome.[86]

The ensuing silence in the conference room at these revelations was broken by Louis Joinet, who declared that he also had been under pressure, and he added in a jocular manner, it made him feel "very important." In view of these developments, and given the secret ballot, the size of the following affirmative vote for the no-action motion on Tibet (17 in favor, 6 against, and 2 abstentions) was remarkable. It was received with shock by NGOs, who regretted Palley's initial overly hasty tactics which had produced an unfavorable reaction among the experts. However, the two main arguments for supporting the motion, the "politicization" of the issue and the Palley revelation that discussions on Tibet were ongoing and had therefore to await an outcome, appeared insufficient to justify the size of China's victory.

The Tibet vote had a decisive impact on the mood of NGOs in the conference room. Late in the afternoon of 26 August, a spokesman for a number of NGOs took the floor in a joint statement that expressed concern that the long-standing cooperation between the experts and NGOs was in danger of changing, as indicated by certain instances in the session. He stated: "NGO representatives are unable to contribute freely if pressured by veiled or direct threats by governments not to address certain issues. This is particularly disconcerting where persons are threatened by repercussions to their family members, as happened during this session of the Sub-Commission. Equally, NGO representatives regard with deep concern the increased governmental interference and pressure that hinder the independence of experts."[87]

Summarizing the outcome of the session, experienced NGO spokesmen attributed the unprecedented negative vote on Tibet to a variety of factors. First, the UN human rights system as a whole was seen as suffering from fatigue after the Vienna Human Rights Conference.[88] In addition, it was believed that the Chinese government had used the Vienna process to consolidate its position. Although China's representatives had not achieved their main objective of offsetting universality with cultural and historical relativism, as they had sought in the preceding preparatory conferences, they were still pursuing relativity as a lively and current issue. At Vienna, the Chinese had claimed the U.S. wanted strategic control and had thereby rallied the South around them. Of the South, only the Latin group had moved on allegiances; during the forty-fifth session they either voted with

China or abstained. They had sought to avoid controversy and had broken out of this pattern only with their vote on East Timor, because of their ties with Portugal. Because of the strong support for China from states of the South, a vote on China's human rights would not have been successful. A vote on Tibet was rendered even more problematic because of deep-seated concern about the divisive influences of self-determination.

The West, in contrast, was seen as not united. Complex reasons such as guilt about the historical depredations of imperialism, Western support for China's market reforms, concern lest Chinese instability produce a flood of Chinese refugees, and a fear of isolating China all combined to prevent a united Western front. Western states were also afraid of taking an isolated stand on China's human rights in case they lost out economically vis-à-vis other states who did not. In their lobbying activities, the Chinese had harnessed a swag of diplomatic arguments that exploited each and all of these fears. Yet, China's reaction to its success was essentially defensive. Speaking privately after the vote, Chinese diplomats hailed their success as a sign that China was no longer "a victim." Relief was also apparent that a vote that might have cast a shadow on China's still lively hopes for hosting the year 2000 Olympics had been avoided.

Monitoring, 1993–94: Swing to the Multilateral

Only six months later, in March 1994, both the multilateral UN mechanisms and the bilateral MFN mechanism were simultaneously put to the test. At the fiftieth session of the Human Rights Commission in February–March, the draft resolution, "Situation of Human Rights in China," called upon the government of China to take further measures to ensure the observance of all human rights, invited the government to continue to cooperate with all special rapporteurs and working groups and requested the Secretary-General to bring the resolution to the attention of China's government and prepare a report for the Commission at its fifty-first session on the situation of human rights in China.[89] As at the preceding Commission session, the Chinese themselves proposed a no-action motion, which was carried on 9 March by 20 votes to 16, with 17 abstentions. The narrow majority of four was one less than the preceding year. An analysis of the vote suggests that, had Poland and Romania continued to vote against the motion as in 1993, instead of abstaining, and had two Latin American states also voted against it, the result would have been a tie of 20 against and 20 in favor, resulting in the overturning of the 1994 no-action motion on China for the first time in Commission history. The contingent nature of China's success was underlined by the fact that up until the vote, the Polish delegation had insisted it intended to vote against the no-action motion — but at the last minute China's Foreign Minister had persuaded Poland's Foreign Minister to change.[90] Poland in turn persuaded Romania.

Thus, although one NGO observer complained that the narrow margin of the vote could not be regarded as "any great success" for the China lobby group, it nevertheless suggested that the Human Rights Commission was becoming a more likely forum for the successful monitoring of China's human rights than the Sub-Commission. Over a period of three years the Commission vote had changed from 27 in favor of the no-action motion to 15 against with 10 abstentions (1992), to 22 in favor, 17 against, and 12 abstentions (1993), to 20 votes in favor, 16 against, and 17 abstentions (1994). The decreasing majority was due not to the change in numbers against, which remained reasonably constant, but to an increase in the number abstaining rather than voting in favor. That change mainly reflected the alteration in the Eastern European and Latin American vote away from support for China. But the changing margin did not detract from continuing success of the no-action motion. In Geneva, the Chinese diplomats had worked extremely hard and been very effective in their lobbying, organizing supporters to speak on their behalf. In contrast, the American and European group had misjudged the Commission's mood and, two days before the vote, were still certain that a no-action motion would be defeated by perhaps a majority of four against China.[91] Some NGO observers and journalists claimed that the U.S. State Department was not sufficiently determined to criticize China's human rights record, since the U.S. could have obtained the numbers to defeat the no-action motion. On the U.S. side, diplomats claimed that they had lobbied vigorously but, owing to the difficulty of obtaining a draft acceptable to all, had once again been faced with a problem of inadequate time.

It was ironic that at this time there was criticism within the U.S. that the State Department was too committed to monitoring China's human rights on a bilateral basis.[92] Detailed examination of U.S. monitoring of China's human rights suggests that, contrary to general belief, since 1990 China had indeed complied with some of the conditions laid down by the U.S. for the renewal of MFN, even if often only on paper. Over a period of five years, as the 1993 executive order and previous congressional bills had required, Chinese authorities had released political prisoners, often through the good offices of U.S. businessman in Hong Kong, John Kamm, in timing that revealed a direct correlation with looming congressional voting, or with the final point of the presidential decision to renew MFN, on 3 June each year. China had also agreed to ensure that goods made with prison labor were not exported to the U.S., had arranged the emigration of some political prisoners, and had agreed to discuss Red Cross visits to Chinese political prisoners.[93] The success of U.S. pressures in eliciting compliance in specific areas, notably with political prisoners, was also measurable negatively, by reference to China's diminishing cooperation once MFN and human rights had been delinked.[94]

Nevertheless, the debate over the linkage between human rights and

MFN in the United States in late 1993 and early 1994 demonstrated the lack of domestic unity on the issue, with the business community in particular opposed to the linkage. This lack of unity was perceived by China's leadership as underscoring China's vital importance to the U.S. economy. Furthermore, as the introduction of market reforms made China increasingly powerful in economic and strategic terms, its hold on domestic stability diminished. A swing to a more nationalistic stance reflected the increasing power of the military, which, from April 1993, signed a number of anti-U.S. petitions that strongly opposed bartering away China's independence in exchange for MFN.[95]

For all these reasons, China was no longer prepared to tolerate the challenge to its sovereignty that U.S. bilateral monitoring represented. A final source of obduracy was the humiliating failure of China's bid to host the Olympics in the year 2000. As U.S. Secretary of State Warren Christopher's exchanges with his counterparts in Beijing from 11 March indicated, China was no longer responsive to the pressures that had earlier influenced the release of prisoners of conscience and the publication of the human rights White Papers.[96] Indeed, China's readiness to reject these pressures even became a means of legitimation for the current leadership. The noninterference argument that had almost disappeared from China's self-defense in multilateral human rights forums was now resurrected, with respect to both bilateral and multilateral monitoring.[97]

A month later, these tactics were modified. The release of two leading dissidents, Wang Juntao in late April and Chen Ziming in May, and an agreement in principle to the visit of the International Red Cross to its detention centers appeared to signal China's return to what Asia Watch has called its "hostage politick."[98] Other dissidents, however, continued to be arrested as the fifth anniversary of the Tiananmen crackdown approached. A Human Rights Watch/Asia report, subsequently repudiated by China, identified a further five hundred lesser known Tiananmen protesters still imprisoned since 1989.[99] The principal figure of China's Democracy Movement, Wei Jingsheng, was again detained on 1 April after a temporary release and reports, again denied by China, circulated that he was about to be tried for treason as a result of his meeting with US Assistant Secretary of State John Shattuck on 27 February (7). On 12 May, in talks with visiting Malaysian Prime Minister Dr. Mahathir Mohamad, President Jiang Zemin claimed that "Tiananmen was a bad thing turned good."[100]

The inconsistency of this "hostage politick," and the arbitrary change in tactics only confirmed the contingent nature of China's human rights responses in the context of its ongoing domestic power struggle and its concerns about social instability. The obdurate treatment of the visiting Australian Minister for Foreign Affairs and Trade, Senator Gareth Evans, and the French Prime Minister, Edouard Balladur, particularly in relation to the detention of Wei Jingsheng, further demonstrated the extent to which internal imperatives of stability were impeding China's response to bilateral monitoring by middle powers.[101] These push-me-pull-you tactics came to an end on 26 May 1994 with President Clinton's announcement of the formal delinkage of human rights and MFN. A new era in Sino-U.S. relations began in which the pursuit of U.S. human rights objectives took a different turn.

The most notable positive outcome of the 1994 Clinton decision was a renewed U.S. focus on multilateral forums, partly in reaction to China's triumphalist response to the delinkage. As early as December 1994, U.S. diplomats began channeling their energies into lobbying for the forthcoming vote on China at the 1995 Human Rights Commission. When U.S. National Security Adviser Anthony Lake visited Zimbabwe, Gabon, and Ethiopia, the Geneva resolution was on his agenda. So it was for Geraldine Ferraro, then head of the U.S. delegation to the Commission, when she visited Latin American capitals.[102] This expression of renewed U.S. political will, in part aimed at undermining domestic criticism of the President's decision, had a powerful effect. For almost six weeks in the Commission, China was "the most intensively discussed and lobbied issue."[103] In a dramatic roll call, on the morning of 8 March 1995, the no-action vote on the draft China resolution was overturned for the first time. It was rejected by 22 votes to 22, with 9 abstentions, and because it required a majority to pass, it failed on the tie. This failure highlighted the weaknesses of this procedural motion and its inability to shield China from UN human rights scrutiny once the U.S. had shifted its attention from bilateral monitoring mechanisms to multilateral ones.

The 1995 vote, in contrast to that of 1994, saw growing opposition to nonaction and a decrease in the numbers abstaining. This time those voting against the motion included former communist states (Poland, Romania, and the Russian Federation) and Latin American states (Ecuador, El Salvador, and Nicaragua) as well as the Philippines. The results suggested the success of the Ferraro visit, if not that of Anthony Lake. The unprecedented failure of the no-action motion was attributed to the strength and the sustained nature of U.S. lobbying; the number of countries in the 1995 Commission favorable to the West, compared with the past; and specific problems in China's bilateral relations, such as its strategic disagreement with the Philippines over the Spratlys.[104] It indicated that the condition of China's human rights was now deemed by the Commission to be requiring its attention, even though the draft resolution, "Situation of Human Rights in China," was subsequently narrowly rejected by a margin of one, in a vote of 21 to 20, with 12 abstentions.[105] The Russian Federation, which had opposed the no-action motion, had subsequently changed its vote to oppose the substantive resolution.

China on the Offensive, 1995–98: Back to the Bilateral

The narrowness of its victory in the 1995 Commission changed China's tactics to ones combining more aggressive lobbying of all states members of the Commission and observers to the Sub-Commission with more frequent use of the right of reply during sessions. Attack became the best form of defense. The period coincided with a move by authoritarian states of the South to combine to challenge the UN monitoring mechanisms. This challenge was conducted on two fronts, overturning customary procedures. First was the change in the role of the Sub-Commission in relation to Item 6 on human rights violations. Keen to avoid the political pressures associated with Item 6, experts decided to forgo discussion on country situations already being dealt with by the Commission. This decision undermined the Sub-Commission's role to circumvent conflicts within the Commission. It also meant that the China issue would no longer be discussed in the more objective and rarified forum of the human rights experts, but was now more highly politicized and relegated to discussion by states members of the Commission. Already, the replacement in 1994 of mild-mannered expert Tian Jin with the forthright former UN Ambassador Fan Guoxiang had made it less likely that the China issue would get a hearing in the Sub-Commission.

Second was a more insidious move to introduce the idea of "cooperation" to replace "confrontation" on human rights, specifically by moving away from country-specific resolutions and toward bilateral human rights dialogue. During the 1996 session of the Commission, China clarified the purpose behind its championing of this new approach. Ambassador Wu Jianmin stated that "the correct way to promote human rights was through dialogue and cooperation. However . . . under agenda item 10, 67 countries, almost all developing countries, had been 'put in the dock' since 1992. . . . In considering country situations, the Commission should . . . oppose double standards and put an end to North-South confrontation. In principle, China did not favour country resolutions; if deemed necessary, they should be the subject of consensus."[106]

The outcome of this new tactic was a Sub-Commission resolution, tabled in August 1997 by China's expert, Fan Guoxiang, formally establishing a new human rights standard to overcome the alleged "politicization" of human rights—the promotion of dialogue, "public or closed," among experts, governments, and NGOs. It invited "members of the Sub-Commission and governmental and non-governmental observers to carry out constructive dialogue and consultations on human rights, so as to enhance understanding and to search for effective and commonly agreed solutions to the promotion and protection of human rights in all countries, taking into account the important role of the Sub-Commission as a 'think-tank' in this regard."[107] Fan had earlier outlined three subjects for human rights dialogue, which included the avoidance of "well-organized attacks with a view to forcing country-wise resolutions [which] run counter to the objective of promoting human rights."[108] Previous fears that China could act to limit the powers of the Sub-Commission now appeared justified.

A similar move against the Commission was foreshadowed in a subsequent speech by Liu Xinsheng, the alternate representative of the Chinese delegation at the substantive session of the ECOSOC in July 1997, in which he outlined another three-point proposal, this time for reform of the Commission. He recommended "setting straight the ideas guiding the activities of the Commission on Human Rights" on the basis of "the Universal Declaration of Human Rights and the Vienna Declaration and Programme of Action [which] have clearly provided for the ideas guiding international activities in the field of human rights, i.e., conducting international cooperation on the basis of equality and mutual cooperation." He called for members of the Commission to consider the interests and demands of the developing countries, insisting that "in particular, they must . . . increase the proportional weight given the right to development, economic, social and cultural rights, [and] change the existing imbalance in the membership of the Commission and in the geographical distribution of personnel in the Centre for Human Rights." His third proposal was equally explicit, recommending that the "removal of the confrontation between countries should be the number one task in reforms." Referring to the initiative of the fifty-third session of the Commission on developing consultation, dialogue, and the spirit of consensus, he advocated that "with this as the premise, reform for the Commission should seriously reconsider the direction followed in the consideration of the item of country situations, so that it will promote cooperation between countries instead of aggravating confrontation between them."[109]

The most publicized challenge in this period, however, was China's extension of the open lobbying tactics it had hitherto used only towards the states of the South, to those of the North. Its main goal was to drive a wedge within the WEOG states, primarily between the European Union and the U.S., on the China resolution. Already, as analysis of the 1993 Sub-Commission reveals, human rights experts from the North had been threatened with commercial consequences to their state of origin should they vote against China. These threats, however, had been carried out circumspectly and behind closed doors. Increasingly, China's treatment of Western states became more openly threatening and blatant, with no pretense of respecting diplomatic conventions. Its tactics constituted a mix of diplomacy, with the use of both carrot and stick in the form of manipulation of the West's historical guilt about treatment of China and commercial promises and threats. The response of the West was not, as could have occurred, the formation of a coordinated united front but, on the contrary, utter disarray and confusion in Western ranks.

Thus, in the 1996 session of the Commission, Chinese diplomats attempted to portray the draft resolution on China as an example of Western hegemonism. Throughout 1995, Chinese leaders visited Europe, finalizing the China-EU Airbus sale, to the dismay of Boeing in the U.S., and offering to sign and ratify both International Covenants if the Commission resolution could be dropped. This offer was reportedly in response to a list of ten requirements put to China by the European Union at the Bangkok meeting of the Euro-Asian Summit in March 1996, which included the ratification of the two International Covenants and invitations to the High Commissioner for Human Rights and the UN Working Group on Arbitrary Detention to visit China.[110] China's subsequent failure to sign the Covenants, however, meant that the French-initiated push to drop the resolution failed.[111] Nevertheless, the late start to European lobbying, and the lack of enthusiasm on the U.S. side, contributed to the substantial loss of support for the resolution in 1996 as compared with 1995 (4). The draft resolution, as tabled by the European Union, was inspired by the reports of the special rapporteurs on torture, extrajudicial executions, and religious intolerance and the Working Group on Enforced Disappearances. As before, China presented a procedural motion to prevent voting on the draft resolution. The no-action motion was adopted by 27 votes to 20, with 6 abstentions.[112] On this occasion there was a noticeable increase in the numbers supporting the no-action motion, with the addition of Belarus, Benin, Guinea, Madagascar, Mali, Uganda, and Ukraine, and the departure of Togo and Sudan, which had previously supported the motion, from the Commission.

It was in the 1997 Commission, however, that China's political pressure on the West reached a climax. The pre-Commission politics and the politics of the session form a study in themselves.[113] As early as November 1996, Western powers placed the onus on China to initiate concrete steps to avoid confrontation. This allowed China to engage in delaying diplomatic tactics and to withhold its response until the last minute, thus facilitating its own room for maneuver in its lobbying sweep though Africa, Latin America, Asia, and Europe, while ensuring that American and European leaders themselves had little time left to lobby. For the first time, the united front in EU human rights policy in the Commission was formally breached. Despite common expectation that the European Union would as usual table a draft resolution on China, France expressed its opposition to the draft prepared by the Dutch presidency and was quickly supported in its arguments by Germany, Italy, and Spain. The Dutch delegation decided not to present a draft resolution on China on behalf of the European Union unless its members could agree on a text. Finally, the Danish Minister for Foreign Affairs announced that Denmark would sponsor the resolution.

In response to this political imbroglio, China held out both stick and carrot. To those preparing to cosponsor the draft resolution, it openly threatened loss of trading and diplomatic opportunities; to those deciding to abandon their cosponsorship, it offered the promise of future dialogue, as well as the renewed possibility that China might sign the International Covenants. In particular, the Danish Ambassador was told that he "would regret" his country's efforts; and China published a list of Danish corporations it intended to exclude from future contracts.[114] It also circulated a position paper in the United Nations, arguing that tabling the draft resolution on China was improper, as it was not "pursuant to the purposes and principles and rules of procedure" and was intended to exert political pressure on China (1). As it turned out, Australia, Canada, France, Germany, Italy, Spain, and Japan failed to cosponsor the resolution as they had in previous years, even though those that were members of the Commission subsequently voted against China's no-action motion. By a tactic of divide and rule, China had succeeded in bilateralizing a multilateral process. Consistent with its policy of open threats, China immediately announced measures of economic reprisal against Denmark and the Netherlands after the vote. Vice-Premier Zhu Rongji cancelled a planned trip to the Hague and traveled to Australia instead.

The result of the vote on the no-action motion on the 1997 China resolution — 27 in favor, 17 against, and 9 abstentions — was not very different from the same vote in the 1996 Commission — 27 in favor, 20 against, and 6 abstentions. Crucial to the abstentions was the swinging Latin American vote. Of eight Latin American states visited by Chinese Trade Minister Wu Yi and Premier Li Peng between June and November 1996, all but Peru were members of the 1997 Commission. Of these, only Chile eventually supported the West in the no-action motion. Cuba and Colombia (which in 1996 had abstained) voted with China, and five others, including Brazil (which in 1996 had voted with the West), abstained. Part of the Eastern European vote was also supportive of China, marking a partial swing back to the situation existing before the collapse of communism in Eastern Europe. In both the 1996 and 1997 sessions of the Commission, Belarus and the Ukraine voted with China, whereas the Russian Federation abstained, even though it had voted with the West on the no-action motion in 1995.[115] The diplomatic triumph proclaimed for China was thus more a reflection of the number of Western, Eastern European, and Latin American states now troubled about the China resolution, and the priority China gave the proceedings, than a function of the numerical margin of its success.

However, the politics surrounding the vote clearly had a profound impact on the effectiveness of the UN human rights system as it applied to China, and perhaps even beyond. The means by which success was obtained, the openly threatening nature of China's response to those sponsoring and cosponsoring the resolution, the compliant attitude of some Western states, including Australia, Canada, France, and Germany, toward China's tactics, and their failure to express solidarity with the beleaguered northern European states reflected a qualitative change from the past that had disturbing implications for the continued credibility of Commission resolutions. In particular, China's painfully public claims to the right to special treatment and special exemption on human rights in the UN system represented a rejection of the values of universality and nonselectivity of human rights finally adopted by consensus at the UN World Human Rights Conference in Vienna in June 1993. That China made the claim in the name of developing states, moreover, carried with it the possibility of future collective claims to exemption. The decision by both the European Union and the U.S. not to sponsor a resolution against China in the 1998 session of the Commission represented the final nail in the coffin of Commission credibility vis-à-vis that state.

The paradox was that the split within the European Union was engineered by Western states, under pressure from China, who argued the greater effectiveness of cooperative dialogue with China. By this divisive action, they were effectively transferring their faith and their monitoring energies away from the multilateral arena and back to the bilateral. The decision not to sponsor a resolution in the 1998 Commission did not serve to heal that breach; rather, by uniting the European Union behind a policy that weakened UN procedures, it highlighted it. Yet the fact that China was prepared to go to the extremes of challenging the entire global community to avoid the resolution, and that, in subsequent bilateral dialogue with countries such as Australia, it was still busy trying to persuade Western states not to sponsor the China resolution in the 1998 Commission session, simply underlined the importance China placed on the vote and, conversely, undermined the West's excuse that the annual Commission resolution was not "effective." So too did the human rights concessions China offered to avert a resolution. Its promises in 1996 to sign the International Covenants in exchange for a promise to drop the resolution were not honored immediately, but in all probability influenced its final decision to sign the ICESCR in 1997 and the ICCPR in 1998. These seemingly hopeful signs, welcomed by NGOs and governments alike, were partially offset by Chinese Foreign Minister Qian Qichen's simultaneous statement that China was committed to the pacts but needed more time to research their implications before they could be fully implemented.[116] A senior Chinese Foreign Ministry official also noted the lengthy NPC discussions that were required before ratification of the Covenants could take place.[117]

Other indications of cooperation included China's decision in 1997 to invite the UN High Commissioner for Human Rights, Jose Ayala Lasso, the China visit of the Rapporteur on Religious Intolerance in 1995, and the invitation to the UN Working Group on Arbitrary Detention to visit China in October 1997.[118] Human rights dialogues were commenced with a number of cooperating states, Australia, Brazil, Canada, the European Union, Norway, and Sweden.[119] China first proposed the idea of dialogue to Brazil, which in the 1996 Commission had changed its vote on China to opposing the no-action motion, before the 1997 Commission, and dialogue took place from 18–27 February 1997, just prior to the beginning of the session. Imme-diately after the Commission session, on 10 April Australia announced the beginning of dialogue with China, on 14 April Canada announced dialogue, and in September 1997 discussions were resumed with the European Union. The release of Wei Jingsheng, and his emigration to the United States in November 1997, was associated with China's effort to head off a China reso-lution in the 1998 Commission session. Finally, China's invitation in January 1998 to the new UN High Commissioner for Human Rights, Mary Robinson, to visit China, was associated with the European Union's effort to present a united front at the 1998 Commission session by finding alternative multi-lateral methods of monitoring China, other than through a China resolu-tion.[120] Such concessions appeared to suggest that the UN-China trade-off might be effective. At the same time, there was a real danger that if the resolution were to be permanently, as opposed to temporarily, removed as a source of pressure on China, China would cease making concessions, just as it had after 1994 once MFN and human rights were delinked.

Thus, astute observer Adrien-Claude Zoller, Director of the International Service for Human Rights, dourly commented at the end of the 1997 ses-sion: "The decisions of the Commission are [now] removed from the con-cerns and needs of human rights defenders throughout the world . . . The dominance of commercial relations over human rights concerns, falsely described as 'constructive dialogue,' creates a distance between the Com-mission and such realities. The States that follow this logic, whether they be manufacturers of Airbus or the beneficiaries of Chinese aid, bear respon-sibility for the Commission's loss of credibility."[121]

Conclusion

Of all the multilateral human rights bodies to be analyzed in these case studies, the UN Commission on Human Rights and its Sub-Commission offer, on one hand, the clearest potential for public scrutiny of China's human rights, and, on the other, the greatest susceptibility to lobbying, coalition building, and manipulation by powerful states. They are large forums composed of government representatives and human rights experts that, through their resolutions, call international attention to any state's domestic human rights abuses and submit that state to a process of rein-tegrative shaming. Because of their composition, on the other hand, these Charter-based bodies have shown themselves to be particularly susceptible to the impact of international geopolitical and geoeconomic change. Al-though the defection of the former Soviet Union and Eastern European states from the "Eastern" bloc has strengthened the Western human rights bloc, it has left China as the sole great power within human rights forums championing the values of the South. This status has allowed it to engage in political and commercial horse trading in exchange for an agreement to avoid a resolution on China in the Commission. Its new-found economic and strategic strength has also altered its status in the eyes of the West/North. For the West, facing economic downturn, geoeconomic pressures have gradually prevailed over geopolitical ones. Consequently, China's increasingly assertive and even ruthless tactics in UN forums have encountered less organized resistance from both North and South since the high points of UN censure in 1989 and 1991, and the structural political changes within the international community resulting from the easing of the Cold War have not been reflected in a substantively different outcome on the China vote. Even the financial crisis in the Asian region as of late 1997, which potentially undermines Chinese economic power, has not wrought any discernible change in the West's susceptibility to China's human rights "diplomacy," precisely because China is now seen as the bastion of regional, and hence global, financial responsibility.

Thus, in the nine years of strong monitoring by the United Nations, China's relations with the human rights regime have changed perceptibly, in line with its growing power within the international community. Its relations with the Commission on Human Rights and its Sub-Commission have highlighted, and clearly influenced, change within these bodies. Initially, the Sub-Commission took the lead in censuring China for its human rights violations, in a context characterized by a united front between the West and some Asian and Latin American states. However, by 1994, with President Clinton's separation of MFN from human rights and the narrowing margin of success for the no-action motion on the China resolution within the Commission, the political focus shifted to the Commission. This was partly because Western states perceived that a multilateral forum offered a more congenial environment in which to deal with a state so sensitive about issues of sovereignty. Initially, this switch in focus brought the West close to another successful resolution on China, this time in the Commission. By 1996, the enhanced status of the Commission was reflected in the Sub-Commission experts' decision to avoid political pressures by ceasing to monitor country situations being handled in the Commission. Needless to say, such a move undermined the Sub-Commission's key role of circumventing conflicts within the Commission. By 1997, even the fortress of the Commission was crumbling. By openly threatening the European states sponsoring and cosponsoring the China resolution in the 1997 Commission session, China successfully bilateralized a multilateral forum. Commission powers were dealt a further blow by the adoption of the resolution in the Sub-Commission, tabled by China, emphasizing "cooperative dialogue." The decision by the European Union and the U.S. not to even sponsor a China resolution in the 1998 Commission virtually demolished the effectiveness of this monitoring route. The result was the redirection of states' attention back to bilateral monitoring of China through the purportedly new mechanism of constructive dialogue, which had such resonances with the earlier period of human rights delegations. Both were arrangements whereby states could more easily be persuaded to trade human rights for other national interests and wherein the confidentiality of discussions between China and other states on human rights could be guaranteed.

This case study demonstrates the difficulties of monitoring a large power, particularly in a noncrisis situation. Ongoing, systematic abuse of human rights clearly represents a more difficult challenge to human rights bodies than conditions internationally perceived as a human rights crisis. The resolution on China in the Sub-Commission in 1989 was more easily adopted than the equivalent resolution in the Commission in 1995. Similarly, China's compliance was more easily attained in the early 1990s than in the second half of the decade. As the forty-first and forty-third sessions of the Sub-Commission in 1989 and 1991 indicated, a certain basic consensus had been built up over the decades within UN human rights bodies that the gross and systematic abuse of human rights within a state was the business of the international community, regardless of the principle of noninterference. It had long been accepted by both North and South that monitoring should focus on civil and political rights, even if many states also wished to expand the scope of monitoring to include economic, social, and developmental rights. The actual process of China's interaction with these bodies from 1989 to 1993 gradually instilled acceptance of such custom-based and historically evolved norms. Indeed, as the above analysis has indicated, China's self-defense was invariably formally based on its reading of its obligations under the UN Charter and international human rights law, even if for tactical purposes it often resurrected Article 2, Paragraphs 4 and 7. In structural terms, the Commission and Sub-Commission also showed themselves capable of procedural adjustments designed to avoid excessive political pressure from powerful states through such measures as the introduction of the secret ballot in the Sub-Commission for consideration of cases under Item 6. This capacity was partly a function of their democratic structure, which allowed a significant voice to NGOs and individual agents.

By 1993, however, changes within China set back this process of socialization. As it became more powerful and mastered the procedures of these bodies, its influence on their norms and procedures became correspondingly greater. From the beginning, its responses had shifted between the extremes of invoking the principles of sovereignty and noninterference, attempts to undermine norms, attempts to reoperationalize existing human rights norms, procedural compliance, and procedural innovation. Even from 1989, it had challenged some Sub-Commission and Commission conventions, such as the independence of experts, the democratic interaction with NGOs, and an unspoken gentleman's agreement on the allowable limits of diplomatic lobbying. By 1993, however, these efforts had intensified. In particular, the move after 1996 to cease consideration in the Sub-Commission of country situations under review by the Commission and the

China-sponsored resolution in the 1997 Sub-Commission to eschew "confrontation," conformed with China's view of the Sub-Commission's proper functions as a human rights transmitter and standard setter rather than a human rights monitoring body.

Nevertheless, three positive effects of China's interaction with the Commission and Sub-Commission should be reiterated. First, were the long-term socializing effects of the process of China's interaction at the international level that have already been discussed. Second, as Chinese dissident Wei Jingsheng has pointed out, the Commission and Sub-Commission resolutions on China indisputably served to strengthen the morale of those within China struggling for democracy and liberalization.[122] Third, the effort to evade Commission and Sub-Commission censure involved China in activities effectively renegotiating its sovereignty, if only for short-term gains. Although its signature of the ICESCR and ICCPR and invitations to special rapporteurs and working groups do not necessarily reflect any long-term internalization of norms by China, they have effectively constituted China's acknowledgement of the importance of the International Covenants and of the international community's right to monitor its human rights conditions *in situ.*

However, it must be emphasized that the source of China's long-term learning has been the normative and structural robustness of these human rights bodies. Developments in the 1997 Commission undermined the resilience of both institutions and seriously set back this process of socialization. The decisions taken on the China resolution not only reflected a lack of Western unity, but, ironically, on the eve of a review by the Commission of progress in human rights in the five years since the UN World Human Rights Conference in Vienna, pressured the UN regime to the extent of imperiling some of its norms and procedures. The UN Secretary-General Kofi Annan and the UN High Commissioner for Human Rights, Mary Robinson, both expressed satisfaction that the Chinese government had invited Robinson to China and that it had signed the two Covenants.[123] However, the question yet to be resolved is whether, by accepting this trade-off, the United Nations is more effectively incorporating China into the human rights regime, or merely facilitating the undermining of UN norms and procedures by China. The readiness of the international community to treat China as a club of one in the 1997 and 1998 meetings of the Commission will not necessarily provide a model for its subsequent treatment, as EU representatives and Mary Robinson have been at pains to point out. Yet the new emphasis on "cooperation" has long-term implications for both bodies, undermining the important process of reintegrative shaming through country-situation resolutions which has been applied so effectively to China and many other states. If this new approach to China were to be maintained, Philip Alston's gloomy assessment of the Commission's effectiveness, rather than his more up-beat analysis, would the most likely scenario: "The Commission is far more responsive to violations and more interventionist vis-à-vis governments than most observers would have dared to hope as recently as ten years ago. But, if we apply a different measure, the Commission remains depressingly detached from most of the atrocities that occur in the world today and its role remains less that of a protector than a recorder of facts and a much needed forum for post-mortem examinations."[124]

Chapter 3
China and Torture:
Treaty Bodies and Special Rapporteurs

Long before China's ratification of the Convention against Torture, its Constitution and legislation had clearly stipulated that acts of torture must be prohibited and persons guilty of such acts must be severely punished. Since the ratification, considerable progress had been achieved in developing and implementing legislation. . . . The Committee would find that the recommendations that it had made on the conclusion of its consideration of the supplementary report in 1993 had already been adopted in varying degrees or were being implemented through measures in line with China's specific circumstances.

—Ambassador Wu Jianmin, before the
Committee Against Torture, 3 May 1996

Freedom from torture is a right which must be protected under all circumstances, including in times of internal or international disturbance or armed conflicts.

—Vienna Declaration and Program of Action, 25 June 1993

The practice of torture is an issue that goes to the heart of the rule of law and rights of due process. Its eradication is a major priority of the United Nations, in the light of its understanding that "in all the instruments relating to human rights, the prohibition of torture derives from the group of rights from which no derogation is possible."[1] The right not to be tortured is fundamental to the innate dignity of the human being, the recognition of which constitutes the moral foundation of human rights. Thus, it forms part of the cluster of rights conceived by philosopher Henry Shue as the right to physical security, defined as the "right that is basic not to be subjected to murder, torture, mayhem, rape or assault."[2]

The issue of torture is intrinsic to the culture of China's human rights, for it has historically been practiced to obtain confessions of guilt. It was "not the wanton torture of the subject based on the desire of the inquisitor but, rather, a finely regulated and monitored process of inquisition to extract 'truth'."[3] Its practice has therefore been coupled with another aspect of the Chinese legal system that conflicts with the rights of due process, the absence of a presumption of innocence. It has been the subject of many NGO reports on China's human rights, starting with the first Amnesty report on China in 1978, *Political Imprisonment in the People's Republic of China.*[4] The issue of torture is also central to the distinction between Chinese and Western concepts of human rights, since, in the Chinese conceptual hierarchy, the right to physical security, as part of the right to life, is seen as of lesser importance than the economic right to subsistence.[5] However, the practice of torture in specific circumstances is prohibited by Chinese law, if not specifically by constitutional provisions. Chinese authorities also conducted an antitorture campaign from 1985 to 1989, which, paradoxically, saw a dramatic increase in the volume of torture cases.[6] During this period China signed (12 December 1986), ratified (4 October 1988), and enforced (3 November 1988) the Convention Against Torture and Other Cruel, Inhuman or Degrading Treatment or Punishment.

The importance of freedom from torture as a basic human right enshrined in the major international human rights instruments, and the actual prohibition of its practice in Chinese law but its continuing role in the extraction of confessions, make it an appropriate thematic subject for a study of China's international socialization. It is an issue that is also important by default, since, in view of China's failure to date to ratify the International Covenant on Civil and Political Rights (ICCPR), it is one of the few aspects of civil rights in China closely supervised by a treaty body, the UN Committee Against Torture (CAT), and a Special Rapporteur.

The following chapter seeks to ascertain the nature of China's compliance with both these supervisory mechanisms, while at the same time assessing their effectiveness. It approaches the issue from three different directions: a detailed study of China's formal responses to the monitoring bodies; an analysis of the comments and recommendations of these bodies, together with the critiques by NGOs; and a brief comparison with China's interaction with other UN treaty bodies, thematic special rapporteurs and working groups that monitor related aspects of China's civil rights.

Historical and Institutional Context

In his first report as Special Rapporteur on Torture in 1986, Peter Kooijmans called torture "the plague of the second half of the 20th century."[7] Although his work was premised on the assumption that all states were capable of practicing torture, it was a problem that in his view particularly afflicted authoritarian states: "It is . . . in cases where there is a very authoritarian government not tolerating differences of opinion and where political opposition is next to impossible that torture is the most frequent and may take on a systematic character and where public authorities may be the instigators or prove compliant in this regard."[8]

Unlike some other rights, the right not to be tortured was taken up as a core issue by the United Nations only a few years after its establishment. Article 5 of the Universal Declaration of Human Rights declared simply that "no one shall be subjected to torture or to cruel, inhuman or degrading treatment or punishment." Over the years the UN adopted universally applicable standards in international declarations and conventions. These included the 1949 Abolition of Corporal Punishment in Trust Territories, the 1955 Standard Minimum Rules for the Treatment of Prisoners, the 1961 draft principles on Protection Against Arbitrary Arrest and Detention, and the Code of Conduct for Law Enforcement Officials.[9] Article 7 of the ICCPR of 1967 repeated Article 5 of the Universal Declaration and added: "In particular, no one shall be subjected without his free consent to medical or scientific experimentation."

On 9 December 1975, the UN General Assembly adopted the Declaration on the Protection of all Persons from Being Subjected to Torture and Other Cruel, Inhuman and Degrading Treatment or Punishment, the first article of which defined torture as "any act by which severe pain or suffering, whether physical or mental, is intentionally inflicted by or at the instigation of a public official on a person for such purposes as obtaining from him or a third person information or confession, punishing him for an act he has committed or is suspected of having committed, or intimidating him or other persons." The General Assembly's adoption on 10 December 1984 of the Convention Against Torture and Other Cruel, Inhuman or Degrading Treatment or Punishment was regarded as having "rounded off the codification process to combat the practice of torture."[10] Consisting of thirty-three articles, this Convention, which one hundred and five states parties had ratified or acceded to as of 1998, entered into force on 26 June 1987.

Finally, the 1993 Vienna Declaration and Program of Action contained strong provisions on the prohibition of torture. Section 5, "Freedom from Torture," consisted of eight paragraphs, describing the act of torture as "one of the most atrocious violations against human dignity," which "destroys the dignity and impairs the capability of victims to continue their lives and their activities."[11] It reaffirmed that freedom from torture was a right that must be protected "under all circumstances" and "urge[d] all states to put an immediate end to the practice of torture," calling on them to cooperate fully with the Special Rapporteur on Torture.

Although the Convention Against Torture established four procedures for the monitoring of the implementation of the Conventions by the states parties to it, the only mandatory part of the Convention's monitoring procedure is that states parties are obliged to report to the Committee on the measures they have adopted to implement the Convention. Nonmandatory forms constitute Article 20, a confidential procedure whereby the Committee can investigate reports of torture on its own initiative through confidential inquiries or fact-finding missions on the state's territory; Article 21, covering interstate complaints; and Article 22, allowing individual complaints. A state party is bound by Article 20 unless at the time of ratification or accession it expressly declares its unwillingness to accept the competence of the Committee, whereas Articles 21 and 22 require an explicit declaration of acceptance of the Committee's competence.[12]

The principal instrumentalities set up by the UN system for monitoring states' compliance with these instruments were a treaty body, CAT, and the Special Rapporteur on Torture appointed by the UN Commission on Human Rights. The treaty bodies have been described as "an indispensable cornerstone for the activities of the United Nations human rights programme as a whole."[13] CAT, established pursuant to Article 17 of the Convention, began to function on 1 January 1988 and first met in April 1988. It consists of ten experts, mainly lawyers but including medical specialists, "of high moral standing and recognised competence in the field of human rights."[14] They are elected by secret ballot from among States Parties, for an initial period of four years.[15] The Committee is one of the newest expert supervisory bodies established under human rights treaties.

The Committee's tasks, as set out in Articles 19 to 24 of the Convention, are to receive from states parties reports on the measures they have taken to give effect to their undertakings under the Convention; to invite the state party to cooperate in the examination of reliable information on its practice of torture and to make a confidential Committee inquiry if it is warranted; to receive and consider communications from a state party that claims that another state party is not fulfilling its obligations under the Convention, provided the state party under scrutiny recognizes the competence of the Committee; to receive and consider communications from, or on behalf of, individuals subject to its jurisdiction who claim to be victims of a violation of the Convention by a state party (again provided that the state party recognizes the Committee's competence); and to submit an annual report on its activities to the states parties and the UN General Assembly.[16] As of February 1993, of the seventy-one states parties to the Convention, only thirty-one, not including China, had accepted the Committee's competence to consider matters relating to inter-state disputes and communications from, or on behalf of, individuals.[17] The fact that the Convention had one of the lowest memberships among treaty bodies made China's decision to accede more interesting. By 1996, slightly less than 50 percent of states (95 of 193) had not become parties to the Convention.[18] By 1998, however, the number of non-states parties had declined to 45 percent of UN members.

The definition of torture on which both the CAT and the Special Rapporteur base their monitoring is encapsulated in Article 1, Paragraph 1 of the Convention:

For the purposes of this Convention, the term "torture" means any act by which severe pain or suffering, whether physical or mental, is intentionally inflicted on a person for such purposes as obtaining from him or a third person information or a confession, punishing him for an act he or a third person has committed or is suspected of having committed, or intimidating or coercing him or a third person, or for any reason based on discrimination of any kind, when such pain or suffering is inflicted by or at the instigation of or with the consent or acquiescence of a public official or other person acting in an official capacity. It does not include pain or suffering arising only from, inherent in or incidental to lawful sanctions.[19]

This definition is broader than that of the 1975 Declaration on Torture, which limits torture to acts "intentionally inflicted by or at the instigation of a public official." Both CAT and the Special Rapporteur have the task of substantive interpretation of the Convention. They have to grapple with the problem of distinguishing between "torture" and "cruel, inhuman or degrading treatment or punishment." Although the Convention is aimed primarily at protecting detainees, the problem is to determine whether the Convention also applies to those confined in state institutions other than prisons, such as mental hospitals, or even to maltreatment involving different degrees of official complicity.[20]

Pursuant to Article 19 of the Convention, within one year after the entry into force of the Convention for the state concerned, each state party must submit to the Committee, through the UN Secretary-General, reports on the measures taken to implement the Convention. Thereafter, periodic reports are to be submitted every four years on any subsequent developments. The guidelines for initial reports are much the same as for the Human Rights Committee.[21] The reports are to be divided into two parts, describing in the first the constitutional and legal framework within which the Convention will be implemented, and detailing in the second the means whereby individual articles in the Convention have been implemented, providing specific details of cases and situations where the guarantees have been enforced.[22] The periodic reports are expected to provide information on new legislative and administrative developments since the previous report.[23] The Committee invites representatives of the state party to attend the meetings when reports are considered, so that in the afternoon session they may respond to the questions put in the morning session by the Committee and clarify aspects of the report. Under Article 19, Paragraph 3 of the Convention, the Committee may make general comments on the report and may indicate whether some of the obligations of the state concerned under the Convention have not been implemented.

Under all its monitoring procedures, the Convention and rules of procedure allow for the formal involvement of NGOs, although CAT has not made any formal decision to invite NGOs to participate in its work or to circulate their material formally as Committee documents, as they do in the Human Rights Sub-Commission.[24] However, CAT has adopted a rule of procedure whereby it may formally invite NGOs with consultative status to provide it with information in its review of states parties reports. Because its sessions are public, its members believe that the NGOs and the press should be present during its discussions.[25] While supplying valuable information, however, NGOs, according to interviews, have shown only a limited interest in attending actual CAT proceedings.[26] This is despite the fact that a close reading of the China session documents reveals CAT members' dependence on the evidence of the Special Rapporteur on Torture and on NGO reports, as reflected in their constant references to this material.

For states that are parties to both the International Covenant on Civil and Political Rights (ICCPR) and the Convention, there is a substantial overlap between CAT and the UN Human Rights Committee, particularly in the reporting on the measures undertaken to meet obligations under the two treaties (541). However, for a state such as China, which has not ratified the ICCPR, the primary area of overlap is between the work of CAT and that of the Special Rapporteur on Torture. As well as drafting the text of the Convention Against Torture, on 13 March 1985 the UN Commission on Human Rights, in resolution 1985/33, appointed a Special Rapporteur on Torture who, as one of the Commission's thematic reporters, was required to report to the Commission on torture in general and make recommendations on the measures taken to prevent its practice. In pursuit of this mandate, the Special Rapporteur requests information from governments on the measures taken to prevent torture, receives allegations of torture from various sources, and seeks a response from the government in question. He or she may visit countries at their invitation to consult on matters of torture, compiling reports that contain recommendations to specific governments. He or she also receives requests for urgent action, which are transmitted to governments in order to ensure the individual's right to physical and mental integrity.[27]

Although the government reports required by both bodies entail considerable duplication of CAT and Special Rapporteur functions, there are significant differences between the two authorities in the nature, scope, and the handling of their mandates. There exists what is called "a division of labor . . . whereby the special rapporteurs, representatives or experts [of the Commission on Human Rights, etc.] would remain responsible for urgent appeals, whereas the treaty bodies would focus mainly on State party reports."[28] Unlike CAT, whose mandate is confined to states parties of the Convention, the Special Rapporteur's task extends to all Member States of the United Nations and to all states with observer status. His or her function is preventive. The Special Rapporteur can raise allegations with any governments, unlike CAT where Article 20 is binding only in the case of those states parties to the Convention which has accepted its competence. The Special Rapporteur's mandate is a reflection of the fact that the prohibition of torture is seen by the international community to be "an obligation *ergo omnes* for each and every state."[29] However, the rapporteur does not take a stand on whether allegations are well founded but simply requests the Government concerned to look into the matter.[30] CAT, on the other hand, has a quasi-judicial role, ascertaining whether the state concerned has violated its obligations under the Convention, and thereby establishing state responsibility.[31] Finally, although the Special Rapporteur's mandate has been confined to torture, his concern with ill-treatment in a variety of contexts has led to expansion of the definition and reinterpretation of part of Article 1, Paragraph 1 of the Convention against Torture. Thus: "the final sentence of article 1, paragraph 1 of the Convention against Torture, which states that the term 'torture' does not include pain or suffering arising only from, inherent in or incidental to lawful sanctions, has to be interpreted as meaning that such lawful sanctions must be in conformity with international standards. No State should be allowed to perform acts as a lawful sanction which in any other form are generally condemned as a serious human rights violation."[32]

From the above it is clear that, although it has been suggested that the Special Rapporteur should focus only on states that are not parties to the Convention, in the case of those states resiling from Articles 20–22 of the Convention against Torture, he continues to have an important function.[33] In the case of China, which has not accepted the competence of the Committee in these optional articles, both bodies have a complementary and mutually supportive role to play. The guidelines for the Special Rapporteur's investigations state that an allegation of abuse by a governmental or nongovernmental organization will be transmitted only if it is sufficiently detailed, if it corresponds to the general condition of human rights in the country concerned, and if it is corroborated by other more general information.[34] The allegation's veracity can be tested only through an investigation on the spot by the national authorities.

In the view of the Special Rapporteur, a government's reply is required to contain information about the authority responsible for the investigation, the persons questioned, the results of the medical examination and the identity of the person who performed it, the decision on the complaint that is eventually filed, and the grounds for this decision, as well as any other relevant material. Finally, "a flat denial or a reference to the prohibition of torture under national law or to the fact that the individual has not submitted any complaint or has been released cannot be seen as satisfactory replies. . . . If the authorities are of the opinion that the allegations are made for the sole purpose of smearing the Government, they can always invite the Special Rapporteur to carry out an investigation himself" (para. 10, at 3).

Although it is clear that the Special Rapporteur on Torture has a complementary function to CAT, the effectiveness of this monitoring mechanism is influenced by the wide scope of the Rapporteur's responsibilities across the entire membership of the United Nations, by its dependence on the Human Rights Commission to follow up on thematic reports, and by the requirement that the Special Rapporteur may visit countries to investigate allegations of abuse only with the permission of the state being monitored. As Philip Alston has observed: "The thematic rapporteurs have . . . begun to evolve a significant capacity for prompt responses. They are, however, confined to the use of telegrams and the like and have not yet moved very far towards seeking the immediate mobilization of public or governmental opinion (an option that many observers would, in any event, counsel them not to use). The Commission's other rapporteurs have been more timid in this regard, perhaps assuming that such interventions would jeopardize their fact-finding and conciliation functions."[35]

China and the Committee Against Torture

China not only ratified the Convention Against Torture; it also claimed to have taken a leading role in helping to draft it.[36] In ratifying the Convention it became subject to the obligation in Article 2 to "take effective legislative, administrative, judicial or other measures to prevent acts of torture in any territory under its jurisdiction."[37] However, China both explicitly repudiated the Committee's competence to act on the provisions of Article 20 and failed to make a declaration of acceptance on the competence of the Committee with respect to Articles 21 and 22.[38] Because China did not accept the optional articles of the Convention, UN officials have speculated that it became a party to the Convention mainly because of its obligations as a large power.[39]

Although China's constitutions do not contain provisions explicitly prohibiting the practice of torture, Article 32 of the 1979 Criminal Procedure Law provides that "it is strictly prohibited to use torture to coerce statements (*yanjin xingxun bigong*) and the gathering of evidence by threat, enticement, deceit or other unlawful methods."[40] Yet reports by human rights NGOs indicate that torture is still a systemic problem often instigated by the authorities. The source of the problem has been identified as:

1. Failings in the legal system, including an incomplete conception of torture; the lack of an independent judicial system; the denial of the right of the accused to early access to legal counsel; the acceptance by trial judges of evidence obtained by torture; and the prevalence of administrative detention, outside the purvue of the criminal law;
2. Aspects of judicial practice, wherein cases of torture have been handled in an "overly tolerant manner"; and
3. Chinese Communist Party policies on law enforcement, wherein the

> Public Security Bureau and State Security organs are given vast powers
> to maintain social order and to investigate crimes without adequate
> monitoring.[41]

Of these reasons, perhaps the most basic is the incomplete nature of
China's conception of "torture." There are two conceptions of torture
in the Criminal Law, the first being to "coerce a statement" (Art. 136),
the second being to subject imprisoned people to corporal punishment
and abuse for this purpose (Art. 189) (8). This definition is purposive and
fails to encompass either the general practice of torture or the expanded
reinterpretation by the Special Rapporteur of the meaning of the last sentence in Article 1, Paragraph 1 of the Convention Against Torture, emphasizing that "lawful sanctions must be in accordance with international
standards." In addition, it has a temporal specificity, in that it refers to
the moment of interrogation, and does not appear to apply generally to
the periods of detention, arrest, and subsequent imprisonment. Needless
to say, the Chinese definition does not include the concept of mental torture, a sanction which dissident Wei Jingsheng has identified as the most
difficult form to bear.[42] Thus, at the hearing of the second periodic report before CAT, Ambassador Wu Jianmin admitted that "China's domestic legislation did not incorporate the definition of torture appearing in
Article 1 of the Convention." His defense was merely that China's "domestic legislative provisions designated *various forms* of torture as criminal
offenses."[43]

An Amnesty International report published six months after China had
signed the Convention Against Torture, and based primarily on Chinese
sources, found that "most torture victims are criminal suspects who are
tortured to force them to confess" and that "their torturers are usually
police officers, or Communist Party officials and members of the many
informal security units who illegally detain individuals they suspect of committing crimes."[44] The role of police officers in the practice of torture was
confirmed as late as January 1998, with the issue of three decrees "forbid-
ding officers from accepting favours from suspects, extracting confessions
by torture and bullying complainants."[45]

One of the difficulties in understanding the practice of torture in China
concerns the lack of accurate statistics and their conflicting nature. As Human Rights in China has pointed out, in 1988 the procuratorates received 1,
048 complaints about torture to coerce a statement, of which only 170 were
filed for investigation.[46] Consequently, the statistics later provided by China
to CAT of more than 400 cases filed suggested that the actual cases of torture
could be much greater. As China's Ambassador to the United Nations, Wu
Jianmin, admitted in May 1996 to the CAT, "hundreds of complaints concerning torture were filed every year."[47]

China's Report to the Committee Against Torture, December 1989

On 1 December 1989, only one month after the deadline for its presentation, China produced its initial report to CAT. The report of only eleven pages represented a brief monument to formalism: it outlined China's formal constitutional provisions, legislation and regulations pertaining to torture as evidence that the rights of the Chinese citizen were protected and torture outlawed, as well as that remedies existed through the provisions of the Administrative Procedure Law. It thus merged evidence of *de jure* compliance with claims of *de facto* compliance. The main admission of the actual practice of torture was contained in a short passage: "As with other criminal offences, so torture, an act which endangers society, has yet to be eliminated completely in China. Due to a weak sense of legal system, the serious influence of privileges and the rather low professional level among some State functionaries, the phenomena [*sic*] of torture still exists in some localities."[48]

The report then listed steps taken to redress the situation that included, besides legislative, judicial, and administrative measures, increased legal education and expanded mass media coverage. Its content thus conformed with the first part of the requirements for the initial report, which were to describe the institutional and legal context within which the Convention was to be implemented.[49] However, in failing to detail the means whereby individual articles in the Convention had been implemented in practice, the report fell far short of the second half of the requirements.

Prior to the Committee's response in late April 1990, the International League for Human Rights published a detailed rebuttal of the Chinese report.[50] It challenged the report's claim that the People's Republic of China was resolute in opposing torture and that its legislative, judicial, and administrative measures for the implementation of the Convention were "wholly in compliance" with the requirements of the Convention against the facts of widespread practice of torture in China. It identified an array of related legal, procedural and practical problems "not yet adequately addressed by the Chinese government" that "contribute to the persistence of torture and . . . merit the most serious international scrutiny" (1–2). It included in its analysis material relating to torture in China from both before and after China signed the Convention, as support for its contention that "the methods of torture employed, the circumstances in which most torture occurs, the legislative structure which makes lawful conditions conducive to the occurrence of torture and the inability or unwillingness of public authorities and the legal system to stamp out the practice remain today essentially unchanged from the position before the Convention entered into force for China" (2).

In contrast to the report's claim that torture was an aberrant feature of

Chinese law enforcement, it viewed torture as a "routine part of the *modus operandi* of [China's] law enforcement officials" (5).

In view of the "incompleteness" of the Chinese report, the League recommended that the Committee request a further report from China remedying the deficiencies in the report; that China accept the competence of the Committee under Articles 21 and 22 and withdraw its reservation to Article 20; that the Chinese government invite the Special Rapporteur on Torture to visit China to investigate claims of torture; and that China utilize the advisory services and technical assistance available through the Centre for Human Rights (Supplement, 4–5).

The information in this NGO report, together with other NGO material and the Special Rapporteur's report, was privately described by a source close to the Committee as "alarming."[51] It influenced both the nature of the Committee's response and the Chinese oral presentation. On the morning of 27 April 1990, the Chinese Ambassador, Fan Guoxiang, and four other Chinese delegates appeared before the Committee. In a statement with repercussions far beyond the actual Committee, Fan addressed the thorny issue of the relation between domestic and international human rights law in broad and sweeping terms, claiming that "All the relevant provisions of the Convention were reflected in Chinese legal instruments, including the Constitution, the Criminal Law, the Criminal Procedure Law, the Administrative Procedure Law and the Regulations on Arrest and Detention. In addition, under the Chinese legal system, an international convention came into force as soon as it was ratified. There was therefore no special legislative procedure for incorporating an international convention into domestic law."[52]

The questioning that followed from nine of the ten Committee members concentrated on the very general nature of the Chinese report and its failure to provide factual detail on the application of the Convention article by article. Christine Chanet in particular found Fan's claim "quite unusual," and asked for details of Chinese legislation corresponding to each article in the Convention. The questions sought to explore the gap exposed by the League report between China's legal provisions and its actual practice with respect to torture. Dimitar Nikolov Mikhailov, although the most sympathetic of questioners, regretted that "the report, which gave a good idea of the general situation, did not give enough information about the judicial aspects of the application of the Convention and *did not follow the Committee's guidelines for the submission of a report*" (para. 52 at 8). Two other members proposed that a supplementary report filling in the gaps in the report be submitted by China. A battery of questions followed. They included queries about the practical application of each of the Convention's provisions to China, the judicial aspects of the application of the Convention, the jurisdiction of the different courts, the practice of the death penalty, the number of prisoners and the practice of reform through labor, information on administrative detention and incommunicado detention, legal safeguards for detainees, and the number of officials prosecuted for torture. Most of the members echoed their colleague Ricardo Gil Lavedra's reference to the "impressive amount" of information from NGOs and the Special Rapporteur on Torture, "which revealed a grave pattern of gross violation of human rights" (para. 42 at 7).

In the afternoon session, Chinese delegate Shen Jinchu made a lengthy statement and responded to questions. Regarding the impact of the Convention on China's domestic legislation, he spoke in terms that differed only marginally from those of Ambassador Fan. However, in his seven-page statement he sought to respond to, and elaborate on, the questions raised in the morning session. Once again, the response was long on generalities and formal legal provisions and short on practice and specific detail. In addition, Shen denied that there had been summary arrests or detentions of peaceful demonstrators, summary executions, or widespread torture after the Tiananmen demonstrations in 1989. He also claimed that no cases of political imprisonment or secret detention existed in China.[53] Members of the Committee required more details for their doubts to be dispelled, or called for an additional more detailed and analytical report. Bent Sørensen in particular requested "a supplementary report with the missing answers to the questions on articles 2–16 arranged in systematic fashion as requested in the Committee's guidelines, and full information on the various cases of torture, with details of investigations carried out and their results, the punishment of torturers and the rehabilitation of victims" (para. 43 at 10).

The Chairman therefore agreed that "the Committee should, in accordance with rule 67, paragraph 2 of the rules of procedure, request an additional report, if possible by the end of the year so that it could be considered at the spring session in 1991" (para. 49 at 11). He thanked the Chinese representatives and concluded with the requirements for the supplementary report: "The report should be set out in accordance with the Committee's guidelines: after a description of the judicial, police and prison systems, with general and legislative details, information should be provided in the order of the articles of the Convention. In addition, the Committee would like to have answers to the questions to which replies had not been given" (para. 52 at 11).

A summary of the outstanding questions under the different articles of the Convention was subsequently provided by the Committee in its report to the forty-fifth session of the UN General Assembly.[54]

The Chinese representatives were reported to have been visibly upset by Committee members' reaction to its report, which was subsequently privately described as "completely inadequate." They were undoubtedly aware that the request to provide a supplementary report was not a regular occurrence.[55] Their general reaction was astonishment that ten Committee members could question the condition of 1.2 billion Chinese citizens.[56] This response was substantiated at a national level over subsequent days by public officials in China admitting that some mistakes had been made. Chinese delegates asked the Committee for explanations about procedure and, in particular, inquired whether allegations from NGO sources should be accepted.

For their part, Committee members reportedly experienced major difficulties with the first report because Chinese officials always responded the same way, no matter how the questions were angled.[57] Although, in contrast to their behavior in the ILO Governing Body Committee on Freedom of Association (CFA), Chinese representatives did not complain of Committee interference in front of the Committee members, they were known to have made complaints behind closed doors.[58] Later, in November 1990, during the UN General Assembly debates, the Chinese delegation reportedly complained that CAT was acting beyond its mandate and that the information from NGOs should not be accepted by them. At the same time, the Chinese Ambassador called for understanding from the Committee, asking it to assess China's problems in the context of a country in which medieval concepts and cultural behavior had to be changed.

Although the supplementary report was not provided within the recommended time limit of 31 December 1990, it was produced two and a half years later, in October 1992. In the meantime, in July 1990, Asia Watch had produced a substantial report on torture in China, which explored the gap between the formal system and the substantive reality.[59] This report was based on the submission of Asia Watch to the Committee Against Torture. It analyzed the main factors contributing to the high incidence of torture as: (1) inadequate legal safeguards for the rights of detainees; (2) a strong emphasis by the police on obtaining confessions to facilitate prompt convictions; (3) failure by the authorities to investigate, pursue and punish the criminal responsibility of police officers who used torture; and (4) torture arising from extrajudicial forms of detention (3–13).

It was possibly partly in response to the NGO critiques, and to the supervision of the Committee and the Special Rapporteur, as well as to China's concerns about the U.S. and MFN, that, two months before its report, China published a second White Paper on human rights in August 1992, this time devoted entirely to the issue of criminal reform, and to prisoners' rights.[60] This was produced in addition to the October 1991 White Paper, which also contained a section on prisoners' rights. Both White Papers contained references to torture. The first White Paper, *Human Rights in China*, stated that "it is strictly prohibited to extort confessions by torture (*xingxun bigong*)."[61] It indicated that in 1990, China's procuratorial organs had filed for investigation 472 cases that involved extorting confessions by torture and observed that "this has not only protected citizens' personal rights effectively, but also taught law enforcement officials a lesson" (23). The second White Paper, *Criminal Reform in China*, stated that "it is strictly forbidden to torture (*yanjin dui zuifan shijia kuxing*), insult, or otherwise maltreat prisoners."[62] It also stated that "criminals have the right to protection against assault on their human dignity or personal safety under all circumstances. In response to any illegal action on the part of a warden or guard, such as obtaining a confession by torture (*xingxun bigong*), administering corporeal punishment or otherwise maltreating a prisoner, the victim has the right to appeal to the People's Procuratorate, the People's Court, the people's government or any other institution to expose and report such treatment" (4).

The White Paper admitted that in 1990 and 1991 a total of twenty-four wardens and guards had been sentenced to prison for inflicting "corporeal punishment" (*tifa nuedai*) on prisoners (6). Humiliation of prisoners was also forbidden. At the same time, it stated that "the legal and moral education of criminals in reform-through-labour institutions emphasizes the need to plead guilty" (12). And awareness of the many forms humiliation and mental torture could take was absent in the statement that "sometimes, the prison staff have to talk to a prisoner ten, twenty or even a hundred times before their concern can move the prisoner" (17).

China's Supplementary Report, October 1992

China's 1992 supplementary report suggested that, at least at a procedural level, China had learned from the mistakes of its 1990 report. This time its officials demonstrated a marked effort to comply with the Committee's requirements. The 1992 report was described as the first time that Chinese authorities had recognized that the Committee had the right to question them and that they had the obligation to respond.[63] It itemized the questions asked by the Committee at the hearings for the first report with a cross-reference to its answer in the text. At the CAT session in April 1993 to discuss the report, China's seriousness was further underlined by the large size of its delegation and the senior status of its representation. Ten representatives in all appeared before an equal number of Committee members; the principal respondent to the Committee's questions was the Chinese Ambassador to the Chinese Mission in Geneva, Jin Yongjian.[64] Both these developments were in marked contrast to the 1990 session.

The new report was a substantial document of thirty-nine pages divided into two parts.[65] Following Committee guidelines, the first section consisted of an outline of China's political, legislative and judicial systems, whereas the second part dealt with China's implementation of Articles 2–16 of the Convention under the heading of each article. It repeated Ambassador Fan's earlier acknowledgment of the primacy of international law over domestic law, a remarkable concession of sovereignty not equaled even by Western democracies.[66]

The supplementary report was also more forthcoming on matters of actual practice. It described cases of abuse of citizens' personal (*renge*) rights, and of cases of torture. It reported that in 1990 the procuratorates had received 279 cases of torture from the investigatory service, 207 of which led to prosecutions; and in 1991 these figures had increased to 304 and 279 respectively (para. 108, at 27). However, these figures did not conform with the higher figure of 472 cases for 1990 cited in the White Paper, *Human Rights in China.*

In between the receipt of the Chinese report in October 1992, and the Committee hearings to consider it in April 1993, a substantial report on torture in China was produced in December 1992 by Amnesty International. It stated that "torture has become endemic in many places in China and the abuses suffered by prisoners are now far more severe than they were ten years ago."[67] It claimed that "in the four years since China ratified the Convention, no . . . effective measures have been taken and no fundamental safeguards have been introduced to lessen the risk of prisoners being subjected to torture or other ill-treatment . . . the incidence of torture in China's prisons and detention centres has, if anything, increased" (1). In support of this finding, it provided a detailed documentation of the methods of torture practiced in Chinese prisons and examples of more than fifty individual cases of torture of prisoners of conscience between 1991 and 1992, of which six had allegedly ended in death.

Despite these negative findings, on this second occasion Committee members did not have such difficulties reaching a final conclusion. In the beginning, some members were reportedly not satisfied.[68] They still expressed doubts, especially on the issue of administrative detention and on Tibet. However, as the questioning proceeded and the responses from China's Ambassador proved both detailed and specific, they gradually found the report more acceptable. The Ambassador furnished details of the practice of torture, with higher figures than the report had contained, but did not give figures of deaths in custody or capital punishment. Unlike the issue of torture, whose practice was ritually denounced, during all the hearings, and in interviews, China's UN diplomats did not express disapproval of capital punishment; if anything, they attempted to justify it.[69] In response to a question about the use of organs of executed prisoners, for instance, the Ambassador said that the removal of organs without prior permission of the person or his family was not "standard practice," although "there were cases in which permission had been given and the organs were duly removed and donated to patients" (at 5).

Subsequently, NGOs were reportedly critical of the Committee for being too sympathetic towards China's position, arguing that it should have been more concerned about the substantive issues.[70] But the mere fact of procedural compliance with the Committee's requirements elicited final Committee approval of China's report, despite its revelations of substantive noncompliance at the domestic level. Not only was the report found to comply with report guidelines, but it drew the approving comment from Alexis Dipanda Mouelle that "China was one of the few countries to have annexed to its report all the questions put by the Committee and . . . this was an initiative to be encouraged."[71] Peter Burns, then co-rapporteur for China, also congratulated the Chinese Government on its detailed report, and welcomed the presence in the delegation of the Director of the Supreme People's Procuratorate (paras. 24–25, at 6).

This shift in the Committee's response was due partly to its need to reward China for its progress in complying with the Committee guidelines and its members' requests. Because the purpose of reporting was to establish a dialogue to assist the reporting state in the implementation of its treaty commitments at both international and domestic levels, members were concerned to give credit for procedural as well as for substantive compliance. This concern was reflected in the Committee's 1993 report to the forty-eighth session of the General Assembly on China's response. In its conclusions and recommendations, the Committee "expressed its gratitude for the detailed report submitted by the Government of China, which was in conformity with the Committee's guidelines, as well as for the explanations provided by the delegation." It also "took note with satisfaction of the many legislative, judicial and administrative measures which had been adopted by the Government in order to comply with the various provisions of the Convention."[72] It thus gave China credit for a degree of formal *de jure* compliance at the domestic level.

However, the Committee drew a distinction between *de jure* compliance and the substantive *de facto* lack of compliance at the domestic level. It expressed sympathy with "the obvious difficulties facing China," but exhibited concern at NGO reports of the use of administrative detention and cases of torture, particularly in Tibet. It requested energetic measures of prevention and punishment of those responsible, calling for precise statistical data on the number of persons in administrative detention, sentenced to capital punishment and executed (para. 425). It also called for further legislation providing extensive guarantees for arrested or detained persons, with separation between the authorities responsible for detention and for interrogation, the monitoring of the conduct of interrogations and "limitations on the use of instruments, equipment and weapons by the security forces" (paras. 427–428, at 68). It appealed to the Chinese government to consider making declarations with regard to Articles 21 and 22 of the Convention and withdrawing the reservation to Article 20. Finally, the Committee hoped that China's political will and legislative measures would promote research into the causes of torture and the means of ending, "or at least reducing," its incidence (para. 426, at 67).

Within the discrete international context of the reporting process, China's leaders thus demonstrated a sharp learning curve at the procedural level and, to some extent, in the view of the Committee, at the level of domestic *de jure* compliance. However, a question mark hovered over the issue of China's next periodic report, which was due on 2 November 1993. Two years later, no report had been received. Reminders had been sent, but there had been no indications as to when the report could be expected.[73] Finally, in December 1995, it arrived, breaking the apparent hiatus in China's procedural compliance.

China's Second Periodic Report, December 1995

China's second periodic report was a reasonably lengthy document of twenty pages. Like the supplementary report, it took the articles of the Convention one by one and documented the way in which their provisions had been implemented in China's criminal and administrative law, in particular, the Criminal Law, the Criminal Procedure Law, the State Compensation Law, the People's Police Law, the Prison Law, and the Detention Centre Regulations. However, unlike the supplementary report, and despite the continuing requests of the Committee, it did not deal in any meaningful way with issues of practical implementation. Instead, Part 11 addressed additional information previously requested by the Committee, but only as it pertained to new or existing legal provisions and administrative procedures. China's Ambassador argued that the purpose of providing such information was to demonstrate the ways in which the recommendations made at the conclusion of consideration of the supplementary report in 1993 "had already been adopted in varying degrees or were being implemented through measures in line with China's specific circumstances."[74] The final paragraphs, 88 to 95, dealt only with details of training classes in 1994 for custodial staff on injunctions against "torturing, humiliating, beating, abusing and mistreating prisoners and inmates," thereby, by implication, distinguishing the concept of torture from the other acts described.[75] The report failed to discuss the statistics of the practice of torture as it had been invited to do or to address in any detail efforts taken to remedy and punish the perpetrator, citing only one example to this effect (20).

Otherwise, it was notable that the emphasis was very much on the future — the need for public education on the legal prohibition against torture, for the reinforcement of the supervision of law enforcement (which supervisory body was not identified), and for action on the victim's right to compensation and on mechanisms of prevention. Such mechanisms were identified as social pressure, including supervision by watchdog mechanisms; the placement of inspectors in prisons and reform centers by the People's Inspectorate; establishment of disciplinary offices inside prisons and reform centers; and impromptu visits by delegations from different levels of people's congresses (at 6, 8).

Prior to examination of the report, the NGO Human Rights in China met with the Secretary of the Committee. In April, on the eve of China's examination by the Committee, Amnesty International produced a report on China's second periodic report, as did Human Rights in China. In Amnesty's opinion, the report showed that "seven years after it ratified the Convention against Torture, the government has still not taken measures to prohibit all acts of torture by law, as required by the Convention. Basic safeguards to prevent torture and ill-treatment, such as early and regular access to lawyers, are still lacking, and the ineffectiveness of the measures taken by the government is demonstrated by the continuing high incidence of torture in China."[76]

Amnesty itemized the reasons why torture continued: inadequate legislation, the practice of incommunicado detention as "the norm for most detainees," inadequate investigations, and a "climate of impunity." Apart from its criticism of the inadequacy of China's report in failing to comment on implementation of Articles 7 and 12 of the Convention in the past four years, and its failure to cite torture figures, Amnesty invited the Committee to "look at the extent of deaths in custody in China, which remains largely unacknowledged by the authorities" (13). For its part, Human Rights in China believed that "torture remains routine in many Chinese detention centers, prisons and labor camps and that the Chinese government has generally failed in its responsibility to implement the provisions of the Convention." It concluded with seven recommendations, including the revision of legal provisions in the Criminal Law and Criminal Procedure Law regarding evidence obtained through torture, the prohibition of the practice of employing inmates to perpetrate torture at the instigation of officials, and the elimination of all forms of administrative detention without judicial process.[77]

On the morning of 3 May 1996, the Committee met with eleven senior Chinese representatives. Ambassador Wu declared that the second periodic report "followed the Committee's guidelines regarding the form and content of reports." His oral presentation listed changes in China's legal provisions that had introduced greater safeguards against the practice of torture since the earlier hearings.[78] Thus, if there was insufficient evidence to substantiate an indictment, the court now had an obligation to dismiss the charges on the ground of insufficient evidence. More specific stipulations on the division of labor among the courts, procuratorates, and public security organs under the amended Criminal Procedure Law meant that cases involving extraction of confessions by torture now fell within the jurisdiction of the procuratorates. In addition, strict procedures had been laid down with regard to detention and other coercive measures, abolishing examination during police custody; participation by lawyers in criminal proceedings had been expanded; and the Administrative Punishment Law now entitled citizens and victims to compensation for harm suffered. According to Ambassador Wu, the state had further improved the inspection of law enforcement institutions and had "promptly investigated complaints of corporal punishment and ill-treatment of prisoners or detainees." He also noted that by the end of 1995, permanent inspectors had been assigned to all the countries' prisons. Through these means, "the public authorities had succeeded in reducing the number of cases of torture" (3). Ambassador Wu acknowledged some of the ambiguities involved in China's definition of torture and the difficulty of providing accurate statistics on torture.

There followed substantial discussion, in which members of the Committee politely, but resolutely and methodically, teased out the ambiguities, vagueness and gaps in China's second report. As before, Committee members' questions and comments focused on the important divergence between legal provisions and practical implementation and China's intentions concerning its reservations under Articles 20 and 22 of the Convention. They also addressed China's definition of torture, the presumption of innocence in China's new criminal legislation, and the protection against torture in the system of administrative detention.

In particular, Peter Burns, rapporteur for China in the Committee, took the different paragraphs of the Chinese report and examined them against both the claims in NGO reports and the internal contradictions in Chinese legislation. He wondered whether, in the absence of a precise definition of acts constituting torture, accurate statistics could be compiled and whether universal jurisdiction could be exercised. In the absence of any reference to a criminal penalty, he queried the report's affirmation that obedience to an order from a superior could not be invoked as an excuse to justify an act of torture. He observed that "regardless of the rules formally in force, *de facto* impunity did seem to exist for the perpetrators of acts of torture." He inquired about a new form of administrative detention, detention for questioning, and about the existence of a guarantee in Chinese law comparable to *habeas corpus*. Citing the Amnesty International report, he asked about the practice of keeping most detainees incommunicado and requested the statistical data for deaths that had occurred in detention in 1994 and 1995. He observed the incompatibility between Article 12 of the new Criminal Procedure Law, which laid down the general principle that no one should be presumed guilty before being convicted by a court, and Article 35 of the same law which seemed to run counter to the presumption of innocence by stipulating that the defense must present material evidence proving that the defendant was innocent, that the offense was minor, that the penalty should be light, or that the defendant was not criminally responsible. Referring to Amnesty International figures of 2,780 death sentences and 2,050 executions in 1994, he asked whether it was correct that capital punishment could be imposed for a very large range of offenses, thus running counter to the spirit of Article 1 of the Convention, which stipulated that the death penalty could be imposed only for very serious offenses. Finally, in view of their critical role in safeguarding the rule of law, he inquired about the role and status of procurators in the system, since they were located at the lower levels of the hierarchy (5–7).

That afternoon, Ambassador Wu and his delegation met with the Committee for a closed meeting at 3:00. At 3:30, the public part of the meeting was called to order and Ambassador Wu responded to most of the morning's questions.[79] He decried the Committee members' dependence on reports by Amnesty International, since "that body was known to be politically motivated." He reiterated the claim made in earlier meetings that once the National People's Congress (NPC) approved China's accession to international legal instruments, "such an instrument was binding upon the Government, which was obliged to incorporate its provisions into domestic law, the international instrument always taking precedence in the event of any discrepancy." He announced that in the three years from 1993 to 1995, the Supreme People's Procuratorate had investigated a total of 1,194 allegations of torture. Increasing numbers were being investigated, he affirmed, because China's legislation on torture had been improved, the Procuratorate had stepped up the number of investigations, and citizens were now reporting cases of torture. This statement seemed to contradict his earlier observation that cases of torture had decreased. He did not address the question about deaths in custody, except to promise to inquire about a case of forty-one deaths as a result of torture reported in Yunnan Province.

Allegations that torture was widely practiced in Tibet, he charged, stemmed mainly from the Tibetan separatist movement and from NGOs "with an anti-China bias." He insisted that the death penalty "could be decreed only for particularly serious crimes." He affirmed in answer to Burns that, under the amended Criminal Procedure Law, there was no conflict between Article 12, which established the presumption of innocence, and Article 35: the burden of proof would lie with the prosecutor and not with the accused or the defending counsel. In response to a question about the system of heads of cells or trusties, which could enable prison staff to evade liability for ill-treatment of inmates, he denied the existence of such a system. It was notable that Wu referred in his responses only to the specific prohibition on "extorting confessions under torture" and not to prohibition on acts of torture in general. It was also clear that, while he responded to most points made by Committee members, his failure to address specific cases or to give detailed replies on practical implementation undermined the effectiveness of his response, and the members' questions continued to reverberate in the aftermath of his presentation.

Three days later, and following a second closed meeting, the Committee read out their conclusions and recommendations.[80] Wu remarked at the conclusion that he regretted the reliance on material from NGOs for one section of the conclusions, since these drew their information from "so-called 'dissidents' who made their living out of accusing and blaming China." If, he insisted, "the conclusions of the Committee were based on misinformation, they could not be considered objective." As revised, the formal concluding observations of the Committee stated that "the second periodic report of China follows the Committee's guidelines and meets them satisfactorily."[81]

This was despite the failure of the second half of the report to meet the requirement that it should detail the means whereby individual articles of the Convention had been implemented in practice, and that it should provide specific details of cases and situations where the guarantees had been enforced. The Committee observed that although the report had been due on 2 November 1993, since China had produced its supplementary report only a year before, "the timing of this report is quite satisfactory." Positive aspects of the Chinese report were seen to be the amendments to the Criminal Procedure Law; the reported instances of police officials being prosecuted for acts of torture; steps being taken by the Ministry of Public Security to educate personnel on the prohibition of torture; the provision of effective criminal and administrative compensation to victims of abuse; and the government information that "heads of cells and trusties" did not exist in China.

But the observations also decried the evidence in NGO reports that "torture may be practised on a widespread basis in China"; China's failure to incorporate the crime of torture into legislation in terms consistent with the definition in Article 1 of the Convention; claims that torture occurred in police stations and prisons in situations that often did not result in investigation; NGO claims that the Procuratorate had yet to establish its authority over the police, prison, and security services; the fact that some methods of capital punishment might be in breach of Article 16 of the Convention; claims by NGOs about maltreatment and even death of persons held in police custody and prisons in Tibet; the failure to provide access to legal counsel at the earliest times of contact with authorities and NGO claims that incommunicado detention was still prevalent; and the "important number" of deaths apparently arising out of police custody.

The Committee therefore made nine recommendations: that China enact a law defining the crime of torture in terms consistent with Article 1 of the Convention; that a comprehensive system be established to oversee the effective management of complaints of maltreatment; that methods of execution of prisoners sentenced to death, and that conditions in prisons, be brought into conformity with Article 16 of the Convention; that access to legal counsel be granted to all those detained, arrested, or imprisoned as a matter of right and at an early stage of the process; that China consider the establishment of a branch of the International Rehabilitation Council for Torture Victims in Beijing; that it continue with its "most welcome reforms" to its criminal penal system and continue training legal professions; that it consider withdrawing its reservations to Article 20 and declare in favor of Articles 21 and 22 of the Convention; and that measures be taken to ensure the objectives of the Convention and the autonomy/independence of the judiciary in China.

It was clear that, substantively, the Chinese position was as obdurate as ever. Moreover, despite the clear improvement in its procedural compliance, as the proceedings before the CAT ended, the Chinese Ambassador excoriated the Committee for failing to understand China's cultural conditions and the problems faced by the Chinese government.

China and the Draft Optional Protocol to the Convention Against Torture

In addition to its reporting to CAT, China participated closely in the drafting of the draft Optional Protocol to the Convention against Torture. On 3 March 1992, at its forty-eighth session, the Commission on Human Rights had decided, in its resolution 1992/43, to establish an open-ended working group to elaborate a draft Optional Protocol to the Convention against Torture. The aim of the working group was to elaborate a mechanism for the inspection of all places of detention of states parties, and, on periodic and ad hoc bases, to examine the treatment of detainees and ensure states were taking adequate measures for the prevention of torture and cruel, inhuman, or degrading treatment. This would enable CAT, through a sub-committee, to move from passive to active monitoring. During the first and second readings, it became apparent that the fundamental issue was whether, in ratifying the protocol, states were agreeing in advance to prison visits or whether ratifying states could grant or withhold consent to a request for a visit. Discussion particularly focused on whether parenthetical language should be allowed in Article 1, which read: "A State Party to the present Protocol shall permit visits in accordance with this Protocol to any place in any territory under its jurisdiction where persons deprived of their liberty by a public authority or at its instigation or with its consent or acquiescence are held or may be held [provided that full respect is assured for the principles of non-intervention and the sovereignty of States]." China, Cuba, Colombia, and Mexico could not understand the position of states that argued there was no need to add the bracketed material. As the International Service for Human Rights pointed out, at the heart of the discussion was not the question of whether states were sovereign, but "whether in ratifying the optional protocol, States are agreeing in advance to prison visits or whether ratifying States may grant or withhold consent to a request for a visit."[82] Article 8, which dealt with the arrangements for the visit to be conducted between the proposed sub-committee and the state party, was also a source of debate.

During the second reading in October 1997, China's representative, "while recognizing the importance of the sub-committee being allowed to exercise its functions on the territory of a State party and agreeing that it would enjoy certain privileges, felt that the principles of non-intervention and prior consent were also important and must have their place in the text." He also stated that, in terms of validity, "the text of articles 1 and 8, as adopted as the outcome of the first reading, should still be recognized as a major foundation for future work."[83] China's position, and that of Cuba,

Mexico, Uruguay, Syria and Nigeria, threatened the viability of the future Optional Protocol, since if states had the option to refuse a visit by the proposed subcommittee, its purpose would be undermined. Although at this reading China was reported to have been less assertive and to have "accepted quite a lot of suggestions from the group," its strict position on sovereignty remained a barrier to progress in the drafting. Regarding Article 12, most states expressed concern about the notion of making visits to prisons and prisoners subject to national laws, because this could impede the mission's work. China and Cuba, in contrast, insisted that national laws be respected. Some unexpected alliances were also formed, in that China stood with the United States in favor of allowing reservations to the Optional Protocol, and China and Australia favored a high number of ratifications before the Optional Protocol could enter into force.[84] Common to all these positions taken by China was the issue of state sovereignty. It was interesting that China considered it so important to influence the content of the Optional Protocol, when its obvious option would have been simply to fail to accede to the Optional Protocol once it was formally adopted.

China and the Special Rapporteur on Torture

The first Special Rapporteur on Torture, Peter Kooijmans, saw his mandate as more active than the Committee's, and as designed to enable the adoption of preventive measures.[85] Despite this preventive role, he is not on record as having transmitted any allegations on the practice of torture to China from 1985 to 1987, nor did he address *notes verbales* requesting information from China on measures taken or envisaged to prevent or combat torture.[86] His first public communication with China involved an urgent appeal sent on 2 December 1988 concerning four Tibetan nuns allegedly tortured after being arrested in a prodemocracy demonstration in Lhasa.[87] On 21 April 1989, he also sent a letter transmitting information on the alleged torture of twenty-seven Tibetans convicted for involvement in demonstrations, another Tibetan allegedly tortured in detention, and five Catholic seminarians arrested in Hebei Province. Further, on 29 November 1989 he sent an urgent appeal concerning a Tibetan in Lhasa allegedly tortured in detention.[88]

On 21 July 1989, the government of China replied to the Special Rapporteur's letter of 21 April with respect to the five Catholic seminarians. Although some information about the case was given, it did not cover the detail stipulated in the guidelines for a reply to the Special Rapporteur, particularly as the allegations were claimed to be "sheer fabrications" (para. 42).

The Rapporteur's first communication relating to the 1989 Democracy Movement was an urgent appeal of 13 June 1989 regarding alleged beatings of "a large number of persons," including five individuals arrested during the first week of June for participating in demonstrations. The June action also attracted the attention of special rapporteurs with related mandates, S. Amos Wako, Special Rapporteur on Summary and Arbitrary Executions, and Leandro Despouy, Special Rapporteur on States of Emergency.[89]

The Chinese government twice responded to communications from Wako (at 21–22). On 3 July 1989, it replied to the telegrams of 5, 16, and 20 June, claiming that a counterrevolutionary insurrection had broken out in Beijing. The Chinese account claimed that six thousand officers and People's Liberation Army soldiers and more than three thousand demonstrators and bystanders had been wounded at the beginning of the "insurrection," and that dozens of military and "more than 200 evildoers, students and civilians" had been killed. In this case, as in Shanghai, the Chinese authorities stated that only those who had broken the law had been dealt with, and then according to strictly legal procedures. On 14 September, a similar response to the Chengdu allegations was sent by the government, in answer to the Special Rapporteur's letter of 13 July.

During 1990–91, the Special Rapporteur on Torture sent urgent appeals to the Government of China concerning Tibetans allegedly tortured and one concerning torture of a philosophy lecturer detained in Chengdu. The Chinese government denied the allegations in the case of the Tibetans and denied knowledge of the philosophy lecturer.[90]

Between 1991 and 1992, three urgent appeals to the government of China, of 28 August, 17 September and 10 December 1991, were addressed by the Special Rapporteur, alleging torture of five Tibetans and two Chinese, Wang Juntao and Chen Ziming. On 14 February 1991, he addressed a letter to the Chinese government alleging torture of six Tibetan prisoners, leading to the death of one.[91] The Chinese government replied on 9 May with information on two of these individuals, denying the allegations of torture, and denying totally the existence of the other four cases (at 15–16).

In 1992–93, the Special Rapporteur on Torture stepped up his efforts, communicating information on their practice of torture in general to some countries, besides detailing the cases of individuals. The states addressed in this expanded fashion were Brazil, the Cameroons, China, Djibouti, Egypt, Greece, Haiti, India, Indonesia, Iran, Israel, Mexico, Myanmar, Pakistan, Syria, Turkey and Venezuela. Only Brazil, China, Egypt, Greece, Indonesia, Myanmar and Turkey replied, while Argentina and Mexico produced their periodic report. On 28 October, China responded in detail to the allegations on its practice of torture in general, a report reproduced in its entirety at China's request.[92] It coincided with its supplementary report to CAT, although the content of the two documents was not identical. It failed, however, to provide the detail required by the Rapporteur, such as evidence of medical examination. China also admitted that "Chinese law enforcement authorities investigate and punish individuals guilty of torture every year, mostly State employees who use torture to extract confessions and prison warders who inflict corporal punishment on or mistreat inmates" (para. 80.4, at 26). However, it denied the allegation that torture in Tibet and China was "routine," as "nothing but fictitious and malicious rumours" (para. 80.7, at 27).

In 1993, the new Special Rapporteur on Torture, Nigel Rodley, transmitted to the government of China a letter containing a summary of allegations received with regard to the practice of torture in China, as well as information on thirty-four individual cases. He also made four urgent appeals on behalf of persons who were reportedly at risk of being tortured. The Chinese government sent some information, sometimes minimal, on all but two of them: this time, it did not attach a detailed defense. The Rapporteur's report on China was a substantial brief of ten pages. It concluded with observations of unusual frankness:

The consistency of the reports reaching the Special Rapporteur and his predecessor over the years compels acknowledgement of the serious grounds for concern about the persistence of an extensive problem of torture and severe ill-treatment of prisoners in various parts of China, despite the existence of legal provisions aimed at repressing it. The Special Rapporteur is aware of the relevant conclusions and recommendations of the Committee against Torture (A/48/44, paras. 423–429) and associates himself with these, in particular the recommendations aimed at preventing prolonged incommunicado detention and bringing to justice persons responsible for torture. The Special Rapporteur recommends that, in accordance with the Standard Minimum Rules for the Treatment of Prisoners, and the Body of Principles for the Protection of All Persons under Any Form of Detention or Imprisonment, resort to prolonged solitary confinement and the use of shackles should be abandoned.[93]

Finally, on 15 July 1994, the Special Rapporteur once again sent a letter to China detailing information on the practice of torture, with special reference to a number of individuals. He also sent five urgent appeals. According to Paragraph 91 of the report, in China "[a]mong the most common methods of torture reported were severe beatings or whippings, the use of cattle prods to induce electrical shock, and shackling with handcuffs or leg-irons, often tightly and with the victim's body in a painful position. In those prisons which also serve as labour camps, working conditions were reportedly physically gruelling and at times posed a threat to the health and safety of the prisoners. Persons detained for political reasons were reportedly subjected to especially brutal treatment."[94]

In reply, the Chinese government supplied information on some of the cases but did not attach a general defense. In his Observations, Rodley pointed out: "The Special Rapporteur appreciates the replies the Government has provided in respect of some of the cases. He notes the absence of replies in respect of others and the absence of information on pending investigations. He also finds that where some of the replies contradict the allegations, the Government has not explained the nature of the investigation on the basis of which its position has been reached, nor has it provided material to document the assertions made" (para. 128, at 27).

Accordingly, he stated, the observations in his previous report, Paragraph 172, stating support for CAT's conclusions still "remain[ed] applicable" (at 27).

During 1995, Rodley approached the government of China with a view to receiving an invitation to visit. However, as of 1998 that request had not been granted.[95] In 1995, he transmitted 113 urgent appeals to 43 governments concerning some 410 individuals as well as groups, and sent 55 letters to 48 governments (para. 18 at 7). Of these, he transmitted 25 individual cases to the Chinese government, all Tibetans, and sent an urgent appeal on behalf of the political detainee Tong Yi. He received replies from China with respect to two urgent appeals he had transmitted in 1994 on behalf of political activist Zhang Lin and journalist Gao Yu (para. 46 at 11). His main concerns were that he continued to receive information indicating that the use of torture and ill-treatment against persons held in police stations, detention centers, prisons, and labor camps was "occurring with frequency." Moreover, "many persons detained for political reasons were convicted of offences partly or wholly on the basis of 'confessions' that had been obtained through the application of torture during interrogation" (para. 43 at 10).

During 1996, Rodley sent 68 letters to 61 governments containing some 669 cases of alleged torture and transmitted 130 urgent appeals to 45 countries on behalf of some 490 individuals. Of these, he wrote one letter to China and transmitted allegations on sixteen individual cases and two urgent appeals on behalf of two persons. The government replied to one of the urgent appeals. In his letter of 5 July 1996, Rodley advised the government that he had received information indicating that "torture and other ill-treatment had continued to be used on a widespread and systematic basis against both criminal detainees and persons detained for political reasons." Periods of incommunicado detention might last for some months or even years, and criminal suspects were allegedly tortured to coerce "confessions" or to elicit information about other persons. Torture was alleged to occur frequently in situations of administrative detention, including reeducation through labor (*laodong jiaoyang*) and "Retention for In-Camp Employment" (*liuchang jiuye*).

Contrary to Ambassador Wu's oral presentation before CAT, the Special Rapporteur reported that torture was allegedly carried out by inmates known as trusties and that it included beatings, shackling, and prolonged solitary confinement (at 13). This was apparently to protect prison officers from having to assume legal responsibility. Forms of torture endemic to police stations and detention centers in Tibet included "kicking; beating; application of electric shocks by means of batons or small electric generators; the use of self-tightening handcuffs; deprivation of food; exposure to alternating extremes of hot and cold temperatures; enforced standing in difficult positions; enforced standing in cold water; prolonged shackling of detainees spread-eagled to a wall; placing of heated objects on the skin; and striking with iron rods on the joints or hands" (at 13).

Rodley concluded that "the information reaching the Special Rapporteur continues to justify concern at the situation. Recent legal developments could make a positive contribution, the impact of which would be a focus of a visit to the country should he receive an invitation as requested in 1995."

By the end of 1997, Rodley made it clear that, despite the improvements in China's responses over the years, particularly in 1992, and despite legal developments, its compliance with the antitorture bodies of the international regime was inadequate, both in procedural terms and in terms of substantive change to its domestic practice of torture. This assessment contrasted with CAT's approval of China's procedural compliance, and of a degree of *de jure* compliance, if not of its substantive implementation of its obligations at a *de facto* level. The rapporteur's yearly reports were extremely useful in providing a continual review of China's practice with respect to torture, contrasting with the periodic deliberations of the Committee, which measured change over time and which were dependent on the answers by China's representatives to elicit information. Despite these findings, his observations in the 1996 and 1997 reports lacked the critical edge of those in 1993 and 1994. This was presumably because his main concern was now to obtain a favorable reply to his 1995 request to visit China. As he himself implicitly acknowledged, because of the lack of follow-up to his reports by the Commission on Human Rights, unless China extended him an invitation to visit, his observations risked becoming submerged under the avalanche of thematic reports piled up in UN archives, only to be uncovered by the zealous scholar.

Comparison with China's Interaction with Other Treaty Bodies, Thematic Special Rapporteurs, and Working Groups

It might be thought that China's interaction with the Committee Against Torture and the Special Rapporteur on Torture would represent a special situation, given the sensitive nature of the issue of torture. However, independent research on China's interaction with two Committees monitoring aspects of its economic, social, and cultural rights, the Committee on the Elimination of All Forms of Racial Discrimination (CERD) and the Committee on the Rights of the Child (CROC) reaches similar conclusions.[96] Although China's reports to these two bodies had shown increasing candor over the years, the information they provided focused on relevant domestic legal and administrative procedures rather than on the practical implementation of necessary measures (22). During the debate on China's initial report to the CROC, experts complained that the report failed to elucidate how the provisions had been implemented in practice and what problems had been encountered in the process. The required statistical data was also not presented at the level of detail required by the committees. Thus, the concluding observations of both CROC and CERD took note of the inadequacy of the Chinese reports.[97]

The timing of the reports had also been somewhat haphazard. In the case of CERD, China's fifth periodic report, submitted in a document combining fourth, fifth, and sixth reports in January 1996, had been overdue since January 1991. Although states parties were supposed to submit a report every second year, no overdue report procedure had been used in China's case. In the case of the Committee on the Elimination of Discrimination Against Women (CEDAW), China's second report was submitted in 1988 and examined in 1992. The third periodic report was due in September 1990 and the fourth in September 1994. It was not until 1998 that both were received in a combined report. However, just as in the case of CAT, both CERD and CROC were able to raise a range of substantive concerns that clarified the existing situation in China and raised a number of sensitive issues. The concluding observations in both cases contained detailed criticism and comments, constituting, in the case of CROC, forty-five paragraphs, and in the case of CERD, thirty-six paragraphs. They compared very favorably with CAT's concluding observations on China's second periodic report, which constituted a mere twelve paragraphs.

The experiences of other thematic special rapporteurs and working groups monitoring aspects of China's civil rights had varied. As in previous years, the 1994 report of the Special Rapporteur on Extrajudicial, Summary or Arbitrary Executions, Bacre Waly Ndiaye, regretted "the extensive use of the death penalty [in China], imposed after proceedings which were said to fall short of internationally recognized fair trial standards."[98] He referred to one record of 2,564 death sentences in 1993, at least 1,419 of which were believed to have been carried out. In his observations, he thanked the Chinese government for information both on the legislation and practice of capital punishment in China, and expressed appreciation for "the willingness of the authorities to cooperate with his mandate."[99] However, he was concerned at the recurrence of reports on capital punishment in China and, in view of "the persistent contradiction between the numerous allegations received from credible sources and the information provided by the authorities," expressed interest in visiting China to study *in situ* questions relating to capital punishment (para. 99, at 33). He observed that the government had not yet replied to this request, first forwarded in November 1992 and repeated in September 1993 and September 1994. He noted China's procedural compliance with its obligations, but raised doubts about its substantive compliance at the domestic level. He also suggested that procedural compliance lacked effective meaning in the absence of an invitation to visit China to investigate the reality on the ground.

The 1994 report of the Working Group on Arbitrary Detention referred to contacts begun in 1993 with the Chinese authorities to visit their country which had "so far not yielded any concrete results."[100] Of the twenty-nine states contacted, China was responsible for 89 of the 293 new reported individual cases; it was also one of the sixteen governments that replied to the Working Group.[101] In 1995, the Working Group transmitted sixty-three individual communications to the Chinese government, as well as five urgent appeals on behalf of ten individuals. On 27 June 1995, the Chairman of the Working Group, Louis Joinet, sent a communication to the government regarding the incommunicado detention of Wei Jingsheng. He twice requested an invitation to visit China in 1995.[102]

However, the Working Group's 1994 report had elicited a strong response from Chinese authorities. On 16 February 1995, at the UN Human Rights Commission, Zhang Yishan complained that "unlike the reports by other rapporteurs and working groups, this report seems to style itself as a 'grand judge' over and above all sovereign states and allows itself to call out 'arbitrary detention' at random. It even takes upon itself to declare legislations of sovereign states to be invalid . . . instead of playing a fair game, it politicizes human rights issues and launches arbitrary attacks against sovereign states."[103]

He argued that the Working Group had exceeded its mandate, that its report was "fraught with examples of double standards and selectivity," and that it was "politically prejudiced and unfair" (1–3). He stated that: "The Chinese government attaches great importance to cooperating with relevant United Nations mechanisms. We have seriously investigated into all accusations of arbitrary detention forwarded to us by the Working Group. On the other hand, the Working Group has ignored the replies provided by the Chinese government" (3).

Responding to the Working Group's wish to be invited to China, Zhang claimed that China had "always stood for strengthening cooperation for the promotion of human rights" but that "this kind of cooperation should be conducted on the bases of equality and good will." The Working Group had disregarded China's explanations and had described legal action against "criminals who have done serious harm to the state or the society" as cases of arbitrary detention. "How," he declaimed, "can one speak of visits and cooperation within such atmosphere?" (4).

In contrast with this strong emphasis on state sovereignty and noninterference, in 1994 China took the hitherto unprecedented step of inviting a special rapporteur to China. The Special Rapporteur on Religious Intolerance, Abdelfattah Amor, visited China in November 1994. The purpose of the invitation appeared to be China's wish to counter criticism of its policy on ethnic minorities, which was building up towards a resolution that could possibly go against it in the 1995 Human Rights Commission.[104] Although Amor's specific mandate was only partly related to the individual's right to physical security, freedom of religion was also highly sensitive in the eyes of a nervous leadership, in the sense that many of the religions practiced in China owed allegiance to an authority beyond the Chinese state. In a double sense, the symbolic importance of this invitation for modifying in practice China's formal, legalistic position on sovereignty was clear.

This symbolism was recognized by the Special Rapporteur, who welcomed "the openness shown by the Chinese government and its efforts, its sustained interest and its desire to cooperate." He also observed that "China has for some time been engaged in a process of fundamental reforms in every field, including that of human rights . . . the visit resulted in a better understanding of Chinese realities and at the same time the identification of certain fields of progress and aspects where further development may be hoped for."[105] In his conclusions, Amor noted some progress in China's policy on religious freedom, particularly in its legislation, but made recommendations on the need to amend some legal texts and adopt others guaranteeing specific aspects of religious freedom (at 131–134). He noted a "political determination to apply legislation and policy in the field of tolerance and non-discrimination against religion and belief," but stated that "some adjustment of traditions and modes of behaviour seems to be needed if a new culture among administrative and prison authorities is gradually to take shape."[106]

The Special Rapporteur's report represented a careful blend of tact, aimed at encouraging Chinese authorities to continue their invitations, with a readiness to address outstanding and often sensitive issues. His visit clearly reflected an advance in China's response to monitoring, proceeding for the first time beyond a mere reply to communications to an actual invitation. China's cooperation during the visit allowed Amor further access to information, whether of a positive or negative nature. Despite its often damaging revelations, China welcomed the subsequent report, expressing admiration for Amor's "serious and business-like attitude" and appreciation for the efforts of the UN Centre for Human Rights.[107]

China's contrasting responses to the different monitoring bodies suggested that it had no fixed policy on investigatory missions dictated by considerations of sovereignty, but that considerations of sovereignty came into play when determining in which cases China could afford to be flexible. One interpretation of this flexibility could be that it was a deliberate policy to distract and confuse actual and potential detractors. An alternative interpretation was that mandates pertaining directly to the right to physical security and due process were more sensitive than issues of religious intolerance, while China also claimed to discriminate according to the attitude shown by the particular monitoring body. It was also clear that there could be competing claims on sovereignty. The loss of national status, and hence the threat to sovereignty, involved in a resolution against China in the Commission on Human Rights clearly prevailed in importance over the loss of sovereignty entailed in a visit by a UN body. Hence, despite China's strong objections to the findings of the Working Group on Arbitrary Detention, as the 1998 session of the Human Rights Commission approached, it overcame its extreme sensitivity and invited the Working Group to visit China in October 1997.

Conclusion

In acceding to the Convention Against Torture in October 1988, China took the first step in recognizing the importance of the issue, the competence of the Committee, and its own responsibilities as a Permanent Member of the UN Security Council. Beyond that point, its interaction with the Committee revealed procedural learning at the international level in its response to its reporting obligations. In comparison to other least-likely states, its record of responses to the Special Rapporteur has been shown to have been reasonable.[108] This progress was noted by both CAT and the Special Rapporteur on Torture, although the latter also complained about the inadequacy of the replies. In addition, China made substantive concessions to the norms of the antitorture regime, in accepting the prohibition on torture and in entrenching that acceptance, to some degree, in domestic legislation. Unlike the Special Rapporteur, CAT acknowledged this qualified *de jure* compliance. In contrast, international NGOs challenged the *de jure* adequacy of Chinese provisions. At the same time, CAT, the Special Rapporteur, international NGOs, and Chinese authorities themselves were at one in recognizing the gap between substantive *de jure* and *de facto* compliance at the domestic level in China, even if they differed as to the size of that gap.

Consequently, at the international levels of compliance and, to a limited degree, domestically at the *de jure* level, the conclusion that may be drawn from these case studies is that China's learning process with respect to the prohibition on torture was tactical, strategic, and, to a limited degree, cognitive. Cognitive learning at the international level, however, had yet to be translated adequately into the more significant levels of domestic law and, more obviously, of domestic practice. The fact that the Committee could commend China for procedural compliance while at the same time understanding torture to be continuing in China was in itself an indication of the limitations of the Committee's jurisdiction. Such was the dilemma that necessitated adoption of the Optional Protocol.

With respect to China, the two monitoring bodies carried out a division of labor. The annual review by the Special Rapporteur filled in the gaps in the periodic four-year, and perhaps longer, review by CAT, which tended to measure changes in compliance over time rather than to monitor continuing compliance. The Special Rapporteur's mandate was to comment annually on a state's performance, with or without the consent of the state in question, whereas, even to fulfill the mandatory aspects of its supervisory functions, the Committee was ultimately dependent on China's political will. Within that constraint and noting the qualification that China's reports to the Committee lacked information on practice, both bodies exhibited a critical rigor that enabled them not only to place steady pressure on China but to expose in detail the information that continued to seep through the country's permeable boundaries. This integrity was recognized by NGOs, one of which commended the CAT and the Special Rapporteur for "their excellent monitoring of individual cases of torture in China reported to them."[109]

Despite this ongoing monitoring of China's substantive obligations, the key obstacle to CAT's effectiveness was clearly China's denial of the Committee's competence under Article 20 to undertake confidential inquiries or fact-finding missions on its territory. An additional obstacle was China's unwillingness to accede to Article 21, which would have allowed other states parties to allege that China was not discharging its obligations under the Charter, and Article 22, which would have allowed the Committee to examine communications by individuals claiming to be victims of a violation of the Convention. Unwillingness to be bound by these Articles was a measure of China's continuing attachment to sovereignty and the principle of noninterference, and of its compliance with the letter, but not the spirit, of its obligations. It constituted an example of China's conditional acceptance of regimes.

In the case of the Special Rapporteur, the main obstacle to progress was China's unwillingness to accept his overtures to make an *in situ* visit. The importance of these visits to the fulfillment of the rapporteur's active mandate had long been stressed by the previous Rapporteur, Peter Kooijmans, particularly since he distinguished between CAT visits, seen as falling into the category of "investigative missions," and his own visits "for consultative purposes [which] should be seen much more as falling into the category of advisory services."[110] It was also reflected in the declaration by the Commission on Human Rights that "experience has proved that the effective implementation of human rights is greatly facilitated by activities *in situ.*"[111] In the absence of this facilitating mechanism, it was difficult for both the Committee and the Special Rapporteur to establish a link between the international human rights process and the domestic one. It prevented them from moving from passive monitoring to active monitoring. In addition, the Special Rapporteur's effectiveness was hampered by the failure of the UN Commission on Human Rights to follow up on his report.

However, as the cases of the Special Rapporteur on Religious Intolerance and the Working Group on Arbitrary Detention demonstrated, China did not place a blanket prohibition on visits by UN investigatory bodies. It was concerned, rather, to reserve its decision-making authority as to which body it should invite and when, and not to accept blanket obligations. As in the case of its interaction with the Human Rights Commission and Sub-Commission, the actual process of its involvement in the overall human rights regime built up an obligation to prove its cooperation in selective and discrete areas, and to be seen to be making practical concessions to regime norms. In extending the invitation to the Special Rapporteur on Religious Intolerance and, later, the Working Group on Arbitrary Detention, China in theory established a precedent for other visits, and in practice accepted the more relative and political interpretation of sovereignty implied by the acceptance of investigatory missions on its own soil.

Although insistent on retaining the diplomatic initiative, Chinese authorities themselves, as the different reports indicate, were concerned about the gap between the *de jure* prohibition against torture and its continued *de facto* practice within China. Once again, however, the limits of their concern were measured by the extent to which they were prepared to tolerate the erosion of Chinese sovereignty that an invitation to the Special Rapporteur on Torture, or acceptance of Article 20 of the Convention Against Torture, would have entailed. Their position on the drafting of the Optional Protocol in arguing the right of the state to refuse proposed sub-committee visits perfectly exemplified their continuing unwillingness to make such concessions. The observations by the Special Rapporteur and CAT about the need for efforts to be made by Chinese authorities to identify the philosophical and practical sources of this gap between the law and its practical implementation went to the heart of the problem. So did the observation by the Special Rapporteur on Religious Intolerance that the gap was a manifestation of a deep-rooted political and legal culture that required time, political will and education to eradicate. The gap persisted, despite the practical and specific proposals for bridging it continually forwarded to the UN bodies by international NGOs.

Thus, despite China's heightened consciousness of the problem of torture and some efforts to counteract it, Peter Kooijmans's complaint in 1991 still had resonances in the Chinese situation in 1998: "Much has been accomplished, but the final aim has not been achieved. Everything seems to be there to make the campaign against torture a successful one and nevertheless all human rights reports speak loudly of failure. All the rules are there but they remain formulas instead of living in the minds of men."[112]

In much the same way, an official Chinese newspaper described the practice of torture in China as "a stubborn illness that has not yet seen a recovery in spite of a long treatment."[113]

Chapter 4
China and the UN Specialized Agencies: The International Labor Organization

> The All-China Federation of Trade Unions actively participates in ILO activities because it is a forum for extensive contacts with other countries and a platform for publicising China's viewpoint and policies, an important channel for international exchange and cooperation on labour and social problems, as well as a window for understanding international labour movement news.
>
> — *Seventy Years of the All-China Federation of Trade Unions*
> (Beijing: China Workers' Press, July 1995)

> The aim of freedom of association is to improve working conditions and promote peace.
>
> — Chinese spokesman, ILO Governing Body Committee on
> Freedom of Association, February 1990

The International Labor Organization (ILO) is a UN specialized agency that has played a crucial role in monitoring China's human rights. As a functionally specific international organization concerned with labor matters, its focus correlates with the formal raison d'être of the system of government of the People's Republic of China. As a self-proclaimed workers' state, at least in theory, China is inevitably affected by the opinions of such a body. Its importance is underlined by the fact that since China has signed, but not yet ratified, the International Covenant on Economic, Social and Cultural Rights (ICESCR), the ILO is one of the main bodies that monitors China's economic, social, and cultural rights, as well as its civil rights, as they apply to occupational groups. Other aspects of its economic, social, and cultural rights, as they apply to nonoccupational groups, are monitored by the Committee on the Elimination of Racial Discrimination (CERD), the Committee on the Elimination of Discrimination against Women (CEDAW) and the Committee on the Rights of the Child (CROC). The ILO's importance is highlighted by the fact that had it not been for the intervention of the International Confederation of Free Trade Unions (ICFTU) and the ILO, the plight of the unknown workers involved in the 1989 Democracy Movement crackdown would not have been exposed, given the immediate emphasis by governments, NGOs, and even UN monitoring bodies on the situation of the better-known students and intellectuals.

In many ways, China's interaction with the ILO has been more important and sensitive for it than its relations with any UN human rights body. On one hand, the ILO has the reputation of being an effective body in the monitoring of workers' rights.[1] Its potential for influencing China is considerable, whether with respect to standard setting or specific issues of Chinese workers' rights. China has been clearly concerned about the good opinion of other ILO members, and about being seen to abide by the ILO Constitution.[2] Moreover, it has shown considerable interest in the rights of its workers in foreign investment enterprises (FIEs) established throughout China since 1979. On the other hand, trade union or industrial rights, in the critical sense of the individual's right to form and join the trade union of his choice without previous authorization and the union's right to independence from the state, have not constituted an integral part of China's socialist, or presocialist, history, and have only recently emerged, like the fabled Trojan horse, as an issue of economic modernization. Precisely because of the ILO's standard-setting role, and in particular its strong support for the right to freedom of association, Chinese leaders have been anxious about the effect industrial rights might have on the consciousness of a vast workforce that, as a result of industrial rationalization and, in particular, the 1997 decision to rationalize state-owned enterprises (SOEs), is in the process of radical downsizing.[3] China's changing responses to ILO pressures have therefore reflected the conflicting pressures of economic modernization, its authoritarian political system, and its expanding participation in global regimes.

In theory, China does not reject the principle of the right to freedom of association, the basic norm of the ILO Governing Body Committee on Freedom of Association (CFA) that monitored Chinese workers' human rights after June 1989. Indeed, it has continued to insist that this freedom is guaranteed by the Chinese Constitution. However, unlike China's unqualified theoretical support for the norms of the Committee Against Torture (CAT), even its theoretical support for the right to freedom of association has been equivocal. Its provisions for the right of workers to form and join trade unions have been heavily qualified by the requirement that this activity should be carried out "according to law"; and it has omitted in its definition reference to the key requirement that the unions should be "of their own choosing" and established "without previous authorization." This has meant that, effectively, China has not supported the substantive content of the norm even in theory. For this reason, the process of China's interaction with the ILO Committee has been marked by vigorous and protracted debate about first principles and fundamental issues, a debate the Committee has joined with single-minded determination.

This is not to assert that over the years China's attitude to some labor standards has not changed: in the 1990s, as the following analysis demonstrates, numerous formal and informal changes took place in China's labor relations in response both to domestic pressures and to China's organizational and status interests in the ILO. Nor is it to suggest that the ILO has been immune to China's standing as a permanent member of the UN Security Council and as a regional leader. While the ILO has pursued the issue of workers' rights in China since Tiananmen, both the history of China's ILO membership and the nature of China's impact on the ILO since 1989 indicate the difficulties inherent in its delicate balancing act between the promotion of Chinese workers' interests and the maintenance of China's particular role in the organization. The following analysis involves a detailed examination of the process of China's interaction with the ILO Governing Body CFA against the larger background of China's participation in the ILO and domestic developments in its labor relations. This contextual approach throws light on the holistic nature of China's socialization process.

Historical and Institutional Context

René Cassin has observed that the general protection of human rights first took shape with the establishment of the ILO, whose work has provided the basis for a system of universal customary common law protecting the essential individual freedoms.[4] The process that led to its establishment in 1919 was similar to the two major attempts to promote collective security through the League of Nations and the United Nations.[5] Both were the results of extensive efforts by enlightened individuals whose ultimate success was one of the direct effects of a world war.[6] As part of the new world order enunciated in the League Covenant, the ILO represented the institutionalization of the concept of international labor legislation that had evolved through the nineteenth and early twentieth centuries. It was the product of "wartime bargains between the state, big business and organised labour . . . whose mission was complex: to homogenise labour practices across competing economies, blunt social unrest, and promote 'social justice'."[7]

The main concerns of the ILO are freedom of association, rights of collective bargaining, and the expansion of welfare programs. Its principal activities include the formulation of international standards; the collection of cross-national statistics; the dissemination of information on working conditions; technical assistance; and promotional and educational activities (240– 241). Groups targeted include worker and employer organizations protected by the ILO's conventions on freedom of association: those subject to discrimination in employment and work on the basis of race, color, sex, religion, political opinion, national extraction or social origin; women at work; children and young workers; migrant workers; disabled workers; and indigenous and tribal peoples.[8] Conventions are formulated by annual sessions of the International Labor Conference. Ratification of conventions is considered the equivalent of ratification of an international treaty, requiring states parties to enact and implement the convention's provisions. As of 1998, 181 conventions had been adopted. The Conference also formulates recommendations which are not legally binding but which act as important guidelines for states. After ratification of a convention, the state is required to report on its implementation.

A state is not obliged to implement a convention it has not ratified. However, the ILO Constitution (Article 19, Paragraph 5) requests states members to submit unratified conventions to their national "competent authorities" (normally the legislature) for enactment of legislation or other action, and to report on means taken, or contemplated, to give effect to the Convention. Nonratified conventions at the very least provide standards for the state and its citizens to aspire to. Conventions and recommendations thus form a kind of "international common law."[9] However, in the case of the principle of freedom of association, implementation is required even without the ratification of the relevant conventions, the Freedom of Association and Protection of the Right to Organise Convention (No. 87, 1948) and the Right to Organise and Collective Bargaining Convention (No. 98, 1949). On the basis of the claim of the ILO Constitution and the appended Declaration of Philadelphia (1944), the standing tripartite CFA has successfully established that all ILO members are subject to its jurisdiction *sine die*.[10] This is because, when the ILO's special freedom of association machinery was established in 1950, it was not known how many states would ratify the conventions on freedom of association: a need was therefore felt to establish mechanisms that could operate even in the absence of ratification (105–106).

Freedom of association is a right encapsulated in Article 20 of the Universal Declaration of Human Rights and in Article 23, Paragraph 4, which states that "everyone has the right to form and to join trade unions for the protection of his interests."[11] The International Covenant on Civil and Political Rights (ICCPR) provides for the right to freedom of association and the right to form and join trade unions in Article 22; the ICESCR is even more explicit.[12] The right to freedom of association is acknowledged as a fundamental principle in the preamble to the ILO Constitution and, together with the principle of freedom of expression, was reaffirmed in the 1944 Declaration of Philadelphia. The ILO's provisions for freedom of association, as contained in Convention No. 87, constitute a number of articles, of which Article 2 states: "Workers and employers, without distinction whatsoever, shall have the right to establish and, subject only to the rules of the organisation concerned, to join organisations of *their own choosing without previous authorisation*."[13]

Freedom of association is seen to include a number of principles: the right of all workers and employers to establish organizations; the free administration of these organizations; the right to join federations and confederations; the right of organizations not to be suspended or dissolved; protection against discrimination; the right to collective bargaining; the right to strike; and the right to exercise basic civil rights.[14]

Worker and employer organizations are seen by the ILO to require specific protection because "Both the organisations and the individuals composing and representing them are subject to attack and discrimination . . . If trade unions have acquired considerable influence in some developed countries, in most of the developing world they remain subject to manipulation and exploitation by governments and by employers. Their leaders are often the subject of arrest and imprisonment, torture and exile . . . Employers' organisations can also be subject to brutal repression."[15]

The ILO's supervisory system is based on dialogue and persuasion, although in recent years there has been discussion about the advisability of introducing some sanctions such as linking labor standards with trade, and debate on the introduction of a Declaration on workers' fundamental rights. The ILO uses different terminology than UN bodies, utilizing the term "supervision" rather than the term "monitoring." However, "supervision" is also used in an imprecise generic sense, ranging in meaning from "general surveys" and "reports," which can be understood as passive monitoring, through to "direct contacts," which can be understood as active monitoring. Some observers also claim that the nature of ILO monitoring differs in a number of ways from that of UN bodies.[16] The ILO has avoided the dualism afflicting UN human rights bodies between civil/political and economic/social/cultural rights, viewing, for instance, the freedom of association as both a civil right and an economic right. Its procedure for the adoption of conventions has been reportedly more systematic, and its supervisory procedures have been judged to be more efficient and effective (581).

The ILO is not as accessible as the United Nations to nonoccupational NGOs; but it has been argued that its tripartite nature is "unique, providing for the full participation of non-governmental occupational organizations in all ILO deliberative bodies and activities, as well as in the drafting of ILO conventions and recommendations and in their implementation."[17] It has also been argued that the activities of the Director-General of the ILO, as the head of a key organization whose goals are implicitly and specifically human rights goals, are more unambiguously focused on the issue of human rights than his counterpart in the United Nations, who presides over two basic, and inherently contradictory, axioms of the UN Charter: the protection of the sovereign equality and territorial integrity of states members and the encouragement of respect for human rights and fundamental freedoms for all.[18]

The ILO has a number of procedures monitoring the implementation of its standards as embodied in its conventions. The main method is the regular supervisory system used by other international human rights organs, whereby states report on their compliance with norms they have accepted and the committees examine their reports. The reporting system applied in the United Nations was in fact first introduced by the ILO on the basis of its original Constitution and expanded by amendments to it.[19] Reports are prepared and submitted by national governments but employer and worker organizations are entitled to make written observations that are examined together with the governments' reports (8).

In addition to the regular supervision system, an ILO freedom of association system has been set up. In 1951, the Governing Body CFA was established.[20] Meeting three times a year before each session of the ILO Governing Body, and representing government, workers, and employers, it has gradually become the major ILO body for examining allegations of infringements of freedom of association. It is a nine-member tripartite committee with nine alternates and an independent chairman that reaches its decisions by consensus. From 1989 to 1992, its Chairman was not a member of the Governing Body but of the World Court.

The CFA has a special procedure for urgent cases "involving human life or personal freedom or new or changing conditions offsetting the freedom of action of a trade union movement as a whole, and cases arising out of a continuing state of emergency and cases involving the dissolution of an organisation" (604). Its neutrality is ensured by the checks and balances underpinning its activities: its members are elected members of the Governing Body, and its recommendations are subject to examination by that body. It has no authority without the Governing Body's endorsement, and its findings may be rejected or amended by it. According to one expert, it is the Governing Body's authority which ultimately persuades member states to agree to directions, recommendations and conclusions aimed at them as a result of CFA deliberations.[21]

By July 1991, the Committee had presented findings and recommendations to the Governing Body for decision in almost sixteen hundred cases of allegations of infringements of freedom of association. Of these cases, almost half came from Latin America, followed by Western Europe, North America and the Caribbean, whereas African and Asian cases were relatively few.[22] As in the United Nations itself, this imbalance was due, paradoxically, to the existence of highly self-conscious workers and vocal unions in Latin America, while the weakness of union activity in Asia contributed to the lack of a genuine domestic critique. Adding to this imbalance was the fact that, unlike the 1503 procedure in the United Nations, complaints could be submitted to the CFA by workers' or employers' organizations, such as the ICFTU, or by governments but not by individuals. Once a complaint was received, the Director-General might allow the complainant time to furnish further substantiation; the complaint would then be communicated to the government concerned, which was then invited to comment.[23]

Other monitoring mechanisms of applicability to China included constitutional complaints procedures, commissions of inquiry and "direct contacts." The first two procedures, which have rarely been used, derive from the provisions of Articles 24–26 of the ILO Constitution, and allow for the filing of complaints against states for failing to implement ratified conventions and for the establishment of commissions of inquiry in case of severe dereliction. "Direct contacts," carried out discreetly and for a short period, are personal visits by ILO officials or an independent person named by the Director-General, to ILO member states to help address difficulties in the implementation of a ratified convention or to fulfill other ILO member responsibilities.[24]

In one respect, the ILO and UN human rights bodies exhibit a similarity in that the norms and standards they monitor are of Western origin. ILO standard setting was originally established in the context of pluralist democracies whose labor was "politically organized but not politically dominant." Communist states have denied the principle of pluralism that is fundamental to the ILO.[25] The lack of independence of their worker and employer representatives has meant that they have had little input into the ILO process. Developing countries also encounter problems due to "authoritarian regimes or excessive control or interference by administrative authorities in the establishment and functioning of unions as well as anti-union discrimination by employers" (167). The participation of developing states in the ILO in the 1950s and 1960s simply brought a greater emphasis on technical assistance programs.[26] It has therefore been argued that only in the context of pluralist democracies can the ILO have substantial influence in constructing a more progressive social policy: it is seen to have little direct influence on authoritarian states like China where labor is politically subordinated.[27] Yet the ILO has had a direct effect on workers within authoritarian states, as, for instance, through its support for Solidarity in Poland.[28] In such cases, where workers believe they have a right not to be politically subordinated, ILO standards may have a profound influence on their attitudes and actions, if not on those of their state.

China and the ILO Before June 1989

Between its resumption of ILO membership in 1971 and the Democracy Movement crackdown in 1989, China's relations with the ILO were based on its claims to "specific exemption" and "specific entitlement," that is, on its claims to special rights while seeking special exemption from its organizational responsibilities, with respect to both labor standards and financial and other obligations.[29] Only in the mid-1990s did it begin to take its obligations more seriously and to invoke ILO standards as a protection against labor unrest and foreign exploitation as it had in its pre-1949 history.

The early history of China-ILO relations is documented in several publications.[30] As a member of the League of Nations, China was a founding member of the ILO in 1919. The ILO was held up by China as a positive influence to improve the Chinese labor situation in general, and to obtain the uniform enforcement of Chinese labor laws in enterprises situated in foreign concessions and settlements.[31] The relationship was regarded as "the cornerstone of the international dimension of the Chinese labor situation": before 1949 China had ratified all applicable conventions passed by the annual Conference (16). In 1923, the Chinese government established an office in Bern to deal with its relations with the ILO, and in 1934 China was elected a member of the ILO Governing Body.

After 1949, the existence of two Chinas created problems for the ILO, which, like the UN system proper, chose to validate the credentials of Taiwan.[32] However, Taiwan's credentials were regularly challenged in ILO forums between 1950 and 1971, particularly by socialist states (116). Following the decision of the UN General Assembly in 1971 to recognize the People's Republic as the only legitimate representative of China in the United Nations, the Assembly called on the other UN bodies and specialized agencies to consider their own attitudes. Since the restoration of the rights of the People's Republic took place after the 1971 session of the ILO Conference, the Director-General placed the decision about restoration of China's rights in the ILO before the 184th session of the Governing Body. Some states, like the United States, urged that Resolution 2758 be referred to the Conference at its 1972 session, whereas the workers' group, together with socialist and developing states, upheld the competence of the Governing Body (122–23). According to Victor-Yves Ghebali, "the legal arguments put forward on both sides ill concealed the political nature of the debate and of the stakes involved" (123).

In its role as titular head of the ILO between conferences, the Governing Body took the unilateral decision in 1971 to restore China's rights as a member, without knowing whether China had the desire or ability to assume the obligations of membership (124). It was more than ten years before the People's Republic of China began to effectively participate in the work of the ILO or to comply with its obligations (including financial ones). The destruction of the trade union movement in China during the Cultural Revolution made it difficult to apply the rules of tripartism with respect to China. As in the United Nations, China declared that it needed "time to increase its understanding of the ILO and become familiar with it."[33] It was thus classified as a nonactive member (*buhuodong chengyuanguo*).[34]

Nevertheless, the Director-General, Francis Blanchard, made it his personal responsibility to bring China into the fold as a fully functioning member.[35] Apart from the value of involving a large and powerful state, the ILO's success with other communist states like Poland contributed to the view that it was easier to deal with China as an ILO member, subject to the ILO Constitution, than to allow it to remain outside the organization.[36] Between 1980 and 1982, Blanchard visited China twice to discuss the issue with the government, and in June 1983 China sent its first post-1949 delegation to the sixty-ninth session of the International Labor Conference.[37] At this session, the Conference made a "substantial gesture" by canceling the accrued debt representing China's statutory contribution due since 16 November 1971 (US$37,220,652) and the arrears owed by Taiwan (US$1,624,059).[38]

This decision, based on a Governing Body proposal, clearly represented a special concession to China, since it was approved by the Finance Committee of Government Representatives at the Conference only on the understanding that the case would not constitute a precedent which might be used in future as an argument for cancellation of other arrears (125). It was also a decision made in response to China's express wish to the Director-General that it be relieved of obligations decided unilaterally at a time when it was not taking part in the work of the organization (125). Another interesting departure from normal treatment was that in the ILO's list of members, which normally records any period of lapsed membership, China's membership is listed as uninterrupted since 1919. China's own records state that the People's Republic became a member in 1971 and a full participant in 1983.[39]

After 1983, as a state of industrial importance, China effectively occupied one of the ten nonelective Governing Body seats; from 1 February 1984, the ILO had a Chinese Assistant Director-General. The latter position, however, which had also been held by the Soviet Union, was not linked to a "line area," or department, and was seen to have little effective power. The 1984–94 decade has been seen by China as a period of substantial development in the relationship.[40] Until June 1990, a member of the All-China Federation of Trade Unions (ACFTU) also occupied a worker seat in the Governing Body. In January 1985, the ILO opened a branch office in Beijing that administered and monitored the technical assistance program, and in 1985 PRC experts were assigned to an ILO technical cooperation project for the first time.[41] However, in contrast to the Soviet Union, which accepted that ILO standards applied to it with some differences in interpretation, China's attitude was seen as closer to that of other Asian states that denied the applicability of ILO standards.[42] In regional seminars, for instance, its position was similar to that of the Association of Southeast Asian Nations (ASEAN) states that claimed not that ILO standards were too Western, but that they were not realistic goals for their present stage of development. Because China did not ratify Conventions 87 and 98, it reportedly believed that, as a result, freedom of association standards did not apply to it. The Chinese government regarded itself as responsible for its own internal affairs and was seen to overlook its overall responsibilities as a member.

Despite its formal participation in ILO activities after 1983, it was not until 1986–87 that China assumed a more assertive role in the organization.[43] This followed the support expressed by Premier Zhao Ziyang, who praised the ILO's positive contribution and promised that China would make the organization's struggle against unemployment and poverty its own mission (428). After that date, in a development seen as part of an overall evolutionary change in its policies in Geneva as well as a policy response, China sought to realize its power organizationally, both in the Governing Body and in offices in the committees, and to invoke its rights to technical assistance.[44] It actively participated in all ILO activities, particularly those meetings and conferences relating to elimination of racism, the promotion of employment and social security, and the protection of the environment. It also expanded its participation in ILO activities in the Asian region.[45] It has been speculated that the Chinese Foreign Ministry may have had more effective responsibility for China's participation in the ILO than was the case of the foreign ministries of other states.[46] However, the formal responsibility for China's ILO policy was undertaken by two divisions in the Ministry of Labor's Department of Foreign Affairs, the Division of ILO and the Division of Technical Cooperation.[47]

According to the requirements of tripartite organization, which required representation of government, employers, and workers, the ACFTU also played a role: thus, it was claimed, "the government always consults the employers' and workers' organizations on important labour matters and informs them about the activities conducted by the government" (57). Regional seminars included among their participants the Division Chief of the International Liaison Department of the ACFTU.[48] The Secretary of the ACFTU, Fang Jiade, was the Chinese worker representative on the ILO Governing Body. He did not make many interventions, and those that he made were usually in support of communist bloc countries.[49]

Central to China's relations with the ILO was the governmental and unitary character of the ACFTU, the single body responsible for all union matters in China affiliated with the Chinese Communist Party (CCP). Key officials were appointed by the Communist Party, while the higher organs dictated the appointments, functions, and powers of lower-level ACFTU bodies.[50] An ACFTU directive to all its subordinate unions in 1990 and again in 1995 required that "unions in China should resolutely uphold the unitary leadership of the Party. Unions at all levels should maintain a high degree of unanimity with the Party politically, in ideas and actions."[51] Thus, Chinese workers were effectively denied freedom of association, in the sense of both the right to organize and join trade unions of their choice without previous authorization, and the freedom to organize their unions independently of Communist Party control. Moreover, the state-controlled and unitary character of the ACFTU was contrary to the ILO structural norm of tripartite organization. After 1989, these differences were at the heart of the debate among the Chinese government, the ILO Governing Body CFA, and the ICFTU.

Like many other Asian states which have been criticized for exhibiting only symbolic conformity to ILO standards and responding mainly to ILO technical assistance, China early placed a heavy emphasis on the benefits of technical cooperation. At an ILO Asian-Pacific Symposium on Standards-Related Topics in New Delhi, from 14 to 17 March 1989, Guan Jinghe stressed the particular character of each developing state and their actual social and economic conditions that required "more flexibility and guidance."[52] She emphasized the importance of supervising labor standards within the context of the overall aim of the ILO "to maintain social justice and ensure that the workers of all countries have the right to live and work in a peaceful environment" (57). She also highlighted the importance of ILO regional seminars and training courses and claimed China's extenuating circumstances in relation to labor standards: "Since China is a large country and only officials responsible for handling standards-related matters from departments concerned in the Ministry of Labour grasp the significance of labour standards, it is not possible to meet with the requirement of extensive application of ILO Conventions and Recommendations" (57).

China's attitude to standards was also reflected in its ratification of only a few conventions after reentering the ILO. By 1998, of 181 ILO conventions, China had ratified only 19, all but 5 before 1949.[53] As a declaration of sovereignty, the Chinese Foreign Minister, Wu Xueqian, had notified the ILO in 1984 that although China would continue to recognize (*chengren*) all fourteen conventions ratified by China prior to 1 October 1949, it would abrogate (*feichu*) all of the twenty-three conventions subsequently ratified by Taiwan in the name of China.[54] Of the five subsequently ratified, the most significant was the Tripartite Convention No. 144. This Convention brought China closest to formally embracing the right to freedom of association, since it required that the workers' and employers' organizations taking part in the consultations in question should enjoy freedom of association.[55] In terms of important standards, the number ratified by China was judged by ILO officials to be extremely small. ILO technical cooperation with China was also deemed not large given the country's size and importance.[56] As of May 1993 the ongoing projects, all but one of which had been initiated before 1989, were valued at US $17,570, 836.[57] China and the ILO had, however, cooperated in numerous activities involving the regulation of social and labor issues in SOEs and FIEs.[58]

Before 1989, the ICFTU, the world trade union organization enjoying consultative status with the ILO, had extensive bilateral contact with the All China Federation of Trade Unions (ACFTU). The ICFTU, established in 1949 in London by seventy trade unions in fifty-three countries, and subsequently based in Brussels, also had a regional organization, the ICFTU Asian and Pacific Regional Organization (APRO).[59] Under its aegis, between

1984–1989, almost all national trade unions had visited Beijing. According to an ICFTU source, before Tiananmen the unitary Chinese trade union was attempting to address the issue of grievances in the workplace, but not worker participation.[60]

China and the ILO, June 1989–98

The crackdown on the Chinese Democracy Movement in June 1989 was reported by one interviewee as "almost the end of ILO cooperation with China," and by another as setting back the process of China's integration into the organization.[61] Certainly, it marked the end of the period of "specific exemption" and "specific entitlement" for China in the ILO. The large numbers of workers killed or injured throughout China during and after the early June events, and the deliberate government attack on the Workers' Autonomous Federation (WAF) tents in Tiananmen Square on 3–4 June were subsequently deemed to be in contravention not only of the basic tenets of freedom of association but also of the ILO Constitution.[62] The June crackdown precipitated a period in which, it is argued, the ILO applied universal standards to China and China began slowly to accept the costs as well as the benefits of organizational participation.

Much international attention has been focused on the student-led democracy protests in Tiananmen that culminated in the tragic crackdown. Less attention has been paid to the fact that during this same movement the WAF hoisted the first banner of an independent union movement in China since the founding of the People's Republic of China in 1949. It has been claimed that only when the workers, a small number of peasants, and the general public joined the movement did the government feel impelled to suppress it.[63] The movement's potential to ignite labor unrest was underscored by the fact that, initially, even the official ACFTU supported the students' movement and donated funds to the student hunger strikers.[64]

The WAF's presence in Tiananmen Square represented a clear sign to the Chinese government of the potential dangers inherent in a merger between students and workers following the model of Poland's Solidarity movement. WAF organizers distributed leaflets criticizing the existing labor policies and the official union structure.[65] Their main grievances were the wide wage discrepancy between workers and plant managers, lack of workplace democracy, the lack of genuine worker participation in the policy-making process, poor labor protection and working conditions, and the deterioration of workers' living standards. However, workers made it clear they wanted to organize the WAF through constitutional means and stated that they did not oppose the rule of the CCP (15).

By the height of the movement in Beijing, one hundred thousand workers from the manufacturing, service, and building industries, as well as worker intellectuals, from Beijing, the northeast, Tianjin, Shanxi, Jiangsu, Hebei, and Hunan had enrolled in the Beijing federation (13–14). WAFs also established themselves in other major cities in China. During the June crackdown, the workers who had attempted to halt the Army's advance, and the WAF camp on the north-west side of the square, were mowed down.[66] When the first units of the People's Liberation Army force entered Tiananmen Square, the red-and-black banner of the WAF was their first target (242). Those subsequently executed for their involvement in the movement, albeit with charges of having also been involved in acts of physical opposition and destruction, were almost all workers; students who were arrested were imprisoned but did not suffer the death penalty.

The ILO's response to these developments was to draw a fine line in its policies between displays of disapproval to indicate that it was "not business as usual," and avoidance of action that would undermine the fundamental interests of Chinese workers. Existing programs of technical assistance continued, but no new ones were introduced until CFA Case 1500 had examined the problem. After June 1989, the Director-General had to personally screen any application of technical assistance for China. In principle, it was reportedly ruled that there were to be no activities in relation to the Chinese government, only to tripartite activities within China. However, as one ILO official observed, the difficulty was to determine who was who and, since real workers appeared not to be well represented, to ascertain which activities were *not* governmental.[67] ILO training programs continued in the south of China, because the Director-General believed that, in accordance with strict ILO guidelines which saw technical assistance as an integral part of standard-setting, they were in the interests of Chinese citizens. However, an ILO seminar which was to be held in China in September 1989 was postponed until May 1991. In addition, a supplementary report containing a Declaration of the Government of the People's Republic of China with reference to the future relationship between the Hong Kong Special Administrative Region (SAR) of the People's Republic of China and the ILO from 1 July 1997 was held up. Due to come before the Governing Body at its 244th session in Geneva from 13–17 November 1989, it was held over until its 245th Session, from 26 February–2 March 1990, when it was accepted without debate.[68]

Because China had not ratified Conventions 87 and 98, in principle it would have been possible for the ILO to respond to the crackdown on the incipient free trade union movement with a fact-finding commission of inquiry, although a commission visit would also have had to receive China's consent. However, the Director-General himself reportedly overruled such an approach.[69] There was also reported to be a lot of discussion within the ICFTU as to whether to ask for direct contact. In the end, despite the belief that the Chinese authorities would probably have given their permission for such contact, it was decided that it was not the appropriate time to do so, since there were no independent trade unions in China that could have acted as interlocutors against the government's claims.[70] Consequently, the ICFTU decided to bring its complaint through the CFA procedure, which had also been applied to many other states that had not ratified the relevant conventions. This meant that, like the situation with CAT and the Special Rapporteur, ILO monitoring of China fell into the passive rather than active category.

Ironically, just prior to the suppression of the Democracy Movement in June 1989, China had been chosen as the representative of the Asian region to provide a spokesman to farewell the retiring Director-General, Francis Blanchard, who had been so successful in achieving China's full ILO participation. A few days after Tiananmen, the Conference presided over the embarrassing occasion, addressed by the Chinese representative.

In response to ICFTU complaints on 19 June, 22 June, and 20 July 1989, containing allegations judged by the Governing Body to represent a contravention of the ILO Constitution and the Declaration of Philadelphia, Case 1500 on China was established by the ILO Governing Body CFA. It required the Chinese government to supply detailed information of allegations of human rights abuses on 3–4 June and after, particularly in respect of the treatment of leaders and members of the WAFs set up during the course of the Democracy Movement. Following the events of June, the ICFTU also cut contacts with the ACFTU, while, among affiliates, bilateral contacts were cut off. In addition, in June 1990, partly as the result of the ICFTU decision not to support him, the Chinese ACFTU member on the ILO Governing Body was not reelected.

China's relations with the ILO have been described by one interviewee as "characteristic of a bureaucratic state," with respect to the behavior of both the Mission and those Chinese who worked in the ILO Office.[71] However, in both the International Labor Conference and the industrial committees, China's representatives emphasized China's role as a workers' state. The dual identity of a great power that also built its domestic legitimacy on claims of worker representation made China peculiarly vulnerable to ILO criticism. Apart from this special connection, its overall relationship with the ILO was a composite of many separate parts, including the program of technical assistance, China's organizational activities and ambitions, its regional commitments, and its obligations under the ratified conventions. The stormy passage of its involvement in two CFA cases did not preclude the continuation and, after 1991, even improvement of its position in other areas. Indeed, it is argued here that its overall organizational involvement helped China absorb the impact of the CFA cases, whose sensitivity was suggested by the failure of China's foreign policy documentation to record them.[72] Nevertheless, the CFA examination subjected China to a grueling process of organizational learning that had an impact on its overall participation and on its status within the ILO.

When the ICFTU brought down its complaints against the Chinese government in June and July 1989, Chinese officials were indignant and angry.[73] As has been noted, they had thought to avoid the standards imposed by the freedom of association by not ratifying Conventions 87 and 98. Only at the time of the complaints did they realize that, by virtue of the ILO Constitution and the Philadelphia Declaration, all member states were bound by its provisions. Members of the CFA were not so much shocked by the extreme Chinese reaction as they were bemused at the extent of their distress. Members of the Chinese Mission in Geneva constantly rehearsed the procedures of the inquiry and reportedly attempted to influence the Secretariat at all levels, from the humble Office to the Director-General.[74] These tactics were unsuccessful, since, as one ILO official observed, "we couldn't say it was possible to take the case off the books."

The Committee pursued polite relations with the Chinese Mission and union representatives, and attempted to persuade them to comply with its requirements. The then Chairman of the Governing Body, Douglas Poulter (Australia), mediated in numerous, informal, behind-the-scenes meetings with members of the Chinese Mission. He argued that China could meet the requirements of the Committee and the Governing Body by providing factual information on the events concerned, together with details of trials that had been held and advice as to the whereabouts of designated individuals. To ignore the requests made would be construed as a direct attack on the Governing Body, he stated: as a member of the ILO, the Chinese government had obligations under the Constitution as well as rights. These obligations included the commitment to respond positively to legitimate requests made by the Governing Body which related to its supervisory responsibilities insofar as the Constitution was concerned with fundamental rights such as freedom of association. China's arguments annoyed the members of the Governing Body in a case exposed to such publicity: its refusal to discuss the facts was subsequently compared unfavorably with Poland's situation under martial law, where, despite complaints, the facts had been addressed. Its most conspicuous error was seen by ILO officials as its claim to the right to noninterference. Only Chile and Poland had ever made this claim, which meant that "China was in poor company."

Between 1989 and 1995, the Governing Body CFA inquiry into the rights of Chinese workers was divided into two main cases, Case 1500 and Case 1652. Case 1500 addressed the problem of the crushing of the WAFs in June 1989 and related violations of trade union rights. China's responses in this case passed through three main stages.[75] In the first stage, it denied the right of international organizations to interfere in China's affairs. Chinese authorities claimed that the WAF was an illegal organization, not related to freedom of association, and that, in any case, freedom of association should be understood as meaning to "improve work conditions and promote peace."[76] They insisted that China was unable to accept the Committee's conclusions and recommendations. This period lasted until October 1990. The second phase, which lasted until March 1992, combined a denial of the right to interference with a preparedness to provide information. The final stage, from March 1992, saw both an end to China's references to interference and a readiness to report. Consistency was maintained throughout, however, on China's judgement of WAFs and independent trade unions as "illegal." Likewise, China emphasized the resort to physical violence by some workers, thereby attempting to place the WAF movement as a whole outside the purview of the CFA, which was restricted to consideration of cases involving peaceful measures only.

In CFA Case 1500, as in other UN human rights bodies, China went through an extreme learning curve, moving from a position of denial of the applicability of ILO norms and procedures to it to one of compliance with the formal requirements. It reflected a process of instrumental/adaptive learning that emphasized "how" rather than "that," demonstrating overall an evolving understanding of how to use the rules rather than a readiness to internalize them. The process of interaction with the Committee indicated a growing awareness on China's part that to refuse compliance was more destructive to its reputation and sovereignty than to cooperate. The Committee's continuing insistence that China respond according to the guidelines made it clear that only compliance would remove the pressure and publicity from the issue. Thus, China gradually changed from a position denying the applicability of rules to one in which it invoked its compliance with treaty requirements and a reading of its obligations under UN instruments, in order to deflect the impact of the critique. It did not comply substantively, however, since it was not willing to make the cognitive leap to accept all the provisions integral to the right to freedom of association.

This partial compliance was reflected in the CFA's conclusions and recommendations at the end of Case 1500. It first reminded China that upon joining the ILO, it had undertaken to respect the fundamental rights set out in the ILO's Constitution and Declaration of Philadelphia, including the freedom of association. It noted the great disparity between the ICFTU's account of events on and after 3–4 June and that of the Chinese government. On the basis of WAF grievances concerning the "lack of workplace democracy, the lack of genuine workers' representation, the poor working conditions and the deterioration of the workers' living standards," which had not been denied by China, and given China's acknowledgment that the Provisional Memorandum of the Beijing WAF accepted the Constitution and the law of the country, it ruled that "the WAF organizations would therefore appear to have been workers' organizations in the sense given to them by the ILO." Regarding acts of violence that China alleged had been committed by the WAFs, the Committee stressed that they all concerned events "when the WAFs were reduced to acting illegally." It judged that in the context of the abuse of civil rights entailed in the deaths, detention, and ill-treatment inflicted on the WAF's leaders and activists, all meaning was removed from the concept of trade union rights. It pointed out the omissions in the Chinese response: the government had "not yet supplied sufficiently detailed replies" on the deaths and detentions of WAF leaders and activists, particularly those that had occurred during the assault on Tiananmen Square.

The Committee therefore requested further information on the events and on general and specific cases. It expressed "its deep concern that the constitutional and legislative provisions currently in force in China are in clear contradiction with the right of workers to set up organizations of their own choosing and with the right of these organizations to function freely." And it drew the government's attention to the principle that "if the conditions for granting registration of a trade union are tantamount to obtaining prior permission for the public authorities, this would undeniably constitute an infringement of the principles of freedom of association."[77]

The Committee's second case on China, Case 1652, introduced in response to a new ICFTU complaint of 2 June 1992, addressed issues arising from China's new Trade Union Act of 3 April 1992 and debated the more general problems of a unitary trade union, as well as seeking to prevent the ongoing suppression of the underground free trade union movement.

The underground free trade union movement was a product of the suppression of the Democracy Movement. After June 1989, the labor unrest exposed by the movement had been driven underground and to some extent had been disguised by the economic upsurge that began in late 1991. This unrest, like that among other social groups, was born of the restructuring of China's economic system and its concomitant problems of corruption, unequal distribution, unemployment, and the erosion of socialist welfare policies.[78] Dissident workers' organizations, which totaled more than a dozen in Beijing alone, learned the lessons of 1989 and began operating deep underground in the strictest secrecy, like the Communist Party cells in China in the 1920s and 1930s.[79] These underground unions were reportedly responsible for a number of strikes during 1991, and were viewed with apprehension at a meeting of the Chinese security services and leaders of the judicial system in December 1991.[80] Of particular concern to both Chinese authorities and the ICFTU was the Free Labor Union of China, a new, independent, clandestine organization founded on 15 May 1992. Sixteen of the members of this organization were arrested and, in May 1994, received prison sentences of seven to twenty years.[81] The process of Case 1652 was thus of crucial concern to the Chinese government, and ICFTU complaints, the government's reply, and the Committee's responses were lengthy and impassioned.

In relation to the new Trade Union Act, the principal sources of ICFTU and CFA concern were that it demonstrated China's "utter disregard for the principle of freedom of association"; it denied unions the right to formulate their own programs; it provided for local unions to be under the control of the ACFTU and the CCP; and it ensured that local unions could not acquire legal personality unless approved by the ACFTU (8–11). Yet, relative to the Chinese context, the Trade Union Act did represent some progress. It contained provisions allowing the establishment of basic level union committees by a minimum of twenty-five members of an enterprise or organization, delineated trade union powers in a manner that transcended their normally narrow confines of protecting welfare and ensuring production, and assigned labor unions the role of mediators in labor disputes within enterprises.[82] It also prohibited antiunion discrimination. It was still more progressive in its requirements regarding union participation in Sino-foreign equity joint enterprises and wholly foreign-owned enterprises.[83]

Toward the conclusion of Case 1500, the Committee showed its responsiveness to China's more conciliatory stance, as well as a measure of sheer exhaustion. With the introduction of Case 1652, however, its energy was renewed. The test of whether the procedural learning curve demonstrated by China in Case 1500 had long-term, rather than purely short-term, tactical significance depended on the continuation of this process during Case 1652. One specific index was whether in this succeeding case the government abandoned its complaint of interference in its internal affairs. It did not: China once again protested. However, it soon moved back to a condition of procedural compliance.[84] Nevertheless, as the Committee's recommendations suggested, it did not comply substantively. Once again, the Committee requested that the Trade Union Act be amended so that it fully recognized the rights of association and freedom to organize; that the government take the necessary measures to enable workers and their organizations to exercise their right to strike; that Han Dongfang be allowed to return to China to exercise his trade union rights; and that all cases of detained workers raised by the ICFTU complaint be reexamined and the persons concerned be released.[85] Although there was no immediate response to these requests, China's sensitivity to the CFA critique was later detectable in some of the provisions of the new Labor Law and in its release of a few workers mentioned in the ICFTU complaint.

By contrast, in January 1995 a third case (1819) was lodged with the CFA by the ICFTU and the International Transport Workers' Federation (ITF) on behalf of three Chinese seamen who were arrested in Tianjin because of their involvement in a dispute with the owners of a foreign-owned vessel on which the Chinese seamen were regularly beaten and underpaid. The intervention of ITF on behalf of the Chinese seamen was seen as interference by the Chinese government, since the only union recognized by China was the ACFTU. The seamen were therefore arrested on their return to China for "letting out our important state secrets and causing serious economic losses to their despatcher." Three of the seamen were detained for two and a half years and their documentation and evidence of qualifications were confiscated. On 8 August 1993, their case was heard before the People's District

Court and judgment was reserved. Chinese authorities released the three seamen on bail, but as of 1998, the ILO had not received an official reply to the complaint.[86] At its meeting in June 1996, the CFA requested that the government ensure that the seafarers were compensated for economic losses suffered during their detention. It referred to its communication of 15 June 1996 when the government indicated that there had been no progress on the case. In other words, China showed responsiveness to the complaint by releasing the prisoners, but did not show a readiness to comply with the request to recompense them or to respond to inquiries. In 1997, besides continued noting of Case 1819, the 308th Report of the Committee on Freedom of Association listed two new cases with respect to China, Case 1930 (China) and Case 1942 (China/Special Administrative Region/Hong Kong).

In June 1998, in Case 1930, the 310th Report of the Committee on Freedom of Association published a further complaint by the ICFTU on 4 June 1997 against the Chinese government for violations of freedom of association.[87] As in the past, the ICFTU criticized aspects of China's new labor legislation and called upon China to amend parts of both the Trade Union Act and the new Labor Law. However, its attention was focused primarily on the lack of enforcement of the positive aspects of the new laws, particularly new provisions for collective bargaining, and on the continued ill-treatment, and in some cases, torture of large numbers of independent labor activists who had remained in jail or labor camp since 1989, despite repeated demands by the CFA for their sentences to be reexamined and the prisoners to be released. The ICFTU was also disturbed by the increasing use of administrative sanctions, bypassing the judicial process, to detain independent labor activists. In particular, it described the repression of members of the Free Labor Union of China, of the League for the Protection of the Rights of Working People, and of the "Workers' Forum" in Shenzhen.

The Chinese government's reply demonstrated the progress which had been made in China's procedural compliance with the Committee, as it contained no denial of its accountability. While strongly regretting the submission of the complaint, it stated that it had 'undertaken vast inquiries" with the Minister of Public Security, the Minister of Justice, the ACFTU and a number of cities and provinces to assess the truth of the allegations. It claimed that "collective bargaining is practiced in over 90,000 enterprises covering over 40 million employees" in China, and that "the unionization rate of enterprise employees has reached 80 percent." However, as before it insisted that the independent organizations of workers referred to in the complaint were "not actually unions, but rather groups of individuals who, instead of defending workers' interests, are devoted to illegal activities endangering state security. The prohibition of such groups, therefore, ensures a better defense of workers' fundamental interests." After giving information on some of the cases named in the complaint, it concluded that "As concerns standard-setting activities in China, the Government asserts that the competent authorities take sufficiently into account the principles and provisions contained in relevant standards (whether or not ratified) when drafting and revising legislation so that Chinese legislation is in harmony with international standards and common practice. For developing countries, including China, the constraints resulting from historical factors and present conditions dictate that the ratification of Conventions be a gradual process."

Following lengthy interim conclusions, the CFA focused on China's lack of substantive compliance with its earlier recommendations. It recommended that China amend parts of its labor legislation contrary to freedom of association, to the right to collective bargaining and the right to strike: sections 4, 5, 8, 9, 11, and 13 of the Trade Union Act; and sections 34, 46, and 79 to 83 of the Labor Law. It called for the release of all trade unionists who had been the subject of earlier complaints before the Committee, including Tang Yuanjuan and Wang Miaogen, and requested the release of members of the free labor unions including Yuan Hongbing, Xiao Biguang, Gao Feng, Li Wenming and Guo Baosheng. It required investigation into allegations of torture, and further information on cases not addressed by China.

Throughout all its China hearings, the Committee insisted on the applicability of universal labor standards to China, regardless of China's protests. In this respect, its expectations contrasted with the more relativist position adopted by some individual ILO officials, who, within the larger context of China's total interaction with the ILO, made reference in interviews to China's special status as a great power and as a developing, socialist Asian power with different historical and cultural traditions and different labor conditions.

Committee on Freedom of Association Cases and the Learning Process

China's greater responsiveness in the second examination of Case 1652 and in Case 1930, despite its continuing obduracy on basic provisions of freedom of association, suggested that a degree of long-term procedural adjustment had been initiated. However, the swiftness of the change also occurred against a background of related domestic and external developments.

Paradoxically, from the early 1990s, the same indications of worker and peasant unrest that had initially prompted China's resistance to ILO standards, and that were responsible for a more authoritarian and nationalistic foreign policy stance in 1993, began to combine with international organizational imperatives to produce new instances of China's compliance with ILO standards. Nationalistic sentiments that focused attention on the condition of Chinese workers in FIEs also encouraged China's informal development of collective bargaining practices, particularly in Western-dominated enterprises.[88] Because trade union officials found it easier to take an adversarial position towards employers in FIEs, foreign enterprises formed a convenient base on which to experiment in appropriate mechanisms for worker participation. There was also growing Chinese government awareness that as modernization and the rationalization of industry proceeded, social restructuring had to keep pace: for this purpose, external standards promoted by the ILO provided a convenient and readily accessible model.

In addition, China's interest in obtaining organizational power within the ILO was clearly thwarted by the opposition of the worker and even employer groups that formed half of the ILO's democratic tripartite system of organization and two-thirds in the case of the CFA. This resistance became a concrete obstacle to China's interest in assuming chairmanship of the ILO Governing Body when the position rotated to the Asian group in 1994. Such a goal required the confidence of others in the Asian group, which included states as far west as Pakistan and the Middle East. China's failure to meet standards such as freedom of association reportedly made it an unacceptable spokesperson for all groups, and its candidacy waned in the face of a clear lack of support.[89] In the end, the Governing Body position was taken by the Philippine Secretary of Labour and Employment Nieves Roldan-Confesor.

For these reasons, China's informal compliance with selected ILO standards began to differ both from its earlier position and from the more obdurate position it had adopted after 1993 towards bilateral monitoring and in some UN forums. Indications of compliance at the international level were noticeable a few months after the second examination of Case 1652. They were also reflected in China's declaratory policy on other ILO standards. Following the issuance of the Provisions on Minimum Wages in Enterprises on 24 November 1993 by China's Labor Ministry, China had supplied a report for examination by the Committee of Experts in relation to Convention 26 (Minimum Wage-Fixing Machinery, 1928), ratified by China in 1930.[90] In response to the Committee's request that, with reference to Convention 26, the government supply information on the progress made in the preparation of the regulation on minimum wages, China's delegates appeared before the Committee on the Application of Standards. In the Committee's preliminary discussions, both China's government and worker representatives emphasized the relevance and necessity of ILO standard setting.[91] They also indicated China's intention to ratify ILO Convention 170, the Chemicals Convention of 1990. However, the most unequivocal support for the ILO and ILO standards came from the government representative appearing before the Committee on the subject of Convention 26.

At this meeting, China's representative stressed China's new interest in

ILO labor standards, in view of its transition to a market economy, which required "more emphasis on the role of labour legislation in protecting the basic rights of workers" (25/82). She stressed China's "positive attitude of cooperation" in its written reply to the ILO, "for which the opinions of China's employers and workers had been solicited," and gave information on the purpose and process of the 1993 legislation. She referred to new labor legislation submitted to the National People's Congress (NPC) for discussion, and emphasized the importance her country attached to the application of ILO standards. The workers' delegate of China also confirmed that the Chinese trade unions had "participated actively in the promotion and formulation of the November 1993 regulation." These statements contrasted with Guan Jinghe's disclaimer in 1989 of China's ability to comply with ILO labor standards.

China's new attitude to the ILO was acknowledged in the response of employers' delegates to the Committee on the Application of Standards, who pointed out that this was the first time that a case concerning China had been discussed in the Committee. While noting that the November 1993 regulation was the first provision concerning minimum wages in enterprises adopted since China's ratification of Convention 26, the workers' delegates also observed that "it was at least possible to see a change in the attitude of the [Chinese] Government to the extent that a report had been supplied for examination by the Committee of Experts and information had been made available concerning the application of the Convention."[92] The workers' delegates pointed out that, in the area of labor relations, China's legislative framework had not been adapted to the challenges of the market economy, and requested further detailed information on the outstanding points in Case 1652. Nevertheless, they noted that "the Government had undertaken the commitment, during the general discussion, to attach more importance to international labor standards" (25/83). China's new responsiveness to standards was remarked on by interviewees who attended the June 1994 ILO Conference.[93] It was also apparent in China's response to a campaign initiated by the ILO after May 1995 to encourage ratification by all states members of seven core conventions, Conventions 29, 87, 98, 105, 100, 111 and 138. China had already ratified Convention 100 (Equal Remuneration Convention) and began the process of ratifying Convention 138. Although it was not prepared to ratify Conventions 87 and 98, it undertook to continue discussions on the others with the idea of moving toward them.[94]

However, China's interest in ILO labor standards was not unconditional, but premised on the maintenance of China's autonomy within the organization. It remained deeply suspicious of ILO developments that had the potential to threaten its sovereignty by involving it in labor standards through the back door. Consequently, it took a firm position in the debate surrounding the proposal at the June 1997 ILO Conference to adopt a Declaration on workers' fundamental rights, based on the right to freedom of association and including a follow-up mechanism, which would apply automatically to all member states. In the debate, China's representative, Minister of Labor Li Boyong, objected that "the nature of this proposal forces Members who have not ratified the standards to undertake the same obligations as those that have ratified them." This, he insisted, was "not consistent with the provisions of the [ILO] Constitution." He concluded: " Such practice of imposing labor standards by means of pressure can only intensify disputes and it would not achieve the objective. We stand resolutely opposed to any attempt to transform the ILO into an international tribunal." Echoing his Minister, the Workers' delegate, Li Qisheng, asserted that "we stand for the strengthening and improvements of the ILO supervisory mechanisms, but we are opposed to any abuse of them."[95] At the 86th ILO Conference in June 1998, China bargained hard to keep the obligations involved in the Declaration as weak as possible. For its part, the ILO reassured states that support for the Declaration would not mean that its conventions were immediately applicable, but only that states must work toward them. Following marathon debates in the special Conference committee, both China's state delegate and workers' delegate reportedly voted for the Declaration, which was adopted at the closing plenary session of the Conference with 274 votes in the affirmative, none in the negative and 43 abstentions.[96] According to the ILO, the *Declaration on Fundamental Principles and Rights at Work* "reaffirm[ed] the commitment of the organization's member states 'to respect, to promote and to realize in good faith' the right of workers and employers to freedom of association and the effective right to collective bargaining, and to work toward the elimination of all forms of forced or compulsory labour, the effective abolition of child labour and the elimination of discrimination in respect of employment and occupation."[97]

China's sensitivity about sovereignty in labor standards was heightened by Hong Kong's reversion to China. Before reversion, Hong Kong had amended labor legislation and taken administrative measures to apply forty-nine ILO conventions. Under the Basic Law, China also undertook to adhere to these, which included Conventions 87 and 98 on freedom of association and collective bargaining. On 6 June 1997, in a letter informing the ILO Director-General that the PRC would exercise sovereignty over Hong Kong from 1 July 1997, the Chinese government communicated to the Director-General forty-six notifications concerning forty-six conventions that would continue to be applied to the Hong Kong Special Administrative Region (SAR).[98] However, in March 1997, under a provision of the Basic Law, the Standing Committee of the NPC had already moved to alter the 1991 Bill of Rights Ordinance and to scrap recently liberalized laws on demonstrations and political parties. Following a public outcry, the laws were not scrapped, but amendments were announced to the existing Public Order Ordinance that reintroduced licensing for demonstrations and allowed police objections on grounds of national security. ILO Convention 98, the Right to Organise and Collective Bargaining Convention, had been applied to Hong Kong without modification since 1975. Consequently, when on 29 October 1997, the Provisional Legislature passed government-sponsored legislation to repeal labor legislation, including the Employees' Rights to Representation, Consultation and Collective Bargaining Ordinance, the ICFTU was critical and the ILO warned that it would investigate any formal complaints lodged by union members over government actions to repeal or amend collective bargaining or other labor laws.[99] The discrepancy between the nineteen conventions applicable to China proper and the forty-six applicable to Hong Kong increased the likelihood of tensions arising over labor issues between the SAR and the PRC government.

Despite China's overt resistance to implementing the main principles of the right to freedom of association in domestic practice, by mid-1994 evidence emerged of its selective internalization of some basic standards in new legislation. The PRC Labor Law was promulgated on 5 July 1994 and became effective in 1 January 1995. Its 107 articles, which applied to enterprises as well as to state authorities and social organizations, covered all kinds of employment, holidays, safety and health, salaries, career training and insurance. In some fundamental areas it showed no change. It contained no specific provision allowing workers the right to strike or act directly against their employers. Article 7 of its General Provisions contained no provision, as UN and ILO standards on freedom of association enjoined, allowing the right of workers to form and join the trade union of their own choosing, without previous authorization. It stated simply: "A worker shall have the right to join and organize a trade union in accordance with the law."[100]

China's new Labor Law thus maintained similar provisions to those in the Trade Union Act of April 1992 that had been criticized by the CFA in the hearings on Case 1652. Yet the second paragraph of Article 7 provided that "A trade union shall represent and protect the lawful rights and interests of workers, and organize its activities autonomously and independently (*duli zizhu di kaizhan huodong*) in accordance with the law."[101] In Article 8, the Law also provided that workers should "participate in democratic management or consult on an equal level with the employing unit about the protection of lawful rights and interests of workers through staff meetings." It showed acceptance of ILO standards of tripartism and collective bargaining, thus superseding a 1988 law that allowed collective bargaining only by workers in private enterprises. It adopted ILO language in referring specifically to the state's responsibility to "formulate labor standards" (*zhiding laodong biaojun*). It made no reference to the right to work formally guaranteed in China's Constitution, but endorsed a list of workers' rights, including "equal rights in obtaining employment and choosing occupation" (*laodong-zhe xiangyou pingdeng jiuye he xuanze zhiye di quanli*), a right not previously extended. Most important, unlike any of its precursors, in Section 12, legal liability, the new Labor Law introduced a list of penalties in the form of fines, compensation to workers, revocation of business license, and criminal liability that were to be imposed by the labor administration department on employing units for violations of the Law's provisions.[102] It demonstrated selective compliance with some standards integral to freedom of association at the level of domestic *de jure* compliance. Over the longer term, it thus reflected some cognitive learning, besides the instrumental learning indicated in the CFA proceedings, in relation to ILO standards.[103]

However, while this new law reflected the government's recognition that the new market-oriented economy placed workers in a less favorable position that required special protection of their rights, it also provided guidelines for the expansion of the scope of labor contracts to all workers and a range of procedures for dismissals, layoffs, and resignations.[104] It also continued the assumption in the Trade Union Act, much criticized by the ILO Committee on Freedom of Association, that it was the state's right to guide labor relations, rather than its obligation to facilitate worker independence. And as the CFA noted in Case 1930, sections 34 and 46 of the Law restricted the freedom of workers and employers when bargaining collectively, while sections 79 to 83 "appear[ed] to codify exactly the same type of mediation and arbitration system as the regulations which the Committee had previously criticized," thereby undermining the right to strike.[105] In other words, while representing a symbol of workers' rights, the new Labor Law had a two-fold purpose: it "represented the regime's effort to address workers' concerns while maintaining the state's monopoly on power . . . entrenching the Party-dominated labor union system as the basic mechanism for enforcing workers' rights."[106]

Moreover, as the ICFTU pointed out in its complaint in Case 1930, little compliance was yet exhibited by China at the *de facto* level of domestic implementation of ILO standards. Weak implementation was due, inter alia, to the marked increase in managerial autonomy within the enterprise, an unclear relationship between the labor contract system and the contract responsibility system, the decline in authority of the official union, and the "blurred line between the local governments and businesses [which] creates an environment where those designated as the protectors of labor are either intimately connected with or even the same as those who are violating workers' rights."[107] There were some differing reports about the degree of practical implementation of the rights on paper: in contrast to the Chinese government's claim in Case 1930, according to one source, by 1996 union and labor officials had reported only a few instances of collective bargaining, while according to another there were more.[108]

The contrast between more progressive legislation and continuing suppression of labor activists, however, provided the most clear-cut evidence of the gap between the different levels of domestic compliance. Continued

Chinese government efforts to suppress labor activists, continuing poor labor conditions and a mounting number of labor disputes were irrefutable evidence that practical implementation of the new law had a long way to go.[109] Throughout 1993 and 1994, Chinese authorities had continued the drive to apprehend members of underground free trade unions.[110] Particularly significant was the case of the League for the Protection of the Rights of Working People, established in 1994. In March 1994, a petition calling for workers to assert "freedom from exploitation," the right to strike, and the right to organize nonofficial trade unions was circulated in Beijing. Zhou Guoqiang, Yuan Hongbing, and Wang Jiaqi were detained after they presented a petition. Zhou was subsequently sentenced to three years' reeducation through labor. In gathering support from several hundred activists across the country, the League revealed dissident support for labor rights. Many of its founders had been arrested after they tried to register their group with the government openly.[111] Despite this suppression, however, and despite the fact that the right to strike had been struck from of the 1982 Constitution, there were an estimated 1,870 strikes throughout the country in 1995.[112] Already, between 1986 and 1994, a total of 60,000 labor disputes had been recorded.[113]

By 1998, the picture on the labor front was ambiguous.[114] A number of labor activists, including Zhou Guoqiang, Li Wenming and Guo Baosheng, all of whom had been subjects of CFA appeals, were released between late 1997 and early 1998. In May 1997, in a significant decision possibly anticipating the annual ILO Conference in June, court authorities quashed one of the two principal counts ("organizing a counterrevolutionary group") on which labor activists Tang Yuanjuan and Li Wei were originally convicted, leading to their surprise release from prison in July 1997. Tang in particular had been the subject of active CFA lobbying for his release. However, on 18 September 1998, he was once again arrested, this time in relation to his meeting with a number of activists around China to establish a China Democracy Party (CDP). He was formally charged with "making contacts with illegal organizations."[115] His re-arrest exemplified the continued repression of workers protesting against massive layoffs throughout China and particularly of those seeking to register free labor unions or associations.[116] However, in the diplomatic merry-go-round of dissident repression, only a day before China's signing of the ICCPR on 5 October 1998, he was released once again.

Nonlabor associations were initially treated more generously. Although Communist Party regulations required that all professional and social organizations be officially registered and approved, within a few years fifteen hundred national-level quasi-NGOs and two hundred thousand similar lower-level organizations registered with the Ministry of Civil Affairs. These organizations came under some government control, but they increasingly developed their own agendas. In this way, although the registration requirement was counter to the spirit and letter of the right to freedom of association, civil society in China managed to expand. In January 1997, however, the Ministry imposed an indefinite nationwide moratorium on the creation or registering of any new "social bodies." It also attempted to maintain control over them through a high-level circular stipulating that any social group that had been approved for registration by the organization in charge of the registration and management of social groups should establish a grassroots party organ if there were more than three party members in the staff of their standing bodies.[117] Moreover, on 25 October 1998, the State Council promulgated new Regulations on the Registration and Management of Social Groups, as well as Provisional Regulations on the Registration and Management of People-Organized Non-Enterprise Units. These regulations substantially raised the requirements for the establishment of a social group, allowed for extensive government interference and increased government controls, and removed any possibility for appeals against decisions taken by the registration authorities.[118]

Clearly, the most meaningful level of learning, the extension in practice of freedom of association to all China's citizens, and in particular, its workers, had yet to be attained. Until that happened, China could not be judged to have complied substantively with regime norms. Admittedly, some of the ILO standards that had earlier been a subject of dispute between China and the Committee in Case 1652 were now met in the formal provisions of China's new law. Yet the same period witnessed rigorous government attempts to suppress the sources of such activity. It was clear that, despite the role of ILO standards in providing models for Chinese labor legislation, the actual challenge to the leaders' authority implicit in the existence of genuinely free trade unions in China, independent of both Party and state, would not be tolerated by them.

Conclusion

From its entry into the ILO in 1971, China had moved from a situation in which it claimed "specific exemption" and "specific entitlement" to one in which it had accepted, after considerable resistance, the organization's right to monitor its workers' rights. Like the case studies already examined, ILO monitoring was passive rather than active. In this case, however, the decision to eschew such active mechanisms as direct contacts rested less on China's consent and more on the mismatch between the ILO's tripartite organization and the essentially unitary character of China's official trade union, which made it difficult for the ILO to enlist its trade unions as interlocutors against government claims. However, the rigor of the monitoring that did occur belied the description of "passive." China's interaction with the ILO Governing Body Committee on Freedom of Association between 1990 and 1998 was a tough, unrelenting process, with ILO officials persisting in the application to China of universal ILO standards against strong, and at times vituperative, Chinese opposition.

China's organizational learning curve was reflected in two discrete CFA cases, and, in both cases, moved from outright denial of its reporting responsibilities to partial, and then, grudging if not total, acceptance. The gradual nature of this curve was in line with the ILO's experience that the internalization of standards was an evolutionary process.[119] However, China began its reporting from a less advanced position in terms of normative compliance than it had with the UN Committee Against Torture, and, at least in Case 1500, made slower progress. In the first Case, the process of China's interaction resulted in a learning curve that moved from overt resistance to procedural compliance, and thence to learning "how" to protect its interests. Thus, it ultimately showed instrumental/adaptive learning at the international levels.

In Case 1652, China moved from renewed resistance to once again accepting its reporting obligations. As a result of domestic and organizational pressures, it also showed indications of cognitive learning by internalizing selected ILO standards. However, because China did not in fact accept freedom of association in its intrinsic sense of allowing workers the freedom to form and join the trade union of their own choosing without previous authorization, it evinced little substantive learning with respect to this specific and crucial standard at the international and domestic levels. Not only did it fail to accept all the principles inherent in the right to freedom of association, but it continued to arrest, sentence, imprison, and execute workers for whom the ICFTU and the CFA had pleaded clemency. Moreover, official suppression of free labor unions continued, in defiance of CFA and ICFTU recommendations. With Case 1930, the Chinese government protested only mildly, undertook investigation of the complaints and released some of the workers for whom the CFA had appealed, although general repression still continued.

It may be concluded that China failed to show deep compliance with the Committee's requirements at the level of practical implementation. However, within the larger context of its labor unrest and its participation in the ILO, it became aware of its inability to ensure domestic stability and greater organizational power without accepting some ILO standards. The learning process thus involved both the domestic and international arena. It brought a gradual recognition of the need to comply, or to be seen to comply in theory, with selective ILO standards, in particular tripartism, worker participation, and the right to collective bargaining. These standards were reflected at the domestic *de jure* level in the new Labor Law. Such internal and external pressures ensured that China's relations with the ILO regime were not interrupted, as in the other case studies, by China's hard-line foreign policy after 1993. In this case, the effectiveness of ILO supervision depended in part on the conjunction of external and domestic pressures.

It is equally clear that organizational imperatives determining CFA procedures, the relatively fixed process of the examination and the Committee's obligation not to depart from its body of case law, impressed themselves on Chinese authorities.[120] In addition, the very process of reporting brought a vital transparency to the administrative and judicial treatment of China's dissident workers that had hitherto been totally hidden from public and international scrutiny. The Committee exhibited the same persistent robustness as CAT and other treaty bodies and special rapporteurs. By virtue of its tripartite worker/employer/government structure and long experience in objective standard setting, moreover, the ILO was arguably less vulnerable to China's power claims than were other UN human rights bodies.

Yet, notwithstanding its manifest strengths, the ILO Governing Body CFA had a tougher road to hoe with China than the UN Committee Against Torture and other treaty bodies and special rapporteurs. China's procedural compliance was initially weaker, partly because of the different terms on which China had become a member of the organization, but mainly because, unlike the case of CAT and the Special Rapporteur on Torture, the standards integral to the mandate of the ILO Committee were in practice anathema to the aging and authoritarian Chinese leadership. Although by 1997 improvements had been made in legislation on related standards, the battle over the basic principles of the right to freedom of association, which provided such an authoritative and inspirational model of industrial organization for China's workers, and which was perceived by its government to be so threatening to the survival of the existing political system, continued to be waged in the ILO Governing Body CFA, albeit with fewer procedural obstacles in its path.

Chapter 5
Theory, Policy, and Diplomacy Before Vienna

China has made its due contribution to enriching the concept of human rights and encouraging the universal respect of human rights in the world. China attended the World Conference on Human Rights held in Vienna in 1993 and the preparatory work of the conference.
— Ren Yanshi, 28 October 1997

The previous chapters have documented the Chinese response to specific aspects of the UN human rights regime. They have detailed its interaction with the UN Commission on Human Rights and the UN Human Rights Sub-Commission, and have followed the process of China's compliance with its reporting responsibilities to the UN Committee Against Torture and the Special Rapporteur on Torture, to other treaty bodies and special rapporteurs and to the ILO Governing Body Committee on Freedom of Association. Each of these cases saw different degrees of Chinese compliance and noncompliance with international monitoring. In much the same way, China responded to U.S. bilateral sanctions by releasing important dissidents at crucial times, yet in other respects took action that ran completely counter to both the letter and the spirit of the changing requirements invoked by the U.S. But, when domestic pressures in the form of social unrest and power struggle intervened in late 1993 and 1994, China rejected the right both of the international community and of individual states to monitor it, reiterating the principle of noninterference, and taking a harsh line with domestic dissent.

However, an examination of case studies alone, and of specific responses, does not do justice to the larger environment within which China responded to pressure, from both the international community and its own domestic population. China not only was faced with the need to defend itself against the international critique but, in defense of the sovereignty about which it was so sensitive, also had to be seen by its citizens as taking the lead. In particular, to remain passive in the face of the UN critique was to implicitly accept the United Nations status as a supranational organization with the right to bypass the Chinese state and interact with its citizens. In its effort to regain the initiative, China was led to modify its formal, legalistic interpretation of sovereignty and conform with international standards in some respects. It entered into activity that on the one hand was consistent with UN human rights norms, and that, on the other, sought to establish a new hierarchy of human rights that fundamentally contested their universality, equality, indivisibility, and interdependence.

This broad, public response was first activated domestically in late 1990, at a time coinciding with the looming shadow of the MFN debate in the U.S. Its conceptual foundations were documented in a report by a research group of the Propaganda Department of the Chinese Communist Party (CCP) Central Committee, which sought to address the perceived danger of the Western theory promoting the peaceful evolution (*heping yanbian*) of socialist political systems into liberal democratic systems and the problem of Western attacks on China's human rights.[1] The report, which saw human rights as a political weapon of the West that had developed steadily under every U.S. President since Jimmy Carter, called for research to be carried out on human rights, using Marxist theory and analyzing compilations of material on bourgeois, democratic socialist, Western, Third World, and international theories of human rights, as well as Chinese legal material. It issued a clarion call for Chinese scholars to "organize and throw themselves into the battle" (*zongzhi yao zuzhi qilai touru zhandou*).

The period of active engagement began at a theoretical level, with official encouragement of a limited "hundred flowers" period in academic conferences and the proliferation of publications on human rights. It saw clear governmental leadership with the publication of major White Papers on human rights and the setting up of institutions, such as an "NGO" to study human rights. The China Society for Human Rights Studies (CSHRS) was established by government, contained government officials, and was headed by Zhu Muzhi, former Director of the Information Office of the State Council, former Director of the Xinhua News Agency, and former leader of the Foreign Propaganda Department of the CCP Central Committee. Nevertheless, its establishment at least reflected official acceptance of the role NGOs were expected to play in the international human rights regime. Subsequently, China engaged in human rights debate with Western human rights delegations and official visitors, and sought to test its human rights theory during official visits to Asia and Africa. Finally, it sought to institutionalize the fruits of its human rights policy at the regional Bangkok Preparatory Meeting of March 1993 and the UN World Human Rights Conference at Vienna in June 1993.

This chapter documents the theoretical, institutional, and practical initiatives undertaken by China in the human rights field after 1989. It describes the internal theoretical debate of 1990–91, culminating in the publication of the first Chinese White Paper on human rights in October 1991. It looks at the practice of China's human rights diplomacy (*renquan waijiao*) — contrasting with its day-to-day interaction with specific parts of the regime, and defined as a discrete set of diplomatic endeavours asserting China's primacy in human rights discourse — at a bilateral and, finally, multilateral level. In particular, the chapter subjects the principal statements made by China at the Bangkok Meeting and the Fourth Preparatory Comittee preceding the Vienna Conference to comparative analysis. Chapter 6 then scrutinizes the process of Chinese involvement in the Vienna Conference and compares Chinese statements at Vienna with those at the lead-up conferences. By these different avenues the study seeks to ascertain to what extent China was able to influence the direction of the international debate, and to what extent its views underwent modification as a result of the process of interaction.

Chinese Theory

Institutional and Academic Developments

Legal education in China was resurrected only after the devastation of the Cultural Revolution in 1978. From this time, with the beginning of the first democracy movement — the Democracy Wall Movement — interest in human rights was stimulated. As Chapter 1 has documented, a number of articles challenging socialist dogma appeared, but with the end of the movement in 1981, interest in the subject correspondingly waned. It did not effectively resurface until the latter part of the 1980s, when the government itself began to encourage activities such as symposiums on jurisprudence, involving debates on rights and duties, and the symposium of December 1988 to celebrate the fortieth anniversary of the Universal Declaration of Human Rights in Beijing.[2] The same year saw the publication of a slim volume on human rights by Zhang Chunjin, *Renquan lun* ("On Human Rights"). In the first quarter of 1989, on the eve of the second democracy movement, China's expert on the Human Rights Sub-Commission, Tian Jin, published an article on the development of the international human rights movement.[3]

However, renewed interest in human rights under official guidance was quashed with the suppression of the Democracy Movement in June 1989.[4] Academic journals continued to publish articles on human rights: but Chinese authorities bitterly rejected the entire international human rights critique and contested the international community's right to intervene in China's internal affairs. The first clear signs of a return of official interest and support for academic endeavour was a conference on human rights convened in September 1990 by the Research Centre for Social Science Development of the State Education Commission.[5] Over the next two years, a veritable human rights fever (*renquan re*) developed, with the holding of symposiums, setting up of human rights centres, and publication of books and articles. These activities were actively supported and given financial assistance by the Chinese government.[6] Even Chinese students studying abroad were mobilized in the massive effort to collect material on human rights in general and foreign accounts of China's human rights in particular.[7] Chinese students were not the only source of information. In 1992, a number of foreign scholars were involved in joint research projects on human rights with Chinese institutions.[8] By 1993, however, at which time a Chinese theory had emerged fully developed and China was turning to multilateral forums, this interest in foreign involvement appeared to have waned. Coincidentally, China became more outspoken in its critique of human rights conditions in the U.S. and of U.S. human rights diplomacy (*renquan waijiao*).[9]

There were two main types of Chinese academic and government activity.[10] The first were academic symposiums held from the end of 1990 to 1992 with government encouragement or sponsorship, whose purpose was to build up expertise in human rights and create a theory of human rights with "Chinese characteristics." Topics under discussion included the concept and content of human rights; historical origins of human rights ideas; bourgeois theories and how to deal with them; the relationship between human rights, international law and international politics; the relationship between state sovereignty and the international protection of human rights; the enrichment of Marxist theory on human rights; and human rights protection and human rights research in China. The second form of activity followed the publication of the three White Papers on human rights beginning in October 1991 and consisted of national government forums to discuss their significance and application.[11]

By the end of 1992, at least a dozen institutions were carrying out study or research projects relating to human rights.[12] They included a human rights research center established in 1991 by the Chinese People's University in Beijing, staffed by a large group of scholars of law, sociology, philosophy, and politics.[13]

Academic Theories

The development of official theories after 1989 occurred against the backdrop of an enormous output of articles in academic journals and books on human rights. A Chinese bibliography published in 1992 listed 296 articles on human rights in major newspapers, weeklies, social science journals, and legal journals published between 1979 and 1992.[14] Of these, 240 were published between 1989 and mid-1992. Analyzed chronologically, 32 (13 percent) were published in 1989; 46 (19 percent) in 1990; 120 (50 percent) in 1991; and 42 (17 percent) in the first half of 1992. Numerically, and in terms of their content, the efflorescence of publications and the development in human rights concepts clearly occurred in 1991. From 1989 to 1997, a substantial number of books on human rights were also published.[15] This was in addition to a veritable explosion of publications on Chinese law and in particular, criminal law; on specific laws relating to human rights like the Administrative Procedure Law, the Press Law and the Labour Law; handbooks on citizens' rights; books on the *laogai* (reform through labor) system and on public security; and discussions of related concepts such as freedom.[16] Although many of the human rights publications focused on issues emphasized in the official theories, the debate ranged widely and was not constrained in its development of theory, or in the theoretical questions it addressed. So rich and diverse was the output that attempts to encompass it in analysis have inevitably resulted in surveys of a number of discrete aspects, rather than a detailed and comprehensive analysis.[17]

Although for the most part the Chinese literature did not liberally cite Western sources, apart from Marx, much of the discussion had its origins in Western theories and theorists and closely followed the themes of Western human rights discourse, even if it took divergent positions.[18] This was the case particularly as it related to debates on questions of individual versus collective rights, universal versus basic rights, the universal versus the particular, and state sovereignty versus humanitarian intervention. It is to be noted that, generally speaking, the debate was theoretical: the literature did not on the whole apply this theory to the practice of human rights in China, as had some articles in the late 1970s. Clearly, it was not yet an appropriate time to consider the application of liberal ideas to China's political realities. But their development at a theoretical level meant that when the time came to implement them, China would be well prepared. In the meantime, debate better equipped it to deal more effectively with the external challenge.

According to one Chinese taxonomy, from 1988 to 1989, four principal areas formed the subject of discussion and debate, each containing subcategories:

1. the concept and content of human rights, the basic nature of bourgeois human rights, and the emergence and development of human rights theory;
2. the Marxist view of human rights: (a) the socialist view of human rights; (b) the social and economic aspect of human rights; (c) the view of human rights as concrete; and (d) the historical, developmental view of human rights;
3. socialism and human rights, considering three basic views of the relationship: (a) that human rights was simply a bourgeois slogan; (b) that

human rights contained within itself the requirements of socialism; and (c) that on the basis of a critique of reactionary bourgeois human rights theory, a scientific view of Marxist human rights could be constructed; and

4. the international protection of human rights: (a) the issue of international human rights law and domestic law; and (b) human rights principles and the basic principles of international law.[19]

The sophistication and diversity of Chinese discourse is best indicated by identifying some of the outer parameters of the debate. The most significant of the literature bearing on this study was the material produced before the publication of the official White Paper in October 1991, as it not only fed into the thinking of the White Paper, but also was not inhibited by it. Chinese diplomat Pang Sen's book was largely written before October 1991, a fact noted in his Introduction. Another important precursor was the Chinese Academy of Social Sciences Symposium in June 1991, which wrestled with, and helped inform, many of the issues later addressed in the White Paper. However, its papers, published as *Dangdai renquan* ("Contemporary Human Rights") did not appear until August 1992, allowing subsequent revision.

For this reason, one of the best guides to the parameters of the pre-White Paper academic debate remains the proceedings of the different conferences, published immediately after their completion in the *Renmin ribao* ("People's Daily") or in legal journals.[20] At the State Education Commission conference in September 1990, debate flourished. As its title suggested, its main purpose was to build a Marxist view of human rights that could counter the human rights diplomacy of capitalist states: however, its proceedings demonstrated many differences of opinion on the scope and content of human rights, albeit on the basis of a common-denominator view that Marxist human rights and bourgeois human rights were in opposition to each other. Already at this early date, some participants spoke of "ren di jiben quanli, juti shuo, ji shengcun, fazhan, pingdeng he ziyou di quanli" (man's basic human rights, specifically, the rights of subsistence, development, equality, and freedom).[21] The way had already been prepared for this basic rights argument in an April 1990 speech at the Fourteenth Conference on the Law of the World by China's expert to the UN Human Rights Sub-Commission, Tian Jin. He pointed out that "the developing countries underscore such collective rights as the right to survival, right of self-determination of nations, right to sovereignty over natural resources, and the right to development."[22] Foreshadowing the content of China's official statement at Vienna, he also contended that "respect for national sovereignty (*guojia zhuquan*) should be the prerequisite for realising human rights."

The right to subsistence was not mentioned in the report on the March

Conference of the Law Society of China, which was couched in rather general and rhetorical language.[23] Nevertheless, the right to subsistence was well established as a basic and prior right by early 1991: on 14 April, during a meeting with former President Jimmy Carter, Premier Li Peng stated that, in China's view, "human rights are primarily the people's right to subsistence (*shengcun quan*) and the national right to independence, and if these two basic conditions were not guaranteed, there would be no human rights to speak of."[24] At this point *shengcun quan* was translated in the *Beijing Review* as "the right to live" rather than "the right to subsist."[25]

By 20 April 1991, at the Conference of the Law Faculty of People's University, the Chinese emphasis on the right to subsistence was well established as one of the major lines of scholarly argument. Six main areas of debate were reported: (1) the significance of theoretical research on human rights questions; (2) the precise content of human rights; (3) the question of how to treat bourgeois human rights theory; (4) the struggle between human rights and international law and international politics; (5) the correct treatment of human rights conditions in China; and (6) the promotion of the theoretical research of human rights questions.[26]

On the question of the content of human rights, conference participants held five main perspectives: (1) the majority of scholars believed that human rights, democracy and freedom were the same in being political concepts: they were not universal, supranational, or without boundaries, but were concrete, and had both a class character and a sovereign character; (2) some scholars understood human rights to be the same as citizens' rights; (3) some scholars believed that human rights included the right to subsistence (*shengcun quan*), to freedom, property, and physical security (*ziwei quan*); (4) some believed that human rights and citizens' rights were not the same: citizens' rights grew out of the basic rights of subsistence, development (*fazhan quan*), and freedom and equality; and (5) still others believed that human rights had a class character, and should be concretely analyzed to reveal that some had a class character and others, "such as the right to subsistence (*shengcun quan*) and personal (*renge*) rights," a common character; these rights were "the common possession of mankind" (46–47).

Finally, the Chinese Academy of Social Sciences Symposium held in June 1991, which convened together seventy specialists and scholars, debated five main issues: the concept of human rights; the boundary line between the Marxist human rights view and the Western view; the analysis and critique of the bourgeois human rights system; human rights protection in socialist China; and the principle of sovereignty and the international protection of human rights.[27] The majority disagreed with the view of some scholars that the subjects of human rights were only workers, peasants, scholars, and nationalists who were loyal socialists; they insisted that even individuals who were enemies of the people had the right to life (*shengming quan*) and to personal rights (*renge quan*). Others held that the subject (*zhuti*) of rights was the citizen, others that the subject of human rights was not the citizen, but all humankind (*yiqie ren*) (121).

Some conference participants argued that human rights were empirical rights (*shiyou quanli*), others that they were law-based (*fading quanli*), others that they were moral rights (*daode quanli*), others that they were essential or "ought" rights (*yingyou quanli*), and still others that they comprised four aspects — essential rights, legal rights, customary rights (*xiguan quanli*), and empirical rights (121). Some believed that rights were the product of the commodity economy; others contested this view. There was a debate over whether human rights were class-based (*jiejixing*) or universal in character (*pubianxing*), or a combination of both (122). There was recognition of Marxism's impact in placing pressure on the capitalist system to improve workers' rights, and thus the function of Marxism in developing the concept of human rights. Some scholars believed that to discuss, research, and propagandize human rights was the way to raise the flag of socialist human rights; others disagreed (123).

Such debates were reflected in individual articles in scholarly legal journals, with a particularly long drawn-out discussion arising from the publication of Zhang Wenxian's essay "Lun renquan di zhuti yu zhuti di renquan" ("On the Subject of Human Rights and the Human Rights of the Subject").[28] This provoked a series of articles appearing in *Zhongguo faxue* ("Chinese Legal Science") over the next few years, focusing in particular on the issue of individual versus collective rights, the priority of rights, and basic and non-basic rights. Zhang, for instance, challenged the idea that economic and social rights were more important, claiming that civil and political rights, as well as economic and social rights, all contained some basic rights. He also disputed the thesis that Marx regarded economic, social, and cultural rights as the basis of civil and political rights.

The most restricted and sensitive aspect of the debate related to the international protection of human rights versus the principle of state sovereignty. The bottom line was general agreement with the official position that state sovereignty (*guojia zhuquan*) could not be undermined under the pretext of international human rights protection. However, there was still room here for considerable scholarly disagreement, even after the publication of the White Papers on human rights and the statement at the Vienna Human Rights Conference in June 1993 by China's Vice-Foreign Minister, Liu Huaqiu. For instance, at the opposite pole of Liu's strong position on state sovereignty stood Li Ming, who argued that the principle of noninterference was difficult to adhere to because the international community was paying increasing attention to the protection of human rights, and because "respect for human rights is a demand of modern times."[29] It is to be noted that Li Ming's article was published in the same month as Liu Huaqiu's statement at the Vienna Human Rights Conference. In between these two positions stood Chinese scholar and UN diplomat Pang Sen, who argued that "respect for, and protection of, human rights was one principle of the United Nations Charter, and respect for each state's sovereignty was also an important principle of the Charter."[30]

The Academy of Social Sciences Symposium of June 1991, and its published papers of 1992, concentrated on this issue. During the Conference, some scholars argued that human rights had national boundaries (*guojie*); others disagreed. The most interesting arguments centered on the relationship between human rights protection and state sovereignty and the question of the universality and the particularity of human rights. Some participants held that the question of international human rights protection and the principle of state sovereignty should not be set up in opposition to each other, but that the international protection of human rights rested on the principle of respect for state sovereignty (*guojia zhuquan*), so that human rights and state sovereignty were one (*liangzhe ju you yi zhixing*).[31] There were five reasons for this: (1) every international treaty was set up on the basis of the sovereign equality of states; (2) every human rights organ was constituted by delegates of sovereign states; (3) only when domestic remedies had been exhausted could human rights organizations receive complaints about human rights abuses; (4) the state could limit human rights through law; and (5) except in the case of a state defeated in war, the international protection of human rights had to receive the consent of the monitored state (123).

Some scholars believed that rights were both universal and particular. Reasons given were that (1) the Universal Declaration of Human Rights laid down universal standards; (2) states had together signed the international human rights treaties; (3) states had participated in the condemnation and sanctioning of states such as South Africa and Israel; and (4) in the areas of the environment, space, and peace, every state participated in international cooperation. Notwithstanding the depth of scholarly disagreement, there was general acceptance of the notion that "human rights were principally a matter of state sovereignty, and the product of the differences in a state's politics, economy, culture, society, history and religion, so that the understanding, explanation and purposes of a state's human rights were different" (123).

In the 1992 volume of the Conference papers, *Dangdai renquan*, most of the contributors recognized that the relationship between human rights and state sovereignty was a crucial issue. Zhang Liang claimed that state sovereignty was the precondition of human rights, without which human rights were not possible, and that state sovereignty often limited individual freedoms. Moreover, in every situation he insisted that the state's rights were always superior to individual rights.[32] Other contributors conceived state sovereignty in more restricted terms as a basic principle of international law and the foundation on which human rights protection should be carried out.[33] The principles were the same, but with a shift in emphasis. Eventually,

Zhang Liang's hard-line interpretation was adopted in the government's human rights statement at Vienna.

By June 1991, all the themes contained in the Chinese government's White Paper on human rights had been thoroughly explored and debated in academic forums. Academic debates were not, however, the only source of official thinking. Articles published in official journals such as the *Beijing Review* or official newspapers like *Renmin ribao* ("People's Daily") gave official sanction to human rights policy positions. Guo Jisi's article entitled "China Promotes Civil Rights" claimed that "the pace of progress in the construction of democracy and law has been especially great since the adoption of the reforms and the open-door policy" and that "the judicial organs have made serious efforts to protect the legitimate rights and interests of the citizens."[34] Against this more liberal position, from 1990 to 1991 official Chinese statements on human rights in international forums, in particular the UN Human Rights Commission, alternated between uncompromising statements on the priority of state sovereignty and national independence and more conciliatory efforts to identify the most important rights, whether the right to development or the principle of the self-determination of peoples.[35] There seemed to be different views on which rights were premises or preconditions of human rights and which rights were merely important rights. There were even constructive calls to the international community by Zhang Yishan to strengthen international cooperation on the formulation of human rights standards. He argued that all rights were indivisible and interdependent, and that it was not acceptable to emphasize only civil and political rights.[36] The White Paper, which provided an official standardization of concepts, simply picked up some themes among these myriad views and excluded others. Although a young scholar, Dong Yunhu, was later given a scholarly award for his development of the concept of the right to subsistence, the seeds of this theory, as argued below, had already been sown in foreign soil, in which Chinese scholars and students had been diligently digging.

The State's Theories

The most important, broadly based, and influential of China's official publications on human rights was the White Paper, *Zhongguo di renquan zhuangkuang* ("Human Rights in China"), published in October 1991.[37] The reasons cited for publishing the first White Paper suggested China's need to defend its human rights conditions, both for internal and external purposes, as well as to institute a new set of priorities that constituted a creative theoretical input. Its purpose as stated in a *Renmin ribao* article was to meet the needs of both Chinese and foreigners who lacked a clear understanding of human rights in China and to provide "a powerful rebuttal and counterattack to those who have spread rumours and made fabrications to attack

China over its human rights situation."[38] The White Paper was considered so important that news of its publication occupied the main headlines and an editorial on the first page of the *Renmin ribao*, the official Party newspaper, which published the whole White Paper over subsequent days.

The preface of the White Paper paid tribute to the activities of the United Nations in setting up human rights standards. However, it also quickly affirmed the values of cultural relativism and the importance of national independence with respect to human rights. On the basis of China's claim that "countries differ in their understanding and practice of human rights," it put forward the basic essence of its theory. This was that "for any country or nation, the right to subsistence is the most important of all human rights, without which the other rights are out of the question." In addition, it was claimed, "without national independence, there would be no guarantee for the people's lives."[39] In other words, China was proposing not a specifically Chinese interpretation of human rights, but a basic common-denominator right that could provide the foundation of universal understanding and experience. Its character as the *fons et origo* of all other rights gave the right to subsistence, a right of the individual, automatic priority over the collective state right to development.

However, China's creativity was not so much a native invention as an adaptation of a theory already in circulation in Western thought. Henry Shue's 1980 concept of the basic rights to subsistence and to physical security had already been widely cited internationally and used as a basis of John Vincent's equally influential work, *Human Rights and International Relations*.[40] It also informed the argument in a Western book on China's human rights completed just after the publication of the White Paper.[41]

Henry Shue fell into a category of philosophers seeking a cluster of core rights that had the status of prior rights (that is, without which other rights could not exist) within the three generations of rights. These rights were foundation rights seen as common to all cultures. This group of thinkers, or "essentialists," distinguished themselves from those who gave priority to one set of rights, like Maurice Cranston, and from the universalists, like Jack Donnelly, who claimed the applicability of "all human rights for all."[42] Shue argued that the guaranteed right to physical security and the guaranteed right to subsistence were "inherent necessities" for the exercise of any other rights.[43] Physical security was defined as a civil right "that is basic not to be subjected to murder, torture, mayhem, rape or assault" (20). The right to subsistence, in contrast, was an economic/social right to "unpolluted air, unpolluted water, adequate food, adequate clothing, adequate shelter and minimal preventive public health care" (23). These rights, Shue argued, were also "basic" in that they represented "everyone's minimum reasonable demands upon the rest of humanity" (19).

According to the Chinese description, *shengcun quan* appeared to represent an amalgam of Shue's right to physical security and right to subsistence.

Literally translated, *shengcun quan* was more properly rendered "right to existence," or "to survival," than "right to subsistence," because its meaning in Chinese combined the notions of physical security and subsistence.[44] However, one twist in the argument occurred during the adaptation of Shue's theory to Chinese experience. China could not place emphasis on the right to physical security in the post-1949 era because, according to Chinese theory, the physical security of the Chinese people had been chiefly undermined during the period of colonialism and foreign exploitation. With the establishment of communist China in 1949, such threats to physical security were seen to have largely disappeared. Second, not only was the right to life of the fetus a contemporary issue in Chinese family planning, but, as has been indicated in an earlier chapter, capital punishment formed a prominent part of the post-1949 Chinese system of legal control. Thus, while the Chinese term *shengcun quan* encapsulated both of Henry Shue's meanings, and literally meant the right to existence rather than to subsistence, the content given it in Chinese discourse focused on its economic and social rights aspects, literally the right to subsistence, rather than on the right to physical security.[45] Paradoxically, therefore, it was this inability to face the implications for current Chinese human rights practice of the civil right to physical security that distinguished the actual content of Chinese theory from Henry Shue's theory. Another specifically Chinese aspect of its claim was that national independence was the precondition for the satisfaction of a prior right.

The Chinese White Paper was thus characterized by a theoretical duality that corresponded to its dual purposes of theoretical offense and defense. On one hand, it projected China's uniqueness, while articulating a prior right seen to have universal, rather than purely specific, application. On the other hand, in its overall structure, as has been observed elsewhere, the White Paper concentrated more on the civil rights issues stressed in Western critiques than on China's own human rights priorities.[46] The achievements it claimed in economic and social rights were more descriptive of the Maoist past than of the real economic and social issues with which China was currently grappling. The paper was a mix of Maoist norms, of new and old priorities of rights and guarantees of rights that either no longer existed in substance or were already at the point of being discarded. The main categories of domestically protected rights it addressed were the right to subsistence; China's political rights; its economic, social, and cultural rights; guarantees of human rights in China's judicial work; the guarantee of the right to work; the citizens' enjoyment of freedom of religious belief; the guarantee of the rights of minority nationalities; family planning and the protection of human rights; and the guarantee of human rights for the disabled. Of these rights, two aspects were later developed into White Papers on the rights of Tibetans and the reform of criminals. Other White Papers followed over succeeding years — on women's rights, on the rights of the child, on family planning — as well as two more general updates on the original White Paper, in 1996 and 1997, and, finally, another on Tibet in 1998.[47]

This mix of Western and Chinese rights priorities was reflected in Chapter 10 of the 1991 White Paper, "Active Participation in International Human Rights Activities." On one hand, it stressed China's conformity with the international human rights regime, and on the other, its nonconformity. Such ambiguity was consistent with its articulated goal of "strengthening international cooperation in the realm of human rights on the basis of mutual understanding and *seeking a common ground while preserving differences.*"[48]

Chinese conformity with the human rights regime was manifested in four principal ways. First was its declared respect for the UN Charter and its Foreign Minister's positive assessment in September 1988 of the Universal Declaration of Human Rights as "the first international instrument which systematically sets forth the specific contents regarding respect for and protection of fundamental human rights. Despite its historical limitations, the Declaration has exerted a far-reaching influence on the development of the post-war international human rights activities and played a positive role in this regard" (58).

Second, China stressed its positive role in UN human rights activities, including its attendance at every Economic and Social Council (ECOSOC) session, and its involvement in the UN Human Rights Commission and Sub-Commission. Third, it claimed it had been active in drafting and formulating international legal instruments on human rights within the United Nations and had sent delegates to participate in working groups charged with drafting these instruments, including the Convention on the Rights of the Child (CROC) and the Convention Against Torture (CAT). Finally, the White Paper emphasized that China had successively "signed, ratified, and acceded to" seven UN human rights conventions.

At the same time, China made clear in the paper its support for the specific rights stressed in the developing world: the right to development; the right to national self-determination; support for the principle of non-interference; and the need for "consideration [to] be given to the differing views on human rights held by countries with different political, economic, and social systems, as well as different historical, religious and cultural backgrounds" (61).

The most significant aspect of the White Paper was that, while it referred to the importance of state sovereignty, it did not bind that principle into an integral part of its new theory. It took issue with the Western view on noninterference: "The argument that the principle of non-interference in international affairs does not apply to the issue of human rights is, in essence, a demand that sovereign states give up their state sovereignty in the field of human rights, a demand that is contrary to international law" (61). However, the principle forming the basis of the right to subsistence was seen to be not state sovereignty (*guojia zhuquan*) but national independence (*guojia duli*). Implicit in this difference was the notion that once the state had independence, the right to subsistence as a basic right was no longer under continual threat. This view of the relationship between national independence and the right to subsistence was sustained in the book published to answer, and expand on, questions emerging from the White Paper.[49] Like the White Paper, it saw national independence as the precondition for the right to subsistence.

By May 1993, however, on the eve of the Vienna Human Rights Conference, this more benign view had evolved into a more state-centric position. In his article in the 31 May *Renmin ribao* on the right to subsistence, Liu Fenzhi of the State Council, one of the authors of the first White Paper, substituted the principle of state sovereignty for the principle of national independence as the precondition for the enjoyment of basic rights. He thereby implied not only the need for national independence but the priority of states' rights over individual human rights, and the continuing need to defend the state's preeminence, a view achieving its full articulation two weeks later in Liu Huaqiu's Vienna statement that "if the sovereignty of a state is not safeguarded, the human rights of its citizens are out of the question, like a castle in the air."[50]

In addition to the development of the concept of state sovereignty, official exegeses of the White Paper enlarged on the main differences between China's view of human rights and those purportedly held in the West. The volume *"Zhongguo di renquan zhuangkuang": Wenti jieda* ("*Human Rights in China*: Answers to Questions") identified the following differences: (1) while China believed human rights standards differed according to economic, historical, and cultural backgrounds, the West believed in a universal standard; (2) on the issue of human rights and state sovereignty, the West, unlike China, did not regard the stipulations on safeguarding state sovereignty encapsulated in Article 2, Paragraph 7 of the Charter as applicable to human rights; (3) whereas China believed the responsibility for the protection of human rights lay with the sovereign state, Western states believed that human rights had no national boundaries; (4) while China believed the Five Principles of Peaceful Coexistence were the basis of relations between states, the West saw human rights as an element in bilateral relations; (5) China denied that rights were abstract and absolute, and saw their protection as based on given social conditions and the protection and constraints of the law, while the West saw human rights as abstract and as not limited by national security or legal protection, even viewing the rights to life and to freedom from torture as nonderogable; (6) China recognized both individual and collective rights, whereas Western states belittled collective rights and emphasized individual rights and freedoms; (7) China emphasized the external aspect of the principle of self-determination, whereas Western states claimed that the beneficiaries of self-determination were not states or governments, but people (*renmin*); (8) China saw the right to development as a collective right bearing on other rights, generating a responsibility in the developed states to assist the developing states, whereas Western states regarded it not as a state right or a collective right, but as an individual right; and (9) China viewed the United Nations as primarily responsible for monitoring the wide-scale abuse of rights of minorities, of colonialism, hegemonism, racism, foreign aggression, and occupation. However, the West wanted to make the United Nations stronger and more efficient to protect human rights and peace and stability, with the ulterior motive of interfering in other states' internal affairs.[51]

China's first human rights White Paper represented not just a standardization of official views but a foundation from which it could refine its evolving human rights diplomacy. That diplomacy extended to both the Western and non-Western world.

The period of Western human rights delegations to China, initiated by the first Australian delegation in July 1991, lasted for three years, and included two Australian delegations, one French, one Swiss, two EC delegations, a Canadian parliamentary delegation, a British delegation, and a Swedish delegation.[52] These visits coincided with the easing of multilateral sanctions against China, and were seen as an alternative to them, deflecting part of the monitoring burden onto individual states: however, their initiation appears to have been one of the more haphazard developments in international human rights diplomacy, being the outcome of informal discussions between Australian and Chinese diplomats in Beijing as to how to improve the overall Australia-China relationship.[53] The practical renunciation of the principle of noninterference in internal affairs that this development represented for China was an example of the contingency and negotiability of its sovereignty in the face of practical diplomatic problems. Developed primarily as a means of protecting China's sovereignty, in the process it had the effect of renegotiating that sovereignty. Between its first visit to China in July 1991 and its second in November 1992, the Australian delegation was able to measure the degree to which China had made concessions to foreign pressures, as well as the changes that had taken place in its human rights institutions (20–23). Taking their cue from the first delegations, most U.S., Canadian, and European state leaders visiting China subsequently included human rights issues on their formal agendas.

The human rights delegations, which virtually ceased in that particular form after President Clinton's delinkage of MFN and human rights in May 1994, represented an important phase in China's interaction with the human rights regime. They provided evidence of China's readiness to make compromises with the international community on human rights when its leadership deemed it necessary. They were also part of a process of mutual education and learning. In lively exchanges, the Chinese government invoked the White Paper as its standard of human rights, and tested its efficacy in encounters with the Western world of human rights. Starting from these basic premises and fundamental differences formulated during three years of intense theoretical debate, and taking into account both the Western and Asian responses, in 1993 China entered the formal arena of multilateral human rights discourse.

Vienna, Bangkok, and the PrepComs: Policy and Process

During 1991 and 1992, as it developed its theory domestically, China had sought to promote and test its views on the right to subsistence and on cultural relativism in the Asia-Pacific region.[54] By July 1991, an Association of Southeast Asian Nations (ASEAN) consensus had been formulated on human rights that agreed that "while human rights is universal in character, implementation in the national context should remain within the competence and responsibility of each country, having regard for the complex variety of economic, social and cultural realities."[55] This consensual position did not refer to the right to subsistence, which was not officially articulated in detail by China until October 1991. However, similarities between the ASEAN view and China's included historical and cultural relativism, the priority of the right to development, the stress on sovereignty and opposition to aid conditionality.

Within this context, a joint statement on 11 January 1992 by China's President, Yang Shangkun, and Malaysia's Prime Minister Mahathir Mohamad, referred not only to the importance of each country's particular values but to the two human rights priorities of development and the corresponding individual right of subsistence.[56] On the same day, China's Foreign Minister Qian Qichen, on a visit to Mali and Guinea, also described the human rights priorities of developing countries as subsistence and development.[57] Apart from bilateral agreements, however, it was not clear that the right to subsistence found collective favor in the Asian region where at that period most states had already moved far beyond a state of "subsistence." In August 1992, State Council official, Liu Fenzhi, did not demur when it was suggested in an interview that the Chinese notion of the priority of the right to subsistence might not be considered appropriate to all the states in the region. In answer, he affirmed that China's human rights position gained its main support from India, Singapore and Malaysia.[58] Moreover, the more open political systems characteristic of most of the ASEAN states represented a crucial difference with China's authoritarian system, so that in arguing their commonality, the ASEAN states and China were forced to highlight their "lowest common denominator: 'Asian-ness' and their status as developing countries."[59] Any attempt China might make to assume leadership of the Asian bloc by promoting the idea of the right to subsistence, however, faced a greater challenge.

Even though its efforts in this respect were ultimately not successful, China's far-ranging bilateral diplomacy in the region at least prepared it for the appropriate strategies to follow when it sought support for its newly honed human rights theories at the Bangkok Preparatory Meeting in March 1993 and at the UN Human Rights Conference in Vienna in June 1993. China's contribution to the Bangkok Meeting was consistent with the desire of the participating Asian/Arab states to formulate a theory of human rights with distinct "regional characteristics." The formal Chinese statement was therefore in line with these aims and showed the effects of its earlier regional diplomacy. However, at Vienna, China took a considerably harder line than at Bangkok.

Historical Background: China and the Preparatory Committees for the UN World Human Rights Conference in Vienna

The World Human Rights Conference began as an idea floated unofficially at the United Nations in Geneva in 1988 and was promoted by a small number of enthusiasts in the heady environment of the 1989 political developments in Eastern Europe, the former Soviet Union, and China.[60] It was originally conceived by Jan Martensen, the UN Under-Secretary General for Human Rights, and was supported by Germany, which was eager to host it.[61] The gearing down of East-West confrontation, moves towards democratization in Eastern Europe, the appearance of more liberal regimes in Africa and Latin America, and increased consensus in the Security Council were not only the product of human rights pressures but developments that increasingly promised to facilitate the promotion of such norms. The idea of the Vienna Conference gained momentum, as a function of both apathy and optimism, as it passed through the various levels of the UN hierarchy. Most states showed little enthusiasm for the project, but passively acquiesced to the initiative of those who believed that such favorable international conditions provided the opportunity both for an assessment of the progress made since the first World Conference in Tehran in 1968 and for a "great leap forward" in the development of the system for the promotion and protection of human rights.[62]

In December 1990, the General Assembly adopted Resolution 45/155 on the holding of the conference and its main objectives. China initially supported the convening of the Conference and hoped that it would "further promote the universal realization of human rights and basic freedoms."[63] Over the next three and a half years the Preparatory Committee (PrepCom) created by the General Assembly held four sessions. In addition, regional intergovernmental preparatory meetings were held in Tunis, San José, and Bangkok, as well as dozens of small meetings in different parts of the world. Their purpose was to conduct analyses of past achievements and failures in human rights promotion and to make recommendations for improved mechanisms.

By the time the Vienna Conference was held, however, hopes for a great leap forward in human rights were being viewed as illusory in the context of an international environment increasingly ridden with ethnic conflict and beset in both North and South with economic and social problems.[64] In this environment, the areas neglected in the previous decade, the issue of self-determination and the promotion of the right to development and economic, social and cultural rights, assumed prominence. Thus, China was influential in pushing for priority to be given to the issue of the relationship between human rights and development.[65] Problems of self-determination offered a challenge to the entire UN system, and were unlikely to be resolved by the Conference. Yet, the working definition of human rights as primarily civil and political rights was destabilized both by the easing of East-West differences, which gave greater political respectability to the issue of economic and social rights, and by mounting concern in both North and South about such issues as unemployment and the social safety net. It became likely that the Conference might be an appropriate forum in which the right to development, emphasized by Latin American, African, and Asian states, could finally be addressed in a meaningful and concrete way. In such a dynamic normative environment, however, UN officials and Western governments increasingly expressed anxiety lest, in the process of expanding the working concept of human rights, the Conference might also diminish, rather than promote, the effectiveness of existing human rights mechanisms. They were also concerned about the possible watering down of such concepts as the universality of human rights.

Such fears seemed borne out by the outcome of the four Preparatory Committees and the regional Meetings. A major source of contention at the Third PrepCom session was the question of NGO participation. In the end, it was decided that only NGOs with consultative status would be allowed to attend regional meetings. However, the final interpretation of eligibility was extended from those with headquarters in the region to those involved in the specified area of activity.

In the light of the failure of the Second PrepCom to adopt an agenda for the Conference, diplomats had worked hard in the summer of 1992 to find a reasonable solution.[66] An informal paper was circulated by the African and Latin American groups that contained a list of key rights: the right to self-determination and elimination of foreign occupation, racism, xenophobia, and all forms of racial discrimination, including apartheid. Western countries had already made concessions to this document in negotiations when Asian states circulated their own draft proposals that, besides the above issues, emphasized terrorism, national particularities and traditions, respect for differing judicial systems and respect for national sovereignty (12). This became known as the Indian Proposal, which, in the opinion of Adrien-Claude Zoller, "aim[ed] to challenge the principle of universality of rights and other hard-won acquirements of the UN human rights system" (13). Despite Western opposition to the list of key rights in the Latin American draft, there were several times when, as consensus was reportedly on the point of being reached, the Asian group met to formulate new requirements to achieve further concessions (12). On the last day of the meeting, the Austrian delegate announced that the Western group would accept the whole draft without any reservations in exchange for a concession from the Asian group.

The Austrian proposal was subsequently adopted, but at this point the Asian group chose to call for a modification of the original agreement. Nearly all the diplomats from the other groups voiced their disappointment, but it was too late to restart negotiations and the Third PrepCom session ended "in failure and confusion," with no agenda for the Conference (12).

The Director of the International Service for Human Rights, Zoller, drew from this experience the moral that "the *consensus requirement* generally applied at this kind of gathering permits *a small group* of Governments to stand in the way of positive developments. It only takes a few 'troublemakers' in the regional group to draw the silent majority into a strategy of confrontation with the other groups. In this case, *Syria, Yemen, India, Pakistan, Indonesia, Singapore and China* transformed the consensus rule into a right of veto and tried to force other delegations to accept their proposal wholesale, even if this meant jeopardizing the success of the entire meeting" (12). He added that "it is obvious that the hard-line states only want to attend the World Conference if it provides an opportunity to dismantle the system and mechanisms which can bring them to book" (13).

Despite this lack of cooperation, in the intervening UN General Assembly session prior to the World Conference, China joined the consensus on many issues such as effective implementation of international human rights instruments, the setting up of regional human rights arrangements, the strengthening of the Human Rights Centre, the strengthening of UN action in the field of human rights and the combating of religious intolerance.[67] In addition, the Conference itself was saved by the timely intervention of its Secretary-General, and then Director of the UN Human Rights Centre, Ibrahima Fall, at the Fourth PrepCom (19 April–7 May 1993). His crucial role at this time once again illustrated the importance of individual human agency in achieving progress on human rights. On the eve of the Conference, Fall reportedly worked day and night to present a working document produced by the Secretariat.[68] This was an unusual initiative necessitated by the Third PrepCom's failure to produce its own draft.[69] An informal working group of twenty members was set up with China, India, Pakistan, Syria, and Yemen representing the Asian group. At the end of the third week, a draft Vienna Declaration was adopted, marked by numerous brackets that represented areas of controversy. Sources of contention included the universality of human rights; the historical debate over civil and political rights versus economic, social and cultural rights; the right to development; the right to self-determination; the right to intervene; the rights of women and the rights of children (issues affecting cultural traditions of some states); and the issue of the High Commissioner for Human Rights.[70]

China and the Bangkok Preparatory Meeting of Asia-Pacific Governments, 29 March–2 April 1993

The defaulting states named by Zoller for the most part formed part of the "Asian" group, constituting forty-nine Asian and Middle East governments which, from 29 March to 2 April 1993, met in Bangkok to produce a regional contribution to the Vienna Conference. China was elected as a Vice-Chairman of the Meeting and took a leading role in the Drafting Committee, a body headed by the chief delegate from Iran and including the chief delegate from Burma. For most of the preceding NGO meeting of 25–28 March, Human Rights in China, based in New York, was the only NGO organization representing China. On the last day, two men representing the China Society for the Human Rights Studies (CSHRS), formed two weeks before in China, attended the NGO Conference, and as in the subsequent Vienna Conference, China's former Ambassador to Bern and expert on the Human Rights Sub-Commission, Tian Jin, joined it for the final plenary sessions.[71] This development was not objected to by other NGOs, since it was believed that "the more the Chinese government encourage[d] the emergence of pseudo-NGOs, the greater their tacit acknowledgement of the value of non-Party organizations."[72]

It has been observed that the Asian governments' inability to agree on an agenda prior to the Bangkok Conference, and the difficulty of negotiations on their declaration, indicated the disunity among governments in the region.[73] Despite this disunity, even greater division was apparent between states and their NGOs, which outnumbered the governments present by more than two to one. In the words of one leading Western NGO representative, at Bangkok "it was clear that there was no single 'Asian' position on anything, and that when it c[ame] to human rights, the most important distinctions [were] neither the East-West nor the North-South, but between the powerful and the powerless."[74] A central issue dividing Asian governments and NGOs was universality. Other issues included the indivisibility of human rights, the use of human rights as a condition for aid, the attitude toward NGOs, and self-determination.[75]

China's Statement, 30 March 1993

Under the umbrella of this major contradiction, the principal interstate division at Bangkok saw Japan, Thailand, Nepal, South Korea, and the Philippines assuming a more liberal interpretation of human rights, and China, Indonesia, Iran, and Burma taking a more uncompromising stand.[76] China's statement, delivered by Ambassador Jin Yongjian at Bangkok on 30 March 1993, formed an interesting contrast with the final Bangkok Declaration, and both differed in unexpected ways from the subsequent Chinese statement at the Fourth PrepCom on 21 April 1993.

Ambassador Jin's Bangkok speech obscured the boundary between the Chinese and the consensual "Asian" view.[77] It connected Asia with a human rights tradition by emphasizing its prior involvement in human rights concerns. It underlined Asia's "significant achievements in the universal promotion and protection of these rights" as early as 1955 through the Bandung Declaration. It anticipated the achievements of the Vienna Conference in reviewing, evaluating, summing up, and "putting forward feasible and positive proposals" for "the final realization of the full enjoyment of all human rights by all peoples." It called on the Asian countries to "first demonstrate solidarity among themselves," and stressed two sets of priorities. The first were collective Maoist human rights values of opposition to racism, colonialism, foreign aggression and occupation. The second was state sovereignty, defined as "the basis for the realization of human rights." Ambassador Jin thus retracted the earlier priority of the rights of subsistence and national independence established in the 1991 White Paper. The right to development was mentioned, but only as one right among others. Not only was subsistence not cited as a prior right, it was described as a condition rather than a right. This signal change was probably due to the less than favourable regional reception which had greeted China's earlier defined priorities.

Ambassador Jin's statement mentioned universality only in the context cited above, but acknowledged the interdependence and indivisibility of all rights and the necessity for international cooperation. However, the most interesting aspect of his speech was the use of the principle of the right of self-determination to promote cultural relativism. Rather than referring to the historical and culturally bound nature of rights, he argued that the right of self-determination, according to which countries and peoples could freely choose their political and economic systems and their own road to development, was a basis for cooperation between Asian states. Therefore, he argued, respect for the right of self-determination had an "important role" in "safeguarding human rights and fundamental freedoms." He thus approached cultural relativism from a new direction. The interesting twist in this argument was that it represented a shift from China's traditional revolutionary emphasis on the external meaning of self-determination, that is, of a state's right to independence and freedom from interference, to the internal meaning of self-determination, or the right of citizens to influence their political system. This more liberal view was presumably due to China's concern to avoid criticism of its policies in Tibet during the Meeting, and to link its interests with Indonesia which had similar concerns with respect to Timor.[78]

The Bangkok Declaration

The Bangkok Declaration has been subject to considerable Western and NGO criticism.[79] One leading Western NGO representative has called it an "execrable official document . . . a patchwork of provisions which some authoritarian governments did not want and have no intention of upholding . . . provisions which [were] hypocritical in the extreme . . . and provisions which reflect[ed] regional interests."[80] Nevertheless, in all aspects apart from the issue of self-determination, it was more enlightened than the Chinese statement. It exhibited a notable ambiguity, balancing liberal clauses against conservative ones. However, the distance between these norms was in itself an indication of the breadth of the parameters of human rights concepts held within the region.

The Declaration not only reaffirmed states' commitment to the principles contained in the UN Charter and the Universal Declaration of Human Rights, but welcomed the increased international attention to human rights. It stressed the universality of human rights, their interdependence and indivisibility, and the need to give them equal treatment. It linked economic and social rights with the "growing trend to democracy and the promotion and protection of human rights." It acknowledged the important role of international institutions, the importance of cooperation and dialogue between governments and NGOs, and reiterated the need to explore the possibilities of establishing regional arrangements for the promotion and protection of human rights in Asia. It called for international cooperation for education and training in the field of human rights, for national institutions, and for the strengthening of the UN Centre for Human Rights.

At the same time, under Paragraph 5, the Bangkok Declaration emphasized the principles of state sovereignty and noninterference, although not, as in the Chinese position, as a prior right. While recognizing that human rights were universal in nature, it insisted that "they must be considered in the context of a dynamic and evolving process of international norm-setting, bearing in mind the significance of national and regional particularities and various historical, cultural and religious backgrounds" (Paragraph 8). It also recognized that states had "the primary responsibility for the promotion and protection of human rights through appropriate infrastructure and mechanisms," yet cautioned that "remedies must be sought and provided primarily through such mechanisms and procedures."[81]

Like China's statement, the Bangkok Declaration expressed opposition to racial discrimination, racism, colonialism, and foreign aggression and supported the right to development, but gave these lower priority (Paragraphs 14 and 17–19 respectively). It introduced opposition to aid conditionality, something not mentioned in Ambassador Jin's speech. It also gave the right of self-determination a completely different interpretation, insisting on its external definition and limiting it to peoples under foreign domination and as a right of the state. It claimed that "the right to self-determination is applicable to peoples under alien or colonial domination and foreign occupation, and should not be used to undermine the territorial integrity, national sovereignty and political independence of States."

The final Bangkok Declaration was adopted by consensus, even though Japan and Cyprus expressed their reservations, disagreement, or disappointment with parts of the document. According to diplomats' reports, the consensus was achieved due to the solidarity of ASEAN delegates, who formed a bridge between Japan and hard-line states such as China, Burma and Iran.[82] Considerable divergence was thus illustrated within Asian views of human rights, suggesting a degree of complicity, and even open support, among some with the Western emphasis on individual civil and political rights. The Declaration also offered formal evidence of the distance between China's position and the consensual Asian view, as well as of the failure of the Chinese view to prevail.

China's Statement, Fourth Preparatory Committee, 21 April 1993

Three weeks after his speech at Bangkok, China's Ambassador, Jin Yongjian, made a second statement on his country's human rights goals at the Fourth Session of the Preparatory Committee for the World Conference.[83] On this occasion, he focused on China's view of what the final Vienna Declaration should contain. His speech revealed interesting contrasts with his earlier Bangkok statement and interesting similarities with the Bangkok Declaration. It reflected the degree to which China's official view had been modified as a result of multilateral interaction at Bangkok.

In contrast with China's Bangkok speech, the statement on 21 April 1993 entitled "China's View on the Final Document" did not presume to represent the Asian region. Nor did it insist on Asian solidarity. Yet, unlike the 30 March speech, it showed considerable sensitivity to the consensual Asian view. It omitted any reference to self-determination, thus avoiding the contradiction between China's internal definition in its Bangkok speech and the Bangkok Declaration's external definition. It no longer gave priority to Maoist anticolonial and antiracist values and, although continuing to accord priority to state sovereignty, no longer defined it as the basis on which all human rights depended.

The extent to which China had adjusted its views to converge with the consensual Asian view was reflected in the large number of Bangkok Declaration articles Ambassador Jin's 21 April speech echoed. He itemized seven main issues that he wished the final document of the World Conference in Vienna to contain. The first consisted of a summary of many of the points contained in Paragraphs 1–7 of the Bangkok Declaration, but represented them as Chinese views rather than as those of the Declaration. They included a reference to China's opposition to aid conditionality, something missing from the 30 March speech. Likewise, Ambassador Jin's second point, on cultural relativism, was framed in terms similar to Paragraph 8 of the Bangkok Declaration, although it omitted the Declaration's concession on universality. His third point, on the interdependence and indivisibility of rights and the need to give equal emphasis to all categories of human rights, echoed the Bangkok Declaration's Paragraph 10. This concession represented a change from China's Bangkok speech, which had sought to establish a hierarchy of rights.

The fourth point of the 21 April speech placed Maoist values of opposition to colonialism and racial discrimination in a subordinate position, echoing Paragraph 14 of the Bangkok Declaration. The fifth point, on the right to development, corresponded to Paragraphs 17–19 of the Bangkok Declaration. Once again, Jin made no reference to the right to subsistence. His sixth point, on the need to protect the rights of vulnerable groups, echoed Paragraphs 22–23 of the Bangkok Declaration and represented an addition not found in China's Bangkok speech. The final seventh point, on the necessity to rationalize UN human rights mechanisms, coincided with Paragraph 28 of the Declaration.

Such parallels did not mean that China's position had been transformed by the Bangkok Meeting. Crucial differences remained, and they were to be found not in any new concepts or old ideas in Ambassador Jin's speech, but in the paragraphs of the Bangkok Declaration his speech omitted to cite. It left out the Declaration's recommendations regarding universality, the right of self-determination, the need for effective monitoring of human rights, the need for environmental protection, and Paragraph 21, condemning terrorism. The most obvious omissions regarded the institutional recommendations in Paragraphs 24–30 of the Bangkok Declaration. Ambassador Jin failed to endorse its support for national institutions and regional arrangements promoting human rights, and its calls for dialogue and cooperation between governments and NGOs, and for strengthening the UN Centre for Human Rights.

Within the Bangkok context, textual analysis thus reveals a degree of responsiveness in China's human rights policy to regional values. It also indicates a reservoir of remaining differences, many of them related to institutional developments, both domestic and international, that had the potential to prise control over domestic human rights conditions from the grip of the Chinese state. Whether this responsiveness constituted anything more than a temporary diplomatic adjustment, however, could only be measured by means of a longer-term comparison between these statements and Vice-Foreign Minister Liu Huaqiu's speech on 15 June before the UN World Human Rights Conference in Vienna.

Chapter 6
The UN World Human Rights Conference at Vienna

> During the World Conference on Human Rights, China expounded its position and views, and helped achieve the smooth adoption of the Vienna Declaration and Program of Action.
> — Ren Yanshi, 28 October 1997

The UN World Human Rights Conference at Vienna in June 1993 presented the world in its own image, a rich, diverse, contradictory, and kaleidoscopic picture at once inspirational and profoundly repugnant.[1] It caught the realities of the evolving post–Cold War era, which had not even begun to make sense of the epidemic of ethnic conflict and destruction of the basic rights to life and subsistence that were its inheritance. Against this it counterposed the heady, ideal vision of the theme of "All Human Rights for All." It revealed the gap between that vision, itself espoused by states as well as NGOs, and the actual will of states to implement it.

A solemn forum of the international community, the Conference offered sophisticated studies of each state's political philosophy, and basic justifications of each state's right to rule. It was a colorful bazaar of NGOs, exposing the dirty, ragged, and bloodstained linen of the world for the world to see. Its aims were many: to review and assess the progress made in human rights since the adoption of the Universal Declaration of Human Rights; to examine the relationship between development and the enjoyment of economic, social, cultural, civil, and political rights; to examine ways and methods of improving the implementation of existing human rights standards and instruments; to evaluate the effectiveness of the methods and mechanisms used by the United Nations; to formulate concrete recommendations for improving these mechanisms; and to ensure the necessary financial and other resources for their promotion and protection by the UN.[2] At the most basic level, John Pace, Coordinator of the Conference and Head of the

Centre for Human Rights, announced the aim of expanding the process started in the 1970s of "bringing home human rights." As he explained: "this process really is tantamount to bringing human rights back into the UN Charter. The commitment is there on paper, but it's not there in spirit. The idea is to bring the Charter to bear in its full sense . . . and to give the promotion of fundamental human rights the same priority as you give to the maintenance of international peace and security and to do so because they are complementary; if you destroy one, then you destroy it all."[3]

He estimated the basic criterion of the Conference's success as "the degree to which the final document reflects truly the common will of governments . . . wherever that is placed. What is needed is a solid point of departure, whether high or low."[4] The only stipulation in this quest for common ground was a gentleman's agreement not to raise country-specific issues and to maintain consensus.

Conference Secretary-General, Ibrahima Fall, brought thematic coherence to the proceedings by conferring beforehand with states' Ambassadors on the United Nations interest in six matters: the question of universality versus particularity; the establishment of new human rights institutions raised by the UN Human Rights Centre; the question of resources; the question of the relationship between development, democracy, and human rights; the issue of conditionality; and the character of the new mechanisms to be set in place.[5]

Behind the formal speeches, the Conference was a political forum involving an intricate process of both power play and mutual accommodation. The power play, engaged in mainly by a core group of Asian and Arab states in opposition to a caricatured "Western" human rights position, but also involving a vigorous Western (and particularly U.S.) defense, explored the political vacuum left by the ending of the Cold War. As one observer commented, "the world is in Vienna, jostling for positions as human rights becomes a new vehicle for defining political relationships."[6] Mutual accommodation, in contrast, sought to bridge the East-West divide still in the process of dissolution after the Cold War, and to mute North-South differences. At least during the Conference proceedings, the North-South divide became differentiated and blurred, with both developed and developing states mixing and merging their positions. The outer parameters of the Cold War debate were still maintained by the U.S. and China, with the U.S. exaltation of the virtues of democracy and the formal hard-line Chinese reaffirmation of the principles of sovereignty, self-determination of peoples from colonial domination, and noninterference in internal affairs. Other states reportedly taking a hard-line position in drafting negotiations included Cuba, Indonesia, Iraq, Libya, Malaysia, Burma, North Korea, the Sudan, Vietnam and Yemen.[7] Yet, contrary to anxious predictions before the Conference that North-South positions would harden, the rest of the world, the majority of states, distributed themselves across a wide spectrum of human rights positions.[8] Some of the states that retained their emphasis on local traditions and culture as determinants of human rights values, like Indonesia and Singapore, nevertheless argued their case persuasively on the basis of their familiarity with Western human rights tradition.[9]

Despite the hard-line position of a core of states, the chief Conference divide, as at the Bangkok Meeting, was less between the states of the North and South and more between states, particularly those of the South, and their NGOs. The emergence of civil society in many states of the South that were experiencing different rates of economic and political liberalization had produced an increasing number of organizations defending the individual's civil, political, economic, and social rights against the state's own championing of communitarian and collective, state-defined, rights. At Vienna, these local African, Asian, and Latin American NGOs found common cause with their Western counterparts, who likewise extended their conceptual horizons. This was particularly so in the case of the groups of the Asia-Pacific area: of all the regional NGO declarations preceding the Vienna Conference, the Bangkok NGO Declaration had been "the most unequivocal in its support for the universality and indivisibility of human rights."[10] This process of mutual accommodation was not wholly peaceful, being partly the outcome of some NGO infighting. Nevertheless, the greater permeability of national boundaries in relation to human rights, articulated in the opening address by the UN Secretary-General, Boutros Boutros-Ghali, was underlined by increased NGO solidarity, and exposed the elites of the South to further pressure, not only from external sources but from within.

The response of these elites to NGO pressures varied. On the one hand, there was a formal acceptance of the pressures, evinced in the establishment just before the Vienna Conference of national Human Rights Commissions by states such as Indonesia, or of officially established "NGOs" by states such as China. On the other hand, the elites organized simultaneous attempts to negate these pressures. Thus, a number of Asian and Arab states at Vienna, and in particular China, attempted to limit the participation of NGOs in the drafting process.

Contradictions abounded at the Conference, characterized as it was by the parallel struggle for power and for mutual accommodation, and presiding over an ideal world of the expanding right to rights and the real world of increased abuse of the fundamental right to life. As it proceeded, underlying tensions often erupted. Initial obstacles in drafting the Final Draft Declaration and Draft Program of Action were presented by the debate over universality versus historical, cultural, and political particularity, a North-South disagreement going back to first principles that was finally surmounted, and by the notion of conditionality, the tying of human rights to technical assistance and trade. Other sources of controversy included the principle of the right of self-determination and the question of whether or not to establish the position of UN High Commissioner for Human Rights.

China and the Vienna Conference Process

As a Vice-Chairman of the Vienna Conference, China played an important role in its proceedings. Even before the formal opening of the Conference on 14 June 1993, it dominated the political agenda and procedural debate. To some extent this was a role forced on it by the Austrian government's invitation to the Dalai Lama and other Nobel Peace laureates to attend the opening ceremonies. To a larger extent, as argued, it was a role China had already carved out for itself at Bangkok and the PrepComs, and one anticipated in the position outlined by its leaders in the days leading up to the Conference. The importance China placed on the Conference was suggested by the size of its delegation, not much smaller than that of the U.S. with two representatives, six alternate representatives, and twenty advisers.[11] The precise timing of the Conference created difficulties for a China intent on a favorable decision by the International Olympic Committee in its choice of host country for the year 2000 Olympics and concerned to deflect criticism of its human rights record. Circumstantial developments and issues of principle as well as a fear of defeat and an unwillingness to be seen to make open concessions combined to place it in a combative and publicly inflexible diplomatic position.

This rigidity was signaled some days before the Conference. In an interview on 10 June 1993, China's Vice-Minister for Foreign Affairs, Liu Huaqiu, declared that the Conference "should reflect different political systems, economic and social as well as historical, religious and cultural differences of countries."[12] He said it was "natural that different countries could have different interpretations on the question of human rights." Although he hoped that the Conference would allow the promotion of human rights for all people, he denounced the use of human rights for political purposes. On the eve of the Conference, the *Renmin ribao* attacked the proposal for a High Commissioner for Human Rights that would be debated during its proceedings: "All attempts to put in place a power or a supranational organization could compromise the foundation of modern international law and eventually lead to the disintegration of the international community."[13]

The article insisted that "the realisation of human rights must be guaranteed by each country." The possibility that, unlike the situation pertaining in Bangkok, China's statement at Vienna would include the right to subsistence had already been foreshadowed by the publication of a *Renmin ribao* article entitled, "The Development of the Right to Subsistence Is a Great Contribution to Human Rights Theory," by Liu Fenzhi, one of the authors of the 1991 White Paper.[14]

At the Conference, China's problem with Tibet was the initial source of its unfavorable publicity. The cancellation by UN authorities of the Austrian government's invitation to the Dalai Lama to attend the opening ceremony had become the focal point of the "upstairs-downstairs" differences that emerged between UN and government authorities meeting in preparation for the Conference on the first floor of the Austria Centre, and the NGO Forum meeting on the ground floor.

In its initial plenary session at the opening of the NGO Conference on 10 June, the Forum had early rejected UN guidelines not to raise the human rights abuses of specific countries in its deliberations, since, without mention of specific countries, the actual abuses could not be raised. NGOs thus became incensed by early rumors that the Dalai Lama had been excluded from the Conference due to Chinese pressure. These rumors were confirmed on 11 June, when the Austrian Foreign Minister, Alois Mock, confirmed that the Dalai Lama had been invited by the Austrian government to attend the opening ceremonies of the World Conference, an invitation canceled by Ibrahima Fall, Conference Secretary-General.[15] On the same day, about two hundred NGO representatives from both North and South demonstrated outside the Austria Centre, and three hundred signatures protesting the decision were handed to UN authorities. NGOs also held their own Joint Planning Committee responsible for blocking the Dalai Lama from participating in the NGO Forum.

A second issue that dogged the Conference, the question of NGO participation in drafting the final document, was also a focus of government debate throughout 11 June, with Asian governments reported by observers to be opposed to any NGO involvement. Some observers predicted a split between Asian and other regional groupings after the meetings.[16] It was reported that on 13 June, after informal government meetings had reached a consensus allowing NGO representatives to observe closed sessions of the Drafting Committee, China, which had reportedly consistently lobbied against an NGO presence, reopened the issue and threatened to take it to the Credentials Committee.[17]

On the morning of 12 June, a demonstration outside the Austria Centre linked these two issues, which both related to China. Chanting "Don't Silence NGOs," demonstrators protested both the restriction on NGO participation and the exclusion of the Dalai Lama. That morning, a South resolution, which received a standing ovation, was put to the NGO Forum plenary: "This Plenary of the NGO Forum unanimously extends an invitation to his holiness the Dalai Lama to attend the Conference." After unsuccessful attempts to reply immediately, at the conclusion of the morning's session, a representative of the NGO from China, the China Society for Human Rights Studies, asserted that the unanimous resolution to invite the Dalai Lama was invalid, since the Dalai Lama was not only a religious figure but a political figure who sought to split China. He said it was out of order to invite the Dalai Lama: his intervention met with boos from the few people left in the NGO conference room.[18]

The Chinese NGO was well represented at the NGO Forum, particularly in the plenaries of the final day. It was one of a number of Asian NGOs described by other NGOs as GANGOs (government-appointed NGOs) or GONGOs (government-organized NGOs), which were seen as a new phenomenon at the Conference.[19] They were described as "Trojan horses for anxious governments who want to keep an eye on what their detractors are saying at the largest forum for the human rights debate in twenty-five years."[20] The activities of the Chinese NGO were criticized by Xiao Qiang of the New York-based organization, Human Rights in China, for their clear political agenda. He commented that it had limited its participation in the Conference to supporting Chinese government policies on issues like Tibet.[21]

In its brochure, the China Society for Human Rights Studies described itself as a "nationwide organization composed of Chinese experts, researchers, institutes and organizations engaged in human rights studies" that had been set up in January 1993.[22] Its aims were "to discuss human rights theories, study the development of human rights in China, promote research work all over the country, publish research work of high academic standard, keep informed of the development of human rights studies and activities in the world and carry out international cooperation and exchanges in human rights studies." This view of the society as composed of academics and of representatives of unions, women's and other mass organizations was also echoed at a press conference with its chairman, Zhu Muzhi, at the end of 1993.[23] The Society's brochure stated that "human rights is one of the major issues of the international community" and that the China Society for Human Rights Studies was willing to establish contact with human rights research institutes of other countries to "promote mutual understanding." Its financial sources consisted of "membership dues, donations from individuals and organizations, and other legal incomes."[24]

Nevertheless, the membership of the society's delegation in Vienna gave the impression of an official delegation. The leader was Li Yuanchao, a high-level secretary in the Chinese Communist Youth League.[25] Other members included Xu Ying, a member of the government-funded Party school in Beijing; Li Baodong, a graduate of Johns Hopkins University who was described as a research fellow, but who had spent five years as a diplomat in the Chinese embassy in Washington; and Li Wufeng, also described as a research fellow. Li Baodong later represented China in the 1997 session of the UN Human Rights Commission. On the whole, its members were reticent about the details of their organization, referring all inquiries to Li Baodong.[26] Xu, however, did not mask his opposition to the Dalai Lama in a newspaper interview, nor did he accept that China was guilty of grave abuses in Tibet: "On the whole, China's human rights record is better than the United States," he said "Tibet's human rights record under the Dalai Lama was terrible, most cruel. It's only after decades of construction and effort by the Chinese that Tibet has made rapid progress politically and socially."[27]

Apart from the Tibetan issue, the China Society for Human Rights Studies became involved in other problems. On the final afternoon plenary of the NGO Forum, Jose Ramos Horta, special representative of the National Council of Maubere (East Timor) Resistance, proposed a minute of silence to honor the victims of torture and human rights abuses, including those in East Timor and Tibet. As the NGO representatives rose spontaneously to their feet, the only people to remain seated were the dozen or so members of the Chinese NGO, including the expert from China at the UN Human Rights Sub-Commission, Tian Jin, and Chinese journalists.[28] At the opening day of the formal Conference, when the prized tickets to sit in the main conference hall were to be allocated, a dispute broke out between Li Bao-dong, who claimed the "China tickets," and Xiao Qiang of Human Rights in China. Xiao Qiang, a member of the Asia-Pacific NGO Coordinating Committee, argued that the passes should be distributed only to independent NGOs. He was supported in his stance by other NGO delegates. At this point, Li Baodong pulled the tickets out of the coordinator's hands and "had to be physically restrained."[29]

At the conclusion of the NGO Forum on 12 June, the plenary adopted the report by the general rapporteur Manfred Nowak, comprising a series of recommendations issuing from the thematic workshops. These were to be presented to the main Conference by a liaison committee. The next day, Secretary-General Ibrahima Fall announced that a certain number of places would be reserved for NGOs in the plenary and the main committee. On the same day the Austrian Foreign Minister, Alois Mock, declared that this would be the first time that the NGOs would be participating in the Conference "on an equal footing and as partners of government." He added that although the Austrian government had invited Nobel Peace laureates, including the Dalai Lama, to the UN Conference, it was up to the UN rules of procedure to determine what happened with Conference facilities.

The latter issue was taken up by Pierre Sané, the Secretary-General of Amnesty International, as delegates began arriving for the opening ceremonies at the Austria Centre on the morning of 14 June. He announced the decision of the other laureates to boycott the ceremonies in sympathy with the Dalai Lama's exclusion and stated: "This Conference is about human rights and we are sending the wrong message to the world . . . we want to revive the agenda and prepare new mechanisms and we start by barring a man of peace." He said that it was unacceptable that the authorities "give in" to China because of business interests, when they would not give in to other states.[30]

China was not, however, seen as the only impediment to Conference harmony. The Director of International Service for Human Rights, Adrien-Claude Zoller, identified Syria, Yemen, Iran, Iraq, Pakistan, Malaysia and Croatia as other examples of states which were "trying to hinder the outcome of this conference."[31] His words echoed former U.S. President Jimmy Carter's observation the day before that "Iran, some elements in Indochina, Iraq, Indonesia, China, Cuba, Mexico, Colombia . . . have always either resisted the application of human rights standards or they've strongly resisted outside inquiries into their internal policies."[32] The former President later received a standing ovation from the delegates of every region at the formal Conference at the conclusion of his keynote speech.

An impressive attempt to bridge the views of the different state groupings was made by the UN Secretary-General, Boutros Boutros-Ghali, in his opening address to the Conference on 14 June.[33] He identified the "three imperatives of the Vienna Conference" as "universality, guarantees, democratization" and declared that "there can be no sustainable development without promoting democratization and thus, without respect for human rights." Democracy was "the private domain of no one" and could take many forms in order to accommodate local realities more effectively.

In an even-handed critique of North and South, the Secretary-General observed that "some states constantly try to hijack or confiscate human rights." But, he stated, "human rights give rise to a new legal permeability. They should thus not be considered either from the viewpoint of absolute sovereignty or from the viewpoint of political interference." He warned that no state had the right to expect absolute respect from the international community, "when it is tarnishing the noble concept of sovereignty by openly putting that concept to a use that is rejected by the conscience of the world and by the law." He continued: "When sovereignty becomes the ultimate argument invoked by authoritarian regimes to undermine the rights and liberties of men, women and children, away from public view, then—I say it seriously—that sovereignty is already condemned by history."

However, neither the procedural nor the substantive issues could be resolved by diplomatic words. A last-minute invitation to the Dalai Lama from NGOs to address them brought a swift Chinese response. A few hours before his appearance on 15 June at the Amnesty International tent and his tour of the NGO area of the Austria Centre, China warned Austria of the possible negative consequences of permitting the Dalai Lama to speak on UN territory. It was rumored that these threats included a querying of the trade agreement recently signed by China and Austria. China's Ministry of Foreign Affairs declared that the presence of the Dalai Lama went directly against the objectives of the event, and that to allow him to speak might endanger the continuation of the Conference.[34] Vice-Foreign Minister Liu Huaqiu, leader of China's delegation, stated that "the Dalai Lama is not a religious figure. He is a political exile who wants to divide China. Austria should take notice of this." The Austrian Chancellor, Franz Vranitzky, replied that "we don't accept any criticism from China concerning the Dalai Lama's presence in Austria" (1).

The Chinese delegation was reported to have left the building while the Dalai Lama toured the NGO area. In keeping with UN guidelines, in his speech the Dalai Lama concentrated on thematic issues and avoided specific mention of China.[35] However, he made a veiled reference to China in his distributed address: "It is not enough . . . to provide people with food and shelter and clothing. The deeper human nature needs to breathe the precious air of liberty."

Amid this atmosphere of mounting political tension, while the Dalai Lama addressed an audience outside the Amnesty International tent not far from the Austria Centre, Liu Huaqiu delivered a tough statement.[36] Although he acknowledged the World Conference as "an important conference linking the past and future," he made few concessions to that future, or to China's more conciliatory post-Bangkok statement. Liu's Vienna statement also showed little sensitivity to the more cosmopolitan views of the broader international community. Its blunt, uncompromising message, for instance, differed from the sophisticated statements by Indonesia and Singapore. It presented a hard-line challenge to the outside world that offered a clear contrast both to the Bangkok Declaration and to the final Vienna Declaration, of which China was one of the key drafting members. This contrast, and its involvement in the Drafting Committee, illustrated the degree to which China's interaction with the international community and the Conference process helped modify its position on human rights, if only for the period of the Conference.

The day after Liu's speech, on 16 June, the procedural issue of NGO participation in the Conference resurfaced. The Chairman of the Drafting Committee, Brazilian delegate Gilberto Vergre Saboia, ruled that NGO observers be excluded from the closed drafting session, which was to precede the committee's first formal session later in the day. He reportedly asked the NGO monitors to leave after a lengthy debate in which several country delegates, including Chile, Costa Rica, Jordan, Pakistan, and the U.S. argued in defense of the NGOs.[37] The New York-based NGO, Human Rights Watch, responded with a press release which "condemned the UN's willingness to submit to blackmail by the Chinese government in deciding to exclude NGOs from the Drafting Committee." However, one European delegate argued that China was not alone, but had many supporters (1).

Speaking to a plenary session on behalf of the thirty-member Liaison Committee shortly after the exclusion, Reed Brody of the International Human Rights Law Group quoted a Chilean delegate as saying the decision had been the result of "imposition" rather than negotiation. He said: "We know that what this means is that the government of China said that if NGOs were present at the final drafting, China would find it very difficult to be present too" (1). Later, at a press conference held by five members of the Liaison Committee, Brody said he had been told by several delegates that in a meeting the previous week on NGO participation, the Chinese delegate had argued that "we don't need babysitters in a room here with us."[38] Lupeti Senituli of Tonga also argued that this example of China pulling its rank was a dangerous precedent given the power vacuum in the new world order. Nevertheless, by the next day, NGOs had abandoned moves to fight the

Drafting Committee's restriction of their access to closed sessions, declaring that they "would not like to be scapegoats for the governments not proceeding with any substantial work."[39]

The next day, during a meeting with American NGOs, the U.S. delegation head, Timothy Wirth, sharply criticized a "handful of nations" for trying to talk the drafting process "to death." He stated: "There's no question that the People's Republic has been at the forefront of that process from the start."[40] He added: "If these people want to walk out [of the Drafting Committee deliberations], that's fine with us."

At a press conference later in the day, Wirth avoided targeting any particular country. He expressed frustration, however, with the drafting process, where there had been little progress through the day and night in reducing more than two hundred brackets in a forty-eight page draft.[41] His particular concern was the fact that UN conferences acted on the basis of consensus and thus gave countries opposing certain proposals "an inordinate amount of power."[42] However, when asked specifically whether it was true that some seventy countries followed China, he quipped: "Seventy, seven or seventeen?" He was nevertheless heartened by the fact that the Chinese delegation, when challenged, had agreed to the universality principle. The only differences they could foresee, he said, lay in the implementation of this principle.[43] He thus foreshadowed a move to the next substantive issues, the establishment of an International Court of Human Rights and of a High Commissioner for Human Rights. These were to become the main focuses of controversy once the thorny issue of universality had been resolved.

China's preparedness to make concessions on a point of principle coincided with its expressed concern about growing criticism of its conference behavior. A US official reported that a senior Chinese diplomat had complained about press coverage that singled out China as the mastermind of moves to exclude the NGOs, insisting that there were other states taking the same position. He was reportedly told, "You can't hide behind others."[44]

By Friday, 18 June, the universality debate was finally resolved with the adoption of a key paragraph.[45] An unnamed U.S. official identified 11 countries — China, Syria, Iran, Iraq, Cuba, Burma, Sudan, Libya, Vietnam, North Korea and Malaysia (in that order) — as being responsible for blocking the drafting process.[46] Some Asian governments accused the U.S. and other Western nations of unfairly blaming the Third World for the "painfully slow progress," with Malaysian Ambassador Redzuan Kushairi in particular taking exception to the accusation that it was "engaged in a lot of bracketing." China's senior delegate told the Main Committee that his country's position had been unfairly presented in the media (1). On the same day, U.S. Chairman Timothy Wirth observed that "the United States has made very clear the problems that we have with China's human rights position." He stated: "We want much greater dialogue over the issue of Tibet, we're very concerned about prison labor, child labor and about their over-all performance. The women's groups are very concerned about transparency of the Chinese and whether they will allow NGOs going to the international conference on women which is scheduled in Beijing. At this point I don't think that in many ways the People's Republic is endearing itself to the human rights community worldwide."[47]

Nevertheless, he stated that "we will continue to attempt to work with China. I think we have made progress" (6).

On 18 June, a press conference was held to issue the first joint statement ever made by all the Chinese human rights NGOs outside China, with the exception of the Tibetan NGO. It pledged mutual support and cooperation in pursuing common goals:

1. We reaffirm our belief in the universality and indivisibility of human rights. No government should be allowed to use the pretext of specific cultural, historical or national situations to deny international standards. Likewise, civil and political rights and economic and social rights are interdependent and mutually supportive. No government can arbitrarily emphasize one group of rights to the detriment of the other;

2. We are convinced that human rights and democracy are inseparable; only when democratic governance and the rule of law are firmly secured will human rights be fully implemented;

3. We demand that the government of the People's Republic of China immediately release all political prisoners and cease all political persecutions;

4. We demand that the government of the People's Republic of China fully respect the right of self-determination as well as the rights of all the minorities in respect of their religions, cultures and languages. The fundamental rights of the people of Hong Kong should be fully respected after 1997; and

5. We demand that the government of the People's Republic of China immediately ratify the two international covenants of human rights; further, it should cooperate with international organizations (including NGOs) and other governments in meeting the obligations under international human rights law.[48]

After 18 June, when a breakthrough finally occurred on the universality issue, there was a race against time in the Drafting Committee to meet the deadline before the end of the Conference on 25 June. The Committee's progress in removing brackets became the main focus of attention. Between 19 and 21 June steady progress was made, but the document still seemed far from completion. A second breakthrough occurred on 21 June, however, when the Chairman separated the Drafting Committee into two groups, with a core group concentrating on the future plan of action, and extended work throughout the night. By 22 June, the Conference Coordinator, John Pace, was confidently predicting "a reasonably good outcome."[49] U.S. Undersecretary of State for Humanitarian Affairs John Shattuck was also confident that there would be "no compromise about human rights."[50]

At the same time, Asian states "led by China and Iran" were perceived by the Conference newspaper, *Terra Viva*, to be on the retreat.[51] Certainly, from 21 June, China ceased to be among those countries named as responsible for further obstruction in the Drafting Committee. In the Main Committee, China's representatives continued to press the need to protect fragile group and developmental rights.[52] At a discussion in the Committee on the relationship of development, democracy and human rights, the deputy leader of the Chinese delegation, Jin Yongjian, insisted on their interdependence. He warned against the one-sided emphasis on civil rights adopted by some in the Conference, and at the same time identified the right to development as a basic condition of rights. Nevertheless, he stated that civil, political, economic, social, cultural and developmental rights should be given "equal emphasis" (*gei yu tongdeng zhongshi*).[53] This represented a considerable concession to prevailing Conference views. The only negative report concerned China's alleged pressure on the UN to cancel a seminar on Tibet organized by Tibetan NGOs.[54] On the last day of the Conference, without pinpointing China, *Terra Viva* summed up the Asian role: "As the most vocal of all regional groups, the Asians played a significant role on some of the more contentious issues at the conference: the indivisibility of human rights, the Special Declaration on Bosnia, the role of non-governmental organizations, terrorism and self-determination."[55]

Despite this, there were some positive outcomes. A few days before the end of the Conference, Asian governments as a whole acknowledged the important role of NGOs, and of international opinion, in the Vienna process. For the first time, and contrary to earlier refusals to do so, they asked for a formal meeting with Asian NGO representatives. At the one-hour meeting, NGOs were able to ask questions about controversial issues in the Conference document. For their part, delegates from the governments of Singapore, Iran, and Indonesia complained that NGOs had created an unfair image in media reports of Asian governments as "bad guys" and requested a change in this "simplistic and counter-productive approach." The day after this meeting, a *Renmin ribao* article complained that "NGOs, manipulated and controlled by Western countries, attacked the position of developing countries without any factual basis."[56]

Post-Conference Analysis: Changing Theory

Whether China's formal participation in the consensus of the Vienna process represented a meaningful development in its policy, or merely a contextual adaptation, may be determined by a textual analysis of China's Vienna Conference statement, by a comparison between the Chinese statement and the Vienna Declaration, and by an analysis of a number of examples of China's reaction to the Final Declaration. Finally, a comparison between China's Bangkok statements and its Vienna statement tests the longer-term effectiveness of the Bangkok process and the significance of China's socialization.[57]

China's Vienna Statement

Liu Huaqiu's 15 June speech at the Vienna Conference was tough and uncompromising; it represented an amalgam of the Maoist concept of human rights, the pre-Bangkok formulations in the 1991 White Paper, and elements of Jin Yongjian's Bangkok speech.[58] It resurrected two crucial aspects of the Bangkok speech: the hierarchy of human rights and the priority of the principle of state sovereignty as "the basis for the realization of citizens' human rights." However, Liu gave state sovereignty an even greater emphasis in his insistence that the idea that human rights questions transcended state boundaries was "counter . . . to the lofty cause of the protection of human rights." He also declared that "nobody shall place his own rights and interests above those of the state and society" and argued that it was necessary "to maintain social stability and ensure the basic human rights of citizens do not contradict each other." He emphasized socialist values, calling for the elimination of "colonialism, racism, apartheid, massive and gross violations of human rights as a result of foreign invasion and occupation, safeguarding the right of small and weak countries to self-determination and the right of developing countries to development."

Unlike Ambassador Jin's Bangkok speech, however, Liu's Vienna statement reverted back to the priorities established in the first human rights White Paper. For the first time in the 1993 statements under analysis, it reiterated the priority of the rights to subsistence and development. Liu also returned to the interpretation of cultural relativism in the 1991 White Paper, according to which "different historical stages had different human rights requirements." He called for the guarantee of each country's right "to formulate its own policies on human rights protection in the light of its own conditions."

The only respect in which the Bangkok Declaration appeared to have retained an influence on the thinking in the Vienna statement was in its itemization of all the rights, including civil and political rights, and the description of them as "interdependent, equally important, indivisible and indispensable." While the notion of "equal importance" seemed at odds with the assertion of the priority of the rights to subsistence and development, the addition of the term "indispensable" seemed to approach the notion of universality recognized in the Bangkok Declaration.

China's Vienna statement represented an attempt to place human rights in the context of international and national change as well as in the context of historical human rights abuses against China. It also described China's current human rights conditions. On the basis of the formal provisions of the Chinese constitutions, Liu claimed that every citizen already enjoyed "genuine democracy and freedom, civil and political rights." Unlike earlier statements, he set only four "principal proposals" before the international community. They were the recommendations to: (1) give primary attention to the massive gross violations of human rights resulting from foreign aggression, colonial rule, and apartheid; (2) establish peace and a favourable international environment for the protection of human rights; (3) respect the right to development; and (4) respect the right of each country to formulate its human rights policies. These principles represented a return to the unreconstructed socialist values of Maoist China.

At the same time, Liu admitted that human rights could be discussed among countries in the spirit of mutual respect and on an equal footing, and offered "to further strengthen exchanges and cooperation with other countries on human rights in the international community." He also affirmed that "China respects and abides by the basic principles of the UN Charter and the Universal Declaration of Human Rights" and that it was "earnestly honouring the obligation" it had undertaken in ratifying eight international conventions on human rights.

Despite these assurances, the overall hard-line of China's statement meant that its concessions were unlikely to comfort an expectant international community, which found itself confronted with a screen placed across the changing everyday realities of human rights in China, and across its increasingly cosmopolitan and sophisticated scholarly human rights discourse.

China's new hard-line position represented its basic negotiating line, which would allow it to end with the concessions it was finally prepared to make. It also represented a clear bid for leadership of the human rights diplomacy of the entire developing world, including not just the Asian but the African and Middle Eastern positions. And it was a response to the pressures of China's growing economic power and domestic instability, mirroring its reaction against U.S. bilateral monitoring. Yet, unlike statements made by other Asian states, the Vice-Foreign Minister's speech made no concession to the increasing sophistication of international human rights discourse. Its unyielding character, retreating well behind the line taken at Bangkok to the point of the first White Paper and before, meant that China's concessions, when they occurred, would only be more obvious in the eyes of the international community. By staking out so clearly the boundaries of state sovereignty, China was rendering them more vulnerable.

The Vienna Declaration and Program of Action

The Vienna Declaration is a long and complex document that, although born of compromise, represented a step towards the mutual accommodation of different human rights philosophies.[59] Under its rubric, developed states for the first time deliberately extended their working concept of fundamental rights to include the collective right to development. For their part, developing states accepted the universality and indivisibility of all rights, and the inseparable link between democracy, development, and human rights.

In terms of the fine print, a preliminary assessment by human rights expert Iain Guest of the views of delegates and observers identified the "winners" in the final document as women, children, and groups such as the Untouchables suffering "extreme poverty and social exclusion."[60] Those seen to have made less progress were refugees, whose right of asylum in receiving states was not endorsed. They were also seen to include indigenous peoples, who were described as "people" rather than the collective term "peoples," and thus seen as enjoying individual rights but not the collective right of self-determination; the NGOs, whose hopes to have their rights as defenders of human rights recognized were not met, although they "should be free to carry out their human rights activities without interference"; and minorities, for whom the language on protection was stronger, but for whom the right of self-determination was identified predominantly as freedom from foreign or colonial rule. In addition, the freedom of the press had been modified, in that its implementation was to be determined "according to law."

Particularly gratifying to Western governments and UN officials, however, were the separate sections in the final document on torture, described as "one of the most atrocious violations against human dignity," and on forced disappearances.[61]

Regarding the implementation and the strengthening of human rights mechanisms, the results were also mixed. The proposal to establish an International Court of Human Rights did not proceed. A proposal to double the annual budget of the UN Centre for Human Rights was overturned in favor of the less specific promise of "an increased proportion" of the annual UN budget. An earlier draft calling for "the proposal to establish a post of High Commissioner for Human Rights" to be "expedited" by the UN General Assembly at its next session was watered down to "begin, as a matter of priority, consideration of the question of the establishment of the position of High Commissioner for Human Rights."

From the point of view of Western states and Western and Asian NGOs, the achievements of the Declaration included the universality provisions, recognition of the human person as the central subject of development, insistence that the right to development not be used as a justification for human rights abuses, strong support for women's rights, the strong paragraph recognizing and supporting the role of NGOs in promoting human rights, and the number of countries forming part of its consensus. Its weaknesses were the lack of change on aid conditionality, a serious watering down of language on press freedom, and the absence of a decision on a

High Commissioner for Human Rights.[62] One assessment by human rights lawyers considered that there had been no conceptual advances in Vienna, and that although the Program of Action contained some positive gains, it fell short of expectations for specific measures to turn accepted principles into concrete action that could address human rights violations and their causes.[63]

Undoubtedly, the greatest feat of the Conference was that, at the following UN General Assembly, China was one of the 171 UN member states that adopted by consensus the final document that reaffirmed, and in some cases strengthened, the basic principles of the Universal Declaration of Human Rights, itself originally adopted in 1948 by less than one-third that number (48 in favor, none against and 8 abstentions), not including the People's Republic.

The consensus requirement to which the document was subject thus not only empowered certain states with a "veto" during the drafting process, as Adrien-Claude Zoller had observed, but also imposed consensus on dissenting states at the conclusion of the process. In this way, China became party to the consensus, in spite of the fact that the final document represented the reverse of many of the priorities established in Liu Huaqiu's Vienna statement. At least a dozen major items in the Vienna Declaration represented issues that China did not support in its policy, had taken issue with in official statements, had opposed during the drafting process in Vienna or had failed to endorse from the Bangkok Declaration. First and foremost was the recognition of the universality of human rights, something China had worked against in the drafting process in Vienna, and failed to endorse from the Bangkok Declaration. Second was the statement of the interdependence and mutually reinforcing nature of democracy, development, and respect for human rights. Third was the statement that "lack of development may not be invoked to justify the abridgement of internationally recognized human rights" in Section I, Paragraph 10.

In contrast, Chinese policy and statements habitually viewed the right to development primarily as a collective right of states, and used economic development and the need for political stability as a "trade-off" argument against the claims of civil and political rights. Moreover, Section I, Paragraph 30 of the Vienna Declaration diluted the effect of its support for the values of antiracism, antiforeign occupation, and domination, values shared by China, by including a list of other violations of which China was clearly culpable, such as torture, summary executions, religious intolerance, and a lack of the rule of law. While recognizing that "the primary responsibility for standard-setting rests with States," a view similar to China's, Section I, Paragraph 38 of the Declaration also recognized the "contribution of non-governmental organizations to this process" as well as the "importance of continued dialogue and cooperation between governments and non-governmental organizations." This recognition, also contained in the Bangkok

Declaration, had been opposed in China's policy, in its Vienna Conference diplomacy, and in its statements before the Human Rights Commission and Sub-Commission. In addition to acknowledging the role of NGOs, Section I, Paragraph 39 "encourage(d) the increased involvement of the media" in human rights activity, something that China would not have supported.

Values not respected in Chinese practice, as opposed to its formal theory, which were given extensive treatment in the Vienna Declaration, included the rights of minorities, the long section on torture, according to which freedom from torture was a "right which must be protected under all circumstances, including in times of internal or international disturbance or armed conflicts" (Section II, Paragraph 56), and the need for an independent judiciary and legal profession (Section I, Paragraph 27).

The areas of the Declaration that most clearly diverged from Chinese policy were the sections on the future development of institutions to enable the expansion of human rights protection. The most important of these was the provision for consideration of the establishment of the post of High Commissioner for Human Rights at the following UN General Assembly, a provision watered down in the Drafting Committee at the behest of a number of powers, including China. China lobbied against the post in the August 1993 Human Rights Sub-Commission, and carried its concern into the UN General Assembly session. In their discussion of the resolution, China's representatives stressed that, in the exercise of his or her duties, the "High Commissioner should show respect for sovereignty, territorial integrity and the principle of non-interference, promote balanced and sustainable development and ensure the realization of the Right to Development."[64] However, in contrast to this restricted vision, the final resolution establishing the High Commissioner, adopted in a plenary session of the UN General Assembly on 20 December 1993, gave the United Nations a senior human rights official who could take up all human rights issues with all countries without awaiting a mandate from the UN Commission on Human Rights or any other political body.[65]

Other institutional arrangements, also endorsed in the Bangkok Declaration but not in any Chinese statements, included the reaffirmation of the constructive role of national institutions (Section I, Paragraph 36) and the need to increase their resources (Section II, Paragraph 74); the "fundamental role" of regional arrangements (Section I, Paragraph 37); the request for an increase in the resources for the UN human rights program; the allocation of an increased proportion of the regular UN budget to the Centre for Human Rights (Section II, Paragraph 10); and the call for each state to draw up a National Action Plan (Section II, Paragraph 71). Finally, where China had called for a rationalization of the UN human rights bodies, the Vienna Declaration highlighted "the importance of preserving and strengthening the system of special procedures, rapporteurs, representatives, experts and working groups of the Commission on Human Rights, and the Sub-Commission on the Prevention of Discrimination and Protection of Minorities" (Section II, Paragraph 95).

The distance between such principles and China's hard-line statement of 15 June made clear the concessions that China had made, if in many cases only implicitly, and the degree to which, at least within the drafting process of the Conference, it had been prepared to modify its hard-line policy in exchange for its wish to be seen as a cooperative member of the international community. Undoubtedly, part of the pressure pushing it toward the consensual position was the utilization by Western states of democratic procedures like press conferences (a mechanism used to effect by the U.S. delegation) and continuing NGO pressures, whereby China's activity within the Drafting Committee was exposed to unfavorable publicity.[66]

Yet, China had reportedly also been instrumental in the Drafting Committee in watering down a number of the proposals. Apart from the provisions regarding the High Commissioner, these had included efforts to avoid requests for new funding, which had been diluted in the final draft to requests for an increased proportion of the regular UN budget. In addition, China had been one of the opponents of the proposal for an International Court of Human Rights. Positive inclusions in the Declaration, from China's point of view, would have been the establishment of a Working Group on the Right to Development and Economic and Social Rights (Section 11, Paragraph 98); the weakening of the right of self-determination in a way which undermined minority rights; the establishment of a Special Rapporteur on Racism; and the condition that food should not be used as a tool of foreign trade. Principles that China had insisted the Declaration should contain — namely, the reference to the role of historical conditions and development, and to the importance of state sovereignty — were mentioned in the document, but in a peripheral and diluted form.

An initial Chinese estimate of the benefits of the Declaration published in the *Renmin ribao* was that it reflected the needs of developing nations in its emphasis on the right to development; in its simultaneous emphasis on the importance of historical and cultural specificity and the universality of human rights; in its opposition to foreign occupation, colonialism, and racism; in its affirmation of the collective rights of women, children, the disabled, and minorities; and in its deferral of the question of the High Commissioner until the following UN General Assembly.[67]

China's Formal Responses to the Vienna Declaration, June–December 1993

The full significance of China's participation in the Vienna Declaration consensus process could be measured only by an analysis of its formal response to the Declaration over a substantial period. Its attitude was indicated in immediate judgements in *Renmin ribao* articles, in a more considered statement by Tian Jin, China's expert to the UN Human Rights Sub-Commission in Geneva in August 1993, and in a press conference with Zhu Muzhi, Chairman of China's human rights NGO, at the end of December 1993.

Responding to the Final Declaration on the last day of the Conference, Jin Yongjian adopted a positive approach, declaring that it indicated that "the protection of human rights was international society's common responsibility and that it was the goal for which every government should struggle."[68] He first listed the Declaration's achievements in the area of China's main concerns: in opposing racism, colonialism, foreign aggression, and attempts by a few countries to impose their human rights values on others, and in affirming the right to development and collective rights. He approved its support for the universal realization of rights and acknowledged the value of the mutual discussion and interchange at the conference. However, he also articulated the ambiguous stance China would adopt thereafter on the question of universality. In his judgement, the Final Declaration "reflected some universal understanding of states towards the question of human rights, and at the same time maintained some different viewpoints among different states." Jin praised the cooperation among developing states that had facilitated the passage of the document, and in particular China's role as Vice-Chairman of the Conference. He was heartened by the support China found for its position from many countries. Regarding the drafting of the Final Document, he maintained that China had adopted "an extremely cooperative attitude." It had introduced "quite a few constructive proposals" and had encouraged the emergence of the Final Declaration. Moreover, he insisted, China would "continue to take a positive attitude in its participation in international human rights activities" (6).

The *Renmin ribao* article of 29 June, also carried in the *Beijing Review*, assessed the achievements of the Final Declaration as its reflection of "some universal understanding and common views on human rights" as well as of "different viewpoints from different countries."[69] Positive developments included the fact that, although recognizing the universality of human rights, the Declaration had also demanded that particularities be taken into account: it had described human rights as interdependent and indivisible; had identified poverty as an obstacle to human rights; and had reaffirmed the right to development as inalienable.

Yet the article targeted "a few Western countries" for "attempting to legalize and institutionalize their interference in human rights"; for attempting to control and manipulate "certain so-called 'human rights organizations' "; and for proposing to establish a UN Human Rights Commissioner and a human rights court. These Western countries had "accused some developing countries and exerted pressure, creating a discordant atmosphere and posing many problems and difficulties for the conference before the successful issuance of the final document."[70] In contrast, developing countries had "displayed flexibility and a cooperative spirit in consultation and negotiations and made a valuable contribution to the final document." In particular, "representatives of the Chinese government [had] expounded their basic stand on the issue of human rights, actively participated in all the work of the Conference and made contributions to the Conference declaration and success."[71]

Although the article described the Final Declaration as "a product of mutual cooperation and compromise," the important question was how conclusive and authoritative the Chinese government judged it to be. Suggestions that it was regarded as not much more than a political and contingent document were indicated in one of the concluding paragraphs: "This Conference has achieved some positive results, though there are evident limitations. The struggle over human rights between the developing countries and a few Western countries will last a long time. However, the position and propositions of the developing countries will increasingly command attention in the international arena in the long run."[72]

This view was reinforced in the more considered and, on the whole, more negative judgement made by China's expert, Tian Jin, before the UN Human Rights Sub-Commission on 6 August 1993. He saw the final outcome as a compromise "which satisfied no one," and predicted that there would continue to be differences of opinion on it. Positive elements he detected in the Final Declaration included its opposition to racism, racial discrimination, xenophobia, aggression, and all forms of new nationalism; the affirmation of the right to development as an inalienable right and the opposition to extreme poverty and external debt; its support for the universality of human rights (though he simultaneously expressed support for the statement allegedly made by the Jordanian Chairman of the Sub-Commission on the need for a delicate balance between the universality of human rights and local historical conditions); and its promotion of the needs of women, children, indigenous peoples, refugees, migrants, and workers. The Vienna Declaration, he concluded, was a document that represented "a new stage in the right to protection of these people," while the Vienna Conference was "a link between past and future."[73] He further remarked that "one state" that was said to have made important concessions on the right to development had reversed its position at the last Economic and Social Council (ECOSOC) session, and that the Sub-Commission should call it to increase its spirit of cooperation.

Similar views were echoed at the Sub-Commission on an informal level by a member of China's observer delegation. He described the Vienna Declaration as a "balanced text" that represented a reasonable compromise. However, everyone was "both satisfied and not satisfied." At the Conference, he maintained, China had been blamed unduly, because "whenever anything goes wrong, they think it is China." Different opinions did not mean noncooperation and yet, he complained, every day China was being blamed in *Terra Viva*. This was because one way to prove oneself right was to prove someone else wrong. But, he stated, "Uncle Sam was beating a dragon [and] now the dragon is equal to Uncle Sam."

A third, even more negative view of an entirely negotiable future was maintained at the end of 1993 by Zhu Muzhi, the Chairman of the China Society for Human Rights Studies. He stated that the Vienna Conference had exposed three main issues: (1) that there were differences on human rights within the world community, particularly between North and South, and great differences in views between Asia and the West, as illustrated in the Bangkok Declaration; (2) that developed nations were always attempting to promote their model of human rights, which they believed to be the only one, and force it on developing countries; and (3) that at Vienna China had been the main target of the West's attack, which concentrated on criticism of human rights in Tibet, interference in China's internal affairs, and an attempt to undermine China's proposals, an attempt that nevertheless had been foiled by support from developing states.[74] Zhu did not acknowledge that the Conference may have had a constructive, positive, or lasting outcome for international human rights. China's official assessments of Vienna had become progressively more negative with the passage of time.

Through the lengthy process of the Vienna Human Rights Conference, China had submitted its human rights priorities to international scrutiny, both in the statement made by its Vice-Foreign Minister and its interaction with the Drafting Committee. Within the drafting process, it had influenced the adoption and wording of some of the articles: but it had also finally accepted the universality of human rights and, through its participation in the consensus mechanism of the Final Declaration, had acknowledged human rights that it had hitherto queried, ignored, or denied. Its immediate analysis of the document suggested that it had accepted the validity of some of its aspects. It also reflected a belief, contradicted by empirical evidence, that China had been cooperative in achieving compromise. Chinese representatives had expressed satisfaction that parts of the document reflected Chinese values. When considering the distance between China's hard-line statement at Vienna and the actual rights embedded in the Final Declaration, China not only had traveled a long way, but, more importantly, in the light of its statist view of sovereignty as underpinning all human rights, had been observed during the Conference to be making considerable concessions.

In this sense, China's involvement in the Conference and its Drafting Committee had been productive. However, the significance of its concessions was quickly rendered problematic by subsequent official judgements that the struggle over human rights would last a long time. This negative view of what was meant to be a landmark human rights conference was entrenched on 6 August 1993 by the statement of Tian Jin, and on 29 December 1993 by the observations of Zhu Muzhi. Their statements signaled that rather than standing as an authoritative beacon lighting the way for future human rights progress, the Vienna Declaration would be seen by China as a document that would continue to cause controversy and disagreement between Western and developing states: that, rather than representing part of a long-term learning curve, for China the UN World Human Rights Conference at Vienna signified only a two-week stop along the road of continuing human rights debate.

Conclusion

The post-1989 development of China's human rights theories and an analysis of the theory and process of China's involvement in the Vienna Human Rights Conference and its preparatory meetings suggest two main conclusions. At a general level, it is clear that after about a year denying the validity of the international critique of China's human rights, China's leaders decided to "take the debate on" rather than continue to deny or fulminate against its existence. This positive decision reflected China's view of its leading role in the international community and its concern to be seen to have control over its domestic and international situation. Paradoxically, its sensitivity about sovereignty impelled China to engage with the international human rights debate. In this way it conceded that it was part of the international human rights regime not only by virtue of its membership in the United Nations but by virtue of its own claims to belong. It also accepted at a practical level the negotiability of its sovereignty. This will to be part of the regime, to "be in it to win it," was manifest first at the theoretical level, with the mobilization of scholarly and official energies to construct a theory of "human rights with Chinese characteristics." Subsequently, armed with this theory, China engaged at the bilateral level in human rights debate and interchange, whether with visiting Western human rights delegations, with visiting Western leaders and scholars, or during official Chinese visits to Asia and Africa. Finally, in 1993, China engaged at the multilateral level, regionally, in Bangkok, and internationally, at the UN World Human Rights Conference in Vienna.

At a second level of analysis, which looks specifically at the learning process manifest in this interaction, the results are more complex. In the process of interaction with the Asia-Pacific region, it became clear to China that the priority of the rights of subsistence and development did not have universal acceptance. Aware that promoting these rights might imperil its human rights leadership in the Asian world, China did not emphasize them at Bangkok, failing even to mention subsistence as a "right." At the end of the Bangkok Meeting, China showed even closer compliance with consensual "Asian" values, as expressed in the Bangkok Declaration. Thus, within the context of Bangkok, China's policy exhibited some adaptation. It should be noted, however, that the causal variable behind this "adaptation" related to

China's effort to assert leadership of the "Third World" position on human rights by reshaping norms, not to its compliance with the regime as it was currently constituted.

The crucial test of the significance of its learning within the international human rights regime was whether China carried these new ideas into the Vienna Conference. This it failed to do. Instead, it delved back into the 1991 human rights White Paper and into Maoist concepts of human rights, reverting to an insistent position on state sovereignty and noninterference. It presented a conceptual world of human rights opposed to the U.S. position, providing the outer parameters of the "developing world's" view. The reason for this policy reversal was that, while at Bangkok China had been courting Asian states, at Vienna it was making a broader bid for leadership of the entire non-Western world. Yet, precisely because of its initial hard-line position at Vienna, China was obliged to demonstrate considerable flexibility in its response to the Conference process. Despite the fact that it regarded such international conferences as part of its human rights defense and as forums in which to establish its leadership of the South within the human rights regime, in the short term and within the discrete contexts of the Bangkok and Vienna Conferences, its interaction with the entire international community also had a socializing effect.

Yet this learning experience on the part of China proved to be neither linear nor continuous. There were three main reasons for its failure to internalize Conference norms in any lasting way. While accepting participation in the international human rights regime, China nevertheless believed that it was within its power to control the adverse (in its terms) effects such membership might have on its domestic policy and political constituency. On one hand, China believed that by diplomatic means it could compartmentalize the impact of its international commitment from domestic repercussions while, within the international realm, its activities could be separated into discrete chronological segments which did not affect each other. On the other hand, China was confident that it could undermine the Western critique and "Western" human rights standards by seeking to refashion the predominant principles of the human rights regime in a way that corresponded with "Third World" (as they were described) needs. A third reason for the failure of cognitive, as opposed to instrumental, learning was the impact of China's domestic policies, and its policy makers, on the learning process. The thesis underlying the notion of a learning cycle is that of a continual and positive feedback effect of a state's foreign policy process on its domestic policies, resulting in a reformulation of foreign policy that once again interacts with the foreign policy environment. In this instance, however, the feedback of foreign policy learning into domestic processes did not produce a positive and cumulative effect. Domestic obstacles to the learning process simply returned China's human rights position back to the status quo ante.

Thus, although China made concessions to international human rights norms in the short term, ultimately the emphasis was more on constructing a theory of human rights with Chinese characteristics that could enable China to lead what it still called "the developing world" in a debate against the West. Such a role was not entirely destructive of the cause of human rights. The effort to achieve mutual accommodation within the Vienna process meant that the developed world made a number of important and constructive concessions, to economic and social rights and the right to development in particular. Such changes not only gave rise to subsequent constructive efforts within the United Nations to work out how these rights could be practically implemented, but facilitated a spirit of mutual tolerance between human rights protagonists. In this sense, pressure from China, as well as from other non-Western states, had a constructive impact.

At the same time, China's insistence on the principles of state sovereignty and noninterference at Vienna did not facilitate the progress of human rights discourse. Nor was the debate advanced in great measure by the considerable concessions ultimately made by China. Within the drafting process and in its own statements during and immediately after the Conference, China's diplomats, as at Bangkok, exhibited a socializing response. But, once again, this response was self-limiting to the particular context and was not sustained in official memory. Despite China's initial support for the achievements of the Vienna Conference, a month later the only new principle that it appeared to be conceding was an acceptance of the principle of universality, and then with the strings of cultural and historical relativism attached. The inconclusive image of the final document that China's official statements subsequently portrayed left it an opening to recommence the human rights debate, starting again from scratch, at another time, in another place.

Chapter 7
After Vienna: China's Implementation of Human Rights

The Chinese Government and people have ... scored impressive achievements in the promotion and protection of human rights by turning their solemn commitments to the Declaration into practice.

— China's Vice-Premier, Qian Qichen, at the International Symposium to mark the fiftieth anniversary of the adoption of the Universal Declaration of Human Rights, Beijing, 20 October 1998

Nowadays, there are laws covering virtually all areas of China's political, economic and social life, and democratic rights of Chinese citizens have been effectively protected with the formulation of these laws, especially the revised Criminal Law and Criminal Procedure Law.

— Zhang Xiufu, Vice-Minister of Justice, 31 March 1997

The Chinese authorities have taken some steps in the past year to give growing acknowledgement to international human rights standards, but in practice, very little has changed.

— Amnesty International, February 1998

China's response to the UN human rights regime has been tested in its ongoing interaction with UN bodies and conferences. However, to measure compliance in the sense of an internalization of human rights norms, uniting words and action, a longer-term perspective that utilizes a broader brush encompassing both the international and domestic dimensions of implementation is necessary. Insofar as Articles 55 and 56 of the UN Charter require all members of the United Nations to promote "universal respect for, and observance of, human rights and fundamental freedoms for all without distinction as to race, sex, language or religion," China is obliged to comply with UN human rights norms, regardless of the fact that it has not ratified the International Covenants. From the mid-1990s, China not only made international concessions to the UN human rights regime but also initiated substantive changes domestically, with amendments to its criminal law and, to a lesser extent, reform of its political system. Since the case studies under analysis here include both the Charter-based bodies of the Human Rights Commission and Sub-Commission, which oversee a broad range of civil and political rights, and the treaty bodies and special rapporteurs that monitor specific civil rights, measurement of China's compliance requires the examination of its reforms to its criminal laws and political institutions as well as of reforms relating to torture and to labor laws. These legal and institutional reforms, however, coexist with a paradox — a continuing record of human rights abuses.

International Implementation

China's implementation of its human rights responsibilities at an international level has been indicated in a number of developments in the second half of the decade. The success of international efforts is measurable according to the degree to which the international community has succeeded in transcending the traditional international / domestic divide to overcome the continuing problem of the compartmentalization between China's theory and its practice of human rights. At a multilateral level, the most important of these developments was China's signature of the International Covenant on Economic, Social and Cultural Rights (ICESCR) on 27 October 1997 and its signature of the International Covenant on Civil and Political Rights (ICCPR) on 5 October 1998. The decision to sign the Covenants was finally reached after more than a decade of consideration and pressure, with expressions of intent often prompted by imminent votes on China in the UN Human Rights Commission. It has been speculated that the decision was finally made for the short-term, tactical purpose of heading off such resolutions as well as to raise China's human rights profile more generally and stem international criticism. Signature in itself merely signaled "a good faith intention to review the treaty with a view to ratification in due course and . . . a weak obligation not to do anything in the meantime which is clearly incompatible with the treaty."[1] However, in a broader sense, signature also represented China's acceptance in principle of the international community's right to monitor the overall condition of its human rights.

When China signed the ICESCR, on the eve of the visit of President Jiang Zemin to Washington, it did not specify a schedule for ratification or whether it intended to enter any reservations. Nevertheless, as we have seen, the International Covenant's potential to induce by other means China's acceptance of its obligation to implement freedom of association, as well as many other workers' and citizens' rights, was clear. Under Article 8 of the ICESCR, states parties undertake to ensure everyone's right to form trade unions and join trade unions of their choice, subject only to the rules of the organization concerned, restrictions prescribed by law, the interests of national security or public order and protection of the freedoms of others. They also acknowledge the right of trade unions to function freely subject to the same limitations; and they assert the right to strike, provided this is exercised in conformity with the laws of the country.[2]

In ratifying the ICESCR, unless it entered specific reservations, China would also be bound to extend to all citizens the right of self-determination; the right to nondiscrimination; "the right of everyone to the opportunity to gain his living by work which he freely chooses or accepts"; the right to "fair wages and equal remuneration for work of equal value"; to safe and healthy working conditions, rest, leisure, and reasonable limitation of working hours; the right to an adequate standard of living; the "right of everyone to the enjoyment of the highest attainable standard of physical and mental health"; and the right of all to education. At a time when China was in the process of downsizing a large number of state-owned enterprises (SOEs), when it had laid off an estimated 11.5 million workers in 1997, and planned to lay off another 3.5 million in 1998, international pressures to move from signature to ratification of the Covenant were counterbalanced by domestic financial pressures to avoid, or at least delay, ratification.[3]

The signature of the ICCPR occurred just after the visit of UN Human Rights Commissioner Mary Robinson to China, and a day before the visit of British Prime Minister Tony Blair. China's Ambassador to the United Nations in New York, Qin Huasun, saw the signature of both covenants as demonstrating "the firm resolve of China to promote and protect human rights" and as "China's concrete deeds to honor the fiftieth anniversary of the Universal Declaration of Human Rights and the fifth anniversary of the Vienna Declaration and Programme of Action."[4] The obligations represented by this core treaty were even more onerous than those under the ICESCR. Under the ICCPR, China would be bound to extend to all its citizens the right of self-determination (Article 1); the right to life (Article 6); the right to freedom from torture and from cruel, inhuman or degrading treatment (Article 7); the right not to perform forced or compulsory labor (Article 8); the right to liberty and security of person, including freedom from arbitrary arrest (Article 9); the right to freedom of movement (Article 12); rights of due process, including the right to equality before the courts, the right to be presumed innocent until proven guilty, the right to defense and the right to be tried without delay (Article 14); the right to freedom of thought, opinion, conscience and religion (Articles 18–19); the right of peaceful assembly (Article 21); the right to freedom of association, including the right to form and join trade unions for the protection of one's interests (Article 22); and the rights "(a) to take part in the conduct of public affairs, directly or through freely chosen representatives; and (b) to vote and be elected at genuine periodic elections which shall be by universal and equal suffrage and shall be held by secret ballot, guaranteeing the free expression of the will of the electors (Article 25)."[5]

The challenges inherent in this treaty were such that, at the time of signature, China indicated its intention to enter reservations with respect to freedom of association, freedom of movement, and the death penalty.[6] Since the U.S. itself had entered five reservations to the ICCPR, including one on the death penalty, the U.S. was unlikely to organize significant international opposition to China's reservations.[7] It thus would be left to the other states parties to the Covenant to object that the proposed reservations were "incompatible with the object and purpose of the treaty."

China's decision to sign the ICESCR and ICCPR may also have been related to complications arising from the handover of Hong Kong on 1 July 1997. Until reversion, both the ICCPR and the ICESCR had applied, with some restrictions, to Hong Kong through the United Kingdom. Under the Sino-British Joint Declaration and Article 152 of the Basic Law, these Covenants continued to apply to Hong Kong. Yet, in October 1996, China stated that it did not consider itself obliged to report to the UN Human Rights Committee on the implementation of treaties to which it was not a signatory. This reflected the ongoing tension between human rights and state sovereignty in China's diplomacy and the potential for conflict with the international human rights regime. The UN Human Rights Committee did not accept that territories or states once covered by the treaty should no longer be so covered; accordingly, the obligations set out under the treaty were deemed to remain in force regardless of changes in sovereignty.[8] Thus, China's signature of the ICESCR on 27 October was followed by its equally surprising announcement on 22 November that, under the principle of "one country, two systems," it would submit reports under both Covenants to the relevant UN Committee. The proximity of the two decisions suggested that China was sensitive to the incongruity of reporting to the Committees on two Covenants to which China itself was not a signatory. Rather than resisting the Committees' jurisdiction, and reneging on its undertakings under the Basic Law, it chose to sign the Covenants and to report on both with respect to Hong Kong. The conflict between China's obligation to report and its concern for its decision-making autonomy had brought progress on two crucial issues, thereby revealing the impact of China's short-term tactical interests in altering its long-term perceptions of sovereignty. Both decisions were greeted favorably by some of Beijing's most trenchant critics.[9]

A further welcome development at the multilateral level was the visit to China of UN High Commissioner on Human Rights Mary Robinson in September 1998. Although aimed primarily at establishing the groundwork for future contacts, the visit had some positive outcomes. President Jiang Zemin and Robinson signed an agreement of cooperation and, on 14 September, conferred for almost two hours. According to Jose Diaz, Robinson's spokesman, "there was talk on all sides of a follow-up visit and emphasis on the need to achieve concrete results such as sending a technical mission to assess the situation." Although denied access to a Tibetan prisoner and frustrated in her inquiries as to the whereabouts of the young Panchen Lama, Robinson also raised "concerns and observations" on a range of issues including arbitrary detention, torture, racial discrimination, religious intolerance, and the rights of the child. However, she was criticized by Chinese dissidents for not holding meetings with them outside her official schedule.[10]

China's new readiness to accept the relevance of international human rights procedures and norms to its domestic practice provided a dramatic contrast with its earlier handling of the UN Women's Conference in Beijing in late 1995.[11] The venue in itself was proof of China's acceptance of the application of regime norms and mechanisms to it. However, because of their concern about the domestic impact of the conference, Chinese authorities insisted that even the area in Beijing officially designated as UN territory would remain partly subject to China's own laws and human rights practice. From the beginning, Chinese authorities maintained strict control over the visa process, with organizations or individuals seen as "unfriendly" refused entry to China, thus restricting freedom of movement. Authorities tried to control NGOs by isolating them a considerable distance away in Hairou, thus restricting freedom of movement and assembly. They initially blocked the publication of the UN conference paper, the *Earth Times*, thereby challenging freedom of the press. They forbade meetings of groups of women in hotels outside the UN premises, further restricting freedom of assembly. On Chinese television, although the activities of NGOs (*feizhengfu zuzhi*) were reported, attempts were made to trivialize them by restricting reports to song and dance routines. In the clash between international norms and procedures and China's domestic law and practice, the latter emerged victorious, even at the expense of the international prestige that had been China's reason for hosting the Conference in the first place.

Despite China's eagerness to host the Women's Conference, its handling of the event, clearly affected by the divergent attitudes of its diplomats and Public Security officers, underscored its determination to compartmentalize its international from its domestic human rights policy, and to prevent international bodies from establishing China's accountability at the more meaningful domestic level. This same determination was reflected in its later treatment of the UN Working Group on Arbitrary Detention, whose visit in October 1997 appeared to be a landmark in China's preparedness to allow monitoring on its own soil. Despite the preliminary spadework for the visit by the Group's former Chairman, Louis Joinet, Chinese authorities did not provide the Group with an English or French version of China's revised criminal laws. Moreover, "on account of the difficulty in getting clearances from the Chinese Government to visit specific centers of detention and particular provinces, it was not possible to prepare an agenda for the visit in

advance." These petty obstacles, and the unwillingness of some local authorities to cooperate with the Working Group, clearly impeded its progress
and its considerable achievements.[12] It is also remarkable that the Working
Group did not take the trouble to equip itself beforehand with the readily
available translations of these revised laws.

China was not only subject to United Nations scrutiny but also made
criticisms of UN bodies. Addressing the fifty-third session of the UN General
Assembly in October 1998, Chinese delegate Xie Bohua welcomed the contribution of the numerous declarations, conventions and other international instruments to the promotion and protection of human rights. Action was, however, necessary to eliminate problems such as over frequent
reporting by states parties, duplication of report content and serious delays
in the consideration of reports by treaty bodies. He suggested that treaty
bodies should work within their mandate, become more efficient, and coor-
dinate their work better, so that states parties could present a comprehensive report in a core document.[13]

Even at the level of declaratory policy, it should be noted, China's attitude
to human rights standards remained ambiguous. On the eve of the fiftieth
anniversary of the Universal Declaration of Human Rights, it expressed
support for a review of the Declaration, and openly identified with the
policies of other states with a poor human rights record. In August 1997,
Premier Li Peng endorsed Malaysian Prime Minister Mahathir Mohamad's
call to review the Universal Declaration of Human Rights as a proposal of
"vision and courage."[14] Later, during talks with the Algerian Foreign Minister in Beijing on 11 January 1998, Foreign Minister Qian Qichen stressed
that, as developing nations, China and Algeria shared extensive consensus
on the issue of human rights.[15] In apparent contrast to this nonconformist
position, on 20 October 1998 China convened an International Symposium
on human rights in Beijing to commemorate the fiftieth anniversary of the
Universal Declaration. Hosted by the China Society for Human Rights Studies and the United Nations Association of China, the two-day "International
Symposium on World Human Rights Towards the Twenty-First Century"
brought together more than a hundred delegates from twenty countries to
discuss the present situation of human rights and future challenges. Delegates were, however, government officials or human rights experts involved
in dialogue with China, rather than foreign scholars of China's human
rights or human rights NGOs. Chinese delegates to the conference expressed support for the Universal Declaration, but, while undertaking to
strengthen judicial protection for human rights, they continued to stress
the priority of the state's right to development and the corresponding individual right, the right to subsistence.[16]

At a bilateral level, the results of human rights diplomacy were even more
mixed. Extensive research by Human Rights in China on the numerous

dialogues China was conducting with Western countries and Brazil revealed a diplomatic game in which both sides were anxious to claim success. Thus, "much of what has been characterized as [China's] 'substantial progress' towards instituting protection for rights, while welcome, is generally more show than substance . . . the Western dialogue partners, wishing to justify their position by showing results, are playing along in this game of passing off shop-worn statements and minimal gestures as signs of 'improvements in China's human rights practices'."[17] Lack of serious intent was suggested, for instance, in the fact that neither of the Australian dialogue delegations in 1997 and 1998, unlike the earlier Australian human rights delegations, contained an expert on China's human rights and each contained only one China expert. The dialogues, one in Beijing and one in Canberra, were held in camera and produced no public report while, during informal NGO briefings, officials were unable to identify progress made since the original human rights delegations in 1991 and 1992. Rather than a bold new initiative, in Australia's case the dialogue idea represented a distinct regression from the earlier format of human rights delegations. The most fruitful outcomes of dialogue were those which led to exchanges between legal experts, particularly between China and the Scandinavian countries. However, there was also a danger of over-supply of expertise. The Ford Foundation, the Canadian government and European states such as Switzerland had early been promoting legal exchanges with China: now, individual European states and the European Union as a whole vied with each other to advise China on the rule of law as part of the dialogue process. There was also a danger that foreign advisers could be associated quite unintentionally with changes that regulated away citizens' rights in the name of legal reform, as happened in the case of the 1998 Regulations on the Registration and Management of Social Groups.[18] Moreover, the lack of coordinated and prearticulated benchmarks by which dialogue achievement was to be measured allowed China the upper hand in threatening an end to dialogue with whichever state supported another China resolution in the UN Human Rights Commission (14).

In contrast to human rights dialogue delegations, bilateral visits to China by Western heads of state tended to combine trade and human rights, thus marking a caesura with the immediate post-Tiananmen years when trade was made conditional on human rights. Whether trade was now the sugared pill concealing human rights, or human rights the crucifix held up to justify trade made little difference in this mismatch between strange bedfellows. That these visits were almost inevitably accompanied by the arrest of Chinese dissidents was one sign of the failure of the approach. It caught the West in the act of praising China's progress in human rights just as news came through that more dissidents had been taken into custody. Such was the fate of British Prime Minister Tony Blair and President of the European

Commission, Jacques Santer, during their trips to China. An interesting legal workshop and a re-enactment of a mock British trial was held during the Blair visit: but the Prime Minister's failure to meet with Chinese dissidents who had requested interviews, and the arrest of dissidents during his visit, were jarring reminders of the minimal impact of this particular bilateral mechanism on domestic human rights conditions.

The only exception to the ineffectiveness of bilateral state visits was President Clinton's visit to China in June 1998. The televised presidential debate between the President and China's President Jiang Zemin on Tiananmen, human rights and China's rule in Tibet represented an important break with China's habitual controls over freedom of the press and freedom of speech in politically delicate areas, for the first time allowing China's citizens to view two world leaders debate sensitive issues on an equal footing. The good natured but vigorous interchange also broke the national taboo on public references to Tiananmen. Although the product of tough negotiating between the American and Chinese sides, it was also a reflection of the good relations between Clinton and Jiang and of Jiang's courageous if calculated risk. As China's environmental activist, Dai Qing, commented: "This was something very rare. Nine years after 1989, this is the first time millions of Chinese had heard someone, even though it was a foreigner, say something like this about Tiananmen. It shows that the whole world, not just we Chinese, has not forgotten what happened. It lifted a weight from my heart to hear it."[19]

Domestic Implementation

The most meaningful test of China's cognitive learning is the extent of its domestic implementation of international human rights norms. As has been pointed out, "The General Assembly and the Commission on Human Rights, treaty bodies, country and thematic special rapporteurs and working groups all agree that the implementation of human rights should be at the centre of international attention."[20] This fact was recognized by Vice-Premier Qian Qichen at the International Symposium in Beijing in October 1998, and in his pledge to "continue to press ahead with the political restructuring, further expand the scope of socialist democracy, improve the socialist legal system, rule the country according to law and make it a socialist country ruled by law."[21] Domestically, China's learning may be measured by the degree of its *de jure* and *de facto* implementation of international norms, a record of which may only be summarized here. The findings, whether in reform of the criminal justice system or in political reform, are more positive with respect to legal implementation than practical implementation. An examination of both gives a broad understanding of the legal, institutional, and empirical basis for human rights protection in China.

In the post-Vienna period, new criminal legislation was introduced in the context of repeated expressions of leadership concern that without popular respect for the rule of law (*fazhi*), China's social and political fabric could well disintegrate. In particular, by late 1997, financial problems and the dismissal of millions of workers from state-owned enterprises raised the possibility of widespread social unrest in China, against which only rule by law appeared to offer any safeguards. In addition, notions of fairness, justice, and equality before the law were superficially attractive to a state that had lost its former Marxist underpinnings of fairness and equality of distribution, and for which a revival of Confucian orthodoxy was out of the question. This development was important, reflecting a realization by the leaders that the rule of law was a source not only of security and stability, but also of political legitimacy, for a state whose principal form of post-1989 legitimation — economic performance — was becoming increasingly fragile.[22] However, its corresponding disadvantage was that its purposes were instrumental rather than based on a normative appreciation, a fact influencing the subsequent interpretation and implementation of the laws. Thus, the need for the rule of law was always placed in the context of either the survival or the reform of the political system. Xinhua News Agency, for example, announced in February 1998 that "Chinese lawmakers have investigated into the enforcement of more than 30 laws over the past five years in an effort to strengthen the condition of government power."[23]

This legal consciousness had been fostered and promoted by the former Chairman of the NPC, Qiao Shi, and the President of the Supreme People's Court, Ren Jianxin, since 1993; and it was formalized in President Jiang Zemin's policy of "ruling by law" articulated at the Fifteenth Party Congress in September 1997:

Developing democracy must go hand in hand with the efforts to improve the legal system so that the country is ruled by law. Ruling the country by law means that the broad masses of the people, under the leadership of the Party and in accordance with the Constitution and other laws, participate in one way or another and through all possible channels in managing state affairs, economic and cultural undertakings and social affairs and see to it that all work by the state proceeds in keeping with law, and that socialist democracy is gradually institutionalized and codified so that such institutions and laws will not change with changes in the leadership or changes in the views or focus of attention of any leader. *Ruling the country by law is the basic strategy employed by the Party in leading the people in running the country.*[24]

In his speech, Jiang Zemin used the term, *yi fa zhi guo* (lit. "by means of law, rule the country"). He also referred to the need to *jianshe shehuizhuyi fazhi guojia* (lit. "establish a socialist rule of / by law country").[25] The Chinese term *fazhi* is ambiguous, as it can be translated either as "rule of law" or "rule by law." Within the context established by Jiang of norms within socialist system, however, the implication here was that *fazhi* should be translated as "rule by law."

Legal Implementation: Reform of China's Criminal Justice System

Much publicity has been accorded the reforms in China's criminal justice system in the mid-1990s, by Chinese authorities, Western scholars, and NGOs. Apart from Western analyses, there has been an outpouring of books and articles in China on various aspects of the reforms, while two White Papers on human rights have given pride of place to the topic of "judicial guarantees for human rights." China has also established web sites for human rights that contain some of these sources.[26] The new legislation has been part of the goal to establish "a legal system with Chinese characteristics" by the year 2010. To properly assess its contribution to the rule of law in China and its significance for compliance, it is necessary to disaggregate the content and meaning of this legal reform. Four sets of questions are relevant. The first has to do with the terminology of the laws themselves, and the nature of their procedures. If discrete reforms give further protection to citizens' rights, do they also contain within themselves contradictory provisions or procedural loopholes and are they overridden by reservations or by competing laws, in the same way as the Constitution itself? The second set of questions relates to the motivation behind them. How are the laws interpreted? Who are they aimed at? Is the articulated aim primarily to ensure social stability, or is it also to protect people's rights? If the latter, what is the balance between these two aims? Does concern for judicial efficiency conflict with the protection of citizens' rights? The third set asks whether international pressures form a significant part of the motivation for criminal law reform, and if so, which form of international pressure has been most influential. Finally, how relevant are China's laws to the Chinese people? Do they — the authorities and the citizens — respect and obey the law?[27]

It is commonly agreed that two major trends characterize the new reforms in China's criminal justice system: the attempt to regularize and affirm state power through efficient administration of the law, and the need to protect people's rights. The two goals are not necessarily in conflict, since the need for the state to give legitimacy to the legal system is motivated by the same reason behind its need to protect the citizens' rights — to obtain popular compliance with the law.[28] Thus, for example, moves to limit the court's discretion serve both the needs of state power and those of citizens' rights.[29] Although Chinese authorities recognize these two separate functions of the new reforms, in official parlance they are often conflated.[30] In other contexts, Chinese official statements have given priority to the securing of "social stability," and have placed a lower priority on the protection of citizens' rights. To distinguish these two frequently conflicting functions in the reform of China's criminal law requires considerable hermeneutic skills. Although examining the details of the recent amendments in the Criminal Procedure Law (hereafter CPL) and the Criminal Law is a crucial step in this process, the overall picture of the protection of citizens' rights can be obtained only by placing it in the totality of the legislation affecting the treatment of the individual in China's criminal law. It must also be read with the understanding that the system of criminal justice in the People's Republic of China "is embedded not only within a legal-political structure which remains highly centralized, but also within a set of 'higher order' values very different from those which underpin the official ideology of law in liberal legal systems."[31] As one scholar has pointed out, these include the practical reality that the Chinese legal system is already "so heavily weighted in favour of crime control that a few due process rights will not make a lot of difference to the police's ability to 'do its job'" (76). It must also be read within the context of ongoing factional struggles within the Party and government over the precise balance to strike between these two functions of criminal law.

From 1994 to 1998, a plethora of new laws appeared to alter the hitherto overwhelming weight of the law in favor of instrumental, security-oriented goals. The Chinese government has claimed that these laws are indicative of its progress in human rights. December 1994 saw the enactment of a new Prison Law designed in part to improve treatment of detainees; and the New Year of 1995 marked the coming into effect of the Labor Law, promulgated in mid-1994. There followed legislative attempts to make political and judicial processes more transparent. In February 1995, the NPC passed three new laws, the PRC Law on Judges, the PRC Law on Procurators, and the People's Police Law, to make judges, prosecutors, and policemen more accountable.[32] Magistrates, who formerly had the general status of public officials, thereby acquired their own specific status. The State Compensation Law adopted on 12 March 1994 stipulated that if the legal rights and interests of citizens were infringed upon by state organs, the aggrieved persons had the right to obtain state compensation. The first Lawyers' Law, promulgated to standardize professional performance, lawyer-client relations, and the administration of lawyers and their forms, took effect in January 1996. It allowed lawyers to practice more independently, and no longer as public officials, in cooperative practices and recognized for the first time that lawyers represented their clients rather than the state.[33] In March 1996, the NPC approved major amendments to the CPL of 1 July 1979, which regulated investigation and trial in criminal cases. It also adopted the Administrative Punishment Law that came into force on 1 October 1996. This regulated the system of administrative punishment, including administrative detention, that existed parallel to the criminal justice system. The new Criminal Law of 17 March 1997, an amendment of the 1979 Criminal Law, came into effect in October 1997 and replaced "counter-revolutionary" offenses with provisions barring "treasonous acts designed to threaten national security."

At the same time, the 1993 State Security Law expanded the scope of legal punishment for such activities and, in targeting external involvement, established a system that linked political dissent with unpatriotic activities, the more readily to control dissident ideas within China. It built on the State Secrets Law, according to which all citizens of China are "duty-bound to safeguard national security, honor and interests." In addition, on 1 March 1996, the Martial Law of the PRC, providing for the suspension of constitutional rights during a state of emergency, was promulgated by the Standing Committee of the NPC. Together, these laws curtailed basic freedoms and criminalized a broad range of activities, including some that had earlier been considered mere disciplinary issues.[34]

This plethora of laws pointed to another obstacle to the realization of the rule of law — the "excessive fragmentation, not merely of legislative, judicial, and administrative jurisdiction, but ultimately of the law itself."[35] There was no specific nomenclature or coding system allowing legal texts to be identified easily in terms of sources and order of ranking, nor was there one official bulletin. The different categories of texts included the Constitution, adopted by the NPC; regularly ratified international treaties; fundamental laws adopted by the NPC; laws adopted by the Standing Committee of the NPC; administrative regulations, decisions, and ordinances adopted by the State Council; local regulations adopted by local people's congresses; and regulations of ministries and local governments.[36]

The most positive development in rights of due process in the 1990s was the revision of the CPL, which represented the culmination of nearly three years of drafting and more years of advocacy from reform proponents.[37] According to Gu Angran, Director of the Legislative Affairs Work Committee under the NPC, "modifications to the Criminal Procedure Law mean[t] substantial improvement in China's judicial system, which traditionally value[d] the results of a trial while neglecting the procedures."[38] Among the key changes undergirding rights of due process and protection of the individual were stricter controls on police powers during detention and longer preparation time for defense lawyers. Under compulsory summons, no criminal suspect was to be held for more than twelve hours continuously, and from the day public prosecution was initiated, the criminal suspect had the right to retain a lawyer to offer him legal advice.[39] Judges were freed from presenting evidence, thus allowing them to concentrate on hearing the case and overseeing court procedures.[40] Under Article 34, as in Article 32 of the 1979 CPL, "the use of torture to coerce statements and the gathering of evidence by threats, enticement, deceit or other unlawful methods [was] strictly prohibited."

These revisions were cautiously welcomed by Human Rights Watch/Asia as representing "a move toward acknowledgement of the principle of presumption of innocence; improved access of the accused to legal counsel; more stringent limits on time in detention before formal arrest; limits on the power of public security bureaus to act without supervision; and a *de jure* change in application of the death penalty."[41] The UN Working Group on Arbitrary Detention approved the revised Law's restoration of "balance" to the proceedings, by altering the balance of police/procuratorate in favor of the procuratorate during the investigation phase, and that of magistrate/lawyer in favor of the lawyer in the hearing phase. According to its interpretation, the new law also reinforced the adversarial principle by strengthening the role of the defense; it "introduced the concept" of the "presumption of innocence" of the accused, although it did not guarantee it; and it introduced "an element of neutrality" in court procedures.[42] Likewise, an international NGO, the Lawyers' Committee for Human Rights, in a report by Jonathan Hecht, concluded in carefully chosen words that

> the 1996 NPC Decision demonstrates that China has *begun to* reorient its basic approach to criminal justice away from a dominant preoccupation with social control toward *a somewhat greater* concern for the protection of defendants' rights. It also sets stricter standards against which the government's actions, including those that contravene the revised CPL itself, can be judged. Perhaps most significantly, some of the specific reforms contained in the Decision—elimination of "shelter and investigation," expansion of the right to counsel, limits on non-judicial determinations of guilt and establishment of a more transparent trial process—*give hope of a trend* toward greater incorporation of international human rights norms into the Chinese criminal justice system.[43]

The reasons for the report's caution are to be found in the introduction of new provisions into the revised CPL that partly offset the apparent gains made in four specific areas of reform, as well as in key issues left unresolved by the revisions. As Hecht has so ably demonstrated, despite the elimination of the category of "shelter and investigation," the arrest standard is now relaxed, while the provisions of categories of persons open to arrest and the length of prearrest detention are expanded, thus still allowing police flexibility (26). Moreover, although the revised law authorizes earlier access to lawyers at the pretrial stage it also allows the police to use "state secrets," a concept very broadly defined, as a justification for denying suspects access to a lawyer during the investigations phase; it is silent on the obligation to give suspects immediate notice of their right to counsel in the same phase; and it fails to provide for free legal assistance for defendants unable to afford legal representation, contrary to international requirement (41–42). Finally, as regards the reform of the trial procedure, the judge's role is more clearly differentiated from that of prosecutor and defense lawyer, and the trial court is given a more important role. However, the revised CPL still restricts the power of the defense lawyer and fails to ensure the defendant's right to examine the witnesses against him. It does not indicate China's acceptance of the independence of the judiciary (57–60).

The key issues left unresolved by the revisions are the presumption of innocence; the failure to eliminate a significant form of administrative sanction, the system of reeducation through labor (*laodong jiaoyang*); the lack of provision excluding evidence gathered by such methods as torture, threats, enticement, and fraud; the failure to take measures to overcome the defendant's reluctance to appeal; the existence of few remedies to the violations of the rights of a criminal suspect or defendant; and the failure to provide a mechanism that would oversee the procuratorate's responsibility to act as legal watchdog (60–76).

For its part, the 1997 Amnesty International report objected to the extension under the revised laws of the maximum permitted length of detention without charge, from ten to fourteen days and, in the case of special categories of suspects, thirty-seven days.[44] It pointed out that, although the revised CPL effected the repeal of a 1983 Decision allowing for summary trials in some cases liable to the death penalty, provisions regarding review of death sentences in the revised CPL are the same as in the 1979 Law (17–18); and the addition in the new law of execution by lethal injection would now require the involvement of doctors in executions, thereby breaching internationally recognized principles of medical ethics. The revised CPL also fails to prohibit the public display and humiliation of prisoners sentenced to death (20). For all these reasons, although the new legislation brought China closer to international standards, it was nevertheless adjudged to fall far short of them.[45]

It should be emphasized at this juncture that the issues of the use of illegally obtained evidence and the presumption of innocence are pertinent to one of the core human rights discussed in this book, freedom from torture.

Under the Convention Against Torture, China was obliged to prevent, forbid, and criminalize acts of torture. As has been pointed out earlier, China's definition of torture is narrow, limited to "torture to coerce a statement," or "corporal punishment or abuse" by judicial officers. The revised CPL "strictly prohibits" the practice of such torture. But it does not cover the use of torture to punish, intimidate, or coerce a person for any reason.[46] Not only, therefore, do the revised laws fail to prevent torture, they fail to forbid all acts of torture as defined under the UN Convention. They also fail to provide a mechanism for excluding illegally gathered evidence.[47] Moreover, because there is no provision allowing the suspect to remain silent, and because of the pressure on police to elicit a confession, the temptation for them to resort to coercion to force confessions is very great.[48] The revised CPL also fails to increase protection against torture in other respects such as prompt and ongoing access to lawyers, judges, or relatives.[49] As the Lawyers' Committee for Human Rights concluded, the revised CPL "represents a clear failure to bring China into compliance with the Torture Convention and make the exclusion of illegally gathered evidence a basic principle of the Chinese criminal process."[50]

Redress for complaints of torture is theoretically available. Under the 1982 Constitution, citizens may file complaints against any state official for "violation of the law or dereliction of duty," while the State Compensation Law, promulgated in May 1994, does provide a mechanism for financial redress against officials who abuse their position, even if it neither prevents torture nor brings the torturer to prosecution.[51] The People's Police Law and the Prison Law also contain a few new provisions against torture (10). Article 247 of the amended Criminal Law stipulates that "judicial workers who extort a confession from criminal suspects or defendants by torture, or who use force to extract testimony from witnesses, are to be sentenced to three years or fewer in prison or put under criminal detention. Those causing injuries to others, physical disablement, or death, are to be convicted and severely punished according to articles 234 and 232."[52] However, the reference to "judicial workers" by implication excludes police activities.

Moreover, the difficulty for complainants lies in enforcing those rights. Although the Administrative Litigation Law allows citizens to sue government officials who infringe upon their rights, citizens cannot bring suits under the current interpretation of the Law because police action is deemed to be an "act of criminal investigation," not an "act of administration."[53] There is also the practical problem that lodging a complaint may just bring further abuse. There have been very few reports of applications to the State Compensation Law known in cases of torture.[54] Regulations governing the supervision of public security organs require supervision by police supervisory teams of "the handling of report of incidents by citizens, their requests for help and their petitions and accusation," but make no explicit reference to acts of torture, or to outside supervisory bodies.[55] The Procuratorate, the body theoretically responsible for monitoring such cases, is demonstrably lacking in power vis-a-vis the public security bodies, as the rapporteur for China in the Committee Against Torture (CAT) pointed out. Moreover, according to the impressions of a visiting observer, the Procurator-General has the same status as a judge, itself quite low, making the task of oversight very difficult indeed.

The second relevant issue is the presumption of innocence. Legal academics lobbied hard to write the principle of the presumption of innocence into the CPL, to no avail. But Chinese commentators suggest that the standard of proof required in criminal cases—that "the facts are clear and the evidence is reliable and ample"—together with the requirement that the state gather all evidence proving guilt or innocence, strongly implies the presumption.[56] This interpretation is open to Hecht's objection that many key rights such as the right to bail, *habeas corpus*, and the exclusion of illegally gathered material, "continue to be severely restricted or completely absent" (63). Also significant is the oral evidence, reported by visiting legal scholars, that Chinese judges do not accept that there is an implicit presumption of innocence.

In other words, the policy in Chinese criminal justice reform seems to be to provide a framework of procedures that imply norms, or that can be invoked to produce different outcomes, either instrumental or normative, depending on the political will and leadership, rather than to articulate values that might become entrenched.

The new Criminal Law, which came into effect in October 1997, was the outcome of a long and tortuous process of consultation begun as early as 1982. In 1988, an initial amendment plan was put forward which, by the time it was examined by the fifth session of the eighth NPC, had twice been submitted to the NPC Standing Committee for examination. It was drafted by the Legislative Affairs Work Committee of the NPC Standing Committee in conjunction with numerous relevant departments and legal specialists and scholars who had "studied . . . (relevant) provisions of criminal laws in foreign countries and the trends of modern criminal legislation."[57] According to Chinese legal specialists, its chief improvements are that it cancels the category of criminal acts by analogy in the 1979 Law, so that acts not stipulated in explicit terms as crimes are no longer considered crimes. Secondly, they argue that it establishes the principle of equality before the law, even though this principle is already guaranteed under the Constitution. Third, it establishes the principle of proportionality, of matching the punishment with the crime. In addition, it abolishes the category of "crimes of counterrevolution," replacing them with "crimes endangering state security" (3–4).

Against these perceived improvements is the problem identified by the UN Working Group on Arbitrary Detention, that "the [amended Criminal} Law may not be applied reasonably in practice."[58] The new law also defines as criminal a number of activities that had previously carried no penalty. As Judge Mai Rongzeng of Guangdong pointed out, such activities as dereliction of duty, fraud in business and insider trading, which previously would have been considered disciplinary offences, are now regarded as serious crimes.[59]

In the view of foreign scholars and NGOs, however, the most notable feature of the amended Criminal Law is the new category of "crimes endangering state security." The idea of abolishing the category of crimes of counterrevolution had initially stemmed from the wish of its Chinese proponents to move toward greater tolerance and to liberalize the legal system. By the mid-1990s, such a category was seen by the state as necessary for several instrumental reasons. As two Chinese scholars put it:

The term, "crimes of counterrevolution," is not conducive to the maintenance of China's national sovereignty and dignity. Counterrevolutionary offenses, under the existing criminal code, have always been viewed internationally as being crimes of a political nature — and the principle of "non-extradition of political prisoners" is universally recognized under international law. However, it would by no means be true to say that all of China's counterrevolutionary crimes are in fact political crimes: quite a few of them are recognized under international law as being common criminal offenses.[60]

The problem of extradition was just one of the international pressures persuading China's leadership to discard the concept: also relevant was the harm done to China's international reputation by its continuation, and the difficulty it posed to the successful implementation of "one country, two systems" in Hong Kong (10–11). The application of the concept of counterrevolutionary crime to activities in a capitalist Hong Kong that was now a part of China was seen to be inappropriate in the majority of situations. Furthermore, the new concept of crimes endangering state security cohered with already existing law on national security in Hong Kong.

The instrumental purpose of this change was underlined by Cai Cheng, Vice-Chairman of the NPC Law Committee. He stated that "At present the country focuses on economic construction, and the highest interests are to safeguard national security, the consolidation of political power and the smooth progress of socialist construction. This is why we are changing 'counterrevolutionary crimes' to 'national security crimes'."[61] Not only did the new term "endangering state security" serve to replace the old term of "counterrevolution," but its jurisdiction was expanded to cover "incitement to subvert the political power of the state and overthrow the socialist system by means of spreading rumors, slander or other means" (Art 105[2]). The original law had not included the category of "other means." And, whereas under the old code counterrevolutionary acts had been defined, no operative description was given the new term.[62] As Human Rights in China and Human Rights Watch/Asia complained, "there is no effort whatsoever in any of these laws to establish standards to determine that any act has actually harmed state security or even could have done so" (21). Finally, the UN Working Group on Arbitrary Detention warned that "under Article 105, even communication of thoughts and ideas or, for that matter, opinions, without intent to commit any violent or criminal act, may be regarded as subversion. Ordinarily, an act of subversion requires more than mere communication of thoughts and ideas." It therefore concluded that "the national security law may be misused and, as long as it is part of the statute, it provides a rationale for restricting fundamental human rights and basic freedoms."[63]

These examples demonstrate the difficulty of assessing the precise balance achieved in China's new legislation between its instrumental use as a mechanism of state power and its normative goal of protecting citizens' fundamental rights. Whereas old concepts, like "counterrevolutionary crime"—which had been the source of international and domestic controversy—were eliminated, new concepts of similar instrumental utility have often replaced them. Whereas old procedures such as "shelter and investigation," and "exemption from prosecution" have been eradicated, new arrangements, allowing police almost as much latitude in their investigations, have taken their place. Clearly, much of the relabeling and refinement has occurred in order to give Chinese criminal law a more international and modern face. To what extent it also represents an internalization of international norms, as opposed to a mere instrumental adjustment, is a more opaque question.

The most significant obstacle to a fair and equitable criminal justice system, moreover, remains very little changed. This is the system of administrative justice, which bypasses the criminal justice system proper. Not only does it provide an alternative form of sanctions to that of the official legal system, it is used by that system to insert loopholes into the impartial administration of justice, since some of its procedures, such as "shelter and investigation," were previously utilized as part of the criminal justice system. It also implicitly works against the effective reform of that system. Despite the Chinese authorities' claim that the revised Criminal Law introduces the concept of equality before the law, the fact that certain categories of administrative punishment are targeted against the lower socioeconomic groups—such as vagabonds, itinerants, and the unemployed—militates against the equal application of the criminal law to all members of society. Increasingly, according to *China Labour Bulletin*, such punishment is also being applied to "workers who have been left out of, or impoverished by, the reform process."[64] Although the use of administrative law as an extrajudicial coercive measure is justified by Chinese scholars as enabling the solution of minor crimes in ways that avoid the imposition of a criminal record, there is no definition of the borderline between acts liable to administrative sanction and a criminal offense. The potential for overlap increases the discretion of the agency.[65] It is also a publicly controversial sanction. In its discussions with Chinese jurists, lawyers and academics, the UN Working Group on Arbitrary Detention was told of their concern that no judge was present when the decision was taken to place a person in administrative detention, thus risking an increase in police abuses.[66]

On paper, by 1996, certain reforms had been effected. An important category of administrative law, "shelter and investigation," was abolished by the same NPC session which promulgated the 1996 NPC Decision revising the CPL. However, as Hecht has pointed out, the provisions of the revised CPL on prearrest detention are simply expanded, so that they now include the same category of persons originally targeted under "shelter and investigation"—those who "do not tell their true name or place of residence or whose identity is unclear" and those "strongly suspected of wandering around committing crimes."[67] The main improvement is that by lifting such crimes out of the area of administrative punishment into the jurisdiction of the criminal law, police activities thereby become subject to the oversight of the procuratorate, and thus to outside supervision.[68]

The most egregious form of administrative detention, however, remains virtually unchanged. Contrary to expectations, the system of reeducation through labor (*laodong jiaoyang*, or *laojiao*), has been retained. Although discussions among Chinese specialists on the revision of the law suggested that this measure should be abolished, the suggestion was not accepted.[69] It was even claimed that reeducation through labor centers offered a "new lease of life" for unemployed people.[70] On the fortieth anniversary of the *laojiao* system in 1997, it was officially estimated that it had taken in more than 2.5 million people.[71] Its legal base is a set of 1982 regulations, of uncertain legality, supplemented in 1992 by Detailed Rules on the Implementation of Law in the Administration of Re-education Through Labor. According to an official account:

> Re-education through labor management committees under the provincial, regional and municipal governments examine and approve decisions on who should be taken in for re-education through labor. In most cases, the time . . . is one year, in a small number of cases the time is about half a year and in extremely rare cases, the time is three years. Those who refuse to accept the decisions on their receiving re-education through labour may make an appeal to have their cases reviewed, or may take administrative proceedings at the people's court in accordance with the Adminstrative Procedural [Litigation] Law. In examining and determining who should receive re-education through labor, re-education through labor committees at various levels strictly follow legal systems and procedures and are supervised by people's procuratorates. (1)

In fact, individuals sentenced to *laojiao* can remain in detention up to four years at a time, a sentence longer than criminal punishments such as control (*guanzhi*), criminal detention (*juyi*) (maximum six months), and penal servitude (*laotuxing*) (minimum six months).[72] The treatment of *laojiao* prisoners differs very little from that suffered by those subject to the criminal sanction *laogai* (reform through labor). Despite the official claim that individuals subject to *laojiao* spend a proportion of their time in study, they have a similar experience of labor and live under similar conditions. Like *laogai* inmates, they can also be subject to cancellation of their urban registration and can be required to remain at the labor camp for the rest of their life as "free laborers" (143). The main difference is that *laojiao* inmates are given basic remuneration.

Those punished under the system of administrative sanctions have limited redress under the Administrative Litigation Law of 1990; the Administrative Review Regulations of 1991; the State Compensation Law of May 1994 (Art. 3); the People's Police Law of February 1995 (Art. 50); the Administrative Punishment Law of 1996; and the Administrative Supervision Law of May 1997.[73] Under the Administrative Litigation Law, research suggests that the number of complaints have surged — but initiating an appeal remains difficult and expensive and may be subject to review before the complainant may proceed to litigation. In 1991, only 20 percent of the cases resulted in an administrative decision being quashed or varied by the courts.[74] Moreover, in appeal, the substantive justice of the procedure cannot be debated: it is simply a matter of whether the official's actions comply with the stated rules (19). The result is that Chinese legislation still allowed more than two hundred thousand people to be detained in 1997 without charge or trial for "reeducation through labor."[75]

Finally, although the Administrative Punishment Law helps overcome past problems of random and unreasonable penalties and gives people liable to receive administrative punishments the right to make a statement and to defend themselves (Art. 32), and even the right to a public hearing (Art. 42), it does not challenge the basis for reeducation through labor and thus cannot be seen as a remedy against arbitrary detention.[76]

Looking at the overall situation of criminal law reform in China, the UN Working Group on Arbitrary Detention concluded at the end of its visit to China that "the revised Criminal Procedure Law is a step in the right direction." It approved the increasing role of lawyers in criminal trials, the implied incorporation of the concept of the presumption of innocence, and the move from an inquisitorial toward a more adversarial system. It believed, however, that "much still requires to be done in terms of the criminal law." This was because the offenses previously listed as "counterrevolutionary crimes" still remained in the statute under the name of offenses "endangering national security"; and many such offenses were vague and imprecise. Finally, the Working Group believed that "the absence of an independent tribunal or judge at the time of committing a person to re-education through labor may make the measure fall short of accepted international standards." It therefore recommended that the government of China further revise both the Criminal Law and the Criminal Procedure Law, so that (1) a provision be incorporated expressly in the CPL stating that under the law a person is presumed innocent until proved guilty by a court or tribunal at the end of a trial; (2) the crime of "endangering national security" be defined in precise terms; (3) an exception be incorporated in the criminal law to the effect that the law will not regard as criminal any peaceful activity in the exercise of the fundamental rights guaranteed by the Universal Declaration of Human Rights; and (4) a permanent independent tribunal be established or a judge be associated with all proceedings under which the authorities may commit a person to reeducation through labor, "in order to obviate the possibility of any criticism that the present procedure is not entirely in conformity with international standards for a fair trial."[77]

Given the plethora of new laws and jurisdictions, the many loopholes, contradictions between laws and regulations, and the practice of relabeling, it is tempting to abandon judgement on the degree to which the new laws protect civil rights until more research can be carried out on their practical implementation. Interim judgements remain unsatisfactory. Clarke and Feinerman have concluded that the prognosis for the rule of law in China is not completely gloomy, since "although law has traditionally been identified with punishment, it is increasingly associated with rules and rule-following."[78] However, this conclusion still begs the question of "rules for whom?" and "rules from where?" Are the rules aimed at serving the state's interests more efficiently or are they also aimed at protecting the individual? Do the laws emanate from international standards or are they primarily laws with "Chinese characteristics"?

In view of the failure of international human rights norms of due process and equality before the law to be adequately reflected in China's revised laws, the extent of international influence on China's law is hard to gauge. Clearly, the law of the international treaties to which China is a party does not automatically become part of the law of the land, and domestic law is not always harmonized with international law. Nevertheless, a relationship between international and domestic law, if elusive and indirect, does exist. In many cases the link is procedural. As some of the examples cited above make clear, new legislation has often been introduced in China with reference to foreign influence, or procedures have been changed in response to an unfavorable foreign reaction. Jonathan Hecht has noted that external pressure clearly played a role in shaping key elements of the 1996 NPC Decision on the revised CPL, especially in the case of "shelter and investigation" — eliminated, according to one Ministry of Public Security official, because of international controversy over the issue.[79] Initially, international influence was partly justified by the globalization of China's economy. Fang Weilan, an official with the Legislative Affairs Work Committee under the Standing Committee of the NPC pointed out that "as the Chinese economy has to be linked to the world economy, economic development inevitably calls for an effort to bring China's legal system in line with international practices."[80] Under the influence of China's legal exchanges with U.S. and European institutions from the 1970s, and of the bilateral dialogue with visiting international human rights delegations to China between 1991 and 1994, that aim spilled over into other areas of law. Thus, a British adviser, Robert Seabrook, QC, played an important role in advising the Chinese government on reform of its criminal codes.[81] China's Minister of Justice, Xiao Yang, claimed in March 1997 that "the adoption of the amended [Criminal] Law has further established a good image of the legal system of our country . . . (and) conforms with the principle of a criminal law with Chinese characteristics and with the principle of a criminal law which is in keeping with international practice."[82] In general, in accordance with the state plan, members of the Eighth NPC and its Standing Committee were expected to "absorb the strong points of legislative activities in various countries and (to) initially establish a scientific and modern legal system in line with international practices."[83] At the same time, there was disagreement at elite levels about the degree of international influence which should be permitted.

Foreign influence has been clear in the extensive borrowing of Western legal doctrines, concepts, and terminology in China's new laws.[84] International human rights standards have been cited as reasons for the incorporation into an annotated draft of a completely revised CPL of the presumption of innocence; the defendant's right to counsel at all stages of the criminal process; and the exclusion of evidence gathered through torture (13 f. 38). More specifically, the UN Convention Against Torture was at one point invoked by those drafting the revisions to the CPL as authority for their argument that all evidence gathered through torture must be excluded in rules on criminal adjudication (68–69). Foreign influence is also apparent in procedural reforms, such as the plan to restructure China's judicial system in 1999 by further opening courtrooms to the general public, increasing independent trial responsibility of judges and establishing a people's jury system.[85] Foreign ideas have been officially welcomed, even if foreign "pressure" has not. In approving the establishment of offices in China by seventeen foreign law firms in February 1998, Xiao Yang stated that such a development increased exchanges and cooperation with foreign lawyers, thus improving the work of Chinese lawyers.[86]

Practical Implementation

The formal adoption of a law in China does not signal the end of the policy-making process. The practical implementation stage, conceived here as the ultimate and most significant level of compliance, involves "an entire 'second campaign' . . . [in which] the key actors will rejoin the battle to define how the provisions of the newly promulgated law will be interpreted and carried out, if at all."[87] In this phase, foreign impact is less apparent and domestic culture and "higher order values" more so. Here the advice foreign judicial experts may give Chinese judges and lawyers reaches the limits of its influence. Here enter the extrajudicial aspects of Party and political interference, and the influence of traditional values and procedures emphasizing outcomes reached through nonadversarial means. Here also enters the habit of the "ceremonial use of rules," deriving from the chasm existing since 1949 between formal laws and their practical implementation. As against these traditional uses of the law, a further layer of complexity has now been added, in the form of the adversarial system instituted in the amended criminal laws, wherein the prosecution must prove its case before a judge.[88] These changes involve not only time and effort in the retraining of lawyers, judges and police, but a total shift in mind-set.

Nor is it simply a matter of whether, and how, different Chinese authorities interpret the new laws and carry them out. It is also a question of how Chinese citizens receive them. As Tom Tyler has observed, "laws and the decisions of legal authorities are of little practical importance if people ignore them."[89] Reflecting this understanding, a spokesman of the Standing Committee of the National People's Congress was reported to have lamented that China had drawn up more than 6,000 laws and regulations since the reform and opening-up began in 1978 and that some departments and personnel had ignored them or even violated them. Xinhua News Agency commented that: "Experts say that the key to turn China into a country with an advanced legal system is to solve the problem that 'laws are usually disobeyed'."[90]

According to Tyler, if people do not trust political and legal authorities, and if they do not have confidence in procedural justice, they are unlikely to comply with the law. A number of elements determine whether procedures are held to be fair: a belief by those involved that they have had a chance to take part in the decision-making process; a perception that the decision-making process is neutral; a perception that people are treated politely and shown respect for their rights and their person; a belief that the motives of the authorities are fair, thereby allowing predictions about their future behavior; and, finally, a perception that the procedures produce fair outcomes.[91] Thus, not only is the just implementation of the law in China dependent on the motivation of the authorities, it is equally dependent on their behavior and on citizens' perceptions of their motivations. However "just" the law, if the citizens distrust public authorities and perceive the outcomes of legal procedures to be unfair, they will refuse to comply voluntarily with the law and a vicious circle will be set in train. The spiral of legal instrumentalism then becomes hard to escape. The success of legal reform is therefore a chicken-and-egg situation, dependent on the citizens having an input into decision making and trust in the political and legal authorities. Further complicating the Chinese situation is the existence of other sources of public morality and dispute mechanisms issuing from different historical phases in China, which vie with the law in contemporary disputes as authority and bases for settlement.[92]

Given the loss of public trust as a result of the violent suppression of the 1989 Democracy Movement, and in view of the corruption and inequality currently characterizing China's political, judicial and economic systems, the restoration of public confidence to the point where law is automatically complied with will clearly require not only an intensive public education program, but also repeated indications of trustworthiness and good intent by the authorities over a sustained period. However, given the instrumental grounding of rule by law, with its primary purpose of legitimizing and protecting political authority, such normative intent is unlikely to be realized, at least at this stage. In March 1997, Qiao Shi, in his role of Chairman of the NPC responsible for creating a "socialist legal system with Chinese characteristics," perfectly encapsulated the obstacles facing any attempt to establish a legal system in China that simultaneously delivered equality before the law and imposed restraint upon the state:

Some of our habits and work methods are not in line with the Constitution or the law. We must correct them with firm resolve. We must establish the social norm of respecting the Constitution and laws and safeguarding the legal system . . . Laws are made for enforcement. We must follow three principles, which Comrade Deng Xiaoping put forward in the early eighties, that we must abide by the law, strictly enforce the law and punish those that have violated the law. We must take powerful measures to stop the phenomena, which have been greatly resented by the vast number of people, that law enforcers themselves are breaking the law, laws are replaced by orders or suppressed by people who wield power, and laws are misinterpreted by bribe-takers . . . To achieve better results in this area, the NPC must, on the foundation that has been established, persevere in intensifying its inspection and supervision over law enforcement for a long time to come.[93]

It is because of these difficulties in practical implementation that China's claims of success in legal reform have focused mainly on the legislative process, and that foreign evaluations of Chinese progress are, if not misguided, then premature.[94] As H.L. Fu has noted: "Amending the CPL will not make the rights real unless they can be enforced."[95] The most effective (and meaningful) index of China's internalization of international norms is obtained not through textual analysis of the new laws but through an analysis of the way laws have been implemented in practice. And here, it has been correctly observed, "the relationship between China's criminal law and the PRC's undertakings with respect to international human rights is as intimate as it is problematic."[96] Or, as Human Rights Watch/Asia has pointed out more bluntly, "it is important to remember that the [legal] reforms are taking place at the same time as widespread arbitrary detention, a stepped up anti-crime campaign, increased controls on information, and heightened repression in Tibet, Xinjiang and Inner Mongolia."[97] In particular, the conflict between the perceived need to depend on the "strike hard" campaign against rising crime and the need to introduce fairer practices illustrates the tension between the instrumental outcome of achieving stability and the normative goal of protecting human rights in China's criminal justice system. Yet, the priority of the former outcome was reiterated in March 1998 when the President of the Supreme People's Court, Ren Jianxin, affirmed that given the fact that "a major task for the people's court is to wage protracted hard struggle against crimes and create a favorable social environment for China's socialist modernization drive," the People's Court would "unswervingly adhere to the principle of 'striking hard' and give heavier and quicker punishment to criminal offenders who jeopardize social security in accordance with law."[98]

This tension between the instrumental/normative *intentions* of the rule of law in China and its purely instrumental *outcomes* is best illustrated in the treatment of dissidents, the issue of torture, the death penalty and labor rights. While other nonpolitical aspects of rights have experienced some liberalization, these areas are regarded by the leadership as critical to regime stability.

Dissidents

The treatment of dissidents is symptomatic of the complex signals on human rights being projected to the world at large by China's leadership. On one hand, controls on nonpolitical social activity have been relaxed, a change that began as early as 1991.[99] By 1996, the U.S. human rights report was able to observe that "looser ideological controls, and freer access to outside sources of information have led to greater room for individual choice, more diversity in cultural life and increased media reporting." On the other hand, the same report stated that, by the end of 1995, "almost all public dissent against the central authorities" had been "silenced by intimidation, exile, or imposition of prison terms or administrative detention."[100] And a 1996 report by Amnesty International concluded that "no one is safe."[101]

Despite government denials that China held political prisoners, on 30 May 1997 Vice-Minister of Justice Zhang Xiufu told a press conference that there were 2,026 prisoners in China jailed for counterrevolutionary crimes.[102] For such individuals, prison conditions continued to be poor, and there were continuing reports of torture and lack of medical care. During 1997, some prisoners were released, and there was a hitherto unprecedented wave of public criticism of the government. Closely monitored by the police, some of these protests were tolerated, some protesters were subjected to house arrest or temporary detention, and others were arrested and sentenced. The new dissident boldness built on a trend beginning in the mid-1990s, when greater public consciousness of democracy and human rights was facilitated by dissidents' recourse to public, traditional, and legal forums, such as open petition letters addressed to the NPC, which also made careful use of the international media's influence within China and abroad. By 1995, Chinese dissidents abroad were reporting that despite suppression of dissidents, the social atmosphere in China was becoming increasingly tolerant of dissident ideas.[103]

In late 1997 and early 1998, dissidents were heartened by a government policy that appeared to be more responsive to international pressures, as evidenced by China's signature of the ICESCR and the release of prominent dissident Wei Jingsheng in November 1997. Anticipating the forthcoming Ninth NPC in March 1998, they therefore sent petitions to the NPC calling openly for the closure of labor camps, a revision of China's 1982 Constitution, the rehabilitation of former liberal Premier Zhao Ziyang, and specific human rights improvements.[104] Five of the twenty or so signatories to one of these petitions were arrested prior to the opening of the Congress. In particular, veteran Chinese dissident Xu Wenli, originally arrested after the Democracy Wall Movement in 1979–81, petitioned for the freeing of labor unions from government shackles, and the repeal of laws requiring unions and other social organizations to register with the government. He called on the NPC to chart a way to implement the ICESCR, and added that Beijing should also sign the ICCPR.[105] There were also calls from those "within the system" such as Professor Sheng Dewen of Beijing University, who in August 1997 publicly espoused a twenty-five year program of political reform that would include the phased adoption of direct elections for senior government officials, a directly elected parliament, an independent judiciary, and a free press.[106] A member of the Communist Party, he stated in March 1998, "Total political control by a single party is out of step with modern reality, and it will have to change. We have competition in the economic area, so we will have to have it in politics as well. . . . The new leaders didn't fight for power the way the revolutionaries did, and people do not believe that they have an automatic right to have it. People ask: 'Why do these people deserve all the power'?"[107]

Similarly, writing in *Reform Magazine*, a leading journal of economic reform, in January, Li Shenzhi, retired Vice-President of the Chinese Academy of Social Sciences, proclaimed that "implementation of political reform will determine the ultimate success or failure of economic reform." His article sparked off a spate of publications on political reform and the need for direct elections.[108] The buildup to President Clinton's visit to China in June 1998 allowed dissidents some months of freedom in which to express their views. Government tolerance of such public expression of opinion was reminiscent of the 1979–81 Democracy Wall Movement, and the 1989 Democracy Movement, when dissent was temporarily allowed because it reflected the views and interests of some in the Party. It was part of "the potent interaction of a divided leadership and state apparatus with impulses for protest from below."[109] The measure of what was tolerated and what was not was clearly based on an arbitrary and changing estimate as to which activities represented a threat to social order and political stability at any given time, an evaluation influenced by inner-Party struggle, by domestic pressures, and by international developments.

One constant, however, was state intolerance for potential organized opposition, even in the apparently innocent form of applications for the establishment of citizens' and social organizations. Freedom of association remained a sticking point. As NPC Chairman Li Peng stated in December 1998, "If they [new organizations] violate the Constitution and the principles of Chinese policy, oppose the socialist market economy and national unity, demand political independence and a multiparty system, or even call the leadership of the CCP into question, then we will not tolerate them."[110] When dissidents in nine provinces and cities began attempts in July 1998 to establish a China Democracy party, a new campaign of government repression began which saw increasing arrests of dissidents, often on the occasion of a visit by a Western dignitary. Among them was Wang Youcai, arrested for establishing a preparatory committee for the China Democracy Party, and, in December, the veteran dissident Xu Wenli. Zhang Shanguang was arrested in July for attempting to organize an association for protecting the rights of laid-off workers. An independent think-tank claiming 4,000 members, the China Development Union, was disbanded in October and three of its leaders detained. Also in October, police shut down an anti-corruption group with one hundred members called "Corruption Behaviour Observers." A Chinese dissident, Chen Zengxiang, was refused access to a lawyer and , after a secret trial, jailed for seven years for "leaking state secrets." One dissident, Cai Guihua, was even detained for ten hours in Shanghai after being found in a park with others reading the International Covenant on Civil and Political Rights.[111]

The climax came in late December, when Wang Youcai, Qin Yongmin and Xu Wenli received jail sentences of eleven to thirteen years, prompting international outrage, especially from the U.S. Congress.

Dissent in Tibet and Xinjiang was also harshly treated. In 1997, two hundred monks and nuns were reported to be in prison in Tibet, out of eighteen hundred in the region imprisoned for allegedly breaking national security laws.[112] More than six hundred Tibetans have reportedly been detained for peacefully advocating independence from China.[113] The increase of repression in 1997, which involved a stepped-up campaign against the Dalai Lama and Tibetan cultural practices, led the International Commission of Jurists to recommend a UN-supervised referendum to ascertain the wishes of the Tibetan people (2). Increasingly, the new rhetoric of ruling by law was applied to the ethnic minority regions of Tibet and Xinjiang. By the Ninth NPC in March 1998, Xinjiang officials said that a two-year police crackdown had succeeded in restoring political stability to the Muslim region, and admitted that some people had been executed, given suspended death sentences as well as prison terms after a succession of large-scale riots and bombings in the region. On the same day, however, a top Chinese official admitted that China might fail to curb separatism in Xinjiang.[114]

However, the most public evidence of the *de facto* human rights situation has been the changing fortunes of China's most famous dissident, Wei Jingsheng. To some extent, Wei's fame turned him from a dissident into a commodity that could be bought and sold in the market of human rights diplomacy. For this reason, it was assumed that Chinese treatment of him would illustrate the way the authorities wished their judicial system to be viewed internationally. The case, however, was to prove more a lesson in the changing criteria of Chinese sovereignty than a model of judicial practice. Wei's rearrest in 1994 occurred in the wake of the increasing repression of China's dissidents. Releases of prisoners sentenced in connection with the Tiananmen crackdown in 1989 had virtually ended with the delinkage of human rights and MFN, and with President Clinton's renewal of MFN in May 1994.[115] New security regulations, the Detailed Rules for the Implementation of the Security Law of the People's Republic of China, had been signed into law on 4 June 1994.[116]

Despite some advances in the rights of due process since Wei's first trial in

1979, the process of his trial in December 1995, its virtually closed nature, the lack of prior consultation with his lawyers, the long period of incommunicado detention that also conflicted with the requirement of Chinese criminal law, the length of his sentence, and the summary rejection of his appeal demonstrated, on one hand, the gap that still existed between Chinese legal practice and Chinese law and, on the other, the gulf that yawned between Chinese legal practice and international human rights law.[117] More important, Wei's sentence to fourteen years' imprisonment was for reasons of "conspiring to subvert the government" by "communicating with hostile foreign organizations and individuals, amassing funds in preparation for overthrowing the government and publishing anti-government articles abroad." Although the 1993 State Security Law was not cited in the judgment, "its logic and method" pervaded the case.[118] Despite the expectation that Wei's would be a model trial, it was later seen as representing a change for the worse, wherein the charges for prisoners of conscience changed from "counterrevolution" to "endangering state security" (40).

The international impact of Wei's sentencing revealed once again the way one part of the human rights regime was played off against another, whether by China or the U.S. Before the sentencing of Wei, Chinese authorities had reportedly been offering continued human rights dialogue with the United States as a quid pro quo for U.S. agreement not to press a resolution against China in the 1996 Human Rights Commission. The U.S. response had been noncommittal, but, once Wei had been sentenced, the Administration announced that it now had no alternative but to press for such a resolution.[119] That decision in turn was seen by the U.S. as a preferable and less expensive alternative to returning to the threat of MFN sanctions.

For this reason, Wei's formal arrest and sentencing was inexplicable to many observers, coinciding as it did with urgent attempts by China to head off the looming resolution on China's human rights. China's concerns on this score were not only conveyed through diplomatic channels, but were visibly indicated by its publication on 28 December 1995 of a new White Paper on human rights arguing China's human rights progress over recent years.[120] This document, and the flurry of articles on human rights appearing in the *Beijing Review* prior to the vote in the Human Rights Commission, may well have influenced the final outcome.[121] That Chinese authorities nevertheless chose to convict Wei in the same month as its publication was once again proof of the leadership's preparedness to jeopardize China's international reputation for the sake of domestic stability.

It was thus all the more interesting that only two years later, China chose to release Wei, and some months later, Wang Dan, to the United States, ostensibly on health grounds. The announcement on Wei was made after President Jiang Zemin's return from the U.S., and could also have been part of a basket of agreed commodities to exchange for a promise from the combined forces of the European Union and the U.S. not to sponsor a resolution on China in the 1998 session of the UN Human Rights Commission. It could also have formed part of a broader context involving China's concern to shore up Western investment in its faltering economy. China's altered assessment of Wei's importance to its vital interests, however, once again demonstrated the salience of China's short-term tactical interests in prompting a renegotiation of its sovereignty.

Torture

Human rights NGOs are unanimous on the problem of the continued practice of torture in China. In a media briefing on its 1996 report, Amnesty International stated:

Torture and ill-treatment remain widespread and systemic in China . . . These violations occur in police stations, detention centres, labor camps and prisons across the country, sometimes resulting in the death of the victims . . . Many acts which constitute torture or ill-treatment — notably the use of torture to punish, intimidate or coerce a person — are not offenses under the law . . . The Chinese government has taken some positive measures in recent years to strengthen and implement the existing prohibition of torture in law. While Amnesty International welcomes these measures, it believes that the government is still failing to acknowledge the true extent of torture in China and the reasons why it continues.[122]

Speaking before the UN Committee against Torture, China's Ambassador, Wu Jianmin, stated that in the three years from 1993 to 1995, the Supreme People's Procuratorate had investigated a total of 1,194 allegations of torture. The 1996 White Paper on human rights cited 409 cases of extortion of confession, implicitly by means of torture and ill-treatment, investigated in 1994, and the subsequent completion of 398 cases.[123] Official Chinese statistics are not published about the torturers, or their punishment, and the cases of torture other than for purposes of extracting confessions are not recorded. From the number of unofficial reports on the practice of torture, Amnesty International has concluded that "few judicial investigations into torture allegations are instigated by the Chinese authorities compared with the high incidence reported."[124] Political and common criminals alike continue to be subjected to torture, frequently during preliminary and pretrial detention in police stations, which in many instances has resulted in death (66–68). One study based on interviews of former prisoners in Xinjiang between 1995 and 1997 documented different forms of torture that included forcing prisoners who did not accomplish enough labor in a day to jog for hours or pull a cart loaded with stones; solitary confinement in cagelike cells; beatings; applying electric stun guns to sensitive parts of the anatomy; forced drinking of urine or eating of garbage thrown in the latrine; and forced work in leg chains. This study also reported that in 1996, two years after the appearance of the 1994 Prison Law, conditions were seen by some prison inmates to be improving, since, as one prisoner put it, "now the *duizhang* (wardens) no longer beat prisoners, because they also study the prison law."[125] Particular excesses have been reported in Tibet and Xinjiang, where Chinese fears of separatist activity have produced extremely violent treatment of dissent. According to one report, "the use of electric cattle-prods on these detainees appears to be general practice and women, particularly nuns, are subjected to the harshest torture, including rape using cattle-prods. A number of political prisoners, young nuns among them, have died in Tibetan jails, allegedly as a result or torture or negligence."[126]

Death Penalty

In August 1997, the *Economist* commented: "Last year may, with hindsight, go down as a milestone in China's legal history, for that was when Chinese law reformers won sweeping changes to the arbitrary way in which people were arrested and imprisoned . . . In the meantime, 1996 will be remembered better for the abandon with which the Chinese state executed its people."[127] In a 1997 report, Amnesty International recorded 6,100 death sentences in China for 1996, with 4,367 confirmed executions. It estimated that the figure was probably a fraction of the unreported total, whose statistics are classified as a state secret. It represented a doubling of 1995 figures, and was the highest number of executions in China since 1983, when a "strike hard" campaign against rising crime was first ordered by the authorities.[128] The 1996 increase was possibly related to new legislation in 1995 which raised the number of crimes punishable by death to 65.[129]

The use of the death penalty, increasingly applied to even nonviolent crimes such as stealing, counterfeiting, and propagation of "superstitions," is reported to have been "elevated to the level of dogma" by the Chinese regime.[130] Measures for the imposition of the death penalty include vague categories of cases "where the circumstances are particularly serious" or when the crime is "heinous." The poor have been the hardest hit. Suspected separatists are another highly vulnerable group, with 42 executed in Tibet and 160 in Xinjiang in 1996.[131] However, following Amnesty's report, Xiao Yang, the Minister of Justice, insisted that "Chinese criminal law lays down extremely rigid limitations and regulations on the death penalty, which is only applicable to those criminals who are guilty of the most heinous crimes." While he reportedly mentioned the possibility of its suspension, Gu Angran, Chairman of the Legislative Affairs Commission of the NPC stated categorically at the same press conference that "The death penalty will not be abolished. It will be handled with strict controls."[132]

Notwithstanding such claims, the ubiquitous resort to the death penalty is clearly in breach of the International Covenant on Civil and Political Rights, which China signed in October 1998. Despite continued official support for the efficacy of the "strike hard" campaigns, Chinese legal specialists themselves have begun to question the policy of using the death penalty to prevent and eradicate what is a growing crime problem.[133] The principle of proportionality, of making the punishment fit the crime, is on trial in this system where "strike hard" goals are clearly overriding all notions of justice, equality before the law, and the most basic human right, the right to life.

Labor Rights

Currently China is at a crisis point in labor rights that may well have a determining impact on the future direction of the rule of law. The wholesale dismantling of SOEs, decided at the 15th Party Congress in 1997, together with the downsizing of the bureaucracy announced at the Ninth National People's Congress in March 1998, is creating an unemployment crisis of unparalleled dimensions. The figure for urban unemployment is officially 3.1percent, or 5.63 million people, while the true figure is put at 7.5 percent, or 15.5 million people. To that number must be added more than 100 million rural migrants traveling through China looking for work. A Chinese economist, Feng Lanrui, has even predicted a jobless figure of 28 percent by the year 2000, with 214 million surplus rural laborers seeking work in cities.[134] Strikes and protests have proliferated, particularly in the populous province of Sichuan, and in the rust-belt provinces in the Northeast. From 1991 to 1994 there were 10,000 labor disputes throughout China annually, but after 1995 the number doubled, with 1,504 in Guangdong alone in 1997. Disputes centered on delayed payment of salaries, bad working conditions, overtime without extra pay and on-the-job injuries.[135] Compounding such pressures are the findings of a 1997 ICFTU report, *Search and Destroy — Hunting Down Trade Unions in China*, that there has been no letup in repression since 1989: "All attempts to organize independent workers' organizations have resulted in the arrest, sentencing or extended detention without trial of those involved," it stated. According to the report, organizations are dismantled as soon as they apply for official registration; arrested trade unionists are systematically tortured and often exposed to contagious diseases; and the families of victims are themselves harassed.[136] The result, as Han Dongfang, China's exiled trade union activist, observes, is that "The labor situation in China is a time bomb waiting to explode" (1). This crisis situation has been acknowledged by China's leaders, in particular Premier Zhu Rongji, who warned that "ensuring the livelihood of laid-off workers and their re-employment are issues that are vitally important for both the reform of state-owned enterprises and social stability."[137]

In the face of mounting labor disputes and widespread demonstrations of discontent, arbitration committees charged with resolving disputes recorded a 56 percent rise in the number of cases in the first half of 1997 compared to the same period in 1996. Most cases were reportedly centered on wage rates, the laying off of workers, and social security disputes. At the same time, the *China Market Economic News* claimed that the new labor laws were an important reason for the number of labor disputes, because both employers and employees were increasingly aware of legal methods that could be used to resolve conflicts.[138] The dispute settlement procedure, which has been in effect since 1987, provides for mediation, two levels of arbitration committee and a final appeal to the courts. In early 1998, Fan Jiang, Director of the Ministry of Labor's Dispute Division, announced that in order to counter the delays arising from the fact that employees could not file grievances in court until government-sponsored arbitration efforts had failed, a new law on procedures to resolve disputes was being drafted.[139]

These developments, combined with the lack of an adequate safety net for an aging and increasingly unemployed workforce, a crisis in medical care, and a renewed push for the privatization of housing, have produced a huge legitimacy crisis for a government still theoretically basing its right to rule partly on the leadership of the working class and the right to work, a right still guaranteed under the 1982 Constitution. In this context, the new rhetoric of ruling by law has a coercive ring. At the very least, a new one-year contract system introduced for workers in a Beijing factory was described by a Chinese worker as the method of "'using the law as a shield' in the drive to force workers onto the unemployment heap [and] attack . . . every single one of us at the factory."[140]

If resort to the law is the only option for a government squeezed on one side by threats of a financial blowout and on the other by fear of social unrest, the form the law will take is already predetermined. The crisis highlights the importance of ILO labor standards which could help mediate the situation, and particularly the need for China's ratification of conventions promoting freedom of association. Even within the limited freedoms currently allowed, a survey of sources of worker discontent suggests the need to enlarge the scope of collective bargaining from its present 15 percent coverage.[141] More crucially, as Han Dongfang pointed out in a letter to former NPC Chairman, Qiao Shi: "An ordinary worker who issues a call for independent trade unions as a way of preventing the spread of even more corruption and of ameliorating the deepening social crisis in China is thrown into prison! Does the CCP want workers to issue calls to arms or even civil war? Would that be better than calling for independent trade unions? Of course, the CCP is confident of its control of the army and should it force people into open rebellion then it can justify this violence to cower the population in general. This strategy may not be written down anywhere, but reality reveals its existence."[142]

The All-China Federation of Trade Unions (ACFTU) has made some adjustments to the present situation by attempting to find work for the millions laid off. At a meeting in November 1997, it put forward ten measures for helping workers in difficulty, for promoting reemployment, and for safeguarding the workers' legal rights.[143] It has also moved toward greater worker participation. In September 1997, the President of the ACFTU, Wei

Jianxing, called on trade unions to explore new democratic management methods and ways to supervise the managers and protect the workers' rights in accordance with the law. He stated that both boards of directors and supervisors should work with democratically elected representatives of trade unions.[144] In a meeting in October 1998 with newly elected leaders of the ACFTU, President Jiang Zemin also called on enterprises to improve democratic management and depend more on workers' representatives to deal with major issues concerning enterprise reforms and workers' interests.[145] Worker participation, along with grassroots democracy, was even cited by Premier Zhu Rongji as evidence of China's move toward greater political liberalization.[146] Such claims coexist uneasily with the findings of the International Confederation of Free Trade Unions (ICFTU) report and the strong implication that the 1994 Labor Law is not being put into practice. Thus, Dang Xiaojie, Deputy Director of the Policy and Legislation Department of the Labor Ministry, insisted in late 1997 that "based on our understanding, the non-compliance with the [Labor] Law on the part of employers is not necessarily deliberate. On the contrary, it is often due to their not having a thorough understanding of the legal requirements or having been misled by incorrect advice." He admitted that individual provinces and cities might need to draw up comprehensive rules and regulations based on the Labor Law, since it was of a general nature and largely addressed matters of principle.[147]

The struggle in Hong Kong over the repeal of the Collective Bargaining Ordinance has also taken the debate squarely into the arena of labor standards. In November 1997, Lee Cheuk-yan, General Secretary of the Confederation of Trade Unions in Hong Kong, lodged a formal complaint with the ILO against the Hong Kong Special Administrative Region (SAR) government for scrapping two laws on collective bargaining and antiunion discrimination.[148] To counter the adverse publicity on its domestic and international policies, the ACFTU has embarked on a vigorous labor rights diplomacy, on one hand wooing foreign unions and on the other attacking the ICFTU for its alleged interference in Chinese affairs.[149]

Political Reform

Whatever the Chinese government's attitude to political dissent in any given period, the formal goal of "democracy" as conceived in the West remains far from its priorities.[150] As NPC Chairman Li Peng declared in December 1998, the "Western model of separation of powers, multiparty system and privatization" could not be transposed to China.[151] For this reason, the freedoms underpinning the exercise of popular political power, freedom of speech, the press, publication, assembly, and association, have not been underwritten by new Chinese laws. Indeed, new laws such as the Law on Assemblies, Parades and Demonstrations of the People's Republic of China of November 1989, or Article 105 in the revised Criminal Law, were drafted as much to inhibit the free expression of opinion as to channel it.[152] For this reason, as we have seen, citizens attempting to exercise freedom of association by seeking to register autonomous political or labor organizations have been harshly dealt with. For this reason, the battle has been joined in post-handover Hong Kong, touted as a model of "one country, two systems." There, despite considerable evidence that Chinese authorities have sought to preserve its freedoms, the repeal of an amendment to the Bill of Rights that gave legal recourse to individuals who claimed their rights had been infringed by others was seen as a breach of the ICCPR.[153] So, too, was the passage on 7 April 1998 of the Adaptation of Laws (Interpretative Provisions) Bill, which exempted both the SAR government and organs of the Chinese government from many local laws. It was seen to reverse "the very premise upon which Hong Kong's legal structure and legal future are grounded, that is, the presumption that government is accountable under the law."[154]

The limits of political restructuring in China have been set at the point at which its instrumental function of legitimizing Party rule and enhancing the efficiency of the state apparatus begins to be overshadowed by its negative impact on Party supremacy.[155] Political reform is therefore associated with the stabilizing effects of legal and institutional reform. Thus, on assuming his position as Chairman of the NPC in 1993, Qiao Shi declared that "democracy must be institutionalized and codified into laws so that this system and its laws will not change with a change in leadership, nor with changes in viewpoints and attention."[156] As a first step, this was a legitimate goal since, as Minxin Pei has pointed out, at the beginning of its modernization process, China lacked the necessary institutions for a market economy, such as a legal system and clearly defined political institutions.[157] Political reform as it was conceived saw the regularization of the administration of political power, with the mandatory retirement of party and government officials, and a two-term limit on all Party and government positions; the introduction of limited competition for Party offices; and the gradual strengthening of the NPC. The latter involved the introduction of limited competitive "selections" that allowed deputies of provincial people's congresses to nominate their own candidates to compete with the Party's choices; the appointment of senior politicians as head of the NPC Standing Committee, thereby giving the parliament more clout; and tolerance of an increasing show of independence by NPC deputies.[158]

Institutional reform reached its zenith in the Ninth NPC's decision in March 1998 to restructure and downsize the state bureaucracy and merge government ministries and commissions, bringing the number down from forty to twenty-nine, and possibly laying off around four million bureaucrats over a four-year period. Debate on the management of this reform was lively, as was discussion about how to achieve the optimum rule of law.[159] Moreover, in the election of former Premier Li Peng as Chairman of the NPC, 10 percent of deputies either voted against him or abstained, while Han Zhubin, a protege of President Jiang Zemin, was nominated as Procurator-General with only a 65 percent approval rating.[160] However, the limits of political reform were suggested by the same forum. The top posts of government, the nation's President and Vice-President, the head of the Supreme People's Court, the Procurator-General, and the NPC's Chairman and Vice-Chairmen were to be held on a one-candidate-per-post basis and nominated through the NPC's 152-member Standing Committee.[161]

Although in his Premier's Work Report to the Ninth NPC Li Peng declared that China's goal was to "strengthen the construction of democracy and a legal system," the achievements he itemized were narrow in scope.[162] They did not, for instance, include any change in the unequal relationship between the Communist Party and the eight noncommunist parties that existed in a system of "multi-party cooperation and political consultation under the leadership of the Chinese Communist Party."[163] Nor did they include initiatives to enhance the accountability of the upper echelons of government. When asked about future democratic election of governmental officials such as China's President or the Premier, Premier Zhu Rongji was evasive, stating merely, " that is a question involving the political restructuring that should be done according to legal procedures . . . it is hard for me to predict when such elections will take place."[164]

Minxin Pei has given political reform an essentially Chinese interpretation in his formulation of three elements essential to any such program: the establishment of norms governing elite politics; restructuring of basic institutions governing relations among parts of the state; and the strengthening of the institutions of political participation.[165] The essential missing ingredient is that while the actual political institutions in China may have been strengthened informally, popular participation per se has not. The fundamental political rights as set down by Article 25 of the ICCPR are the rights "(a) to take part in the conduct of public affairs, directly or through freely chosen representatives; and (b) to vote and be elected at genuine periodic elections which shall be by universal and equal suffrage and shall be held by secret ballot, guaranteeing the free expression of the will of the electors." Whatever form China's "socialist democracy" takes, the absence of this crucial ingredient of popular participation via universal suffrage by secret ballot also means that in the face of the enormous political and social dislocation created by economic restructuring, the political system is incapable of absorbing the strains placed on it by widespread discontent. Instead, the onus for maintaining social stability is placed squarely on the legal system.

The only political lung operative in the system, after some abortive attempts at popular elections for the local people's congresses in Beijing at the end of 1990, is grassroots political reform in the countryside, allowing popular political expression at the most basic level. According to the Organic Law on Villagers' Committees, once every three years villagers are permitted to directly elect directors, deputy directors, and members of villagers' committees. In some provinces, "self-recommendation" has been encouraged to decide the candidates for the villagers' committees and the post of Director has been open for competition. In others, preliminary elections have been held to determine formal candidates for villagers' committees.[166] On 5 November 1998, a newly revised Organic Law on Villagers' Committees was adopted at the Fifth Meeting of the Standing Committee of the Ninth NPC that provided new rules for handling the sensitive relations between village committees and Party Committee branches at the village level.

This grassroots development has been widely touted as the beginning of China's democratization and projected as such to an outside world, particularly the U.S. Thus, a delegation from the Jimmy Carter Center was invited to monitor elections of the villagers' committee in Fujian and Hebei Provinces in March 1997 and, again, to monitor elections in villagers' committees in Jilin and Liaoning Provinces in March 1998. However, the program is not just a public relations exercise. Its introduction was initially justified to allow peasants a chance to express their grievances, and hence to act as a safety valve for rural discontent. In his original announcement of the "villagers' autonomy experiment" in fifty-eight unspecified areas in the country in May 1994, Civil Affairs Minister Doje Cering explained that grassroots democracy was important to rural stability and social development.[167] Subsequent official statements have praised its additional contribution to enhancing peasants' awareness of law and democracy and to strengthening the relations between the Party and the masses.[168] The very fact that social stability is the justification given for this new development suggests that China is only too aware of the role popular political participation might play in channeling popular feeling — but the decision not to expand such experiments into politics at a higher level, so strikingly demonstrated in the move to crush the formation of political opposition parties and social organizations at the end of 1998, is due both to concern to maintain Party supremacy and to fear of unleashing the torrent of popular opinion.

Conclusion

It is clear that China has absorbed the procedures and norms of the international human rights regime to the point where it has been prepared to accede to the right of some UN bodies to monitor human rights in China in return for reciprocal advantages, and to host UN conferences that may bring international prestige. It has also taken the long-awaited step of signing the two core International Covenants, the ICCPR and the ICESCR. However, the significance of this step depends very much on when, and with what reservations, China subsequently ratifies the Covenants. Moreover, the diplomatic context, in which China has made significant concessions primarily to avoid a China resolution in the UN Commission on Human Rights, suggests the contingent nature of its compliance. To date it is clear that both the United Nations and China have learned from their interaction: however so far, in China's case, the learning process appears more instrumental than normative.

On paper, the mid-1990s have witnessed an improvement in legal safeguards for citizens' rights. But layers of opacity obscure the degree to which this formal adjustment has improved the protection of the individual's rights. The first layer is the law itself, involving loopholes, regulations contradicting or limiting the laws, the problem of relabeling, and the problem of the fragmentation of legal authority ensuing from a proliferation of laws and regulations. The ambiguity in the new legal procedures is reflected in the dual meaning of the Chinese term *fazhi*, meaning both "rule of law" and "rule by law." The second layer of opacity is the question of the practical application of the laws, and the obstacles impeding equality before the law, due process, and citizens' redress. The third layer is a political one in the form of a complex factional struggle being waged over the precise meaning of ruling by law. A final layer is the international arena of formal human rights diplomacy, wherein certain specific human rights issues — prominent dissidents like Wei Jingsheng and Wang Dan, the issue of religious freedom, Tibet, grassroots political reform, and Chinese initiatives to invite certain UN bodies and officials and foreign "dialogue" delegations to visit China — have become commodities that can be traded on the international human rights market in exchange for an agreement by the global community not to pursue the issue of China's overall human rights conditions in country resolutions in UN forums. Such diplomacy allows certain valid human rights issues to assume international prominence, but thereby also casts other equally valid issues into comparative obscurity, if not outer darkness. To what extent these layers of opacity obscure a fundamental internalization of international human rights standards by China, and to what extent they merely veil the shadow play of instrumental learning, will take time and thorough empirical research to unravel. In the meantime, continuing human rights abuses in China in almost all areas of international human rights — in particular, torture, the death penalty, and freedom of association — suggest the need for caution in proclaiming a new era of progress in China's human rights.

Caution is also required because of the intimate relationship in China between genuine legal reform and political reform. The nexus Chinese leaders perceive is indeed vital to China's political well-being, but not in the sense that it is currently understood. In the Chinese political system as it is currently constituted, it is hardly possible to have a genuine rule of law without political reform, and vice versa. As we have seen, for citizens to respect and obey the law in the first place requires not only public education, but also a popular perception of government trustworthiness and transparency, which can be achieved only through the auspices of responsible government. For the amendment of criminal legislation so that it properly and unambiguously protects the rights of the individual, and for the establishment of a rule *of* law rather than a rule *by* law, an accountable legislature is required. Whatever form of democracy proves most appropriate, it cannot coexist with Party hegemony, so that changes in the Party's role and structure are inevitable. The power of Party and state must also be restrained if the judiciary is to become truly independent. Unless these preconditions can be satisfied, a rule of law capable of protecting citizens' rights is unlikely to evolve.

It is therefore reasonable to conclude that in the second half of the decade, insofar as China has demonstrated normative learning domestically as a result of the process of its involvement in the human rights regime, it is mainly at the *de jure* level, in response to both internal and external pressures. Whether the loopholes and contradictions within the new laws are exploited, or whether new norms and procedures are implemented to protect the individual, depends on the variables already explored and, most crucially, on the political will from above. The principles contained within the laws are amenable to interpretation on behalf of citizens' rights, just as they are open to instrumental manipulation. However, the limits of compliance are currently set at the point where reform begins to challenge the authority of Party and state. In this context, the introduction into the criminal law of new procedures that move toward international principles of the presumption of innocence and judicial independence, and the ongoing debate over the proper implementation of the rule of law by Chinese leaders, scholars, legal specialists, and dissidents, remain the primary evidence that the reach of the international human rights regime has succeeded in transcending the many obstacles in China that exist to block it.

Conclusion

Some gentlemen in Western states often rely on isolated happenings and distorted, exaggerated and even fabricated facts to make biased comments on China's human rights. . . . On the whole, we think that the fair estimate on the condition of China's human rights should be that great achievements have been made although there still exist some problems and efforts are being made to improve.
— Zhu Muzhi, 25 June 1997

This is precisely the time when support from our friends is most needed.
— Wei Jingsheng, addressing the UN Commission on Human Rights, April 1998

The goals of this book have been to assess the nature of China's attitude toward interdependence in the global community and to evaluate the depth of its international socialization and learning. To this end, the most sensitive of barometers and the most stringent of tests — the international human rights regime — has been employed. Using five main case studies of China's interaction with UN bodies that monitor human rights, three principal questions have been posed: what is the nature of its interaction; what does the process of its participation tell us in general about China's international learning experience and its attitude to international regimes; and what do the case studies reveal about the effectiveness of the parts and whole of the UN regime?

Although the Universal Declaration of Human Rights and the human rights treaties provide an abstract and ideal standard of compliance with the international human rights regime, in reality there is a level of acceptable practical compliance in the light of regime norms and procedures.[1] Moreover, this acceptable level is subject to change across case studies, time, and occasions (201). The level actually achieved by states is also subject to variation. China's compliance with the norms and institutions of the international human rights regime has highlighted this variability and contingency. The evaluation of its compliance is also bound by definition to be provisional, since to date it has failed to ratify the two major international human rights treaties, the International Covenant on Civil and Political Rights (ICCPR) and the International Covenant on Economic, Social and Cultural Rights (ICESCR), even though it has signed both.

In this study, the levels of compliance, learning, and effectiveness have been tested through what Marc Levy and others have called "natural or quasi-experiments," involving comparisons across different issue areas over time within a single evolving regime.[2] Interaction between China and UN bodies has been documented and assessed both vertically and horizontally, that is, according to chronology and issue area. Three main chronological phases in its compliance distinguish themselves, determined by China's domestic situation, its openness to the outside world, its external bargaining power, and the weakness or strength of the regime's application. The first phase of interaction, from 1971, when China entered the United Nations, until 1979, coincided with an expansion in China's relations with the outside world, its continued domestic introspection, and a very weak application of the regime. In this initial phase, China barely conceded its international human rights obligations and avoided, where possible, involvement in UN human rights activities and UN General Assembly human rights resolutions. It was, however, exposed to the regime's routinizing effect in habituating it to its norms and procedures. Significantly, during this period the civil rights violations exacerbated by the onset of the Cultural Revolution continued unabated, but failed to draw international criticism.

During the second phase of interaction, from 1979 to 1989, China was opening up both domestically and internationally, attempted to make restitution to its citizens for the abuse of their rights during the Cultural Revolution, and began voluntary and active involvement in the UN human rights regime. Domestic interest in the theory and practice of human rights expanded, in parallel with the more liberal domestic environment. The still weak application of the regime, however, ensured that China was able to maintain the initiative in the timing and intensity of its participation, and to avoid the potential threat to its sovereignty that a strong application of the regime would have entailed.

The crushing of the Democracy Movement in June 1989 represented a watershed in China's interaction with the regime and to a large extent undermined its control over the nature of its participation. It brought a swift multilateral response, with the imposition of sanctions by international financial institutions and multilateral forums and the adoption of measures by a variety of UN bodies. Ironically, it was the previous phase of China's active and voluntary participation in UN human rights bodies that facilitated the new international critique and encouraged international action.

China's domestic behavior altered its hitherto benign image in the eyes of foreign governments, particularly those of the West. Under the umbrella of the multilateral response, measures were also adopted by a number of states. Initially, the effect of this joint action was China's total rejection of the regime's norms, its denial of their applicability to itself, and the mobilization of arguments invoking highly legalistic interpretations of sovereignty. By 1990, however, with the gradual easing of sanctions, and the resumption by the U.S. of the main responsibility for their continuation, Chinese attention was drawn away from the multilateral monitoring process, and the majority of its protests relating to state sovereignty and interference were targeted at bilateral monitoring, in particular the MFN mechanism wielded by the U.S.

By the end of 1990, a new and more positive sub-phase in the post-1989 era began, with the Chinese government's decision to actively engage in the international human rights debate and to embark on vigorous human rights diplomacy (*renquan waijiao*). This decision involved strong domestic support for human rights research, conferences and scholarly and official human rights publications, the hosting of visiting government delegations, and heightened activity in UN human rights forums. Much energy was expended on forums that attracted maximum international attention and that had the potential to subject China's human rights conditions to unfavorable international publicity. The paradoxical effect of such activity was that in order to reassert its sovereignty and retain the diplomatic initiative on human rights, China was obliged to admit that it was subject both to the norms and mechanisms of the international regime in general and to the jurisdiction of UN human rights bodies in particular.

This positive phase lasted for three years. At a vital point in the strong application of the human rights regime, changes occurred that affected both China's readiness to comply with its obligations and the monitoring ability of the total regime. Already foreshadowed in internal leadership communications in April 1993, in Liu Huaqiu's Vienna statement in June 1993, and in China's stance in the UN Human Rights Sub-Commission in August 1993, a third and more negative subphase was unequivocally proclaimed during the meeting between President Jiang Zemin and President Clinton at the Asia-Pacific Economic Cooperation (APEC) meeting in Seattle in November 1993.[3] As in the first phase of interaction, internal developments began to prevail over China's foreign policy interests to inhibit its human rights responses, and even to interfere with its procedural compliance. The rapid expansion of Chinese economic and strategic power by 1992 coincided with continued low growth in developed economies. These changes enhanced the confidence of the leadership, which was increasingly dominated by senior military figures, that, rather than engaging the world on human rights, it could afford to turn its back on the issue. The gradual shift in the world power balance in Asia's favor bolstered its faith in this new direction. The growth in China's power also coincided with a leadership struggle brought on by Deng Xiaoping's failing health. In addition, frequent manifestations of unrest by large numbers of Chinese workers and peasants aroused fears of social instability. A potent mix of external strength and internal weakness made China resistant to change pressured from outside. Concerns for state security, regime maintenance, and national status were intermeshed in its articulation of the principles of sovereignty and noninterference and repeated expressions of nationalism.

As a result of these developments, continued acceptance of the changing dictates of American bilateral monitoring — an acceptance fragile at best and hitherto borne principally for the sake of economic self-interest — was now seen by China as incompatible with its sovereignty. The subsequent delinkage of MFN and human rights by President Clinton in May 1994, influenced as it was by clear indications of Chinese obduracy as well as by a split in U.S. domestic opinion, served to justify the arguments of Chinese hard-liners and to confirm the leaders in their uncooperative stance. The virtual suspension of effective bilateral monitoring brought to an end specific and open pressures on China to release leading intellectual prisoners of conscience.

The cessation of bilateral monitoring refocused international attention on UN mechanisms. U.S. energies in particular shifted to the coalition-building activities necessary to ensure the success of a resolution on China in the March 1995 Human Rights Commission. Its lobbying was carried on throughout 1994, with senior U.S. envoys visiting different African capitals to obtain pledges of support. The result of this renewed political will in the United Nations was the overturning for the first time of the no-action motion on the resolution on China in the 1995 Commission. Thus, although the forms of monitoring — and their particular focus — changed, the strength of the application of the overall human rights regime was not substantially impaired. U.S. energies were simply shifted back to the multilateral arena of the regime. However, the avenue to the release of political prisoners was now foreclosed, and, in those aspects of the UN regime that required prior Chinese consent or cooperation to succeed, such as reporting obligations to the Committee Against Torture (CAT), even China's procedural compliance had come under question by 1994. China had thus, in some areas, successfully tested its ability to resist regime pressure and direct pressure outward.

This ability was not affected by financial collapse in the Asia-Pacific region in late 1997. Consonant with the greater political stability at the elite level following Deng Xiaoping's death, a new and more peaceful Chinese foreign policy emerged at the Fifteenth Party Congress in September 1997. This change was the outcome of a number of developments, including the demonstrable diplomatic failure of earlier hard-line military tactics, greater domestic political confidence and an awareness that the country faced substantial financial problems which could very well require the goodwill and

support of the U.S. and European Union. Paradoxically, neither this consciousness of a loss in its bargaining power vis-à-vis the West, nor the subsequent collapse of the Thai and other regional economies served to undermine China's diplomatic effectiveness. Whereas previously it had been seen
as the powerhouse of Asia, it now became the bulwark of global financial
stability. The need to ensure that China did not devalue its currency meant
that developed states and international financial institutions continued to
court it. Indeed, China's responsible attitude and cooperation in the face of
its temptation to devalue were invoked by its negotiators at the World Trade
Organization as one of the arguments for China's right to be accepted into
the organization. Consequently, the West continued to be responsive to
China's assertive human rights diplomacy. Despite its new foreign policy of
peace, China maintained its efforts to influence UN norms and procedures
and, in 1997, succeeded in making changes that had a significant and detri-
mental impact on the effectiveness of the UN Human Rights Commission
and the UN Sub-Commission on Prevention of Discrimination and Protection of Minorities.[4]

Compliance

Turning from a vertical chronological to a horizontal case-by-case analysis,
the extent of Chinese compliance has been measured along a five-point
continuum. At the international level, the continuum has been conceived as
(1) accession to human rights treaties, the acceptance of the norms that this
entails, and acceptance by the target state of the right of UN bodies to
monitor its conditions and of its obligation to respond; (2) procedural
compliance with reporting and other requirements; and (3) substantive
compliance with the requests of the UN body, exhibited in international
or domestic behavior. At the domestic level, the continuum proceeds into
(4) *de jure* compliance, or the implementation of international norms in
domestic legislative provisions; and (5) *de facto* compliance, or compliance
at the level of domestic practice.

The preceding chapters have documented the details of China's compliance with different UN bodies and conferences and its impact on the
norms and procedures of these bodies. It is appropriate at this point to
assess the more general significance of the interaction and to evaluate its
quality according to the different character of UN bodies. To revert back to
an earlier question, has China been a taker, shaper — or, indeed, breaker —
of UN human rights norms and procedures?

Three main types of forums have been distinguished in this study. The
first are political forums: the UN Commission on Human Rights; the Sub-
Commission on Prevention of Discrimination and Protection of Minorities;
and the UN World Human Rights Conference in Vienna and the Preparatory Committees and Conferences. Although the first two are UN bodies

and the latter are UN conferences, operating in different ways and with different purposes and functions, they are similar in certain significant respects. As political forums, the former bodies offer the clearest potential for public scrutiny and testing of the overall condition of China's human rights. The conferences, in contrast, provide the opportunity to submit China's theories of human rights to international scrutiny. In enmeshing states in a global environment in which human rights are the consensual focus, they involve them in an acceptance of norms and procedures that can be repudiated only at the price of isolation. Yet both types of forum are highly susceptible to lobbying, coalition building, and manipulation by powerful states. If states are able to mobilize support for alternative norms and procedures, they can effectively destabilize the existing consensus and reshape regime norms and procedures. China managed to do this over the years in the UN Commission on Human Rights and its Sub-Commission. At a basic level, from the early 1980s it began to comply with the norms and procedures in those forums, accepting the right of the international community to monitor the civil rights of member states and the procedures — in particular, the resolutions on "country situations" — adopted to this end. This was so, even though China objected to being made a subject of the same resolutions and attempted by a number of procedural means to deflect international attention. By 1993, however, China's successful challenge of U.S. bilateral monitoring encouraged it to undertake an equally effective challenge of multilateral monitoring. As a result of its procedural dexterity, within the Commission and Sub-Commission at least, it became questionable whether China was being incorporated into the UN regime, as UN officials hoped, or whether it was simply undermining the regime.

Unlike these two UN bodies, the 1993 UN Human Rights Conference in Vienna did not monitor China's human rights: rather, it offered a medium through which China could hope to influence the world. It provided a forum in which existing human rights norms could be evaluated, reassessed, and renegotiated. However, a similar process of enmeshment was involved. At the Vienna Conference and at the preceding Preparatory Committees and Bangkok Meeting, China adopted a mix of approaches by accepting some existing norms, by attempting to reformulate priorities by privileging collective over individual rights, and by trying to negate existing norms or prevent the development of new ones. The initial statement made in each forum emphasized China's different human rights priorities. In Vienna, it gave pride of place to the right to subsistence and the principles of sovereignty and noninterference, and the cultural relativist argument that each state had the right to its own interpretation of human rights. During the course of the Conference, efforts were also made to negate existing provisions, such as acceptance of the universality of human rights, or to head off new ones, such as the plan to appoint a UN High Commissioner for Human Rights. In the Conference Drafting Committee, Chinese pressure fed into the emphasis in the Final Declaration on the right to development, the weakening of the right of self-determination in a way that undermined minority rights, the support for a Special Rapporteur on Racism, the condition that food should not be used as a tool of trade and human rights, and references to the role of historical conditions and development in shaping each state's human rights and the importance of state sovereignty. The last two provisions, although crucial planks of China's human rights platform, were articulated in much weakened form in the Declaration.

However, in these forums China's was only one of the many voices competing to advance their proposals. At both Bangkok and Vienna, it failed to gain significant support and its efforts did not have a negative impact on the final document. On the contrary, the final Chinese statements tended to show positive acceptance of the views of other participants, and to be more supportive of the consensual status quo. Thus, China formed part of the consensus upholding the Vienna Declaration, which contained many provisions it would not have supported voluntarily. On the final day of the Vienna Conference, Ambassador Jin praised the Declaration's achievements in promoting the universal realization of rights and emphasized the value of the mutual discussion and interchange at the Conference.

The procedural compliance evident at the Vienna Human Rights Conference and its preceding conferences was, however, discrete and context-dependent. At the time, the process of its involvement brought a marked improvement in China's compliance with the regime, both procedurally and, in many cases, in its substantive acceptance of international human rights norms. As in other case studies, though, this compliance was limited to the context of each separate international forum.

In the case of all three political forums, compliance at the international level was easily identified. Yet it was almost impossible to attribute changes at the levels of domestic implementation to their influence, precisely because the norms they monitored, or in the case of the conferences, negotiated, were so wide-ranging. What was possible was to identify the concessions on sovereignty China offered as a quid pro quo for human rights concessions by the international community. Some offers were outright bribes or threats, others could be identified as exchanges by dint of the intermittent correlation between the pressures and norms of the regime and related behavior and outcomes. Thus, China is on record as having signed the ICESCR and ICCPR, to have invited a special rapporteur and a working group to China, to have freed Wei Jingsheng and to have invited the High Commissioner for Human Rights, Mary Robinson, to China, all to avoid a forthcoming Commission resolution. Its most important concessions were to sign the ICESCR and ICCPR and to continue reporting on the condition of human rights in Hong Kong. Signature of the ICESCR signalled only a good faith intention to review the treaty with a view to ratification in due course, and a weak obligation not to do anything in the meantime that was clearly incompatible with the treaty.[5] Yet, it represented the beginning of a process that could have a meaningful outcome.

Intermittent horse-trading included China's signature of the Airbus contract with France in 1996 and the offers of bilateral human rights dialogue to Australia, Canada, and Japan after these states refrained from cosponsoring the China resolution in the 1997 session of the Human Rights Commission. This brisk exchange of human rights favors demonstrated the importance China attached to the annual Commission and Sub-Commission resolutions, and its willingness to continually renegotiate its sovereignty in the interests of avoiding the loss of face a successful resolution against it would entail. It also underlined the effectiveness of the resolution procedure in prompting Chinese concessions.

The second category of forums for the purposes of this evaluation are the UN treaty bodies, and the thematic special rapporteurs and working groups. They are nonpolitical, thematically focused bodies which operate, for the most part, away from the glare of publicity and on a regular basis. They consist of experts who apply norms and procedures according to consistent, rigorous, and nonselective rules. The focused nature of their monitoring also makes it easy to assess a state's domestic compliance with treaty provisions. Member states are, moreover, less able to influence the norms and procedures of these bodies. For all these reasons, they provide more congenial environments for learning and socialization. In its interaction with CAT, as with other treaty bodies, China accepted the norms of the treaty and complied progressively with reporting procedures and requirements, to the point where its reports were accepted primarily because of its cooperation. Similarly, it responded to inquiries by the Special Rapporteur on Torture, even if the information it offered was often minimal. However, it did not comply with many of the substantive recommendations of the Committee and Special Rapporteur. Its compliance was conditional, premised on a refusal to allow *in situ* inspection by either the Committee or Special Rapporteur. At the domestic level of legislative implementation, although China's definition of the meaning and scope of torture was not expanded in amended laws, the move towards a presumption of innocence and earlier access to lawyers, as well as other procedural reforms, offered the possibility of modifying the legal culture that favored the practice of torture. Yet, at the level of practical implementation of the prohibition on torture there was little evidence of compliance.

The third type of forum consists of the UN specialized agencies. Unlike the UN bodies proper, the International Labor Organization offers a total organizational framework that places many different pressures on China to comply. It combines the strengths of the first two types of forum in that its activities are both public and focused, with rigorous sets of rules. It is less accessible to nonoccupational NGOs, but at the same time incorporates within its tripartite organization representatives of occupational NGOs—

workers and employers—as well as the representatives of the state. It also has the virtue of longevity, which equips it to deal impartially and consistently with a new and inexperienced member state, just as it has with countless others since 1919. Such in fact was its authority that China eventually accepted the right of the ILO Governing Body Committee on Freedom of Association (CFA) to monitor the conditions of Chinese workers, even though it had initially assumed that the CFA had no jurisdiction over it. Over time, China complied procedurally in its reports to the CFA, and in some instances complied with the Committee's substantive requests. However, although its new Labor Law incorporated some ILO standards, in particular, worker participation and collective bargaining, the vital notion of the freedom of association — the right of workers to form and join unions of their own choosing without previous authorization —was not entrenched. Consequently, as China's industrial and social problems grew in proportion and intensity, the government's temptation was to curb its newly found interest in ILO standards and to invoke instead the less controversial formula of "ruling by law."

International Socialization

What, then, may be said about the nature of China's socialization and learning? In its interaction with UN human rights bodies, have there been "individually or collectively learned inferences from experience that get encoded into governmental learning and decision-making procedures"?[6] If so, has it been learning in a cognitive sense or primarily learning in an instrumental sense? Have norms been internalized or merely utilized? Has China's behavior been adaptive or merely disruptive? Finally, has its membership in these UN bodies given an impetus to its international socialization?

It is clear from the patterns discussed above that China has experienced organizational learning in the human rights regime in an instrumental/adaptive sense. Tactically, it has learned that it is easier to comply with UN and ILO reporting obligations than to seek to avoid them, or to respond only minimally. Indeed, the intensity of its initial resistance, and the praise forthcoming when it finally complied with UN bodies, suggested that its initial obduracy had concentrated the attention of the monitoring authorities at the procedural level, obscuring the importance of more substantive outcomes. Strategically, China realized that to avoid becoming a loser in the serious game of human rights, it had to reassert its initiative and leadership and establish its own human rights priorities, with which to attract the Third World and debate the First and Second. Part of this strategy was the development of its human rights diplomacy, as a result of which many of the debating forums were transferred to China, there to become immersed in generous hospitality and the context of China's impressive civilization and poverty. However, unlike cognitive learning, tactics and strategy are dynamic and may change rapidly in response to new circumstances. Hence the major hiatus in regime learning that occurred in 1993–94, which had a serious impact on bilateral monitoring and, to a lesser degree, on multilateral monitoring

Within that vertical distinction between different phases of human rights diplomacy, a further horizontal one may be made that distinguishes, as in the previous section, between the political forums of the UN Human Rights Commission, the UN Sub-Commission, and the UN World Human Rights Conference in Vienna and its preceding meetings; the treaty bodies, special rapporteurs and thematic working groups; and the UN specialized agencies.

To understand the vertical division, the insights of transnational agenda setting are relevant. As has been noted, politics, including changes in national mood and the nature of the administration and political leadership, may either open windows of opportunity to learning and adaptation or close them.[7] In a partially closed system like China's, as Charles Ziegler has observed of the former Soviet Union, the trend is towards rewarding the status quo.[8] This was particularly true in the case of China's human rights where, as on a range of other issues central to the survival of the domestic regime, decision making was tightly controlled by older generations of leaders whose approach to negotiations and policy was not modern.[9] At the very most, a dilution of the learning process occurred, with China's bureaucrats and political leaders filtering out the stronger messages communicated to them. It should be acknowledged that this occurrence was not unique to China: policy makers rarely have the time or inclination to question the fundamental premises of policy, but make frequent tactical adjustments.[10] In the context of learning within the elite, clublike atmosphere of the United Nations, this dichotomy of perceptions between China's UN diplomats and its domestic policy makers was understandably pronounced. In the domestic context of translating new Chinese laws into practice, a similar gulf existed, between China's judiciary and the Procuratorate on one hand, and its Public Security Bureau, which administered the law, on the other. Where there was radical political change, involving a reversal of national mood and a change in leadership, such as occurred in China in 1993, policy makers were even instrumental in blocking the learning process at the international level. Apart from the case of the U.S. and MFN, this development was most noticeable in the UN Human Rights Commission and Sub-Commission, if not in the ILO.

In the different types of UN bodies, the experience of compliance was complex. In all of them, substantial procedural learning was apparent. Even when, as in the case of the ILO Committee on Freedom of Association, China's best interests did not appear to be served by remaining within the jurisdiction of the Committee, China began, if under considerable protest, to observe its procedural obligations and to work within the rules to improve its situation. In the case of CAT, it learned that procedural compliance with its reporting obligations was a principal determinant of Committee approval. However, the purely instrumental character of China's learning in both these bodies was underlined by its unwillingness to support unreservedly the further entrenchment and more effective projection of their respective norms, which the Optional Protocol to the Convention Against Torture and the ILO's proposed adoption of a Declaration on Workers' Fundamental Rights represented. At the domestic level of legal implementation, in contrast, China demonstrated some cognitive learning in its conscious incorporation of international standards derived from these bodies, even though for the most part this legislation did not alter the incidence of its human rights abuses. Yet, in the more political bodies of the UN Commission and Sub-Commission, China learned its procedural lessons so well that it was able to initiate changes that had the potential to undermine the basic norms and procedures of these bodies.

In the context of such learning obstacles, it is unsurprising that evidence of deeper and unconditional levels of Chinese compliance, at the domestic *de jure* and *de facto* levels, has been generally difficult to discover in the period under review. Such a depth of compliance would have betokened a total cognitive change brought about by the learning experience that is generally not apparent in the case studies. However, what is notable about the amendments to China's criminal laws and to rights of due process is that, rather than providing overwhelming evidence of the state's control of the judicial process, they have now established a legislative framework with the potential to be interpreted in a number of ways, depending on institutional change and on political direction from above. Whereas they were once an unmistakable tool of the state, China's criminal laws now offer greater flexibility and the potential for protection of the individual's rights. To attain that potential, much clearly depends on the leadership's political will and, conversely, the preparedness of Chinese citizens to place their trust in the leadership. Failure in these two areas to date has marked the limits of China's compliance with the UN human rights regime.

For the most part, therefore, it must be concluded that membership in UN human rights bodies has indeed led China to become more internationally socialized but that cognitive/normative learning has been offset by its parallel efforts to reshape and reoperationalize their norms and procedures. Indeed, it could be argued that the very efficiency of China's procedural learning has become a barrier to its cognitive learning. That membership of international organizations has given impetus to its socialization is best exemplified in its changing interpretation of sovereignty in response to different pressures. But, precisely because these changes have not represented an internalization of norms, they have often been made for short-term tactical reasons and have shown no linear or progressive development. Rather, they have been zigzagged, compartmentalized changes characterized by much backtracking. Moreover, in the manner typical of an authoritarian state lacking a tradition of the rule of law, China has not been guided in its actions by its own precedents, but has continued to make up its rules on the run. In short, the ongoing problematic, first raised by Benjamin Schwartz in 1968, as to whether the "provisional" in China's use of international (human rights) law and the machinery of international diplomacy might one day slip over into the category of the "normal" has yet to be resolved.[11]

If China has learned instrumentally as a result of international interaction, the United Nations and its member states have also learned much about dealing with China. In the beginning, the UN Commission and Sub-Commission introduced procedural innovations that allowed them to cope more successfully with the counterpressures of a powerful and influential state. In the face of China's continual testing of UN resolve, however, and particularly during the 1997 session of the UN Commission on Human Rights when China succeeded in bilateralizing a multilateral process, Western states adopted alternative tactics. They called for concessions by China in exchange for giving it special treatment; "cooperation" and not "confrontation," at least temporarily, became the order of the day. Not fully recognized was the need to maintain a unified Western front within the United Nations in the face of this assault on UN norms and procedures and to combine multilateral *and* bilateral monitoring in order to have the greatest impact on China's human rights. In contrast, the less political UN human rights bodies remained fully conscious of the importance of maintaining a steady, consistent, nonselective, and rigorous pressure on China, as they did with respect to all other states parties.

What then may be concluded about China's view of interdependence and the degree of its socialization and learning, as reflected in its interaction with the international human rights regime? To recapitulate Gilpin's words, from 1979 to early 1989 and from 1990 until the end of 1993, China's leaders generally "learn[ed] to be more enlightened in their definitions of their interests and to be more cooperative in their behavior."[12] Such cooperation did not necessarily spring from an acknowledgment of the value of interdependence as such, but, rather, from the need to realize other goals, as well as to be seen to be a cooperative member of the international community. That the latter consideration has served as a constraint on its behavior is in itself significant. It suggests that although China has often felt threatened by the regime, it also sees its sovereign interests as coinciding with participation in it. Moreover, the ultimate result, rather than the precise causal variables leading to it, is of greater interest and importance. However, it is also clear that over time China progressed to a position where it could exploit the innate contradictions between economic and political interdependence. In the Human Rights Commission and Sub-Commission, and in its efforts to sever the connection between MFN and human rights, China has been able to manipulate the increased dependence of Western states on its markets to modify their political pressures and to reshape UN norms and procedures. Within these bodies, China has thus been taker, shaper, and breaker of norms. In contrast, China has not reshaped the norms and procedures in less political bodies, such as the Committee Against Torture, the special rapporteurs and the ILO Governing Body CFA. Yet here its participation, and its acceptance of political interdependence, have been incomplete and conditional, premised on its refusal to lose ultimate control over the monitoring process. The continuing tension between sovereignty and human rights in its diplomacy, and between cooperation and noncooperation, has reflected the sensitivity of this ultimate test of China's compliance with regimes.

Effectiveness

What do these findings reveal about the effectiveness of the different parts of the UN regime under study, and of the regime as a whole? To some extent, this question is a mirror image of the questions about China's compliance and learning and requires the same distinction between types of UN bodies. However, it is also more complex, as the issue of the United Nations impact on the domestic level of a state's human rights conditions involves difficult judgments of causality—that is, to what extent China's domestic compliance has been influenced by UN and other indirect international influences; and to what extent its improvements have been propelled from within.

Membership of the UN Human Rights Commission and Sub-Commission, especially after June 1989, subjected China to the strong application of the regime and to a rigorous learning experience that saw changes in its strategy and tactics to better adapt itself to the challenges. Indeed, the effectiveness of these bodies was demonstrated by the fact that the trade-offs initiated by China after 1994 between various parts of the human rights regime were almost all focused on avoiding a Commission resolution critical of its human rights conditions.[13] The role of the Commission and Sub-Commission was thus primarily one of standard setting, of prompting human rights trade-offs and the post-facto recording of domestic abuses, as well as of influencing the human rights debate within China.

The effectiveness of the UN World Human Rights Conference in Vienna, a forum constituting part of China's human rights defense and diplomacy rather than a monitoring body, may be measured by the distance between the values in China's formal statement at the Conference and the principles in the final Vienna Declaration. The changes in China's position during the drafting process in response to international criticism, and the graceful speech at its closure by the Chinese Ambassador, were both testimony to the effectiveness of the Conference process, at least in the short term, involving as it did the democratic exchange of ideas and values and a process of mutual concessions. However, in the longer term, China's declaratory policy reflected a return to the *status quo ante*.

CAT and the Special Rapporteur on Torture were more successful in obtaining China's procedural compliance with their reporting requirements at the international level and some substantive compliance at the *de jure*, if not at the *de facto*, domestic level. Their experience mirrored that of other treaty bodies and special rapporteurs in their relations with China. Given the latter's preference for formalistic reporting, they all shared a problem in obtaining details of its practical implementation of treaty norms. Moreover, although one thematic rapporteur and one working group obtained an invitation to China, the antitorture bodies were unsuccessful in their attempts to move from passive monitoring in Geneva to active monitoring in China. Ultimately, both bodies remained dependent on China's political will, and its readiness to participate unconditionally in the regime, for the effective discharge of their mandates.

Unlike the United Nations proper, where the different human rights bodies operate largely as separate and discrete units, the ILO offers a total organizational framework within which the various aspects of its human rights regime may be absorbed and, to some extent, reconciled. Nevertheless, on the right fundamental to the normative foundations of the ILO, that of freedom of association, the ILO Governing Body CFA initially faced an uphill battle, given the fears of labor unrest exhibited by China's leaders. To the extent that this struggle brought China into more intimate contact with a broad range of ILO standards, and to the selective acceptance of some, it was successful. The Committee, in conjunction with internal pressures, obtained China's compliance with its procedural reporting responsibilities and, in the longer term, influenced the incorporation of some basic standards into China's Labor Law, if not the vital standard of freedom of association.

At the domestic level, evaluation of the overall effectiveness of UN bodies becomes more complicated. To what extent China's new criminal legislation is a response to UN standard setting and monitoring and to what extent it is a response to domestic pressures is unclear, because the question is already anachronistic. It has been argued here that in a globalized world, the norms of the international human rights regime have penetrated even the sovereign boundaries of an authoritarian state like China. This has been instanced in the lively debate within China on international human rights after 1990 and, in particular, in the ongoing debate among scholars in China as to whether human rights have national boundaries (*guojie*). It has also been reflected in the frequency with which Western legal concepts are cited in Chinese law journals. The increasing interchange in the 1990s between Chinese political leaders and their Western counterparts, between Chinese and Western legal scholars and practitioners, and between Chinese dissidents and international NGOs has provided fertile soil in which theories of human rights and legal concepts have become part of common discourse. Decisions made by the United Nations are transmitted to China via its own media or in fax and e-mail messages from abroad. Foreign television and radio broadcasts are accessible in most parts of China, even though government efforts to block some communications have been partially successful.[14] Domestic and expatriate Chinese dissidents now call on international leaders to promote change within China. It becomes difficult, therefore, to separate international from domestic pressures. Given that strong internal pressures for liberalization within China gave rise to the Democracy Wall Movement in 1979–81, before effective international pressures had been applied, domestic pressures are clearly paramount. Yet Western ideas and ideals, as distinct from Western pressures, were also invoked by the dissidents of that early movement. Today, Chinese political leaders, and legal scholars freely refer to the need to establish a legal system that is both modern and in line with international practice. Chinese lawmakers cite the norms in UN treaties as justifications for proposed legislative change. Chinese lawyers, judges, and legal scholars openly discuss legal issues with their Western counterparts both at home and abroad. Changes in China's criminal law, which move towards internationally validated principles of the presumption of innocence and judicial independence, provide the framework for the future guarantee of individual rights, even if they currently provide overwhelming support for the policy of "ruling by law." The litmus test for the development of a genuine rule of law in China will remain the fate of the existing rule of law in Hong Kong. Already, despite the continuation of the system prevailing before July 1997, danger signals are appearing in the form of threats to the rights of assembly and collective bargaining and to government accountability.[15] In the meantime, throughout China, legal change and ongoing domestic debate about the protection of rights have become part of a global movement of ideas that redounds to the efficacy of UN human rights bodies and their international human rights discourse.

Notwithstanding the clear constraint that China has not yet ratified either of the two major UN human rights covenants, the ICCPR and the ICESCR, the overall human rights regime to which China voluntarily submitted may thus be judged to have been partially effective. From 1979 to 1989, its weak application broadened, rather than deepened, in effect, as China voluntarily joined human rights bodies and acceded to human rights treaties. China initially rejected the strong application of the regime after June 1989, but then grudgingly accepted it. The UN regime obtained China's procedural and, to a limited degree, substantive compliance at the international level. To some degree it was also successful in impacting on its domestic *de jure* but not its actual, human rights conditions. This was partly because China's participation in the regime was conditional and, with significant exceptions, did not allow of active UN monitoring. The effects of this incomplete participation in the regime were demonstrated at the 1995 UN Women's Conference in Beijing, where, rather than showing acceptance of UN norms, China's domestic *de jure* and *de facto* human rights conditions temporarily subverted UN procedures and norms.

In terms of cognitive learning, therefore, the most significant effect of the UN regime has not derived from its supervision of the implementation of China's domestic human rights obligations, since UN monitoring on Chinese soil has required a Chinese consent that, with respect to the case studies, has been withheld. Rather, it has been located in the standard setting and promotional aspects of the UN regime at the international level, imposed not through specific devices, but by means of the long drawn-out, often tedious, process of China's participation in each of the UN human rights bodies and conferences. By dint of its participation, China has gradually begun to indicate an acceptance of basic international human rights procedures and norms in multilateral forums. Whether such learning at the international level is sufficient to judge the UN regime as a whole to be effective is questionable. From the United Nations viewpoint, the conclusion depends in the short term on the evaluation made by each UN body of its principal raison d'être and of the standard that constitutes an acceptable level of compliance. It also has to take into account the finding that, in the protection of human rights, there is "an extreme time lag" between undertaking and performance.[16] However, it is clear that the regime's effectiveness must ultimately be judged by its contribution to the solution of the human rights problems that gave rise to its establishment in the first place.[17] In face of the evidence, it would appear that, despite their best efforts, UN human rights bodies and the broader international human rights community have not succeeded in breaching the divide between China's international human rights policy and its domestic human rights practice, but that they are slowly making some inroads. Against this open conclusion, itself dependent on the continued political will of states to support and maintain the standards of the UN human rights regime, is the ever present possibility that, as in the final phases of post-1989 monitoring in the period under review, China's domestic constraints might once again intervene to block its learning at the international level, so that the effectiveness of UN standard setting remains contingent upon the continuing receptivity of China's domestic political environment.

And here lies the nub of the problematic examined in this book. The ultimate priority of domestic political considerations returns us to our initial arguments. The UN human rights regime does not operate in a vacuum, and to assign direct and exclusive causal influence to it would be to misrepresent reality: for China, it should be reiterated, the human rights regime represents an intervening, rather than an autonomous, causal variable. A schematic restatement of the six principal phases and subphases in China's participation in the UN regime may help to clarify the latter's role:

1. 1971–79: the weak application of the UN regime, combined with little internal pressure → little Chinese compliance with the regime;
2. 1979–89: weak application of the UN regime, combined with increasing internal pressures → voluntary Chinese participation in the regime;
3. 1989–98: strong application of the UN regime to post-Tiananmen China:
   a. 1989–90: strong and sudden application of the multilateral regime through tough international economic sanctions, combined with China's repressive internal measures and weakened internal pressures → Chinese resistance and noncompliance;
   b. 1990–92: consistent and continuing strong application of the UN regime and ongoing U.S. threat of removal of China's MFN status, combined with weak Chinese international bargaining power and the revival of internal pressures → selective Chinese compliance including the release of political prisoners;
   c. 1993–96: weakening application of the overall regime influenced by the delinkage of MFN and human rights, combined with China's strong international economic bargaining position and domestic political and social instability → China's reiteration of principles of sovereignty, nationalism and the weakening of compliance, except in the case of the ILO and at the level of domestic labor, administrative and criminal legislation; and
   d. 1996–98: continued weakening application of the overall regime, combined with China's weaker economic, but strong financial, bargaining position, stronger domestic political situation but heightened social instability → China's new foreign policy of peace and cooperation, some international human rights concessions but the weakening of domestic compliance, continued reiteration of principles of sovereignty, and an increasingly assertive human rights diplomacy.

The issue of sovereignty has been the vital thread integrating these phases. The domestic balance sheet of human rights has also been affected, if less obviously, by considerations of sovereignty, in that any challenge to China's authoritarian leadership, whether emanating from the labor movement or from individual dissidents, has been interpreted as identical to a challenge to the authority of Party and state.[18] However, the interesting point to note about the principle of sovereignty is that it has served different functions in different periods. In 1990, faced with a situation in which it was at an international disadvantage, China was prompted to engage with the international human rights debate, and to negotiate its interpretation of sovereignty: from late 1993, however, its rising international status and weakened internal authority combined to make the principle of sovereignty, now more strictly interpreted, a reason for noncompliance. Sovereignty thus has had both an enabling function in China's human rights policy and a limiting one.

From the above, it is clear that from 1971 until 1998 China's compliance was most forthcoming in an international situation characterized by the combination of a strong application of the overall human rights regime with weak Chinese bargaining power. However, the third subphase, 3c, characterized as it was by a weakening of the application of the human rights regime and strong Chinese bargaining power, nevertheless resulted in some compliance with ILO standards and in amendments to domestic legislation that came closer to international standards. The new causal variable in the latter case was increased internal and in particular, labor, pressures. This finding suggests that, whatever the external balance of power, China's compliance with international human rights norms may still be obtained when national interests, prompted by domestic pressures, and external pressures converge. In other words, despite its enhanced global bargaining power after 1993, China's compliance was obtained when, in the face of labor unrest, perceived foreign exploitation, and rising middle-class expectations, China's leaders decided that the adoption of international human rights standards of labor rights and rights of due process corresponded with the interests of their domestic regime, as well as with those of the international regime.

Conversely, as in the last subphase, when the domestic interests of the regime did not coincide with external pressures, or when external pressures perceptibly weakened, external pressures on their own were unlikely to produce compliance, unless China's bargaining power was also weak. In his excellent study of the effectiveness of UN human rights bodies, Maxime Tardu has observed that external and internal pressures on human rights reinforce each other to produce compliance.[19] In the case of China, particularly after 1993, internal pressures have been shown in many cases to have worked against compliance. Where, in contrast, internal interests, informed by domestic pressures, and external pressures have coincided, domestic progress has been achieved, if still only primarily at the formal level of legislation.

Although China's policies have been more sensitive to domestic than to external pressures, this study has demonstrated that the UN human rights regime matters. In many forums, China has presented a view of human rights opposed to that of the United States and other Western states. It has sought to counterpose statist and cultural relativist values to the universalist principles espoused even by some non-Western states. However, at least until 1997, the forums in which human rights values have been debated and human rights law developed, such as the UN Human Rights Commission, the UN Sub-Commission, and the UN Human Rights Conference in Vienna, enjoyed a status and authority far greater than the sum of the individual states that constituted them. They were not only proof against the destructive impact of the negative policies of member states, but in their final outcomes, such as the Vienna Declaration, benefited from the cut and thrust of radically opposing views. Thus, for instance, the Vienna Declaration produced strong provisions on the right to development with China's support, strong provisions on the prohibition of torture, perhaps without it, and achieved its principal aim of reaffirming the universality of human rights, despite Chinese opposition. The same resilience was evinced in the deliberations of the other UN bodies examined, and was due both to their institutional robustness and to their democratic structure, which allowed NGOs and individual actors an influential, and at times, decisive, voice.

Since 1997, the UN Human Rights Commission and Sub-Commission have become less effective in dealing with China. However, even at this difficult time, the UN treaty bodies, thematic special rapporteurs and working groups, and specialized agencies have continued to maintain their standards and their rigor. UN effectiveness has also been enhanced by the creative ambiguity inherent in the "simulacra" of global human rights norms. Such ambiguity has made possible the coexistence, if not the reconciliation, of different voices; it has also facilitated a degree of complicity among some non-Western states regarding the individual civil and political rights upon which UN monitoring has been based. Through its persistent robustness, and in the outcomes summarized above, the UN human rights regime has clearly made a difference, to both China and the international community.[20] Over a period of convulsive international change, and in the face of severe political challenge, with some signal exceptions it has maintained its basic standards, its authority, its capacity to absorb constructive change, and its resistance to the erosion of values. It has formed part of the complex web of interdependence opposing the centrifugal forces of global change, ethnic tribalism and political atomization in today's world.

Notes

Introduction

1. Thus, the theme of the 1997 Meeting of the American Society of International Law was "Implementation, Compliance, and Effectiveness." China's international socialization and its attitude toward interdependence is explored in Thomas W. Robinson and David Shambaugh, eds., *Chinese Foreign Policy: Theory and Practice* (Oxford: Clarendon Press, 1994); Yoichi Funabashi, Michel Oksenberg, and Heinrich Weiss, *An Emerging China in a World of Interdependence* (New York: Trilateral Commission, 1994); Alastair Iain Johnston, "Learning versus Adaptation: Explaining Change in Chinese Arms Control Policy in the 1980s and 1990s," *China Journal* 35 (January 1996):27–61; Shih Chih-yu, *China's Just World: The Morality of Chinese Foreign Policy* (Boulder, Colo.: Lynne Rienner, 1993); David S.G. Goodman and Gerald Segal eds., *China Rising: Nationalism and Interdependence* (London: Routledge, 1997); and Michel Oksenberg and Elizabeth Economy, eds., *Involving China in World Affairs* (New York: American Council of Foreign Relations, 1998).

2. These new analytical and normative concerns are articulated in Abram Chayes and Antonia Handler Chayes, *New Sovereignty: Compliance with International Regulatory Agreements* (Cambridge, Mass.: Harvard University Press, 1996); Chayes and Chayes, "On Compliance," *International Organization* 47, 2 (spring 1993): 175–205; and in Marc A. Levy, Oran R. Young, and Michael Zürn, "The Study of International Regimes," *The European Journal of International Relations* 1, 3 (September 1995): 268–69, 312.

3. Bilahari Kausikan, "Human Rights: Asia's Different Standard," *Foreign Policy* 92 (fall 1993): 32.

4. I thank John Braithwaite for this insight. China is a least likely state by virtue of its history, cultural traditions, and power. It has historically considered itself to be the "Middle Kingdom"; it lacks a tradition of the rule of law; and it is powerful enough to ignore its international obligations. The function of a least likely case study is that it is "especially tailored to confirmation" of a theory. See Harry Eckstein, "Case Study and Theory in Political Science," in *Handbook of Political Science: Strategies of Inquiry*, ed. Fred I. Greenstein and Nelson W. Polsby (Reading, Mass.: Addison-Wesley, 1975): 119.

5. "China to Report on Hong Kong Rights at UN," Reuters China News, 22 November 1997; and Christine Loh, "One Country, Two Human Rights Reports," *China Rights Forum* (winter 1997–98): 14–15.

6. Harry Harding, *A Fragile Relationship: The United States and China since 1972*

(Washington, D.C.: Brookings Institution, 1992); Tan Qingshan, *The Making of U.S. China Policy: From Normalization to the Post-Cold War Era* (Boulder, Colo.: Lynne Rienner, 1993); Robert G. Sutter, "Changes in Eastern Europe and the Soviet Union and the Effects on China: A U.S. Perspective," in *Asia and the Decline of Communism*, ed. Young C. Kim and Gaston J. Sigur (New Brunswick, N.J.: Transaction, 1992), 253–68; Michel Oksenberg, "The China Problem," *Foreign Affairs* 70, 3 (summer 1991): 1–16; Nancy Bernkopf, "China and America: 1941–1991," *Foreign Affairs* 70, 5 (winter 1991–92): 75–92; Barber B. Conable, Jr., and David Lampton, "China: The Coming Power," *Foreign Affairs* 71, 5 (winter 1992–93): 133–149; George Szamuely, "Clinton's Clumsy Encounter with the World," *Orbis* 38, 3 (summer 1994): 373–394; David Zweig, "Clinton and China: Creating a Policy Agenda That Works," *Current History* (September 1993): 245–52; Harry Harding, *The Evolution of Greater China and What It Means for America* (New York: National Committee on US-China Relations, December 1994); Richard Madsen, *China and the American Dream: A Moral Inquiry* (Berkeley: University of California Press, 1995); David M. Lampton and Alfred D. Wilhelm, eds., *United States and China Relations at a Crossroads* (Lanham, Md.: University Press of America, 1995); and James R. Lilley and Wendell L. Willkie II, eds., *Beyond MFN: Trade with China and American Interests* (Washington, D.C.: American Enterprise Institute, 1994).

7. Robert Drinan, S.J. and Teresa T. Kuo, "The Battle for Human Rights in China," *Human Rights Quarterly* 14, 1 (1992): 21–42; Holly Burkhalter, "Bargaining away Human Rights: The Bush Administration's Human Rights Policy Towards Iraq and China," *Harvard Human Rights Journal* 4 (spring 1991): 105–16; Patricia Wing Lau and Jeffrey Sims, "Human Rights in Tibet: An Emerging Foreign Policy Issue," *Harvard Human Rights Journal* 5 (spring 1992): 193–203; Gary W. Vause, "Tibet to Tiananmen: Chinese Human Rights and United States Foreign Policy," *Vanderbilt Law Review* 42, 6 (November 1989): 1575–1615; Robert A. Manning, "Clinton and China: Beyond Human Rights," *Orbis* 38, 2 (spring 1994): 193–205; Allen S. Whiting, "Chinese Nationalism and Foreign Policy After Deng," *China Quarterly* 142 (June 1995): 295–316; and David M. Lampton, "America's China Policy in the Age of the Finance Minister: Clinton Ends Linkage," *China Quarterly* 139 (September 1994): 597–621; and Alan D. Romberg, "The Role of Human Rights in US Policy and the Implications for Relations with China," in *United States and China*, ed. Lampton and Wilhelm, 169–80.

8. See International League for Human Rights (Timothy Gelatt), *Business as Usual . . . ? The International Response to Human Rights Violations in China* (New York, 29 May 1991); International League for Human Rights (Timothy Gelatt), *Getting Down to Business: The Human Rights Responsibilities of China's Investors and Trade Partners* (New York, July 1992); Peter Van Ness, *Analysing the Impact of International Sanctions on China*, Working Paper 1989 no. 4 (Canberra: Australian National University); and James D. Seymour, *The International Reaction to the 1989 Crackdown in China* (New York: East Asian Institute, Columbia University, February 1990).

9. Fang Lizhi, *Bringing Down the Great Wall: Writings on Science, Culture, and Democracy in China* (New York: Knopf, 1990); Ann Kent, *Between Freedom and Subsistence: China and Human Rights* (Hong Kong: Oxford University Press, 1993 and 1995); Michael C. Davis, ed., *Human Rights and Chinese Values: Legal, Philosophical and Political Perspectives* (Hong Kong: Oxford University Press, 1995); William Theodore de Bary and Tu Weiming, eds., *Confucianism and Human Rights* (New York: Columbia University Press, 1998); and Tahirih V. Lee, ed., *Law, State, and Society in China* (New York: Garland, 1997). See also William P. Alford, "Making a Goddess of Democracy from Loose Sand: Thoughts on Human Rights in the People's Republic of China," in *Human Rights in Cross-Cultural Perspectives: A Quest for Consensus*, ed. Abdullahi Ahmed An-Na'im (Philadelphia: University of Pennsylvania Press, 1992), 65–80; Chad Han-

sen, "Do Human Rights Apply to China? A Normative Analysis of Cultural Difference," *Hong Kong Law Journal* 24, 3 (1994): 397–415; and James T. H. Tang, ed., *Human Rights and International Relations in the Asia-Pacific Region* (London: Pinter, 1995).

10. Nihal Jayawickrama, "Human Rights Exception No Longer," in *The Broken Mirror: China After Tiananmen*, ed. George Hicks (United Kingdom: Longman, 1990), 345–66; Wei-chin Lee, "With Open Arms? China and Human Rights in the United Nations," *Pacifica* 2, 1 (January 1990): 16–36; Philip Baker, "China: Human Rights and the Law," *The Pacific Review* 6, 3 (1993): 239–50; Kent, *Between Freedom and Subsistence*, 100–04, 186–92; Susan Whitfield, ed., *After the Event: Human Rights and their Future in China* (London: Wellsweep Press, 1993); Kent, "China and the International Human Rights Regime: A Case Study of Multilateral Monitoring, 1989–1994," *Human Rights Quarterly* 17, 1 (February 1995): 1–47; and Hatla Thelle, ed., *Political Developments and Human Rights in China: Report from Five Seminars at the Danish Centre for Human Rights* (Copenhagen: The Danish Centre for Human Rights, 1998).

11. Samuel S. Kim, "Reviving International Law in China's Foreign Relations," in *Chinese Defense and Foreign Policy*, ed. June Teufel Dreyer (New York: Paragon, 1989), 87–131; James V. Feinerman, "Chinese Participation in the International Legal Order: Rogue Elephant or Team Player?" *China Quarterly* 141 (March 1995): 186–210; in the same volume, a special issue on China's legal reforms, see Stanley Lubman, "Introduction: The Future of Chinese Law," 1–21; Donald C. Clarke, "The Execution of Civil Judgements in China," 65–81; Anthony R. Dicks, "Compartmentalised Law and Judicial Restraint: An Inductive View of Some Jurisdictional Barriers to Reform," 82–109; and Donald C. Clarke and James V. Feinerman, "Antagonistic Contradictions: Criminal Law and Human Rights in China," 135–54. See also Albert H. Y. Chen, *An Introduction to the Legal System of the People's Republic of China* (Singapore: Butterworths Asia, 1992); Jyh-pin Fa and Shao-chuan Leng, *Judicial Review of Administration in the People's Republic of China*, Occasional Papers/Reprint Series on Contemporary Asian Studies No. 1 (Baltimore: University of Maryland School of Law, 1992); Ronald C. Keith, *China's Struggle for the Rule of Law* (Basingstoke: Macmillan, 1994); Pitman B. Potter, ed., *Domestic Law Reforms in Post-Mao China* (Armonk, N.Y.: M. E. Sharpe, 1994); Potter, "Riding the Tiger: Legitimacy and Legal Culture in Post-Mao China," *China Quarterly* 138 (June 1994): 325–58; and Murray Scot Tanner, "The Erosion of Communist Party Control over Lawmaking in China," *China Quarterly* 138 (June 1994): 381–403.

12. Chen Jie, "Human Rights: ASEAN's New Importance to China" *Pacific Review* 6, 3 (1993): 227–37; Simon Long, "The Tree That Wants to Be Still: The Chinese Response to Foreign Pressure Since June 1989," *The Pacific Review* 5, 2 (1992): 156–161; and Feinerman, "Chinese Participation in the International Legal Order."

13. Andrew J. Nathan, "Human Rights in Chinese Foreign Policy," *China Quarterly* 139 (September 1994): 622.

14. In an earlier article, Nathan covers much the same ground, although devoting one section to discussing MFN as a policy tool. See, "Influencing China's Human Rights," in *Beyond MFN*, ed. Lilley and Willkie, 77–90; and "China: Getting Human Rights Right," *Washington Quarterly* 20, 2 (1997): 131–151.

15. James D. Seymour, "Human Rights in Chinese Foreign Relations," in *China and the World: Chinese Foreign Relations in the Post-Cold War Era*, ed. Samuel S. Kim (Boulder, Colo.: Westview Press, 1994), 219.

16. Feinerman, "Chinese Participation in the International Legal Order," 210.

17. Clarke and Feinerman, "Antagonistic Contradictions," 152.

18. See n. 1.

19. Samuel S. Kim, "China and the World in Theory and Practice," in *China and the World*, ed. Kim, 30.

20. For different regime theories, see the special edition on regimes in *International Organization* 36, 2 (spring 1982); Stephen Haggard and Beth A. Simmons, "Theories of International Regimes," *International Organization* 41, 3 (summer 1987): 491–517; Peter M. Haas, "Do Regimes Matter? Epistemic Communities and Mediterranean Pollution Control," *International Organization* 43, 3 (summer 1989): 377–403; Friedrich Kratochwil and John Gerard Ruggie, "International Organization: The State of the Art on the Art of the State," *International Organization* 40, 4 (autumn 1986): 753–75; Oran R. Young, "International Regimes: Toward a New Theory of Institutions," *World Politics* 39 (October 1986): 110–11; James Keeley, "Toward a Foucauldian Analysis of International Regimes," *International Organization* 44, 1 (winter 1990): 83–105; Barry Buzan, "From International System to International Society: Structural Realism and Regime Theory Meet the English School," *International Organization* 47, 3 (summer 1993): 327–52; and Levy, Young, and Zürn, "The Study of International Regimes," 267–330.

21. Stephen D. Krasner, "Structural Causes and Regime Consequences: Regimes as Intervening Variables," *International Organization* 36, 2 (spring 1982): 187.

22. Haggard and Simmons, "Theories of International Regimes," 493. See a similar judgment in Levy, Young and Zürn, "The Study of International Regimes," 270–74.

23. Stephen D. Krasner, "Regimes and the Limits of Realism: Regimes as Autonomous Variables," *International Organization* 36, 2 (spring 1982): 509.

24. Marc A. Levy and Oran R. Young, "The Effectiveness of International Regimes," paper presented at the Annual Convention of the International Studies Association, Washington D.C., 29 March–1 April 1994, cited in Levy, Young, and Zürn, "The Study of International Regimes," 304–307.

25. Theodor Adorno, *Negative Dialectics* (New York: Seabury Press, 1973), 27.

26. Richard Falk, *Human Rights and State Sovereignty* (New York: Holmes and Meier, 1981), 34. As James Keeley observes, in international relations the "constitutions of public spaces"—here regimes—"are more protean, vulnerable and contested than those of well-ordered civil societies." See Keeley, "Toward a Foucauldian Analysis," 105.

27. See Susan Strange, "Cave! Hic Dragones: A Critique of Regime Analysis," *International Organization* 36, 2 (spring 1982): 479–96.

28. Jack Donnelly, "International Human Rights: A Regime Analysis," *International Organization* 40, 3 (summer 1986): 640.

29. Robert Gilpin, *War and Change in World Politics* (Cambridge: Cambridge University Press, 1981), 227. See also Robert O. Keohane, *After Hegemony* (Princeton, N.J.: Princeton University Press, 1984), 131–32. For socialization and learning theory, see George W. Breslauer and Philip E. Tetlock, eds., *Learning in U.S. and Soviet Foreign Policy* (Boulder, Colo.: Westview Press, 1991); Jack S. Levy, "Learning and Foreign Policy: Sweeping a Conceptual Minefield," *International Organization* 48, 2 (spring 1994): 279–312; Chayes and Chayes, *New Sovereignty;* Chayes and Chayes, "On Compliance," 175–205; Robert Jervis, *Perception and Misperception in International Politics* (Princeton, N.J.: Princeton University Press, 1976); G. John Ikenberry and Charles A. Kupchan, "Socialization and Hegemonic Power," *International Organization* 44, 3 (summer 1990): 283–315; George Modelski, "Is World Politics Evolutionary Learning?" *International Organization* 44,1 (winter 1990): 1–24; and Kim Richard Nossal, "International Sanctions as International Punishment," *International Organization* 43, 2 (spring 1989): 301–22. For empirical studies of learning in a state's foreign policy, see the comprehensive Breslauer and Tetlock volume, in particular, Banning N. Garrett, "The Strategic Basis of Learning in US Policy Toward China, 1949–1988," 208–63; and Allen S. Whiting, "Soviet Policy Toward China, 1969–1988," 504–50. See also Charles E. Ziegler, *Foreign Policy and East Asia: Learning and*

Adaptation in the Gorbachev Era (Cambridge: Cambridge University Press, 1993); and Johnston, "Learning Versus Adaptation," 27–61.

30. See John W. Kingdon, *Agendas, Alternatives, and Public Policies* (Boston: Little, Brown, 1984), 206–15, cited in Sandra L. Gubin, "Between Regimes and Realism — Transnational Agenda Setting: Soviet Compliance with CSCE Human Rights Norms," *Human Rights Quarterly* 17, 2 (1995): 289.

31. The role of international regimes and their organizations as "teachers of norms" has become the focus of a growing body of literature. See Martha Finnemore, "International Organizations as Teachers of Norms: The United Nations Educational, Scientific, and Cultural Organizations and Science Policy," *International Organization* 47, 4 (autumn 1993): 565–597; Audie Klotz, "Norms Reconstituting Interests: Global Racial Equality and US Sanctions Against South Africa," *International Organization* 49, 3 (summer 1995): 451–78; and Michael N. Barnett, "Sovereignty, Nationalism and Regional Order in the Arab States System," *International Organization* 49 (summer 1995): 479–510. Organizational or governmental learning has been conceptualized in terms of "individually or collectively learned inferences from experience that get encoded into governmental learning and decision-making procedures." See Levy, "Learning and Foreign Policy," 289. Governmental learning in international affairs involves a multistage process in which external environmental feedback leads to individual learning. This gives rise to individual action to change governmental procedures, leading in turn to a change in governmental behavior, and thence to further feedback. This notion, which views the learning process as a cycle, is similar to the "second image reversed" theory conceived by Peter Gourevitch. It has also been employed by Andrew Nathan, who states that China's human rights policy exhibits second image reversed characteristics. The present study puts this claim to detailed test. See Nathan, "Human Rights in Chinese Foreign Policy," 622.

32. Among many others, Jack Donnelly has questioned the effort to establish a lowest common denominator of basic norms, thereby implying that all rights are not universal. His position was supported by the theme of the NGO Conference preceding the 1993 UN World Human Rights Conference at Vienna, "All Human Rights for All." In contrast, anthropologists posit a whole range of alternative positions, ranging from the "radical cultural relativists," who argue that universalism represents the particular as universal, to the "cultural diversivists" or "contextualists," who argue that some commonalities need to be established for human rights if cultural diversities are to be defended and maintained. Joseph Chan articulates the tension between universalism and particularism as being that "while the Asian governments acknowledge the universality of human rights and while the West concedes that particularities do matter, the two sides have very different views of how the two ideas should be related." In terms of the specific rights that should be considered universal, philosophers like Henry Shue have argued the priority of the basic norms of physical security and subsistence, thereby establishing a core of civil, political, social and economic rights. This basic needs approach has been extended by Joseph Camilleri into the international arena, as a solution for conflict management and conflict resolution in the Asia-Pacific region. In contrast, Antonio Cassese, an international lawyer, establishes a set of basic rights on the basis of the consensus he perceives in international practice. See Jack Donnelly, "Human Rights and Human Dignity: An Analytical Critique of Non-Western Conceptions of Human Rights," in *Third World Attitudes toward International Law: An Introduction*, ed. Frederick E. Snyder and Surakiart Sathirathai (Dordrecht: Martinus Nijhoff Publishers, 1987), 354; Jennifer Schirmer, "The Dilemma of Cultural Diversity and Equivalency in Universal Human Rights Standards," in *Human Rights and Anthropology*, ed. Theodore E. Downey and Gilbert Kushner (Cambridge, Mass.: Cultural Survival Inc., 1988), 93.

See also Alison Dundes Renteln, ed., *International Human Rights: Universalism versus Relativism* (London: Sage, 1990), who argues that relativism does not undermine the possibility of empirically universal human rights; Joseph Chan, "The Asian Challenge to Universal Human Rights: A Philosophical Appraisal," in *Human Rights and International Relations*, ed. James T. H. Tang, 26; Henry Shue, *Basic Rights: Subsistence, Affluence and U.S. Foreign Policy* (Princeton, N.J.: Princeton University Press, 1980); Joseph A. Camilleri, "Human Rights, Cultural Diversity, and Conflict Resolution: The Asia Pacific Context," *Pacifica Review* 6, 2 (1994): 36–41; and Antonio Cassese, "The General Assembly: Historical Perspective, 1945–1989," in *The United Nations and Human Rights: A Critical Appraisal*, ed. Philip Alston (Oxford: Clarendon Press, 1992), 46–49.

33. Cf. Chayes and Chayes, "On Compliance," 176.

34. UN Committee Against Torture, 4th Sess., Summary Record of the 51st Meeting, Geneva, 27 April 1990, UN Doc. CAT/C/SR.51 (4 May 1990), at 2. This stipulation is not entrenched in China's Constitution. Article 67, Para. 14 of the Constitution simply states that the Standing Committee of the National People's Congress has the power "to decide on the ratification and abrogation of treaties and important agreements concluded with foreign states." See The Constitution of the People's Republic of China, in *People's Republic of China Yearbook 1996/1997* (Beijing: Editorial Department of the PRC Yearbook, 1997), 136–37.

35. For a comprehensive discussion of these issues, see Philip Alston and Madelaine Chiam eds., *Treaty-Making and Australia: Globalisation Versus Sovereignty?* (Sydney: Federation Press, 1995). See particularly Alston, "Reform of Treaty-Making Processes: Form Over Substance?" 5–9. For discussion of the Australian government's new procedures for ratification of treaties, see Sir Anthony Mason, *The Internationalisation of Domestic Law* (Canberra: Centre for International and Public Law, 1996); and George Williams, *Human Rights Under the Australian Constitution* (Melbourne: Oxford University Press, 1999).

36. See John Quigley, "Human Rights Defenses in U.S. Courts," *Human Rights Quarterly* 20, 3 (August 1998), 568.

37. Chayes and Chayes, "On Compliance," 176.

38. Cf. Kathryn Sikkink, who posits a three-stage process in a state's response to human rights, moving from a state's denial of the legitimacy of human rights and refusal to cooperate, to its acceptance of the legitimacy of international human rights practices, to "reconstituted sovereignty," involving recognition of legitimacy and concrete responses to international pressures that change domestic human rights practices. See "Human Rights, Principled Issue-Networks, and Sovereignty in Latin America," *International Organization* 47, 3 (summer 1993): 415.

39. Ernst Haas has distinguished between learning and adapting, George Breslauer between learning "that" and learning "how," and Philip Tetlock between learning in a cognitive sense and learning in an efficiency sense. Tetlock and O. R. Holsti conceive the relationship between the different levels of learning as a triangular formation, with fundamental beliefs and theory at the apex, strategic policy beliefs and preferences (policy) at the middle level, and tactical preferences and day-to-day operations (process) at the base. This model is adapted to the notion of the learning process. See Ernst B. Haas, "Collective Learning: Some Theoretical Speculations," in *Learning in U.S. and Soviet Foreign Policy*, ed. Breslauer and Tetlock, 72. In same volume, see George W. Breslauer, "What Have We Learned About Learning?" 825; and Philip Tetlock, "Learning in U.S. and Soviet Foreign Policy: In Search of an Elusive Concept," 32–36.

40. Cf. Johnston, "Learning Versus Adaptation," 27–61.

41. Explanations for this, and for the variations in the nature of learning or, in the case of regime monitoring, degrees of compliance, over time may be found in the

theory of transnational agenda setting, combining the insights of John Kingdon and Karl Deutsch and applied by Sandra Gubin to the case of the Soviet Union. This paradigm focuses both on the target state and, in the case of bilateral monitoring, on the state or organization seeking to influence it. In the case of the state being monitored, the formulation of policy agendas entails problem recognition, politics, and policy. Politics, including changes in national mood, and the nature of the administration and political leadership, may either open windows of opportunity to learning and adaptation, or close them. The degree to which a state can be influenced is determined in Deutsch's linkage model by three main factors: (1) the resources that can be directed toward influencing the target state; (2) the strength or mobilization of interest groups, interests, actors, or institutions with ties to the international or domestic system; and (3) the ability of the target state to resist pressures or redirect the pressure outward. See Gubin, "Between Regimes and Realism," 278–302; Karl W. Deutsch, "External and Internal Political Relationships," in *Approaches to Comparative and International Politics*, ed. Robert Barry Farrell (Evanston, Ill.: Northwestern University Press, 1966), 5–26, cited in Gubin, "Between Regimes and Realism," 289–90.

42. Ziegler, *Foreign Policy and East Asia*, 166–69.

43. For development of this argument, see Wang Jisi, "International Relations Theory and the Study of Chinese Foreign Policy: A Chinese Perspective," in *Chinese Foreign Policy*, ed. Robinson and Shambaugh, 492–93.

44. Chayes and Chayes, "On Compliance," 179.

45. Maxime Tardu, "The Effectiveness of United Nations Methods and Mechanisms in the Field of Human Rights: A Critical Overview," UN Doc. A/CONF.157/PC/60/Add.5 (1 April 1993), at 37.

46. For analyses of its methods and mechanisms, see UN Centre for Human Rights, *Manual on Human Rights Reporting Under Six Major International Human Rights Instruments* (New York: United Nations, 1991); Felice D. Gaer, *A Guide to UN "Special Procedures" in Human Rights* (New York: International League for Human Rights, October 1992); United Nations, *The United Nations and Human Rights, 1945–1995* (New York: Department of Public Information, 1995); Michael O'Flaherty, *Human Rights and the UN: Practice Before the Treaty Bodies* (London: Sweet & Maxwell, 1996); and Tardu, "The Effectiveness of United Nations Methods."

47. Para. 27, Vienna Declaration and Programme of Action. See also Simon Duke, "The State and Human Rights: Sovereignty Versus Humanitarian Intervention," *International Relations* 12, 2 (August 1994): 38.

48. Jack Donnelly, "Human Rights in the New World Order," *World Policy Journal* 9, 2 (spring 1992): 252, 256–57. For a comprehensive and balanced assessment of the effectiveness of the UN regime, see Alston, ed., *The United Nations and Human Rights*.

49. Tom J. Farer and Felice Gaer, "The UN and Human Rights: At the End of the Beginning," in *United Nations, Divided World: The UN's Roles in International Relations*, eds. Adam Roberts and Benedict Kingsbury (Oxford: Clarendon Press, 1996), 2nd ed., 288.

50. See discussion in C. A. J. Coady, "The Problem of Intervention," in *Ethics and Australian Foreign Policy*, ed. Paul Keal (Canberra: Allen and Unwin, in association with the Department of International Relations, Australian National University, 1992), 66–77.

51. Ann Kent, "The Limits of Ethics in International Politics: The International Human Rights Regime," *Asian Studies Review* 16, 1 (July 1992): 30.

52. See also Hurst Hannum, ed., *Guide to International Human Rights Practice* (Philadelphia: University of Pennsylvania Press, 1984).

53. Philip Alston, "Critical Appraisal of the UN Human Rights Regime," in *The United Nations and Human Rights*, ed. Alston, 21.

54. Chayes and Chayes, *New Sovereignty*, 230; and Chayes and Chayes, "On Compliance," 204.

55. Cited in Jonathan M. Mann, "Global Health Interdependence: An International Public Health Perspective" (seminar, Peace Research Centre, Australian National University, 1993).

56. See Levy, Young and Zürn, "The Study of International Regimes," 280. For their role in the United Nations, see Rachel Brett, "The Role and Limits of Human Rights NGOs at the United Nations," *Political Studies*, Special Issue: Politics and Human Rights, 43 (1995): 96–110.

57. Mark Girouard, "China's Obligations on Economic, Social and Cultural Rights Unfulfilled," *China Rights Forum* (winter 1997–98), 24. Thus, NGOs have forwarded critiques of China's reports to the International Labor Organization and the Committee Against Torture (see following chapters).

58. This indirect causal relationship has been pointed out by most of the representatives of Western and Chinese NGOs interviewed; they have also stressed the importance of domestic pressures from within China. However, in 1998 China began meeting with Amnesty International and has made direct attacks on NGOs such as Human Rights Watch/Asia.

59. For analyses of the "other" Western human rights tradition of "like-minded states," established by the Nordic countries and Canada, see Jack Donnelly, *International Human Rights* (Boulder, Colo.: Westview Press, 1993); and Jan Egeland, *Impotent Superpower—Potent Small State: Potential and Limitations of Human Rights Objectives in the Foreign Policies of the United States and Norway* (Oslo, Norway: Norwegian University Press, 1988)

60. I thank Philip Alston for this point.

61. Chayes and Chayes, "On Compliance," 204. Cf. George W. Downs, David M. Rocke, and Peter N. Barsoom, "Is the Good News About Compliance Good News About Cooperation?" *International Organization* 50, 3 (summer 1996): 379–406.

62. Levy, Young, and Zürn, "The Study of International Regimes," 291.

63. Donnelly, "International Human Rights," 616.

64. Levy, Young and Zürn, "The Study of International Regimes," 294, citing Donald Campbell and Julian Stanley, *Experimental and Quasi-Experimental Designs for Research* (Chicago: Rand McNally, 1966).

65. Alston, "Critical Appraisal," 21.

66. Cf. Nigel Rodley, the Special Rapporteur on Torture, has defined monitoring more broadly as "the assembling, presentation, and dissemination of pertinent data in a form that enables human rights performance to be assessed according to agreed-upon international standards." See "Monitoring Human Rights: Violations in the 1980s," in Jorge I. Dominguez, Nigel S. Rodley, Bryce Wood, and Richard Falk, *Enhancing Global Human Rights* (New York: McGraw-Hill, 1979), 119–51.

67. As Alston points out, "supervision" in the ILO also contains the sense of "control" or "correction by a superior authority" that most states would challenge. The word is also used in an imprecise, generic sense, ranging in meaning from "general surveys" to "direct contacts." In the study, "general surveys" can be understood as "passive monitoring," and "direct contacts" as "active monitoring." Thus, the ILO operates much as the United Nations proper, although it claims that through its peculiar tripartite structure, the effectiveness of each activity is strengthened (hence, it may be inferred, the strength of the word "supervision" is really meant to convey the efficacy of the result rather than to describe the process itself). See Philip Alston, "Establishing Accountability: Some Current Challenges in Relation to Human Rights Monitoring," in *Monitoring Children's Rights*, ed. E. Verhellen (The Hague: Martinus Nijhoff, 1996), 21–3.

68. According to Philip Alston, "standards" comprises setting standards, deepen-

ing normative understanding, and issue analysis. "Promotion" comprises promoting rights-consciousness, encouraging the adoption of international norms in domestic legal systems, facilitating institution building, and developing an international institutional network. "Establishing accountability" comprises development of an accepted international framework, monitoring respect for obligations by authoritative, regular reviews, anticipating and preventing violations; responding to violations through effective fact-finding, mobilization of shame and enforcement through sanctions, and securing relief and redress for victims of violations. See Alston, "Critical Appraisal," 21.

69. This process, which in these UN forums involves resolutions drawing attention to a state's abuse of human rights, but also commending them for any improvements, is conceptualized in John Braithwaite, *Crime, Shame and Reintegration* (Cambridge: Cambridge University Press, 1989).

70. Theo van Boven, "The International System of Human Rights: An Overview," in UN Centre for Human Rights, *Manual on Human Rights Reporting*, 7.

71. World Conference on Human Rights, "Interim Report on Updated Study by Mr. Philip Alston," UN Doc. A/CONF.157/PC/62/Add.11/Rev.1 (Geneva, 22 April 1993), para. 93, at 40.

72. Mark Girouard, "China's Obligations," 24.

73. Vojin Dimitrijevic, "The Monitoring of Human Rights and the Prevention of Human Rights Violations through Reporting Procedures," in *Monitoring Human Rights in Europe: Comparing International Procedures and Mechanisms*, ed. Arie Bloed, Liselotte Leicht, Manfred Nowak and Allan Rosas (Dordrecht: Martinus Nijhoff Publishers, 1993), 22–23.

74. Philip Alston, "The Purposes of Reporting," in UN Centre for Human Rights, *Manual on Human Rights Reporting*, 13.

Chapter 1. The UN Human Rights Regime and China's Participation Before 1989

1. W. Michael Reisman, "International Law after the Cold War," *American Journal of International Law* 84 (October 1990) 4: 861.

2. Perez de Cuellar, "Secretary-General's Address at the University of Bordeaux," 22 April 1991, United Nations Press Release SG/SM/4560, New York, 24 April 1991.

3. Brenda Cossman, "Reform, Revolution or Retrenchment? International Human Rights in the Post-Cold War Era," *Harvard International Law Journal* 32 (Spring 1991) 2: 340. For new importance of human rights, see also W. Michael Reisman, "International Law after the Cold War," *American Journal of International Law* 84 (October 1990) 4: 861.

4. Former UN Secretary-General Boutros Boutros-Ghali has pointed out: "The machinery of the United Nations, which had often been rendered inoperative by the dynamics of the Cold War, is suddenly at the centre of international efforts to deal with unresolved problems of the past decades as well as an emerging array of present and future issues." See Boutros Boutros-Ghali, "Empowering the United Nations," *Foreign Affairs* 71 (Winter 1992/93) 5: 88.

5. See, for instance, Holly Burkhalter, "Moving Human Rights to Centre Stage," *World Policy Journal* 9 (Summer 1992) 3: 417–28.

6. According to the two Covenants, civil rights include freedom of thought, conscience and religion, expression and association, residence and movement; every person's right to life, free from arbitrary killing, torture and mistreatment; freedom from slavery, arbitrary arrest or detention; the right to a fair trial; and equality before the law. They may be loosely divided into two main categories: the rights of freedom

of expression and rights of immunity from the intervention of the state. Political rights may be defined as rights of participation and include the individual's right to "take part in the conduct of public affairs, directly or through freely chosen representatives"; the right of access to public service; and the right of election and recall of government on the basis of "universal and equal suffrage" by secret ballot. Social and cultural rights, in the form of claims of benefits from the state, may be understood as rights of consumption or positive rights, allowing access to social security, to education and to "the cultural life of the community." Economic rights include the right to work, to free choice of employment, the right to strike and the right to equal pay for equal work. Collective rights include the rights of peoples to self-determination and equality of rights, rights relating to international peace and security, the right of permanent sovereignty over natural resources, developmental rights, environmental rights and the rights of minorities.

7. See Bilahari Kausikan, "Human Rights: Asia's Different Standard," *Foreign Policy* 92 (Fall 1993), 29; and Kishore Mahbubani, "The Pacific Way," *Foreign Affairs* 74 (January–February 1995) 1: 111. See also Peter Bailey, Ann Kent, and others, in *Perceptions of Human Rights in Asia*, ed. Anthony Milner (University of New South Wales and Australian Academy of Social Sciences, 1993); and Chandra Muzaffar, "The New World Order: Gold or God?" *24 Hours* (February 1992).

8. Francis Fukuyama has speculated that the current crisis will "puncture the idea of Asian exceptionalism." See Francis Fukuyama, "Asian Values and the Asian Crisis," *Commentary* 105 (February 1998) 2:27. For different scholarly theories about the future direction of the human rights debate, see Cossman, "Reform, Revolution or Retrenchment?" 345; Christopher Tremewan, "Human Rights in Asia," *The Pacific Review* 6, 1 (1993): 29; Ann Kent, *Between Freedom and Subsistence: China and Human Rights* (Hong Kong: Oxford University Press, 1993), Chapter 8; and John Quinn, "The General Assembly into the 1990s," in *The United Nations and Human Rights: A Critical Appraisal*, ed. Philip Alston (Oxford: Clarendon Press, 1992), 100. See also B. G. Ramcharan, "Strategies for the International Protection of Human Rights in the 1990s," *Human Rights Quarterly* 13 (1991) 2: 155–56; and Robert Cullen, "Human Rights Quandary," *Foreign Affairs* 71 (Winter 1992–93) 5: 79–88.

9. Peter van Ham, "The Lack of a Big Bully: Hegemonic Stability Theory and Regimes in the Study of International Relations," *Acta Politica* (January 1992) 1: 46.

10. See also discussions of universalism and cultural relativism in Jack Donnelly, *International Human Rights* (Boulder: Westview Press, 1993), 34–38; Joseph A. Camilleri, "Human Rights, Cultural Diversity and Conflict Resolution: The Asia Pacific Context," *Pacifica Review* 6 (1994) 2: 19–36; Michael Freeman, "Human Rights: Asia and the West," in *Human Rights and International Relations in the Asia Pacific*, ed. James T.H. Tang (London: Pinter, 1995), 17–23; Kent, *Between Freedom and Subsistence*, 19–26; and Fred Halliday, "Relativism and Universalism in Human Rights: the Case of the Islamic Middle East," *Political Studies*, Special Issue, "Politics and Human Rights," 43 (1995): 152–67.

11. Kausikan, "Human Rights," 32.

12. Martti Koskenniemi, "The Future of Statehood," *Harvard International Law Journal* 32 (Spring 1991) 2: 403.

13. Stanley Hoffmann, *Duties Beyond Borders: On the Limits and Possibilities of Ethical International Politics* (New York: Syracuse University Press, 1981), 19. This distinction is also made by R. J. Vincent, "Modernity and Universal Human Rights," in *Global Politics: Globalisation and the Nation-State*, Anthony McGrew and Paul Lewis et al. (Cambridge: Policy Press, 1992), 269–91.

14. Hedley Bull, *Justice in International Relations*, 1983–84 Hagey Lectures, 12–13 October 1983 (Ontario: University of Waterloo, 1984), 5–11.

15. R. J. Vincent, *Human Rights and International Relations*, (Cambridge: Cambridge University Press, 1986), 80.

16. David P. Forsythe, "The United States, the United Nations, and Human Rights," in *The United States and Multilateral Institutions: Patterns of Changing Instrumentality and Influence*, ed. Margaret P. Karns and Karen A. Mingst (Boston: Unwin Hyman, 1990), 261–88. On U.S. government attitude to economic, social and cultural rights, see Philip Alston, "U.S. Ratification of the Covenant on Economic, Social and Cultural Rights: The Need for an Entirely New Strategy," *American Journal of International Law* 84 (April 1990) 2:367; and for U.S. monitoring bias, see Rhoda E. Howard, "Monitoring Human Rights: Problems of Consistency," *Ethics and International Affairs* 4 (1990): 34–37.

17. For an analysis of Western and non-Western identity, see Jacinta O'Hagan, "How the West Was Lost: The Absence of the Concept of the West from International Relations," Paper delivered at the Australasian Political Science Association, Monash University, September 1993; for a broad analysis of culture in international relations, see special issue of *Millenium*, 22 (Winter 1993) 3.

18. For example, Vincent, *Human Rights*, 50; Adamantia Pollis, "Liberal, Socialist and Third World Perspectives of Human Rights," in *Toward a Human Rights Framework*, ed. Peter Schwab and Adamantia Pollis (New York: Praeger, 1982), 1–26.

19. Cf. Daniel A. Bell, "The East Asian Challenge to Human Rights: Reflections on an East West Dialogue," *Human Rights Quarterly* 18 (August 1996) 3: 641–67. For the historical background, see Antonio Cassese, "The General Assembly: Historical Perspective, 1945–1989," in *The United Nations and Human Rights*, ed. Alston, 35–50; and Farrokh Jhabvala, "On Human Rights and the Socio-Economic Context," in *Third World Attitudes Toward International Law: An Introduction*, ed. Frederick E. Snyder and Surakiart Sathirathai (Dordrecht: Martinus Nijhoff Publishers, 1987), 293–319. The increasing "internationalization" of human rights within the UN, under pressure from socialist and Third World states, has also been recognized in Chinese texts. See, for example, Wang Xingfang ed., *Zhongguo yu Lianheguo: Jinian Lianheguo chengli wushi zhounian*, ("China and the United Nations: Commemorating the 50th Anniversary of the Founding of the United Nations") (Beijing: *Shijie zhishi* chubanshe, 1995), 333–35.

20. See Koskenniemi, "The Future of Statehood," 404.

21. For the most comprehensive description and analysis of the UN human rights organs, see Alston, ed., *The United Nations and Human Rights*. See also Jack Donnelly, *International Human Rights*; Jack Donnelly, *Universal Human Rights in Theory and Practice* (Ithaca: Cornell University Press, 1986); Donnelly, "Human Rights in the New World Order," *World Policy Journal* 9 (Spring 1992) 2: 251–52; David P. Forsythe, *The Internationalization of Human Rights* (Lexington, Mass.: Lexington Books, 1991); and Richard P. Claude and Burns H. Weston, eds., *Human Rights and the World Community: Issues and Action* (Philadelphia: University of Pennsylvania Press, 1992), second edition.

22. Philip Alston, "The Commission on Human Rights," in *The United Nations and Human Rights*, ed. Alston, 188. Different views to this effect may be found in Quinn, "The General Assembly," 85; A. A. Cancado Trindade, "La Protection des Droits Économiques, Sociaux et Culturels: Évolution et Tendances Actuelles, Particulièrement à l'Échelle Régionale" ("The Protection of Economic, Social and Cultural Rights: Evolution and Current Trends, Particularly at the Regional Level"), *Revue Générale de Droit International Public* (1990) 4: 945; M. Jean Mayer, "Progrès et Obstacles dans la Mise en Oeuvre des Droits de l'Homme: Bilan de la Période 1945–1992 et Suggestions pour l'Avenir" ("Progress and Obstacles in the Implementation of Human Rights: Balance-Sheet for the Period 1945–1992 and Suggestions for the

Future"), UN Doc. A/Conf. 157/PC/60/Add.1, 1 April 1993, at 13; and Audrey R. Chapman, "A 'Violations Approach' for Monitoring the International Covenant on Economic, Social and Cultural Rights," *Human Rights Quarterly* 18 (1996) 1: 26.

23. See Iain Guest, *Behind the Disappearances: Argentina's Dirty War Against Human Rights and the United Nations* (Philadelphia: University of Pennsylvania Press, 1990); and Manfred H. Wiegandt, "The Pitfalls of International Human Rights Monitoring: Some Critical Remarks on the 1995 Human Rights Watch/Helsinki Report on Xenophobia in Germany," *Human Rights Quarterly* 18 (1996) 4: 833–42.

24. The Editors, "Culture in International Relations: An Introduction to the Special Issue," *Millenium* 22 (Winter 1993) 3: 376. See also Adamantia Pollis, "Cultural Relativism Revisited: Through a State Prism," *Human Rights Quarterly* 18 (May 1996) 2: 316–44. Cf. Samuel P. Huntington, "The Clash of Civilizations," *Foreign Affairs* 27 (Summer 1993) 3: 22. For Chinese assessment of this thesis, see Wang Jisi, "Civilisations: Clash or Fusion?" *Beijing Review* 39 (15–21 January 1996) 3: 8–12.

25. Michael Perry makes a useful distinction between three kinds of relativism: anthropological relativism; epistemological relativism; and cultural relativism. While dismissing the first two, he argues that, because of the very general nature of the norms in human rights treaties, "cultural particularities do and should play a role in determining the shape — for example, the specific institutional embodiment — one or another culture gives to a value (e.g., freedom of the press), represented by a human rights provision." See Perry, "Are Human Rights Universal?" *Human Rights Quarterly* 19 (1997) 3: 508–509.

26. See Bailey, Kent and others, *Perceptions of Human Rights in Asia.* See also Yash Ghai, "Asian Perspectives on Human Rights," in *Human Rights and International Relations,* ed. Tang, 54–67; and Ghai, "Rights, Duties and Responsibilities," in *Human Rights Solidarity,* AHRC Newsletter 7 (September 1997) 4: 9–17. For a comparison between the positions of China and Japan see Robert J. Myers, "Rethinking Human Rights," *Society* 30 (November–December 1992) 1: 61–62.

27. Alston, "The Commission on Human Rights," 162–64. See also Tremewan, "Human Rights in Asia," 17.

28. Geoffrey Best, "Justice, International Relations and Human Rights," *International Affairs* 71, 4 (1995): 788.

29. Ian Brownlie (ed), *Basic Documents on Human Rights* (Oxford: Clarendon Press, 1971), 94–95.

30. Boutros Boutros-Ghali, "Empowering the UN," 98–99.

31. See citation of definition by PCIJ in the Wimbledon case, in Kathryn Sikkink, "Human Rights, Principled Issue-Networks, and Sovereignty in Latin America," *International Organization* 47 (Summer 1993) 3: 413; and Nationality Decrees in Tunis and Morocco (advisory opinion) 1923 P.C.I.J. (ser. B) No 4, at 24, cited in Koskenniemi, "The Future of Statehood," 408.

32. Jarat Chopra and Thomas G. Weiss, "Sovereignty Is No Longer Sacrosanct: Codifying Humanitarian Intervention," *Ethics and International Affairs* 6 (1992): 107–8.

33. Georg Schwarzenberger, cited in Jack Donnelly, " Human Rights: A New Standard of Civilization?," *International Affairs* 74, 1 (January 1998): 13.

34. See also Joseph Camilleri and Jim Falk, *The End of Sovereignty? The Politics of a Shrinking and Fragmenting World* (Aldershot: Edward Elgar, 1992); and Allan Rosas, "State Sovereignty and Human Rights: Towards a Global Constitutional Project," *Political Studies,* Special Issue, "Politics and Human Rights," 43 (1995): 61–78.

35. Vincent, "Modernity and Universal Human Rights," 290. See also Lizius Wildhaber, cited in Ruth Lapidoth, "Sovereignty in Transition," *Journal of International Affairs* 45 (Winter 1992) 2: 345; W. Michael Reisman, "Sovereignty and Human Rights in Contemporary International Law," *American Journal of International Law* 84, 4 (October 1990): 866–76; and Robert Keohane, "Hobbes' Dilemma and Institu-

tional Change in World Politics: Sovereignty in International Society," paper presented at the conference "Economic and Security Cooperation in the Asia-Pacific: Agendas for the 1990s," 28–30 July 1993, National Convention Centre, Canberra, 19.

36. Herbert V. Evatt, *The Task of Nations* (Westport, Conn.: Greenwood Press, 1949), 225–26.

37. See, for instance, World Bank, *China, Long-term Development: Issues and Options* (Washington D.C.: International Bank for Reconstruction and Development, 1984), 16. For analysis of economic and social rights in China before 1979, see Kent, *Between Freedom and Subsistence*, 68–78, 160–66; and Stephen C. Thomas, "Measuring Social and Economic Rights Performance in the People's Republic of China: A Comparative Perspective Among Developing Asian Countries," in *Human Rights: Theory and Measurement*, ed. David Louis Cingranelli (London: Macmillan Press, 1988), 104–19.

38. Kent, *Between Freedom and Subsistence*, 232. See also Philip Baker, "China: Human Rights and the Law," *The Pacific Review* 6 (1993) 3: 239–45.

39. See Susan Shirk, "Human Rights: What about China?" *Foreign Policy* (Winter 1977–78) 29: 109–27; and Roberta Cohen, "People's Republic of China: The Human Rights Exception," *Human Rights Quarterly* 9 (November 1987) 4: 447–549.

40. This analysis is based on Kent, *Between Freedom and Subsistence*, 30–110. For discussions of this issue, see Wang Gungwu, *Power, Rights and Duties in Chinese History*, the Fortieth George Ernest Morrison Lecture in Ethnology (Canberra, Australian National University, 1979); R. Randle Edwards, Louis Henkin, and Andrew J. Nathan, *Human Rights in Contemporary China* (New York: Columbia University Press, 1986), 137–47; Roberto Unger, *Law in Modern Society: Toward a Criticism of Social Theory* (New York: The Free Press, 1979); Albert H. Y. Chen, "Civil Liberties in China: Some Preliminary Observations," in *Civil Liberties in Hong Kong*, ed. Raymond Wacks (Hong Kong, Oxford University Press, 1988), 113–15; Chad Hansen, "Do Human Rights Apply to China? A Normative Analysis of Cultural Difference," *Hong Kong Law Journal* 24 (1994) 3: 397–415; Michael C. Davis, ed., *Human Rights and Chinese Values: Legal, Philosophical and Political Perspectives* (Hong Kong: Oxford University Press, 1995); and Randall P. Peerenboom, "Rights, Interests and the Interest in Rights in China," *Stanford Journal of International Law* 31 (Summer 1995) 2: 359–86.

41. Thus, a U.S. crackdown on the Japanese Communist Party in 1950 was described in official Chinese statements as violation of "freedom of speech" and "fundamental human rights"; a 1958 Chinese statement accused the Thai government of infringing upon the "legitimate rights" of overseas Chinese; and a 1963 statement heralded the black struggle for "freedom and equal rights." See Andrew J. Nathan, "Human Rights in Chinese Foreign Policy," *The China Quarterly* (September 1994) 139: 624–26. See also Hungdah Chiu, "Chinese Attitudes Towards International Law of Human Rights in the Post-Mao Era," in Victor C. Falkenheim and Ilpyong J. Kim, eds., *Chinese Politics from Mao to Deng* (New York: Paragon House, 1989), 242–43.

42. "Joint Communiqué of Bandung Conference," NCNA 24 April 1955, in *Survey of China Mainland Press* (24 April 1955) 1033: 16–17. These principles were earlier encapsulated in the "Agreement between the Republic of India and the People's Republic of China on Trade and Intercourse between Tibet Region of China and India, April 29, 1954," reprinted in Jerome A. Cohen and Hungdah Chiu, eds., *People's China and International Law: A Documentary Survey*, vol. 1 (Princeton: Princeton University Press, 1974), 122.

43. 1978 Constitution, art. 44, in *Peking Review* 21 (17 March 1978) 11: 13.

44. Louis Henkin, "The Human Rights Idea in Contemporary China: A Comparative Perspective," in Edwards, Henkin, and Nathan, *Human Rights in Contemporary China*, 32. Although the Chinese constitutions contain no prohibition on the subject

of torture, it is prohibited by law. See James Seymour, "Human Rights and the Law in the People's Republic of China," in *Chinese Politics from Mao to Deng*, ed. Victor C. Falkenheim and Ilpyong J. Kim (New York: Paragon House, 1989), f. 42, 295–96.

45. Alice E. Tay, "Communist Visions, Communist Realities and the Role of Law," *Bulletin of the Australian Society of Legal Philosophy*, 13 (December 1989) 51: 240.

46. For this concept, see Carol A. Heimer, *Legislating Responsibility*, American Bar Foundation Working Paper, # 9711 (Chicago, 1997).

47. Alice E. Tay, "China and Legal Pluralism," *Bulletin of the Australian Society of Legal Philosophy*, 8 (December 1984) 31: 33.

48. For consequences of modernization policy, see Gordon White, "The New Economic Paradigm: Towards Market Socialism," in *Reforming the Revolution: China in Transition*, eds. Robert Benewick and Paul Wingrove (Basingstoke: Macmillan Education, 1988), 85–90. See also Kent, *Between Freedom and Subsistence*, 83.

49. Tony Saich, "Modernisation and Participation in the People's Republic of China," in Joseph Y. S. Cheng, ed., *China: Modernisation in the 1980s* (Hong Kong: Chinese University Press, 1989), 42.

50. For Deng Xiaoping's promise to move towards "socialist democracy" and "socialist legality," see "Dang he guojia lingdao zhidu di gaige" ("Reform of the Leadership System of our Party and State"), *Deng Xiaoping wenxuan* ("The Selected Works of Deng Xiaoping") (Beijing: Renmin chubanshe, 1983), 282.

51. See details in Shao-chuan Leng, "Legal Reform in Post-Mao China: a Tentative Assessment," in *Chinese Politics*, ed. Falkenheim and Kim, 203–28. See in general *The China Quarterly*, Special Issue: China's Legal Reforms, 141 (March 1995).

52. The Australian Department of Foreign Affairs and Trade, *Report of the Australian Human Rights Delegation to China, 14–26 July 1991* (Canberra: Australian Department of Foreign Affairs, September 1991), Annex 7, 1. For statistics, see Amnesty International, *China, Violations of Human Rights: Prisoners of Conscience and the Death Penalty in the People's Republic of China* (London: Amnesty International Publications, 1984), 9–10.

53. Amnesty International, *1991 Report* (London: Amnesty International, 1992). See also Baker, "China: Human Rights," 240.

54. Asia Watch, "Torture in China" (New York: Asia Watch, July 1990), 3.

55. For these discussions, see Xiao Weiyun, Luo Haocai, Wu Xieying, "Makesi zhuyi zenmayang kan 'renquan' wenti" ("How Marxism Views the Question of Human Rights") *Hongqi* ("Red Flag") (1979) 5: 43; Sheng Zuhong, "Renquan yu fazhi" ("Human Rights and the Legal System"), *Minzhu yu fazhi* ("Democracy and the Legal System") (September 1979) 2: 19–20; Lin Rongnian, Zhang Jinfan, "Tan renquan wenti" ("Discussing Human Rights"), *Xuexi yu tansuo* ("Study and Exploration") (1980) 1:30–37; Li Maoguan, "Gongmin di ziyou he falu" ("Citizens' Freedom and the Law"), *Faxue yanjiu* ("Legal Science Research") (1981) 2: 5–8; and *Gongren ribao* ("Workers' Daily"), 22 March 1979, cited in *The China Quarterly* 78 (June 1979): 44; and *BBC Summary of World Broadcasts* SWB/FE/6075.

56. See, for instance, *Xianfa zidian* ("Constitutional Dictionary") (Jilin: Jilin chubanshe, 1988), 5; *Faxue zidian* ("A Dictionary of Legal Science") (Shanghai: Cishu chubanshe, 1980), 8–9; Lin Rongnian and Zhang Jinfan, "Tan renquan wenti," 30–37; Wang Delu and Jiang Shihe, eds., *Renquan xuanyan* ("Declarations of Human Rights") (Beijing: *Qiushi* chubanshe, April 1989), 1–6; and *Jiandan shehui kexue zidian* ("A Concise Dictionary of the Social Sciences") (Shanghai: Cidian chubanshe, 1982), 17.

57. Xu Bing, "Renquan lilun di chansheng he lishi fazhan" ("On the Origins and Historical Development of Human Rights"), *Faxue yanjiu* ("Legal Science Research") (1989), 3: 1–10.8–9; and Ma Jun, cited in Li Haibo, "China Applauds Human Rights," *Beijing Review* 31 (19–25 December 1988) 51: 6.

58. Shen Baoxiang, Wang Chengquan, Li Zerui, "Guanyu guoji lingyu di renquan wenti" ("On the Question of Human Rights in the International Arena"), *Hongqi* ("Red Flag") (1982) 8: 47–48.

59. Guo Shan, "China's Role in Human Rights Field," *Beijing Review* 30 (9 February 1987) 5–6: 23–24.

60. Shen Baoxiang et al., "Guanyu guoji lingyu," 44.

61. Ma Jun, "Human Rights," 18.

62. For an excellent exegesis of this literature, see Suzanne Ogden, "The Approach of the Chinese Communists to the Study of International Law, State Sovereignty and the International System," *The China Quarterly* 70 (June 1977): 315–36.

63. Jerome Cohen and Hungdah Chiu, ed., *People's China*, 82.

64. For instance, Zhou Gengsheng, "The Persecution of Chinese Nationals and Infringement of the Right of China to Protect Chinese Nationals by the Indian Government are Serious International Delinquencies," cited Oppenheim, *International Law* (London: Longmans, Green, 1955), as support for the Chinese position. See *Renmin ribao*, 22 January 1963, 5, reprinted in Cohen and Chiu, eds., *People's China*, 82.

65. See, for instance, Wang Jisi, "International Relations and the Study of Chinese Foreign Policy," in *Chinese Foreign Policy: Theory and Practice*, ed. Thomas W. Robinson and David Shambaugh (Oxford: Clarendon Press, 1994), 492–93.

66. Cohen and Chiu, eds., *People's China*, 4–5.

67. Truong Buu Lam, "Intervention Versus Tribute in Sino-Vietnamese Relations, 1788–1790," in *The Chinese World Order: Traditional China's Foreign Relations*, ed. John King Fairbank (Cambridge: Harvard University Press, 1968), 179.

68. Cohen and Chiu, eds., *People's China*, 7.

69. See, for instance, Zhu Qiwu, "Looking at the Class Character and Inheritable Character of Law from the Point of View of International Law," *Guangming ribao*, 13 May 1957: 3; Liu Jiaji, "Some Questions Concerning the Nature and Systems of International Law," *Faxue* ("Legal Science") (1958) 3: 44–45; and Yang Zhaolong, "On the Class Character and Inheritable Character of Law," *Huadong Zhengfa xuebao* ("East China Journal of Politics and Law") (1956) 3: 30: all reprinted in Cohen and Chiu, eds., *People's China*, 48–54.

70. Yu Fan, "Speaking about the Relationship Between China and the Tibetan Region from the Viewpoint of Sovereignty and Suzerainty," *Renmin ribao* ("People's Daily"), 5 June 1959: 7, reprinted in Cohen and Chiu, eds., *People's China*, 395.

71. Yang Xin and Chen Jian, "Expose and Criticise the Imperialists' Fallacy Concerning the Question of State Sovereignty," *Zhengfa yanjiu* ("Political and Legal Research") (1964) 4: 6–11, reprinted in Cohen and Chiu, eds., *People's China*, 112.

72. Samuel S. Kim, *China, the United Nations and World Order* (Princeton: Princeton University Press, 1979), 414.

73. Zhou Gengsheng, "The Persecution of Chinese Nationals," 82.

74. See, for instance, Ji Xiangyang, "Smash the New Tsars' Theory of Limited Sovereignty," *Peking Review* 12 (23 May 1969) 21: 20–22, reprinted in Cohen and Chiu, eds., *People's China*, 153–55.

75. Ogden, "The Approach of the Chinese Communists," 318.

76. Guo Qun, *Lianheguo* ("The United Nations") (Beijing: Shijie zhishi chubanshe, 1955), 15, cited in Hungdah Chiu, "Chinese Attitudes," 243.

77. For an excellent discussion of this position, which still pertains today, see Benedict Kingsbury, "'Indigenous Peoples' in International Law: A Constructivist Approach to the Asian Controversy," *American Journal of International Law* 92, 3 (July 1998).

78. Wei Min, *Guojifa gailun* ("Introduction to International Law") (Beijing: *Guangming ribao* chubanshe, 1986), 245.

79. Zhou Gengsheng, *Xiandai yingmei guojifa di sixiang dongxiang* ("Trends in the Thought of Modern English and American International Law") (Beijing: *Shijie zhishi* chubanshe, 1963), 67, 84–85.

80. Zhou Gengsheng, "The United Nations Intervention in the 'Question of Tibet' is Illegal," *Zhengfa yanjiu* ("Political and Legal Studies") (December 1959), no. 6, 8–11, reprinted in Cohen and Chiu, eds., *People's China*, 1330.

81. "Joint Communiqué of Bandung Conference," reprinted in ibid. 123–24.

82. Ogden, "The Approach of the Chinese Communists," 328 and n. 46.

83. Kong Meng, "A Criticism of the Theories of Bourgeois International Law Concerning the Subjects of International Law and Recognition of States," *Guoji wenti yanjiu* ("International Studies") (February 1960) 2: 44–51, reprinted in Cohen and Chiu, eds., *People's China*, 97–98. On the state as basic unit of international law, see James Crawford, "The Rights of Peoples: 'Peoples' or 'Governments'?" in *The Rights of Peoples*, ed. James Crawford (Oxford: Clarendon Press, 1988), 55–56; and Hungdah Chiu, "The Nature of International Law and the Problem of a Universal System," in *Law in Chinese Foreign Policy: Communist China and Selected Problems of International Law*, ed. Shao-chuan Leng and Hundah Chiu (New York: Oceana Press, 1972), 1–33.

84. Wang Tieya and Wei Min, eds., *Guoji fa* ("International Law") (Beijing: Falu chubanshe, 1981), 268.

85. Zhonghua renmin gongheguo guowuyuan xinwen bangongshi, *Zhongguo di renquan zhuangkuang* (Beijing: Zhongyang wenxian chubanshe, October 1991), 65–66; Information Office of the State Council of the People's Republic, *Human Rights in China*, 57–58.

86. For a history of China's relations with the UN in the early years of its establishment, see Wang Xingfang, ed., *Zhongguo yu Lianheguo* ("China and the United Nations") 19–51; and Tao Wenzhao, Yang Kuisong and Wang Jianliang, *Kang Ri zhanzheng shiqi zhongguo duiwai guanxi* ("China's Foreign Relations During the War of Resistance Against Japan") (Beijing: Zhonggong dangshi chubanshe, 1995), 381–90. For relations after 1971, see Wang Xingfang, ed., *Zhongguo yu Lianheguo*; and Kim, *China, the United Nations*. For UN and human rights, see Pang Sen, *Dangdai renquan ABC* ("Contemporary Human Rights ABC") (Chengdu: Sichuan renmin chubanshe, 1992), 209–10; John F. Copper, "Defining Human Rights," in Yuan-li Wu et al., *Human Rights in the People's Republic of China* (Boulder: Westview Press, 1988), 15; and Wei-chin Lee, "With Open Arms? China and Human Rights in the United Nations," *Pacifica* 2 (January 1990) 1: 16–37.

87. Article 55 (c) of the Charter calls for "universal respect for, and observance of, human rights and fundamental freedoms for all without distinction as to race, sex, language, or religion." Article 56 states: "All members pledge themselves to take joint and separate action in cooperation with the Organisation for the achievement of the purposes set forth in Article 55." See text in Ian Brownlie, ed., *Basic Documents on Human Rights* (Oxford: Clarendon Press, 1971), 96.

88. According to Zhonghua renmin gongheguo waijiaobu waijiaoshi bianjishi (Editorial Department, China's Diplomatic History, Chinese Foreign Ministry") *Zhongguo waijiao gailan, 1989* ("Survey of China's Foreign Relations, 1989") (Beijing: *Shijie zhishi* chubanshe, 1989), 459–60, China believed the UN should give priority to issues of racism, colonialism and foreign aggression and occupation, national self-determination and development.

89. Samuel S. Kim, "China's International Organizational Behaviour," in *Chinese Foreign Policy: Theory and Practice*, ed. Thomas W. Robinson and David Shambaugh (Oxford: Clarendon Press, 1994), 431.

90. UN Doc. E/AC.7/SR.699 (30 May 1972), at 143, cited in Kim, *China, the United Nations*, 485.

91. Based on author's analysis of China's voting patterns recorded in the UNGA *Resolutions and Decisions Adopted by the General Assembly*, Press Releases GA/5355–7814, 1971–1988, 25th–43rd session, UN, New York. See also Cohen, "Human Rights Exception," 537–8; and Wang Xingfang ed., *Zhongguo yu Lianheguo*, 342.

92. Jerome A. Cohen, "Due Process?" in *The China Difference*, ed. Ross Terrill (New York: The Asia Society, 1979), 249–50.

93. *Peking Review* 20 (11 March 1977) 11: 24.

94. Kim, "China's International Organizational Behaviour," 431.

95. Pang Sen, *Dangdai renquan*, 210.

96. See UNGA Resolutions, Press Releases GA/5355–6546, 1971–1981, 25th–36th sessions; and Cohen, "Human Rights Exception," 537.

97. 1986 Press release GA/7272, 40th session, 13 January 1986, res. 40/114, at 461–3. It reaffirmed that "all human rights are indivisible and interdependent and that the promotion and protection of one category of rights can never exempt or excuse States from the promotion and protection of the other rights," and stated that "the full realisation of civil and political rights is inseparably linked with the enjoyment of economic, social and cultural rights."

98. See UN Commission on Human Rights, *Report on the Forty-Fifth Session* (30 January–10 March 1989), Economic and Social Council, Official Records 1989, Supplement 2, UN Docs. E/CN.4/1989/2–E/CN.4/1989/86.

99. Wang Xingfang, ed., *Zhongguo yu Lianheguo*, 342–43.

100. Information Office of the State Council of the People's Republic of China, *Human Rights in China* (Beijing, November 1991), 85–86.

101. See *Zhongguo waijiao gailan* 1989, 459.

102. Cohen, "Human Rights Exception," 537.

103. Following is the chronological order of signature [Key: *Y*: China accepted (ratification, accession, or succession); *S*: China signed but not yet ratified; *R*: China made reservations]: Convention on the Elimination of All Forms of Discrimination against Women: *Y* (1980), *R* (Paragraph 1 of Art. 29); International Convention on the Elimination of All Forms of Racial Discrimination: *Y* (1981), *R* (Art. 22); Protocol Relating to the Status of Refugees: *Y* (1982), *R* (Art. 4); Convention Relating to the Status of Refugees: *Y* (1982), *R* (Art. 14. 16); Convention on the Prevention and Punishment of the Crime of Genocide: *Y* (1983), *R* (Art. 9); International Convention on the Suppression and Punishment of the Crime of Apartheid: *Y* (1983); International Convention against Apartheid in Sports: *S* (1987); Convention against Torture and Other Cruel, Inhuman or Degrading Treatment or Punishment: *Y* (1988), *R* (Art. 20, Para 1 of Art. 30). See United Nations, *Multilateral Treaties Deposited with the Secretary-General. Status as at 31 December 1989* (New York: United Nations, 1990), ST/LEG/SER.E/8. See also Lee, "China and Human Rights," 37. For discussion of China's position on these treaties and the rights they incorporated, see Wang Xingfang, ed., *Zhongguo yu Lianheguo*, 343–53.

104. State Council, *Human Rights in China*, 58–59; and Pang Sen, *Dangdai renquan*, 210.

105. *Zhongguo waijiao gailan*, 1989, 461.

106. See ibid.; and Li Haibo, "China Applauds Human Rights," *Beijing Review* 31 (19–25 December 1988) 51: 5–6.

107. Hungdah Chiu, "Chinese Attitudes Towards International Law," 256. Rumors of this possibility continued to surface throughout the next decade. Now that China has signed the ICCPR and the ICESCR, the important issue is how soon it will ratify them.

108. See Andrew Byrnes and Johannes Chan, eds., *Public Law and Human Rights: A Hong Kong Source Book* (Hong Kong: Butterworths, 1993), 46–49.

109. State Council, *Human Rights in China*, 58–59; and Pang Sen, *Dangdai renquan*, 210.

110. See UN Doc. E/CN.4/1988/SR.30, 29 February 1986, at 19–20; and *Summary Record of the 18th Meeting*, Commission on Human Rights, UN Doc. E/CN.4/1989/SR.52 (1989), at 17.

111. Katherine Brennan, Reed Brody, and David Weissbrodt, "The 40th Session of the UN Sub-Commission on Prevention of Discrimination and Protection of Minorities," *Human Rights Quarterly* 11 (May 1989) 2: 295, 302.

112. See UN Doc E/CN.4/1988/SR.27, 25 February 1988, at 10. See also Lee, "China and Human Rights," 26.

113. See *Report by the Special Rapporteur on Summary or Arbitrary Executions*, 12 February 1985, UN Doc. E/CN.4/1985/17, at 2, cited in Cohen, "Human Rights Exception," 538.

Chapter 2. China, the UN Commission on Human Rights, and the UN Sub-Commission on Human Rights

1. *International Response to Human Rights Violations in China* (New York, May 1991); International League for Human Rights (Timothy Gelatt), *Getting Down to Business: The Human Rights Responsibilities of China's Investors and Trade Partners* (New York, July 1992), 43–50; James D. Seymour, *The International Reaction to the Crackdown in China* (New York: East Asian Institute, Columbia University, February 1990); and Seymour, "Human Rights in Chinese Foreign Relations," in *China and the World: Chinese Foreign Relations in the Post-Cold War Era*, ed. Samuel S. Kim (Boulder: Westview Press, 1994), 202–25.

2. Kim Nossal's thesis that the purpose of Australian human rights sanctions was to punish China for the Tiananmen crackdown, rather than to prevent and monitor continuing abuses, is, I believe, generally applicable to the purpose of international sanctions in this 1989 period. See Kim Richard Nossal, *The Beijing Massacre: Australian Responses* (Canberra: Australian Foreign Policy Publications Programme, Australian National University, 1993), 49–52.

3. For analyses of global and regional developments in the post–Cold War era, see Richard Leaver and James L. Richardson, eds., *Charting the Post-Cold War Order* (Boulder: Westview Press, 1993); Andrew Mack and John Ravenhill, eds., *Pacific Cooperation Building: Economic and Security Regimes in the Asia-Pacific* (Boulder: Westview Press, 1993); and James C. Hsiung, ed., *Asia Pacific in the New World Politics* (Boulder: Lynne Rienner, 1993).

4. For the most comprehensive treatments of China's foreign policy in this period, see Thomas W. Robinson and David Shambaugh, eds., *Chinese Foreign Policy: Theory and Practice* (Oxford: Clarendon Press, 1994); and Kim, ed., *China and the World*.

5. For an excellent analysis of this dualism, see Ian Wilson, "China and the New World Order," in Leaver and Richardson, eds., *Charting the Post-Cold War Order*, 194–208.

6. See Hsiung, "China in the Postnuclear World," in *Asia Pacific in the New World Politics*, 76.

7. Human rights violations by Permanent Members of the Security Council have been targeted, but they have either been specific and not wide-scale, or they have occurred outside the territory of the offending state. See, for instance, Egon Schwelb, "The International Court of Justice and the Human Rights Clauses of the Charter," *American Journal of International Law* 66 (1972) 2: 341. He notes the UNGA request that the USSR allow Soviet women married to foreigners to join their husbands in other countries. Cited in Robin M. Maher and David Weissbrodt, "The 41st

Session of the UN Sub-Commission on Prevention of Discrimination and Protection of Minorities," *Human Rights Quarterly* 12 (May 1990) 2: 290, 305 n.66.

8. For articulation of this concept, see John Braithwaite, *Crime, Shame and Reintegration* (Cambridge: Cambridge University Press, 1989).

9. For analysis of the nature and functions of the Commission, see Philip Alston, "The Commission on Human Rights," in *The United Nations and Human Rights*, ed. Alston (Oxford: Clarendon Press, 1992), 126–210; Frank Newman and David Weissbrodt, *International Human Rights: Law, Policy and Process* (Cincinnati: Anderson Publishing Co., 1990), 5–7; Henry J. Steiner and Philip Alston, eds., *International Human Rights in Context: Law, Politics, Morals* (Oxford: Clarendon Press, 1996), 330–459; and Australian Department of Foreign Affairs and Trade, *Human Rights Manual* (Canberra: Australian Government Publishing Service, 1993), 53–59.

10. Alston, "The Commission on Human Rights," 207–209.

11. Tom J. Farer and Felice Gaer, "The UN and Human Rights: At the End of the Beginning," in *United Nations, Divided World: The UN's Roles in International Relations*, ed. Adam Roberts and Benedict Kingsbury (Oxford: Clarendon Press, 1996), 2nd ed., 272.

12. Alston, "The Commission on Human Rights," 144.

13. Farer and Gaer, "The UN and Human Rights," 296.

14. Asbjørn Eide, "The Sub-Commission on Prevention of Discrimination and Protection of Minorities," in *The United Nations and Human Rights*, ed. Alston, 223.

15. Alston, "The Commission on Human Rights," 164.

16. Theo van Boven, "Identifying Policies and Activities Harmful to Human Rights," 15 August 1977, in Theo van Boven, *People Matter: Views on International Human Rights Policy* (Amsterdam: Meulenhoff, 1982), 85.

17. "Joint Statement of Non-Governmental Organisations to the Sub-Commission on Prevention of Discrimination and Protection of Minorities," 45th Sess., 26 August 1993.

18. *Report of the Sub-Commission on Prevention of Discrimination and Protection of Minorities on its Thirtieth Session* (E/CN.4/1271–E/CN.4/Sub.2/399), para.14., cited in van Boven, *People Matter*, 90.

19. Eide, "The Sub-Commission," 252.Cf. Chinese diplomats and scholars see it as having a subordinate role of preventing discrimination, protecting minorities, carrying out research and forwarding proposals to the Commission. See Wang Xingfang, ed., *Zhongguo yu Lianheguo: Jinian Lianheguo chengli wushi zhounian* ("China and the United Nations: Commemorating the 50th Anniversary of the Founding of the United Nations") (Beijing: *Shijie zhishi* chubanshe, 1995), 336–37.

20. The 1503 procedure has been described as a "petition-information" system which allows the confidential processing of complaints about the behavior of governments in the pre-sessional meetings of the Communications Working Group of the Sub-Commission. The Group consists of five Sub-Commission members, each of whom takes responsibility for a special group of rights. An affirmative majority vote is required before the "situation" can be referred to the full plenary of the Sub-Commission. The plenary considers each of the cases adopted by the Working Group and decides by a simple majority vote to send it on to the Commission, to drop it, or reconsider it later. At the third stage of this procedure, the Commission itself establishes a Communications Group to recommend action. One of the Group's options is to transfer the case to the public 1235 procedure. For a full description of this process, see Eide, "The Sub-Commission"; and Alston, "The Commission on Human Rights," 147.

21. Feng Zhuoran and Gu Chunde, eds., *Renquan lunji* ("Collected Essays on Human Rights") (Beijing, Shoudu shifan daxue chuban, 1992), 233; and Wang Xingfang, ed., *Zhongguo yu Lianheguo*, 336–37.

22. Pang Sen, *Dangdai renquan ABC* ("Contemporary Human Rights ABC"). Dangdai renquan yanjiu zongshu (Sichuan: Sichuan renmin chubanshe, 1991), 148.

23. See speeches reported in Zhonghua renmin gongheguo waijiaobu waijiaoshi bianjishi ("Editorial Department, China's Diplomatic History, Chinese Foreign Ministry"), *Zhongguo waijiao gailan*, 1988, 1989, and 1990 ("Survey of China's Foreign Relations," 1988, 1989, and 1990) (Beijing: *Shijie zhishi* chubanshe), 430–31, 410–11 and 423–24, respectively.

24. Pang Sen, *Dangdai renquan ABC*, 150–52.

25. *Summary Record of the 14th Meeting*, UN Doc. E/CN.4/Sub.2/1987/SR.14, at 11; *Summary Record of the 17th Meeting*, UN Doc. E/CN.4/Sub.2/1987/SR.17, at 11–12.

26. Reed Brody and David Weissbrodt, "Major Developments at the 1989 Session of the UN Commission on Human Rights," *Human Rights Quarterly* 11 (November 1989) 4: 586–87.

27. See *Summary Record of the 18th Meeting*, Commission on Human Rights, 45th Sess., UN Doc. E/CN.4/1989/SR.18, at 12–13.

28. *Summary Record of the 52nd Meeting*, Commission on Human Rights, 45th Sess., UN Doc.E/CN.4/1989/SR.52, at 17.

29. *Summary Record of the 56th Meeting*, Commission on Human Rights, 45th Sess., UN Doc. E/CN.4/1989/SR.56, at 2.

30. For detailed analysis, see Nihal Jayawickrama, "Human Rights Exception No Longer," in *The Broken Mirror: China After Tiananmen*, ed. George Hicks (London: Longman, 1990), 345–66 ; and Ann Kent, "China and the International Human Rights Regime: A Case Study of Multilateral Monitoring, 1989–1994," *Human Rights Quarterly* 17 (February 1995), 1: 1–47.

31. Interview with government delegate, 11 August 1992.

32. See "Question of the Violation of Human Rights and Fundamental Freedoms, including Policies of Racial Discrimination and Segregation and of Apartheid, in all Countries, with Particular Reference to Colonial and other Dependent Countries and Territories: Report of the Sub-Commission Established under the Commission on Human Rights Resolution 8 (XXIIII)," Commission on Human Rights, Sub-Commission on Prevention of Discrimination and Protection of Minorities, 45th Sess., Provisional Agenda Item 6, UN Doc. E/CN.4/Sub.2/1993/NGO/16 (1993).

33. *Summary Record of the 15th Meeting*, Commission on Human Rights, Sub-Commission on Prevention of Discrimination and Protection of Minorities, 41st Sess., UN Doc. E/CN.4/Sub.2/1989/SR.15 (1989), at 16.

34. See Jayawickrama, "Human Rights Exception no Longer," 359.

35. *Summary Record of the 17th Meeting*, Commission on Human Rights, Sub-Commission on Prevention of Discrimination and Protection of Minorities, 41st Sess., UN Doc. E/CN.4/Sub.2/1989/SR.17 (1989), at 11–12.

36. *Summary Record of the 19th Meeting*, Commission on Human Rights, Sub-Commission on Prevention of Discrimination and Protection of Minorities, 41st Sess., UN Doc. E/CN.4/Sub.2/1989/SR.19 (1989), at 5–7.

37. *Summary Record of the First Part of the 37th Meeting*, Commission on Human Rights, Sub-Commission on Prevention of Discrimination and Protection of Minorities, 41st Sess., UN Doc. E/CN.4/Sub.2/1989/SR.37 (1989), at 4–5.

38. "Statement by the Chinese Delegation on the Adoption of a Resolution Concerning China by the Sub-Commission on Prevention of Discrimination and Protection of Minorities at its 41st Session, delivered on 31 August 1989," cited in Maher and Weissbrodt, "The 41st Session," 295–96, n. 25.

39. Interviews with NGO representatives, Geneva, August 1993.

40. Maher and Weissbrodt, "The 41st Session," 300, 305.

41. Jayawickrama, "Human Rights Exception No Longer," 362.

42. NGOs concentrating on the situation in China, in order of intervention, were: International Movement for Fraternal Union among Races and Peoples, International Federation for Human Rights, Amnesty International, Pax Christi International, International Confederation of Free Trade Unions, International Human Rights Law Group, International League for Human Rights, International Commission of Jurists, World University Services, World Federation of Trade Unions, World Confederation of Labour and the International Fellowship of Reconciliation.

43. *Summary Record of the 17th Meeting*, UN Doc. E/CN.4/Sub.2/1989/SR.17, at 2–3. Contrary to the claims of Chinese officials, McDermot asserted that "although over two million people had assembled in Beijing, there had been no disorder or riot and at no time had the organised life of the community been threatened." He observed: "China had voluntarily accepted obligations under treaties it had signed which required it to ensure that human rights were enjoyed by its citizens." China was participating in the Commission on Human Rights and had secured the election of an expert to the Sub-Commission. China, he claimed, "had repeatedly acknowledged the right of the international community to scrutinize the human rights performance of other countries and had also voted in favour of resolutions that had sent human rights investigators to countries such as Afghanistan, South Africa and Chile and had joined in consensus resolutions in respect of conditions in other parts of the world." As a result, China was now required "to review and fulfil its responsibilities to its own citizens and its commitments to the international community."

44. Jayawickrama, "Human Rights Exception No Longer," 357–8.

45. The use of secret ballot for Item 6 was initially conceded for the 41st session only; subsequently, an amendment allowed this procedure to continue to be used.

46. Maher and Weissbrodt, "The 41st Session," 300.

47. Adrien-Claude Zoller, "Analytical Report of the 1989 Sub-Commission," *Human Rights Monitor* (October 1989), no. 6, 6. See also *Summary Record of the 36th Meeting*, Commission on Human Rights, Sub-Commission on Prevention of Discrimination and Protection of Minorities, UN Doc. E/CN.4/Sub.2/1989/SR.36 (1989), at 2–3.

48. The Chinese Foreign Ministry later suggested that the secret ballot had been chiefly responsible for China's defeat. See *Zhongguo waijiao gailan 1990*, 411.

49. See analysis of vote, Maher and Weissbrodt, "The 41st Session," 301 n.50.

50. *Journal de Genève*, 5 September 1989, reported in Zoller, "Analytical Report," 10.

51. UN Doc. A/44/504 (6 September 1989), at 2. See also speech by the Chinese Ambassador in *Zhongguo waijiao gailan 1990*, 411.

52. Adrien-Claude Zoller, "North-South Tension and Human Rights," *Human Rights Monitor* (April 1990) 8: 9. One African diplomat reportedly was paid a visit in his tiny hotel by ten Chinese who had come to explain how best to vote in order to avoid unnecessary complications.

53. It endorsed the appeal of the Sub-Commission, welcomed China's lifting of martial law in January 1990 and the release of five hundred and seventy-three persons, urged the full observance of human rights and requested the Secretary-General to transmit further information by the Government of China and other reliable sources to the Commission's forty-seventh session. UN Doc. E/CN.4/1990/L.47, at 12.

54. "Position of the Chinese Delegation on the Draft Resolution, 'Situation in China'," Geneva, February 1990, 1.

55. See Reed Brody, Maureen Convery, and David Weissbrodt, "The 42nd Session of the Sub-Commission on Prevention of Discrimination and Protection of Minorities," *Human Rights Quarterly*, 13 (May 1991) 2: 274; author also drew on confidential advice.

56. *Summary Record of the 23rd Meeting*, UN Doc. E/CN.4/Sub.2/1990/SR.23, at 13; and *Summary Record of the 24th Meeting*, UN Doc. E/CN.4/Sub.2/1990/SR.24, at 8.

57. *Summary Record of the 23rd Meeting*, UN Doc. E/CN.4/Sub.2/1990/SR.23, at 13.

58. *Summary Record of the 50th Meeting*, UN Doc. E/CN.4/1991/SR.50, at 25.

59. Karen Rierson and David Weissbrodt, "The Forty-Third Session of the UN Sub-Commission on Prevention of Discrimination and Protection of Minorities: The Sub-Commission under Scrutiny," *Human Rights Quarterly* 14 (May 1992) 2: 232, 246.

60. Discussion with senior UN human rights expert, Geneva, 18 August 1993.

61. *Summary Record of the 27th Meeting*, UN Doc. E/CN.4/Sub.2/1991/SR.27/Add.1, at 6–7.

62. Interview with government delegate, 19 April 1993.

63. See *Zhongguo waijiao gailan 1992*, 433.

64. Joe W. (Chip) Pitts III and David Weissbrodt, "Major Developments at the UN Commission on Human Rights in 1992," *Human Rights Quarterly* 15 (February 1993) 1: 122, 142.

65. Later, on 3 June, Premier Li Peng especially thanked Third World states for their support in the Commission vote. See *Zhongguo waijiao gailan 1993*, 497.

66. *Summary Record of the 28th Meeting*, UN Doc. E/CN.4/1992/SR.28, at 18.

67. Adrien-Claude Zoller, "The UN Human Rights Commission 1992," *Human Rights Monitor* (April 1992) 16: 24.

68. Pitts and Weissbrodt, "The UN Commission on Human Rights in 1992," 141.

69. Zoller, "Commission 1992," 24; and interviews with NGO representatives, Geneva, August 1993.

70. UN Doc. Decision 1992/116, ch. 11 in E/1992/22E/CN.4/1992/84, Supp. no. 2.

71. See voting on draft resolution, UN Doc. E/CN.4/1992/L.49/Rev.1, in E/1992/22E/CN.4/1992/84, Supp. no. 2, at 286.

72. Adrien-Claude Zoller, "Analytical Report of the 44th Session of the Sub-Commission," *Human Rights Monitor* (September 1992) 17–18: 21.

73. *Zhongguo waijiao gailan 1993*, 497.

74. Zhonghua renmin gongheguo guowuyuan xinwen bangongshi ("Information Office of the State Council of the People's Republic of China"), *Zhongguo di renquan zhuangkuang* ("Human Rights in China") (Beijing: Zhongyang wenxian chubanshe, October 1991). See analysis of the White Paper in Chapter 5.

75. *Summary Record of the 38th Meeting*, UN Doc. E/CN.4/1992/SR.38, at 14.

76. For a detailed analysis of this new right, and the White Paper, see Kent, *Between Freedom and Subsistence: China and Human Rights* (Hong Kong: Oxford University Press, 1993 and 1995), 222–30. For human rights in China, see also Kent, "Waiting for Rights: China's Human Rights and China's Constitutions, 1949–1989," *Human Rights Quarterly* 13 (May 1991) 2: 170–201.

77. *Summary Record of the 40th Meeting*, UN Doc. E/CN.4/1993/SR.40, at 13.

78. *Summary Record of the 45th Meeting*, UN Doc. E/CN.4/1993/SR.45, at 20.

79. *Zhongguo waijiao gailan 1994*, 533.

80. UN Doc. E/CN.4/1993/L.104.

81. Adrien-Claude Zoller, "The UN Human Rights Commission 1993," *Human Rights Monitor* (April 1993), 20: 37.

82. The following account is based largely on the author's own notes, taken at the session. A more extensive version is to be found in Kent, "China and the International Human Rights Regime."

83. Interview with senior UN human rights experts, Geneva, 26 August 1993.

84. Apart from the NGOs formally accredited to ECOSOC, whose representatives were able to make statements from the floor, members of the International Coalition

for Human Rights in China, including the New York-based organization, Human Rights in China, and the London-based June 4 China Support Group, attended the forty-fifth session and took part in lobbying and providing information to experts and governmental observers. Brief criticisms of China's human rights and particularly its Tibetan policies were contained in statements by Habitat and Amnesty International. Major critiques were contained in the statements of the Fédération Internationale des Ligues des Droits de l'Homme on Items 10 and 11, the International Association of Educators for World Peace on Item 10, the International League for the Rights and Liberation of Peoples on Item 10, the World Organization against Torture on Item 6 and Pax Christi International on Item 6. In addition, two briefing sessions on the current situation of human rights in China, publicized in leaflets widely distributed in the Conference room, were held in UN meeting rooms during the month. Screening the TV documentary, "Laogai — Inside the Chinese Gulag," the seminars were supported by the June 4th China Support Group, the Fédération Internationale des Ligues des Droits de L'Homme, International Educational Development and the International Fellowship of Reconciliation. On 13 August, moreover, representatives of NGOs signed a joint Press Statement expressing "deep concern at the possibility that the International Olympic Committee will award the Olympics for the Year 2000 to the city of Beijing." It was co-sponsored by Asian Cultural Forum on Development; International Association of Educators for World Peace; International Campaign for Tibet; International Coalition for Human Rights in China; International Educational Development; International Fellowship of Reconciliation; Korean Council for the Women Drafted for Sexual Slavery by Japan; Observatorie Internationale des Prisons; Swiss Federation of Tamil Associations; and World Organization Against Torture.

85. For instance, it was Martinez who intervened to mediate between Palley and the Chinese Ambassador when the former complained about Chinese pressure on 20 August. Similarly, it was Martinez who threatened to respond to the NGO critique of the Sub-Commission, which included many aspects of Chinese activities, immediately after it was delivered on 26 August.

86. Two years later, at the forty-seventh (1995) Sub-Commission, Palley was to reveal that "the British Foreign Office had made it known to her that some of her oral interventions during the Sub-Commission had caused complaints and difficulties in the relations between the United Kingdom and other countries which had not understood that the members of the Sub-Commission were independent." See Adrien-Claude Zoller, "Not Too Bad . . . ! Analytical Report of the 47th Session of the Sub-Commission (Geneva, 31 July–25 August 1995)," in *Human Rights Monitor* (September 1995) 29: 38.

87. NGO statement to Sub-Commission, see note 17 above.

88. The following analysis is based on an interview with a leading NGO human rights expert, Geneva, 25 August 1993; an interview with Michael Van Walt, Geneva, 27 August 1993; and a discussion with a senior UN human rights expert, Geneva, 26 August 1993.

89. UN Doc. E/CN.4/1994/L. 83.

90. Interview with senior UN human rights expert, 30 May 1994.

91. Communication from Philip Baker, London, 11 April 1994.

92. For instance, Elaine Sciolino, "U.S. Big Business Urges Renewal of China's Trade Ties," *New York Times*, 14 March 1994.

93. Ann Kent, "China, the U.S. and MFN," unpublished paper, 26 July 1995, 34.

94. See "China and Tibet," in *Human Rights Watch World Report 1995: Events of 1994* (New York: Human Rights Watch, 1995), 142–149. A change in China's readiness to comply once MFN and human rights were delinked was noted by all NGO representatives interviewed.

95. Documented in Samuel S. Kim, "China's Pacific Policy: Reconciling the Irreconcilable," *International Journal* 50 (Summer 1995), 475.

96. Elaine Sciolino, "China Trip on a Frosty Note for Christopher," *New York Times*, 12 March 1994, A1, A4.

97. For example, Shi Quan, "Wenhua chuantong yu renquanguan" ("Cultural Tradition and Human Rights Views"), *Renmin ribao* ("People's Daily"), 14 February 1994, 6, which attacked the State Department's newly issued human rights report as using human rights as "a pretext to interfere in other states' internal affairs." The non-interference argument was also used in respect of the 1994 Human Rights Commission vote, when Premier Li Peng interrupted his Work Report at the 8th National People's Congress to acclaim the failure of the Commission vote against China. See John Kohut, *South China Morning Post*, 11 March 1994; and "Western Anti-China Draft Rejected," *Beijing Review* 37, 12 (21–27 March 1994): 37.

98. See Asia Watch, *Detained in China and Tibet: A Directory of Political and Religious Prisoners* (New York, February 1994).

99. Human Rights Watch/Asia report, cited in "The Price of Obscurity in China," *The Australian*, 20 May 1994, 7.

100. Reuters China News, 14 May 1994.

101. Peter Logue, "Chinese Tell Evans: Butt Out," *Canberra Times*, 3 April 1994, 1; and Lena Sun, "China Turns Screws on Dissidents," *Guardian Weekly*, 17 April 1994, 18.

102. Human Rights Watch/Asia, "Chinese Diplomacy, Western Hypocrisy and the UN Human Rights Commission," 9 (March 1997) 3: 4.

103. For account, see John R. Crook, "The Fifty-first Session of the UN Commission on Human Rights," *American Journal of International Law* 90, 1 (1996), 127–28.

104. Observation by Bill Barker, Director of Human Rights International, who was present at the 1996 Commission session.

105. For vote on no-action motion, and for vote on draft resolution E/CN.4/1995/L. 86, see UN Doc. E/CN.4/1995/176.

106. UN Doc Press release HR/CN/96/41, 18 April 1996, at 5.

107. UN Doc. E/CN.4/Sub.2/1997/L.33, at 2.

108. These were: (1) to exchange views and to "change an abnormal exercise of reaching conclusions prior to talks"; (2) to seek common points, such as discussions on the universality and specificity of human rights, and other theoretical issues; and (3) to adopt a "reasonable attitude towards divergences" and to seek for progress, "even partially and temporarily." See Xinhua newsagency, "Chinese 'Expert' on Human Rights Dialogues," 7 August 1997, BBC Monitoring Summary of World Broadcasts, Reuters "China" News, 11 August 1997.

109. For text, see Xinhua, "China Proposes Reforms in UN Human Rights Body," 22 July 1997, BBC Monitoring Summary of World Broadcasts, Reuters "China" News, 28 July 1997.

110. Human Rights in China, *HRIC Participation in the 1996 UN Commission on Human Rights, 52nd Session, Geneva* (New York, 1996), 4.

111. Human Rights Watch/Asia, "Chinese Diplomacy," 4.

112. "Report on the 52nd Session of the Commission on Human Rights (Geneva, 18 March–26 April 1996)," *Human Rights Monitor* (1996) 32–33: 43. For vote, see UN Doc. E/CN.4/1996/177.

113. See Human Rights Watch/Asia, "Chinese Diplomacy," 12–14; and Adrien-Claude Zoller, "Little to Highlight, Nothing to Celebrate: Analytical Report of the 53rd Session of the Commission on Human Rights (Geneva, 10 March–18 April 1997)," *Human Rights Monitor* (1997) 37: 90.

114. Adrien-Claude Zoller, "The Draft Resolution on the Human Rights Situation

in China and China's Attempts to Suppress It: Will Its Tactics Succeed?" (Geneva, International Service for Human Rights, 14 April 1997).

115. For analysis of this human rights diplomacy, see Human Rights Watch/Asia, "Chinese Diplomacy," 6, 10. In 1997, those voting in favor of the no-action motion were: Algeria, Angola, Bangladesh, Belarus, Benin, Bhutan, Cape Verde, China, Colombia, Cuba, Egypt, Ethiopia, Gabon, Guinea, India, Indonesia, Madagascar, Malaysia, Mali, Mozambique, Nepal, Uganda, Pakistan, Sri Lanka, Ukraine, Zaire, Zimbabwe. Voting against the motion were: South Africa, Germany, Austria, Bulgaria, Canada, Chile, Denmark, El Salvador, United States, France, Ireland, Italy, Japan, Nicaragua, Netherlands, Czech Republic, and United Kingdom. Abstentions: Argentina, Brazil, Ecuador, Russian Federation, Mexico, Philippines, South Korea, Dominican Republic, and Uruguay. See Zoller, "Little to Highlight," 90.

116. See Scott Hillis, "UN Chief Says Pleased with China Rights Moves," Reuters News Service, 31 March 1998, Reuters "China" News, 31 March 1998. The Foreign Minister stated: "After the signing, of course, we will comply with the covenants, but there are a few issues we will have to look into. We will have to research whether there are areas that clash with Chinese laws or are unclear."

117. Discussion with responsible Chinese official, Helsinki, 22 August 1998.

118. For details, see Stephanie Nebehay, "UN Rights Boss Ready to Start Talks with China," Reuters "China" News, 20 January 1998; "China Invites UN Rights Chief for Visit — Official," Reuters "China" News, 21 January 1998; and Simon Beck, "Washington Divided over Merits of Geneva Human Rights Censure Motion," *South China Morning Post*, 21 January 1998, Reuters "China" News, 21 January 1998.

119. For excellent analysis of these dialogues and their effects, see Human Rights in China, *From Principle to Pragmatism: Can Dialogue Improve China's Human Rights Situation?* (New York, 1998), available on http://www.hrichina.org/; and *China Rights Forum*, issue on "Dialogue and Debate" (summer 1998). The following information on the dates of the dialogue are derived from this source.

120. The invitation, according to a Chinese Foreign Ministry spokesman, was intended "to strengthen cooperation with the United Nations in the field of human rights." See Justin Jin, "China Issues Formal Invitation to UN Rights Head," 20 January 1998, Reuters "China" News.

121. Zoller, "Little to Highlight," 92. The Director of Human Rights Watch, Lotte Leicht, commented: "By and large, the dialogue has become non-transparent. The annual scrutiny by the UN has been replaced with a behind closed-doors dialogue that is conducted without publicly known agendas and briefings." She argued that the Commission was no longer a credible body for discussion of China and human rights. See Joanne Lee-Young, "Fears the Premier May Be Let Off Lightly," *South China Morning Post*, 30 March 1998, Reuters "China" News, 30 March 1998.

122. Wei Jingsheng has observed that "to seek the support of people from more nations at the Human Rights Conference in Geneva . . . is very important, since it would have major psychological impact for the common people on the mainland." See China News Digest Interview of Wei Jingsheng, Part V, CND, 7 February 1998, 3.

123. Hillis, "UN Chief Says Pleased."

124. Alston, "The Commission on Human Rights," 209.

Chapter 3. China and Torture

1. UN Doc. E/CN.4/1986/15, para. 3, at 1.

2. Henry Shue, *Basic Rights, Subsistence, Affluence, and U.S. Foreign Policy* (Princeton: Princeton University Press, 1980), 20.

3. Michael R. Dutton, *Policing and Punishment in China: From Patriarchy to "the People"* (Cambridge: Cambridge University Press, 1992), 115, 134, 177.

4. Reports include Amnesty International, *Political Imprisonment in the People's Republic of China* (London, 1978); Amnesty International, *China, Violations of Human Rights: Prisoners of Conscience and the Death Penalty in the People's Republic of China* (London, 1984); Amnesty International, *China, Torture and Ill-Treatment of Prisoners* (London, 1987); Asia Watch, *Punishment Season: Human Rights in China after Martial Law* (New York, February 1990); International League for Human Rights and the Ad Hoc Study Group on Human Rights, *Torture in China: Comments on the Official Report of China to the Committee against Torture* (New York, April 1990); Asia Watch, *Torture in China* (New York, July 1990); Lawasia and Tibet Information Network, *Defying the Dragon: China and Human Rights in Tibet* (London, March 1991), 47–57; Amnesty International, *Torture in China*, ASA 17/55/92 (London, December 1992); Human Rights in China, *Words without Substance: The Implementation of the Convention against Torture in the People's Republic of China* (New York, April 1996); and Amnesty International, *Torture and Ill-Treatment: Comments on China's Second Periodic Report to the UN Committee against Torture*, ASA 17/51/96 (Geneva, April 1996).

5. See also Chapter 7. For elaboration of this argument, see Shue, *Basic Rights*; R.J. Vincent, *Human Rights and International Relations* (Cambridge: Cambridge University Press, 1986); for its application to China, see Ann Kent, *Between Freedom and Subsistence: China and Human Rights* (Hong Kong: Oxford University Press, 1993 and 1995), 15–19, 231–38.

6. Asia Watch, *Torture in China*, 3.

7. UN Doc. E/CN.4/1986/15, para. 1, at l.

8. Cited in UN Doc. E/CN.4/1988/15, para. 11, at 3 (transl. from French version).

9. See also Andrew Byrnes, "The Committee Against Torture," in *The United Nations and Human Rights: A Critical Appraisal*, ed. Philip Alston (Oxford: Clarendon Press, 1992), 520.

10. UN Centre for Human Rights, "The Committee Against Torture," *Human Rights Factsheet* No. 17 (Geneva, 1992), 1.

11. See "Vienna Declaration and Programme of Action," in Australian Department of Foreign Affairs and Trade, *Human Rights Manual* (Canberra: Australian Government Publishing Service, 1993), para. 5.55, 195.

12. Byrnes, "The Committee Against Torture," 530.

13. World Conference on Human Rights, *Interim Report on Updated Study by Mr. Philip Alston*, A/Conf.157/PC/62/Add.11/Rev.1 (22 April 1993), para. 54, at 281.

14. UN Centre for Human Rights, "The Committee Against Torture," 1–2.

15. For details on States Parties and members of the Committee, see *Report of the Committee against Torture*, 1994, UN Doc. A/49/44, at 1, 30–33.

16. See Arts. 19–24, in United Nations Centre for Human Rights, *Human Rights: A Compilation of International Instruments* (New York: United Nations, 1993), ST/HR/Rev. 4 (vol. 1/Part 1), 300–304.

17. Australian Department of Foreign Affairs and Trade, *Human Rights Manual*, 71.

18. Philip Alston, *Final Report on Enhancing the Long-term Effectiveness of the United Nations Human Rights Treaty System*, UN Doc. E/CN.4/1997/74 (Geneva, 27 March 1996), para. 16 at 6.

19. United Nations, *Human Rights*, vol. 1, 293–94.

20. See Byrnes, "The Committee Against Torture," 512–515.

21. For guidelines for initial reports, which have been revised on a number of occasions, see A/46/44 (1991), and for second and subsequent reports, A/46/44 (1991), Annex Vlll.

22. Byrnes, "The Committee Against Torture," 525.

23. For guidelines, see also UN Centre for Human Rights, "The Committee Against Torture," 3–5.

24. Byrnes, "The Committee Against Torture," 524.

25. Letter from UN human rights expert, 14 February 1996.

26. Byrnes, "The Committee Against Torture," 524, 529. In China's case, NGOs began to pay more attention to Committee proceedings once MFN and human rights had been delinked in May 1994.

27. See UN Centre for Human Rights, "Methods of Combating Torture," *Fact Sheet* no. 4 (Geneva, 1988), 11.

28. Alston, *Final Report*, para. 79, at 20.

29. UN Doc. E/CN.4/1993/26, para. 10, at 6.

30. See comparison drawn by the Special Rapporteur on Torture in UN Doc. E/CN.4/1988/17, paras. 5–12, at 2–3.

31. It has also been seen to have a judicial role vis-à-vis Article 22. Letter from UN human rights expert, 14 February 1996.

32. UN Doc E/CN.4/1993/26, para. 593, at 131–32.

33. Reported in Byrnes, "The Committee Against Torture," 546.

34. UN Doc. E/CN.4/1991/17, para. 8, at 2.

35. Philip Alston, "The Commission on Human Rights," in Alston, ed., *The United Nations and Human Rights*, 208–209. Tom Farer and Felice Gaer point out that "the theme mechanisms have fundamentally altered what the UN can and to some significant degree does accomplish in aiding victims of human rights violations." But, they add that "the lack of open and sustained discussion and pointed resolutions limits the potential efficacy of the special procedures." See Tom J. Farer and Felice Gaer, "The UN and Human Rights: At the End of the Beginning," in *United Nations, Divided World: The UN's Role in International Relations*, eds. Adam Roberts and Benedict Kingsbury (Oxford: Clarendon Press, 1996), 2nd ed., 288.

36. See *Report of the Committee Against Torture*, UN Doc A/49/44 (1994), at 30, 34; Pang Sen, *Dangdai renquan ABC* ("Contemporary Human Rights ABC") (Chengdu, Sichuan: Sichuan renmin chubanshe, 1992), 210; and Zhonghua renmin gongheguo guowuyuan xinwen bangongshi ("Information Office of the State Council of the People's Republic of China"), *Zhongguo di renquan zhuangkuang* ("Human Rights in China") (Beijing: Zhongyang wenxian chubanshe, October 1991), 66. Interestingly, although there are sections on China's human rights activities in the United Nations and on China's relations with the ILO in the Chinese Foreign Ministry's publication *Zhongguo waijiao gailan* ("Survey of China's Foreign Relations"), the yearly volumes do not discuss China's relations with the Committee Against Torture.

37. See Convention against Torture and Other Cruel, Inhuman or Degrading Treatment or Punishment, in UN Centre for Human Rights, *Human Rights: A Compilation of International Instruments*, 1: 294.

38. *Report of the Committee Against Torture*, UN Doc. A/49/44 (1994), para. 426, at 67.

39. Interview with UN official, Geneva, 6 August 1993.

40. *The Criminal Law and the Criminal Procedure Law of the People's Republic of China* (Beijing, Foreign Languages Press, 1984), Chinese text, 180.

41. For detailed analysis of these three reasons, see the excellent report, Human Rights in China, *Words Without Substance*, 4–21.

42. In an interview in the U.S. after his release, Wei stated that "for people like us, death was not the most dreadful. What we feared the most was the possibility of developing mental disorder, and losing our dignity . . . Those who committed suicide were just as strong as I was, but they might have felt that they could not pull through mentally." See CND interview with Wei Jingsheng, China News Digest, 20 January 1998, Part 11, 12.

43. Committee against Torture, *Summary Record of the 251st Meeting: China. 06/05/96.* UN Doc. CAT/C/SR.251 (Geneva, 5 June 1996), para. 5, at 3. Author's emphasis.

44. Amnesty International, *China, Torture and Ill-Treatment of Prisoners*, 1. See also Hungdah Chiu, "Chinese Attitudes Toward International Law of Human Rights in the Post-Mao Era," in *Chinese Politics from Mao to Deng*, ed. Victor C. Falkenheim and Ilpyong J. Kim (New York: Paragon House, 1989), 259.

45. Xiao Yu, "Crackdown Ordered on Unruly Police," *South China Morning Post*, 19 January 1998, in Reuters "China" News, 19 January 1998.

46. Human Rights in China, *Words Without Substance*, 6.

47. Committee against Torture, *Summary Record of the 251st Meeting*, UN Doc.CAT/C/SR.251 (Geneva, 5 June 1996), at 3.

48. Committee against Torture, *Consideration of Reports Submitted by States Parties Under Article 19 of the Convention: Initial Reports of States Parties due in 1988*, Addendum, "China," UN Doc. CAT/C/7/Add. 5 (Geneva, 1989), para. 53, at 11.

49. For text of guidelines, see Committee against Torture, *General Guidelines Regarding the Form and Contents of Initial Reports to be Submitted by States Parties under Article 19, Paragraph 1, of the Convention*, UN Doc. CAT/C/4/Rev. 2 (1991).

50. International League for Human Rights, *Torture in China.*

51. Interview with UN expert, Vienna, 25 June 1993.

52. Committee against Torture, *Summary Record of the 50th Meeting*, UN Doc. CAT/C/SR.50 (Geneva, 1990), para. 3, at 2.

53. Committee against Torture, *Summary Record of the 51st Meeting*, UN Doc. CAT/C/SR.51 (Geneva, 1990), at 2–4 (esp. para. 15).

54. UN Doc. A/45/44 (1990), at 84–90.

55. The UN manual states that "it is only exceptionally that the Committees . . . request a supplementary report to be submitted." See Fausto Pocar and Cecil Bernard, "National Reports: Their Submission to Expert Bodies and Follow-Up," in UN Centre for Human Rights, *Manual on Human Rights Reporting Under Six Major International Human Rights Instruments* (New York: United Nations, 1991), 28. Apart from China, the Committee has requested additional reports from a number of countries, including Cameroon, Senegal, Chile and Colombia. See Byrnes, "The Committee Against Torture," 528.

56. Interview with UN official, Geneva, 6 August 1993.

57. Interview with UN human rights expert, Vienna, 25 June 1993.

58. Interview with UN official, Geneva, 6 August 1993. The following observations come from this interview.

59. Asia Watch, *Torture in China.*

60. Guowuyuan xinwen bangongshi, *Zhongguo gaizao zuifan di zhuangkuang* ("Criminal Reform in China") (Beijing: Falu chubanshe, August 1992).

61. *Human Rights in China*, 20 (Engl. transl., 22).

62. *Criminal Reform in China*, 7.

63. Interview with UN human rights expert, Vienna, 25 June 1993.

64. The Chinese representatives were Ambassador Jin Yongjian; Liao Jincheng; Zhang Yishan; Chen Weidian; Zhang Jun; Hao Chiyong; Li Yuqian; Shen Yongxiang; Liu Zhenmin; and Li Linmei. See Committee Against Torture, *Summary Record of the Fifth Part (Public) of the 146th Meeting*, "Supplementary Report of China (cont.)," UN Doc. CAT/C/SR.146/Add. 4, para. 5, at 4.

65. Committee against Torture, *Initial Reports of States Parties Due in 1989*, Addendum, "China," Supplementary report, 8 October 1992, UN Doc. CAT/C/7/Add. 14 (1993), Part 1 at 3–16, Part 2, at 17–32.

66. He stated: "In the Chinese legal system, treaties and major international agreements concluded or acceded to by China must be ratified by the supreme organs of

power. Upon ratification, they enter into force in China, which then assumes the obligations arising therefrom. In general, when certain provisions of an international instrument concluded or acceded to by China are not compatible with domestic law, a process of harmonization is necessary. The provisions of the international treaty prevail over domestic law, except where China has entered reservations to the treaty at the time of ratification or accession. Implementation of the Convention against Torture follows this principle." Ibid. para. 61, at 16.

67. Amnesty International, *Torture in China,* 1.

68. Interviews with UN human rights expert, Vienna, 25 June 1993; and UN official, Geneva, 6 August 1993.

69. Interview with Chinese official, Geneva, 17 August 1993. Ambassador Jin also defended the death penalty in that it "had proved an effective way of controlling serious crime." See Committee Against Torture, *Summary Record of the Third Part (Public) of the 146th Meeting,* "Supplementary Report of China," UN Doc. CAT/C/SR.146/Add.2 (1993), para. 20, at 5.

70. Interview with UN official, Geneva, 6 August 1993.

71. Committee Against Torture, *Summary Record of the Third Part (Public) of the 143rd Meeting,* "Report of China," UN Doc. CAT/C/SR.143/Add.2 (1993), para. 13, at 4.

72. UN Doc. A/49/44 (1994), paras. 423–24, at 67.

73. Telephone interview with UN official, Geneva, 14 November 1995.

74. Committee Against Torture, *Summary Record of the 251st Meeting,* para. 2, at 2.

75. Committee Against Torture, *Second Periodic Reports of States Parties due in 1993.* UN Doc. CAT/C/20/Add.5 (Geneva, 15 February 1996), para. 88, at 18.

76. Amnesty International, *Torture and Ill-Treatment,* 1.

77. Human Rights in China, *Words Without Substance.*

78. Committee against Torture, *Summary Record of the 251st Meeting,* UN Doc. CAT/C/SR.251 (Geneva, 5 June 1996).

79. Committee Against Torture, *Summary Record of the Public Part of the 252nd Meeting: China,* CAT/C/SR.252/Add.1 (Geneva, 8 May 1996).

80. Committee Against Torture, *Summary Record of the Public Part of the 254th Meeting: China,* UN Doc. CAT/C/SR.254 (Geneva, 10 May 1996).

81. Committee against Torture, *Concluding Observations of the Committee Against Torture: China,* UN Doc.A/51/44 (Geneva, 9 July 1996), paras 138–150.

82. "Commission on Human Rights, Working Group on the Draft Optional Protocol to the Convention Against Torture, 5th session (Geneva, 14–25 October 1996)," *Human Rights Monitor* (1997), 36: 24.

83. For these statements, see Commission on Human Rights, *Report of the Working Group on the Draft Optional Protocol to the Convention Against Torture and Other Cruel, Inhuman or Degrading Treatment or Punishment,* UN Doc. E/CN.4/1997/33 (Geneva, 23 December 1996), paras. 34 and 46.

84. "Working Group on the Draft Optional Protocol to the Convention Against Torture," 6th session (Geneva, 13–24 October 1997), *Human Rights Monitor* (1997) 39–40: 21–23.

85. See his comparison in E/CN.4/1988/17, para. 18, at 3.

86. See UN Docs. E/CN.4/1986/15, at 17; E/CN.4/1987/13, at 5.

87. UN Doc.E/CN.4/1988/17, para. 12, at 5; and para. 112, at 24.

88. UN Doc. E/CN.4/1990/17, at 11–12.

89. UN Doc. E/CN.4/Sub.2/1989/30/Rev. 2, at 5; and E/CN.4/1990/55. On 8 May 1989, the latter received a letter from the Government of China concerning the imposition of martial law in Lhasa, Tibet, on 8 March 1989, and another on 15 August concerning the imposition of martial law in Beijing on 20 May 1989. Following the lifting of martial law in Beijing on 11 January 1990, the Permanent Representative of China also sent a letter to Mr. Despouy on 12 January. The Special Rapporteur

on Summary and Arbitrary Executions, Mr. Wako, sent a letter to the Chinese government on 26 April 1989 regarding allegations of summary executions of people in Tibet. On 5 June 1989, he sent an urgent telegram to the Chinese government on the incidents of 4 June during which "a great number of people would have been killed as a result of the intervention of the army," appealing to the government to avoid the creation of new victims and to respect the individual's right to life. He invoked Resolution 34/169 of 17 December 1979, the Code of Conduct for Those Responsible for the Application of the Law, adopted in the General Assembly, according to which "those responsible for the application of the law can only have recourse to force when it is strictly necessary and in the measure required for the accomplishment of their functions." Mr. Wako sent a further telegram to the Chinese government on 16 June 1989, seeking information on several hundred students summarily beaten between 4 and 6 June 1989. Four more telegrams were sent, on 20 June, 23 June, 13 July, and 2 November 1989, alleging summary process in the cases of people condemned to death in Beijing, Shanghai, Chengdu, and Lhasa, respectively, calling for the protection of their right to life and for clemency (at 19–21).

90. UN Doc.E/CN.4/1991/17, at 12–13.

91. UN Doc. E/CN.4/1992/17, at 13–14.

92. UN Doc.E/CN.4/1993/26, at 24–27. This cooperation must be seen in the context of the Rapporteur's observation that "it is regrettable that only a minority of the Governments whose comments are solicited provide the Special Rapporteur with a reply" (para. 16, at 7–8).

93. UN Doc. E/CN.4/1994/31, para. 172, at 39.

94. UN Doc. E/CN.4/1995/34, para. 91, at 21.

95. See Commission on Human Rights, *Report of the Special Rapporteur, Mr. Nigel S. Rodley, Submitted Pursuant to Commission on Human Rights Resolution 1995/37*, UN Doc. E/CN.4/1996/35 (Geneva, 9 January 1996), para. 5 at 5; and Commission on Human Rights, *Report of the Special Rapporteur, Mr. Nigel S. Rodley, Submitted Pursuant to Commission on Human Rights Resolution 1995/37 B*, UN Doc. E/CN.4/1997/7 (Geneva, 10 January 1997), at 6. For the following account, see 1996 report for 1995 developments, and the 1997 report for developments in 1996.

96. Mark Girouard, "China's Obligations on Economic, Social and Cultural Rights Unfulfilled," *China Rights Forum* (Winter 1997–8): 20–25.

97. CERD "regret(ted) that the report contained insufficient data on health, education, welfare and other social and economic conditions of life of the different minority groups, which made it difficult to assess properly the implementation of the Convention in the State party," but expressed satisfaction with the additional information provided by the delegation. *Concluding Observation of the Committee on the Elimination of Racial Discrimination: China. 27/09/96.* CERD/C/304/Add.15, at 2. CROC " appreciate(d) the self-critical elements of the report, although it is noted that greater focus was placed in the report on the content of domestic legal and administrative provisions than on their practical application." UN High Commissioner for Human Rights, *Concluding Observations of the Committee on the Rights of the Child: China. 07/16/96.* CRC/C/15/Add.56.

98. UN Doc E/CN.4/1995/61, para. 94, at 31–32.

99. Ibid. para. 99, at 33. In this instance, by implication, China's cooperation was compared favorably with that of a number of countries, which, despite urgent appeals and communications relating to allegations concerning violations of the right to life were clearly, in view of their absence from the list of respondents, among those "other governments [which] have chosen to remain silent." Ibid. para. 18, 20, 22, at 12–13; and Annex, at 136. States cited by the Special Rapporteur for sentencing to death persons under eighteen years of age were China, Pakistan and the United States. China and the United States were also among thirteen states cited for their

"limited or non-existent remedies" in proceedings resulting in death sentences. China was cited as one of five states which had recently expanded the scope of the death penalty through new laws, while, the Special Rapporteur observed, the United States was "said to intend to follow their path." See Annex at 137–138.

100. UN Doc. E/CN.4/1995/31, para. 18, at 5. In its Report, the Working Group attached decisions adopted at its seventh, eighth, and ninth sessions from September 1993–May 1994. Of the Working Group's 26 decisions involving 19 countries, seven concerned China. These decisions declared as arbitrary the detention of scores of Han Chinese and Tibetans, and called upon the Government of China "to take the necessary steps to remedy the situation in order to bring it into conformity with the provisions and principles incorporated in the Universal Declaration of Human Rights and in the International Covenant on Civil and Political Rights."

101. UN Doc. E/CN.4/1995/31/Add. 1, at 3, 5, 33, 35, 36, 43.

102. Human Rights in China, *HRIC Participation*, 15–16.

103. "Statement by Mr Zhang Yishan, Alternate Representative of the Chinese Delegation at the Fifty-first Session of the Commission on Human Rights under Item 10," 16 February 1995, original (translation), 1.

104. At the Human Rights Commission in 1995, Ambassador Jin Yongjian stated that "we hope this visit to be conducive to further the understanding of the Special Rapporteur and the UN Centre for Human Rights of the religious situation in China and the efforts made by the Chinese Government on the protection of the freedom of religious belief . . . In inviting the Special Rapporteur on the Question of Religious Intolerance to visit China, the Chinese government has demonstrated fully its sincerity in developing international cooperation in the field of human rights. Regrettably, however, some Western countries ignored such sincerity." See "Statement by Ambassador Jin Yongjian, Head of the Chinese Delegation at the 51st Session of the UN Commission on Human Rights," (Geneva, 10 February 1995), original document (English translation), 1.

105. UN Doc E/CN.4/1995/91, at 110. His forty page report covered details of his visits to Beijing, Shanghai, Sichuan and Tibet, discussions with the leaders of five principal religions, Buddhism, Taoism, Islam, Catholicism and Protestantism, and three pages of conclusions and recommendations. During his visit he also handed the Chinese authorities a list of allegations concerning believers and members of religious orders detained in China and Tibet, a list of which, with replies from Chinese authorities, was supplied in the Appendix of the report.

106. He also stated that it was essential to secure the principle of religious freedom and its manifestation and limit it "only in exceptional circumstances." He called for greater personal liability for officials under civil and criminal law for interference with religious freedom, and for the freeing of members of religious orders and believers belonging to unofficial religious organisations, including members of sects and Tibetan monks. He recommended that state officials and judges in China be given human rights training, with the assistance of the UN Centre for Human Rights, and that "a culture of human rights and in particular of tolerance should be spread by promoting the creation of human rights clubs in universities (sic)."

107. See "Statement by Ambassador Jin Yongjian," 10 February 1995, 1.

108. For instance, in 1992 the Special Rapporteur approached 55 governments asking for their comments and received replies from only 27. See E/CN.4/1993/26, para. 19, at 9.

109. Human Rights in China, *Words Without Substance*, 22.

110. In his report for 1990, Kooijmans stated: "As the Special Rapporteur said in previous reports, such systems of periodic visits must be deemed to be one of the most effective preventive measures against torture." See UN Doc. E/CN.4/1991/17, para. 298, at 92. He also stated: "A visit by the Special Rapporteur is commend-

able in all those cases where, on the basis of the information received, the situation in a country seems to be problematical and where consultations with the authorities and with non-governmental groups might lead to a clearer picture and to improvements by the taking of certain measures." See UN Doc. E/CN.4/1993/26, para. 16, at 8.

111. See UN Commission on Human Rights, *Building a Partnership for Human Rights*, Report of the UN High Commissioner for Human Rights, 24 February 1997, UN Doc. E/CN.4/1997/98 (Geneva, February 1997), at 8.

112. UN Doc. E/CN.4/1991/17, para. 183, at 89.

113. *People's Public Security News*, no. 661, 27 September 1991, cited in Amnesty International, *Torture in China* (December 1992), 1.

Chapter 4. China and the UN Specialized Agencies

1. See Virginia A. Leary, "Lessons from the Experience of the International Labour Organisation," in *The United Nations and Human Rights: A Critical Appraisal*, ed. Philip Alston (Oxford: Clarendon Press, 1992), 580.

2. Telephone interview with Australian representative to the ILO, Canberra, 6 December 1995.

3. China's concern was reflected in its condemnation of leading labor dissident Han Dongfang for his involvement with the organization. See International Labour Office, *292nd Report of the Committee on Freedom of Association*, G.B. 259/7/14 (Geneva, March 1994), paras. 385–86, at 95.

4. René Cassin, *Human Rights Journal*, 1v–4, 1971, 684–85. See also description of the ILO as "the first of the modern international regulatory agencies," in Abram Chayes and Antonia Handler Chayes, *New Sovereignty: Compliance with International Regulatory Agreements* (Cambridge: Harvard University Press, 1996), 230.

5. For histories of the ILO, see A. Alcock, *History of the International Labour Organisation* (London: Macmillan, 1971); G.N. Barnes, *History of the International Labour Office* (London: Williams and Norgate Ltd., 1926); Robert Cox, "ILO: Limited Monarchy," in *The Anatomy of Influence*, ed. Robert W. Cox and Harold K. Jacobson (New Haven: Yale University Press, 1973), 59–101; Walter Galenson, *The International Labor Organisation* (Madison: University of Wisconsin Press, 1981); Victor-Yves Ghebali, *The International Labour Organisation; A Case Study on the Evolution of UN Specialized Agencies* (Dordrecht: the Netherlands: Martinus Nijhoff, 1989); Ernst B. Haas, *Beyond the Nation-State* (Stanford: Stanford University Press, 1964); James T. Shotwell, *The Origins of the International Labor Organization* (New York: Columbia University Press, 1934); and Nicolas Valticos, "Fifty Years of Standard-Setting Activities by the International Labour Organisation," *International Labour Review*, 100 (1969), 201–37. For an excellent analysis of the history and significance of the ILO in the globalization of labor standards, see "Labour Standards," in *Global Business Regulation*, ed. John Braithwaite and Peter Drahos (publication forthcoming), 209–41.

6. Ghebali, *The International Labour Organization*, 1–2.

7. David Strang and Patricia Mei Yin Strang "The International Labour Organization and the Welfare State: Institutional Effects on National Welfare Spending, 1960–80," *International Organization*, 47 (Spring 1993) 2: 240.

8. United Nations General Assembly, World Conference on Human Rights Preparatory Committee, *Contribution from the International Labour Organisation*, Addendum to Status of Preparation of Publications, Studies and Documents for the World Conference, UN Doc. A/CONF. 157/PC/61/Add. 10 (3 March 1993), at 4.

9. Nicolas Valticos, "The Sources of International Labour Law: Recent Trends," in

International Law and its Sources, ed. Wybo P. Heere (Deventer: Kluwer Law and Taxation Publishers, 1989), 184–85.

10. See, for example, Ernst B. Haas, *Human Rights and International Action: The Case of Freedom of Association* (Stanford: Stanford University Press, 1970), 28; and International Labour Office, *International Labour Standards: A Worker's Education Manual* (Geneva, 1990), Third ed., 105.

11. United Nations Centre for Human Rights, *Human Rights: A Compilation of International Instruments* (New York: United Nations, 1993), vol. 1, at 5.

12. Under Article 8 it provides for: "(a) The right of everyone to form trade unions and join the trade union of his choice, subject only to the rules of the organization concerned, for the promotion and protection of his economic and social interests. No restrictions may be placed on the exercise of this right other than those prescribed by law and which are necessary in a democratic society in the interests of national security or public order or for the protection of the rights and freedoms of others; (b) The right of trade unions to establish national federations or confederations and the right of the latter to form or join international trade union organizations; (c) The right of trade unions to function freely subject to no limitations other than those prescribed by law and which are necessary in a democratic society in the interests of national security or public order or for the protection of the rights and freedom of others; and (d) The right to strike, provided that it is exercised in conformity with the laws of the particular country'." See above, at 11.

13. Convention (No. 87) Concerning Freedom of Association and Protection of the Right to Organise, 9 July 1948, in UN Centre for Human Rights, *Human Rights,* 2: 422, author's emphasis.

14. See Lee Swepston, "Human Rights Complaints Procedures of the International Labor Organization," in *Guide to International Human Rights Practice,* ed. Hurst Hannum (Philadelphia: University of Pennsylvania Press, 1984), 86. See also International Labour Office, *International Labour Standards,* 103; and International Labour Office, *Freedom of Association: Digest of Decisions and Principles of Freedom of Association Committee of the Governing Body of the ILO* (Geneva: International Labour Office, 1985).

15. United Nations General Assembly, *Contribution from the International Labour Organization,* at 4.

16. For a detailed exposition of these differences, see Leary, "Lessons from . . . the International Labour Organisation," 580–619.

17. Rachel Brett, "The Contribution of NGOs to the Monitoring and Protection of Human Rights in Europe: An Analysis of the Role and Access of NGOs to the Intergovernmental Organisations," in *Monitoring Human Rights in Europe: Comparing International Procedures and Mechanisms,* ed. Arie Bloed, Liselotte Leicht, Manfred Nowak and Allan Rosas (Dordrecht: Martinus Nijhoff, 1993), 131.

18. See Sydney Bailey, "The Security Council," in *The United Nations and Human Rights,* 304. See also Hector G. Bartolomei de la Cruz, Geraldo von Potobsky and Lee Swepston, *The International Labor Organization: The International Standards System and Basic Human Rights* (Boulder, Colo.: Westview Press, 1996); and Lee Swepston, *The Universal Declaration of Human Rights and ILO Standards* (Geneva: International Labour Organization, 1998).

19. Theo van Boven, "The International System of Human Rights: An Overview," in UN Centre for Human Rights, *Manual on Human Rights Reporting under Six Major International Human Rights Instruments* (New York: United Nations, 1971), 8.

20. In 1950, a Fact Finding and Conciliation Commission on Freedom of Association was set up, but because it only functioned with the consent of the government concerned, it was used sparingly. See International Labour Office, *International La-*

bour Standards, 106–108. For description of CFA, see Haas, *Human Rights and International Action,* 26–36 ; Breen Creighton, "Freedom of Association," in R. Blanpain, *Comparative Labour Law and Industrial Relations in Industrialised Market Economies,* vol. 2 (Deventer: Kluwer Law and Taxation Publishers, 1990), 19–45; A. J. Pouyat, "The ILO's Freedom of Association Standards and Machinery: A Summing Up," *International Labour Review,* 121 (1982): 287–302; J.M. Servais, "ILO Standards on Freedom of Association and their Implementation," *International Labour Review* 123 (1984), 765–81; and Leary, "Lessons from . . . the International Labour Organisation," 603.

21. Letter from then Australian representative to the ILO, Canberra, 21 February 1996.

22. Creighton, "Freedom of Association," 31.

23. Swepston, "Human Rights Complaints Procedures," 87.

24. Leary, "Lessons from . . . the International Labour Organisation," 609–11.

25. De la Cruz, von Potobsky, and Swepston, *The International Labor Organization* 166.

26. Strang and Strang, "The International Labour Organization," 241.

27. Haas, *Beyond the Nation State,* 447–8; and *Human Rights and International Action,* 117.

28. Telephone interview with Australian representative to the ILO, Canberra, 6 December 1995.

29. For this characterization of Chinese international organizational behavior, see Samuel S. Kim, "China's Pacific Policy: Reconciling the Irreconcilable," *International Journal* L (Summer 1995), 464.

30. Ming K. Chan, *Historiography of the Chinese Labor Movement, 1895–1949: A Critical Survey and Bibliography of Selected Chinese Source Materials at the Hoover Institution* (Stanford; Hoover Institution Press, 1981); *Guoji laogong zuzhi gaiyao ji qi yu Zhongguo zhi guanxi* ("The International Labour Organisation and its Relations with China") (Shanghai: ILO China Branch Office, 1934); *Guoji laogong zuzhi yu Zhongguo* ('The International Labour Organisation and China') (Shanghai: ILO Branch Office, 1948).

31. Chan, *Historiography,* 16.

32. See Ghebali, *The International Labour Organization,* 116.

33. International Labour Conference, 1984, PR9, at 3, cited in Ghebali, *The International Labour Organization,* 125.

34. For Chinese view of early history, see "Guoji laodong zuzhi" ("International Labour Organization") in *Shijie zhishi nianjian, 1994/1995 (World Knowledge Yearbook, 1994/1995)* (Beijing: *Shijie zhishi nianjian* chubanshe, 1995), 814; and yearly surveys in Zhonghua renmin gongheguo waijiaobu waijiaoshi bianjishi ("Editorial Department, China's Diplomatic History, Chinese Foreign Ministry"), *Zhongguo waijiao gailan* ("A Survey of China's Foreign Relations") (Beijing: *Shijie zhishi* chubanshe, 1987), vols. 1987–1995.

35. Interviews with a number of ILO officials and government representatives have suggested that the Director-General saw China's integration into the ILO as an important achievement.

36. Telephone interview with Australian representative to the ILO, Canberra, 6 December 1995.

37. "Guoji laodong zuzhi," 814.

38. Ghebali, *The International Labour Organization,* 125.

39. See "Guoji laodong zuzhi," 814; and Han Nianlong, Qian Qichen, Zheng Weizhi, Zhou Nan eds., *Diplomacy of Contemporary China* (Hong Kong: New Horizon Press, 1990), 406.

40. The 1995 Chinese account emphasizes the ILO contribution of technical

assistance and even of labor standards, but does not mention the hiatus in the relationship caused by the June 1989 crackdown. See "Guoji laodong zuzhi," 814.

41. Ghebali, *The International Labour Organization*, 125.

42. Interview with ILO official, Geneva, 6 August 1993. The following perceptions also derive from interview with government delegate to ILO, Canberra, 26 July 1994; and interview with Australian government representative to the ILO, Canberra, 21 February 1994.

43. Interviews with ILO officials; and *Zhongguo waijiao gailan 1988*, 438; and 1987, 427.

44. Interview with Australian government representative to the ILO, Canberra, 21 February 1994.

45. *Zhongguo waijiao gailan 1987*, 427. For details of its varied activities in the 1980s and early 1990s, see Wang Xingfang, ed., *Zhongguo yu Lianheguo: Jinian Lianheguo chengli wushi zhounian* ("China and the United Nations: Commemorating the 50th Anniversary of the Founding of the United Nations") (Beijing: *Shijie zhishi* chubanshe, 1995), 368–373.

46. Interview with Australian government representative to the ILO, Canberra, 21 February 1994.

47. For organizational structure of China's Labour Ministry, which in March 1998 was enlarged as the Ministry of Labour and Social Security, see International Labour Organization, Asian and Pacific Regional Centre for Labour Administration (ARPLA), *Labour Administration: Profile on the People's Republic of China*, (Geneva: ILO, December 1989), 1–6, 69–71. Within China's Labor Ministry, the Division of ILO was mainly responsible for the work of attending the Conference and Governing Body sessions as well as for dealing with standards setting matters, such as the reporting obligations outlined by Article 22 of the ILO Constitution. The Division of Technical Cooperation was responsible for technical cooperation with the ILO in the fields of vocational training, labor statistics, labor administration, security, wages, occupational safety and health. See also Guan Jinghe, "Country Paper on China," in ILO, *Report on the ILO Asian-Pacific Symposium on Standards-Related Topics* (New Delhi, 14–17 March 1989), ILO Regional Office for Asia and the Pacific, Bangkok (Geneva: ILO 1989), 56.

48. See, for instance, Fu Xushan, "Country Paper on China," in ILO, *Report on the ILO Asian-Pacific Symposium*, 59.

49. Interview with Australian representative to the ILO, Canberra, 21 February 1994.

50. "The Fable of 'Calling a Deer a Horse': An Analytical Report on the All-China Federation of Trade Unions and the Repression of Independent Trade Unions," *China Labour Bulletin*, 27 (November 1995), 3.

51. See ACFTU, "Opinion on the Implementation of the Circular from the CPC Central Committee on the Strengthening and Improvement of the Leadership of the Communist Party of China (CPC) in the Work of Trade Unions, the Communist Youth League and the All-China Federation of Women," 15 April 1990; and statement by Zhang Dinghua, General Secretary of the ACFTU, April 1995, *Workers' Daily*, 19 April 1995, both cited in "The Fable."

52. Guan Jinghe, "Country Paper on China," 56.

53. By 1995, the number of ratifications placed China behind the UK, Russian Federation, India, Australia, Canada, the Philippines, Singapore and Myanmar in terms of the number of Conventions ratified or in force, but in front of the US (11 [rat], 9 [in force]), Thailand, Vietnam, Malaysia, Republic of Korea and Laos. As of November 1998, China has ratified C.7, Convention on Minimum Age (Sea), 1920 (ratified 02.12.36); C. 11, Convention on the Right of Association (Agriculture), 1921 (rat. 27.04.34); C. 14, Convention on Weekly Rest (Industry), 1921 (rat. 17.

05.34); C.15, Convention on Minimum Age (Trimmers and Stockers), 1921 (rat. 2.12.36); C. 16 Convention on the Medical Examination of Young Persons (Sea), 1921 (rat.2.12.36); C. 19, Convention on Equality of Treatment (Accident Compensation), 1925 (rat. 27.04.34); C. 22, Convention on the Contract on Seamen's Articles of Agreement, 1926 (rat. 02.12.36); C. 23, Convention on the Repatriation of Seamen, 1926 (rat. 02.12.36); C. 26, Convention on the Machinery of Minimum Wage-Fixing, 1928 (rat. 05.05.30); C. 27, Convention on the Indication of Weight on Transport Vessels, 1929 (rat. 24.06.31); C. 32, Convention on Protection against Accidents (Dockers) (Revised), 1932 (rat. 30.11.35); C. 45, Convention on Underground Work (Women), 1935 (rat. 2.12.36); C. 59, Convention (Revised) on the Minimum Age (Industry), 1937 (rat. 21.02.40); C. 80, Convention on Final Articles Revision, 1946, (rat. 04.08.47); C. 100, Convention on Equal Remuneration, 1951 (rat. 02.11.90); C. 122, Employment Policy Convention, 1964 (rat. 17.12.97); C. 144, Convention on Tripartite Consultation (International Labour Standards), 1976 (rat. 02.11.90); C. 159, Convention on Vocational Rehabilitation and Employment (Disabled Persons), 1983 (rat. 02.02.88); and C.170 Chemicals Convention, 1990 (rat. 11.01.95). See International Labour Office, *List of Ratifications by Convention and by Country* (as at 31 December 1994), Report 111 (Part 5), 82nd sess. (International Labour Office, Geneva, 1995); and ibid. (as at 31 December 1997), Report 111 (Part 2), 86th sess., (Geneva, International Labour Office, 1998), 254.

54. *Zhongguo waijiao gailan 1987*, 427.

55. International Labour Office, *International Labour Standards*, 104.

56. Interview with ILO official, Geneva, 30 August 1993.

57. As of 10 May 1993, ILO technical cooperation in China consisted of the following projects: Promotion China's overseas contracts and employment (Total budget $661,850); Changzhou entrepreneurs centre (TB $936,395); Strengthening of prog. nl cooper. training centre (TB $886,030); Assistance to national occupations training programme (TB $1,729,510); Professional teacher training centre Cha Yang (TB $772,800); Assistance to advanced vocational training centre (TB $680,465); Development of national safety training centre (INTC) (TB $1,221,550)); Labour safety and health (TB $1,393,229); Development of advanced national tourism training (TB $3,480,563); Social security training and development (TB $1,093,900); Social security development (TB $68,000); Village and township enterprises (TB $50,000); Financing seminar employment promotion strategies (TB $20,000); Study on rural industry SAREC (TB $380,388); Improv. manpower & employment data at Labour Ministry (TB $1,181,135); Training centre for small and medium coal mines (TB US$1,185,162); Training in IGA/FP in Hainan (TB $248,180); and Activities and improvement, family welfare women (TB $300,000). The one project closed after June 1989 was Hotel instructors' training, Suzhou (TB $1,281,679). Information provided by ILO, August 1993. Prior to 1989, more than ten projects with China had been completed or were under discussion: Tianjin and Shanghai Centres for Advanced Vocational Training; Dual-Language Administrative Personnel Training Centre of the Foreign Affairs Institute; Suzhou Advanced Vocational Training Centre for Hotel and Tourism Managers; National Cooperative Training Centre; Training Centre for Safety in Small and Medium-sized Coal Mines; Labour Ministry Computer Centre for Labour Statistics; Beijing and Suzhou Workers' Audio-Visual Education Programmes of the All-China Federation of Trade Unions; Xi'an Rehabilitation Centre for the Handicapped; and Advanced Training Centre on Labour Protection in Jiujian, Jiangxi Province. See ILO, *Profile on the People's Republic of China*, 70.

58. Peng Mao'an, "Report on Study Tours to Asian and European Countries Concerning Labour and Social Policy for Multinational Enterprises in International Labour Office," *Proceedings of the China/ILO National Workshop on Social and Labour*

Practices for Multinational Enterprises Operating in China and Its Special Zones (Shenzhen, December 1988), 113.

59. Union of International Associations, ed., *International Organizations, 1995/ 1996*, Vol. 1 (Munchen: K.G. Saur, 1996), 863.

60. Interview with ICFTU official, Geneva, 19 August 1993.

61. Interviews with ILO official, Geneva, 6 August 1993; and with Australian representative to the ILO, Canberra, 21 February 1994. For a partial account of these post-1989 developments, see also Ann Kent, "China, International Organizations and Regimes: the ILO as a Case Study in Organizational Learning," *Pacific Affairs* 70 (Winter 1997–98) 4: 31–47.

62. Telephone interview with Australian representative to the ILO, Canberra, 6 December 1995.

63. Lu Ping, "A Brief History of the Workers' Autonomous Federation" in *A Moment of Truth: Workers' Participation in China's 1989 Democracy Movement and the Emergence of Independent Unions*, ed. Lu Ping (Hong Kong: Asia Monitor Resource Center Ltd., 1990), 18. First published as *Gongren qiliao* ("Workers Arise") (Hong Kong: Hong Kong Trade Union Education Centre, 1990). See also Leung Wing-yue, *Smashing the Iron Rice Pot: Workers and Unions in China's Market Socialism* (Hong Kong: Asia Monitor Resource Center, 1988).

64. George Black and Robin Munro, *Black Hands of Beijing: Lives of Defiance in China's Democracy Movement* (New York: John Wiley & Sons, 1993), 320.

65. Lu Ping, "A Brief History," 15.

66. For accounts of these developments see essays in Lu Ping, ed., *A Moment of Truth*; and Black and Munro, *Black Hands of Beijing*, 221–45. For accounts of executions, see Lu Ping, "A Brief History," 18–19.

67. Interview with ILO official, Geneva, 30 August 1993. Information on developments also derives from interview with ILO official, Geneva, 11 August 1993.

68. The Declaration, conveyed in this Supplementary Report (GB. 244/18/1), strongly implied that, after its reversion to China, Hong Kong would continue its participation in the same ILO activities and ILO Conventions as it had under its status as a "Non-Metropolitan Territory" of the United Kingdom. It stated: "At present, Hong Kong, under arrangements made by the UK Government in accordance with relevant articles of the ILO Constitution relating to 'Non-Metropolitan Territories,' participates in ILO activities and has International Labour Conventions applied to it. With effect from 1 July 1997 the Hong Kong Special Administrative Region, as an inseparable part of the territory of the People's Republic of China, will not and should not be deemed to be a 'Non-Metropolitan Territory.' However, the Hong Kong Special Administrative Region will be autonomous in the enactment of labour legislation and in the administration of labour affairs. Therefore, for the purpose of enabling the Hong Kong Special Administrative Region to continue its participation in International Labour Organisation activities and to continue to have International Labour Conventions applied to it, the relevant articles of the International Labour Organization Constitution will be applied, by analogy, to the Hong Kong Special Adminstrative Region."

69. Interview with ILO official, Geneva, 6 August 1993.

70. Interview with ICFTU official, Geneva, 19 August 1993.

71. Interview with Australian representative to the ILO, Canberra, 21 February 1994.

72. On the former point, Lee Swepston has argued that "the complaints procedures would not be nearly as effective if they did not form part of the ILO's overall machinery for supervising the implementation of ILO principles and instruments." See Swepston, "Human Rights Complaint Procedures," 92. On the latter point,

Zhongguo waijiao gailan's annual survey of China's foreign relations contains a section on China's relations with the ILO. However, apart from a fleeting reference in the 1991 volume to China's complaint in February 1990 to the ILO Director-General about the ICFTU's "false accusations" (*wugao*) in Case No. 1500, no further reference to the CFA cases has been recorded. See *Zhongguo waijiao gailan 1991*, 434.

73. This account is based on interviews with Australian representative and ILO officials, Canberra and Geneva, August 1993 and comments of then Australian representative to the ILO, 21 February 1996.

74. China's complaint to the Director-General is also recorded in Wang Xingfang, ed., *Zhongguo yu Lianheguo*, 371.

75. The following summary is drawn from International Labour Office, *268th Report of the Committee on Freedom of Association*, Case No 1500 (China), GB. 244/5/6, 244th Sess. (Geneva, November 1989), paras. 671–701, at 158–162; International Labour Office, *270th Report of the Committee on Freedom of Association*, GB. 245/5/8, 245th Sess. (Geneva, February–March 1990), paras. 297–334, at 83–92; International Labour Office, *279th Report of the Committee on Freedom of Association*, GB. 251/8/11, 251st Sess. (Geneva, 11–15 November 1991), paras. 602–41, at 156–65; and International Labour Office, *281st Report of the Committee on Freedom of Association*, GB. 252/9/13, 252nd Sess. (Geneva, 2–6 March 1992), paras. 74–83, at 17–20.

76. See International Labour Office, *270th Report*, para. 302, at 84.

77. For these conclusions and recommendations, see International Labour Office, *270th Report*, paras. 322–334 (c), at 89–92.

78. See Ann Kent, "Standards of Living, Relative Deprivation and Political Change," in *China's Quiet Revolution: New Interactions between State and Society*, ed. David S. G. Goodman and Beverley Hooper (Melbourne: Longman Cheshire, 1994), 64–86.

79. Black and Munro, *Black Hands of Beijing*, 322.

80. Ibid. 321. See also Asia Watch, "Evidence of Crackdown on Labour Movements Mounts" 4 (28 May 1992) 17; Asia Watch, "Economic Reform, Political Repression: Arrests of Dissidents in China since Mid-1992," 5 (2 March 1993) 4; and Human Rights Watch/Asia, "China: New Arrests Linked to Workers Rights," 6 (11 March 1994) 2.

81. See, for instance, Han Dongfang, "A Long Hard Journey: The Rise of a Free Labor Movement," in *China Rights Forum* (winter 1995–96), 8–11.

82. In Section 4, "Union Powers and Responsibilities" (*Gonghui quanli he yiwu*), Article 21 stated that unions could (*keyi*) raise objections (*ti yijian*) if the enterprise violated workers' labor rights, and should (*yingdang*) support and help them if he filed a court action. Normally the terminology used of Chinese enterprises was that the union had "the power" (*you quan*), to take certain actions, while in the case of foreign enterprises it normally declared that the union should (*yingdang*) take action. The only other exception was the case where there were work stoppages or slowdowns in Chinese enterprises, in which case the union should be able to (*yingdang hui*) negotiate a solution between workers and management (Art. 25). See Zhonghua renmin gongheguo guohui fa ("Trade Union Act of the People's Republic of China"), Art. 12, in Jin Qi (ed), *Gonghuifa zidian* ("Trade Union Act Dictionary") (Beijing: Zhongguo zhengfa daxue chubanshe, 1992), 806–7; and Article 20, 808.

83. Article 33, 809. Thus, while Art. 20 merely made a factual statement that China-wide labor unions take part in the mediation of labor disputes within the enterprise, in respect of enterprises involving foreign participation, Art. 33 stipulated that in questions of immediate concern such as wages, welfare benefits, production safety, labor protection and labor insurance, the complaints/objections/views of the trade union should be heard (*yingdang tingqu gonghui yijian*).

84. For details of complaints and proceedings in CFA Case No. 1652, see Interna-

tional Labour Office, *286th Report of the Committee on Freedom of Association*, GB. 255/5/11, 255th Session (Geneva, 1–4 March 1993), paras. 677–728, at 161–171; International Labour Office, *292nd Report of the Committee on Freedom of Association*, GB.259/7/14, 259th sess. (Geneva, March 1994), paras. 374–401, at 92–99; International Labour Office, *297th Report of the Committee on Freedom of Association*, GB.262/ 7/1, 262nd sess. (Geneva, March–April 1995), para. 25, at 10–11.

85. International Labour Office, *292nd Report*, para 401, at 98–99. For detailed summary of Cases 1500 and 1652, see Ann Kent, "China, the United Nations and the International Human Rights Regime, 1971–1994: The Learning Process," Ph.D. thesis (Canberra: Australian National University, June 1996), Appendix 1 and 2, 283–295.

86. International Labour Office, *304th Report of the Committee on Freedom of Association* GB. 266/5, 266th sess. (Geneva, June 1996), at 31–42.

87. See International Labour Office, *272nd Report of the Committee on Freedom of Association*, Case No. 1930 (China), GB.272/5, 272nd sess. (Geneva, June 1998), paras. 271–367, at 64–84.

88. Collective bargaining was to be found in Western FIEs, characterized by "human resource management patterns," rather than in the joint ventures with firms from Newly Industrialized Countries (NICs), often in south China, which adopted a more authoritarian approach to industrial relations. See Anita Chan, "Trade Unions and Collective Bargaining in China," Seminar, Contemporary China Centre, Australian National University, Canberra, 27 March 1996.

89. Interview with ILO delegate, Canberra, 26 July 1994.

90. International Labour Conference, *Report of the Committee of Experts on the Application of Conventions and Recommendations*, Report 111 (Part 4A), C. 26.

91. International Labour Conference, *Provisional Record*, 81st Session, 25 (Geneva, 1994), paras. 11, 30, and 31, 25/5–10.

92. ILO Conference, *Provisional Record*, 81st session, 25/82–25/83.

93. Interview with ILO delegate, Canberra, 26 July 1994.

94. Interview with ILO official, Geneva, 9 September 1998.

95. For debate, see International Labour Office, "Extracts from Statements made at the 85th Session (1997) of the International Labour Conference during the Discussion of the Report of the Director-General Concerning the Universal Guarantee of Fundamental Workers' Rights and the Possible Adoption of a Solemn Declaration," GB. 270/3/1 (Add.) 270th Sess., (Geneva, November 1997), at 10.

96. Interview with ILO official, Geneva, 9 September 1998.

97. International Labour Office, "Clearing the Final Hurdle: ILO Conference Adopts the Rights Declaration, Seeks End to Child Labour Abuses," *World of Work* 25 (1998), 13.

98. These were Conventions: 2, 3, 5, 7, 8, 10, 11, 12, 14, 15, 16, 17, 19, 22, 23, 29, 32, 42, 45, 50, 58, 59, 64, 65, 74, 81, 87, 90, 92, 97, 98, 101, 105, 108, 115, 122, 124, 133, 141, 142, 144, 147, 148, 150, 151, 160. See International Labour Office, *List of Ratifications* (1998), 254.

99. U.S. State Department, "Hong Kong," *Report on Human Rights Practices for 1997* (Washington, D.C., 30 January 1998): 6, 13; Christine Loh, "One Country, Two Human Rights Reports," *China Rights Forum* (Winter 1997–8): 14–15; and "Hong Kong Sets Protest Curbs, Criticised on Labour Rights," Reuters "China" News, 18 July 1997.

100. Article 7, "People's Republic of China, Labour Law," 5 July 1994, Chinese and English text in *China Law and Practice* 8, 8 (29 August 1994), 22.

101. Ibid. author's emphasis.

102. See "Labour Law," arts. 89–105, 34–36.

103. For these reasons, China's dissident labor leader, Han Dongfang, commented

that "China's first Labour Law . . . certainly represents some progress. But there are still serious doubts about the government's ability and willingness to enforce the law. In the eyes of the Chinese government, the law is just like a piece of cloth and the government is a tailor with a pair of scissors. If the government needs something, the scissors simply snip it out. No consideration is given to the final appearance of the cloth. . . ." On the other hand, he claimed, "the objective conditions for the development of a free labour movement have already taken shape in China." See Han Dongfang, "A Long Hard Journey: the Rise of a Free Labour Movement," in *China Rights Forum* (Winter 1995–96): 9–10.

104. Mary Gallagher, "An Unequal Battle: Why Labor Laws and Regulations Fail to Protect Workers," *China Rights Forum* (Summer 1997): 12–13.

105. International Labour Office, GB.272/5, paras. 343–348, at 75–6.

106. Pitman B. Potter, "The Chinese Legal System(?): Continuing Tensions over Norms and Enforcement," in *China Review 1998*, ed. Joseph Y. S. Cheng (Hong Kong: The Chinese University Press, 1998), 35–36.

107. Gallagher, "An Unequal Battle," 13.

108. See US Department of State, "China," in *Country Reports on Human Rights Practices for 1995*, Report Submitted to the Committee on Foreign Relations, U.S. Senate, and the Committee on International Relations, U.S. House of Representatives (Washington, D.C.: U.S. Government Printing Office, 1996), 34; and the same report for 1996, which reported "only a few experiments in collective bargaining," 24. Cf. Chan, "Trade Unions and Collective Bargaining in China."

109. See Gallagher, "An Unequal Battle"; and Anita Chan, "Workers' Rights are Human Rights," *China Rights Forum* (Summer 1997): 4–7. Chan cites cases of forced and bonded labor; control of workers' bodily functions and physical mistreatment; subsistence or sub-subsistence wages; and violence committed by the police and private security guards.

110. See *China Labour Bulletin*, "Trade Union Rights in China," reported in *China Rights Forum* (Fall 1994): 12–13.

111. The League's organizers protested the unfavorable effects of reforms on workers and demanded the establishment of legal safeguards for the rights and interests of workers at the lowest levels of society. Among those detained for post-1989 activities were Liu Jingsheng, arrested in 1992 for helping to organize the Free Labour Union of China and China's Social Democratic Party, China Progressive Alliance and China's Liberal Democratic Party; sentenced with him for between two and twenty-years of imprisonment were other members of the "Beijing 16." Disappeared unionists included Wang Miaogen, Liu Nianchun and his other members of the League for the Protection of the Rights of Working People, Yuan Hongbing, Zhang Lin and Xiao Biguang. Equally significant from the ILO's point of view was China's continued denial of former WAF leader Han Dongfang's right to return home. See Liu Qing, "Devoted to Democracy and Human Rights: the Development of the Dissident Movement," in *China Rights Forum* (winter 1995): 5; and Han Dongfang, "A Long Hard Journey," 9; and "Repression of Independent Trade Unionists," *China Labour Bulletin* (November 1995): 5–8.

112. U.S. Department of State, "China" in *Country Reports* (for 1996), 23.

113. See Potter, "The Chinese Legal System(?)," 34.

114. See generally, Human Rights Watch, *Human Rights Watch World Report 1998* (New York, 1998), "China and Tibet," 170–180; and U.S. Department of State, "China," in *Country Report on Human Rights Practices for 1997* (Washington, D.C., 30 January 1998).

115. "Tang Yuanjuan Arrested," *China Labour Bulletin* 44 (September–October 1998), 10.

116. Between 1992 and 1995, the increases in industrial action in each successive

year were 51, 73, and 74 percent, respectively; a *Workers' Daily* report in May 1996 gave a total figure of 210,000 cases. Throughout 1997, a series of major protests by workers and other urban residents occurred in a number of Chinese cities, in the provinces of Sichuan, Honan and increasingly in the rust belt provinces in the Northeast. Many of these were forcibly suppressed. See Chan, "Workers' Rights," 4.

117. "Circular Issued on Establishing Party Groups in Social Organizations," Xinhua Newsagency, 27 March 1998, Reuters "China" News, 30 March 1998.

118. For detailed analysis, see *Bound and Gagged: Freedom of Association in China Further Curtailed Under New Regulation* (New York: Human Rights in China, 13 November 1998).

119. Telephone interview with the Australian representative to the ILO, Canberra, 8 February 1996.

120. Interview with Australian representative to ILO, Canberra, 21 February 1994.

Chapter 5. Theory, Policy, and Diplomacy Before Vienna

1. Report reproduced in "Yifen yanjiu renquan wenti di mijian" ("A Confidential Document on the Question of Human Rights Research"), *Dangdai Zhongguo* ("Contemporary China"), 15 July 1992, 38–41 and 15 June 1992, 67–70.

2. For analysis of theories of jurisprudence, see Albert H.Y. Chen, "Developing Theories of Rights and Human Rights in China," in *Hong Kong, China and 1997: Essays in Legal Theory*, ed. Raymond Wacks (Hong Kong: Hong Kong University Press, 1993), 125–33.

3. Tian Jin, "Guoji renquan huodong di fazhan he cunzai zhengyi di wenti" ("The Development of the International Human Rights Movement and Current Controversies"), *Guoji wenti yanjiu* ("International Studies") (1989) 1: 4–7.

4. In contrast, a Chinese taxonomy has identified the two waves of human rights interest as (1) from 1979 and (2) from 1988–89 to the present. It did not recognize the impact of the June crackdown as interrupting the process. See Rao Fang, "Renquan yu fazhi lilun yanjiu zongshu" ("A Summary of the Theoretical Research on Human Rights and the Legal System"), in *Zhongguo faxue* ("Chinese Legal Science") (9 July 1991) 4: 41.

5. See summary of Conference proceedings in Meng Chunyan, "Jianchi Makesi zhuyi renquanguan, fandui zichan jieji renquanguan" ("Insist on the Marxist View of Human Rights, Oppose the Bourgeois View of Human Rights"), *Renmin ribao* ("People's Daily"), 17 September 1990, 5.

6. The 1996 White Paper pointed out: "The Chinese government actively supports and aids financially the study of human rights. The research subjects aided financially by the State Social Science Fund, the China Social Science Fund and the Youth Social Science Fund include a certain number of subjects on human rights. Every year a group of subjects on human rights win financial aid from the State Education Commission, the Chinese Academy of Social Sciences and local governments and achieve results. In addition, the China Human Rights Research Fund set up by various social circles collects funds and gives financial aid to research activities on human rights." See Information Office of the State Council of the People's Republic of China, *The Progress of Human Rights in China*, December 1995, text in *Beijing Review*, Special Issue, 39 (January 1996): 25–26.

7. For instance, some Chinese students abroad were requested by their embassy to find material on human rights. A Chinese student in Australia translated a monograph on China's human rights, Ann Kent, *Human Rights in the People's Republic of China: National and International Dimensions* [Canberra, Peace Research Centre, ANU, 1990]), and sent it to the Chinese Foreign Ministry.

8. For instance, the Chinese Institute for Peace and Development Studies in Shanghai had occasional foreign scholars working on human rights attached to it in 1992 and regularly conferred on human rights with visiting scholars.

9. See, for instance, Liu Wenzong, "Lun Meiguo di 'renquan waijiao'," ("On America's 'Human Rights Diplomacy' "), *Guoji wenti yanjiu* ("International Studies") (1993) 3:28–34. However, criticisms were made throughout the 1989–1994 period. See, for example, critique of US record in accession to human rights treaties by China's Foreign Minister, Qian Qichen, 27 March 1991, in "Foreign Minister Qian Meets the Press," *Beijing Review* 34 (April 8–14 1991) 14: 13; and Wei Guoqiang, "The United States Plagued by Domestic Problems," *Beijing Review* 35, 4 (27 January–2 February 1992): 9.

10. For a detailed overview of these activities, see "Recent Human Rights Studies in the PRC," in *Report of the Second Australian Human Rights Delegation to China, 8–20 November 1992* (Canberra: Department of Foreign Affairs and Trade, 10 March 1993), Annex 11, i–iv.

11. They included the Forum on Human Rights, held March 1992 by the Information Office of the Shanghai Municipal Government to discuss the White Paper, *Human Rights in China* (Beijing: Information Office of the State Council, October 1991); the Forum on Criminal Reform in China, held in Beijing on 13 August 1992 and organized by the Law Society of China, to discuss the White Paper, *Criminal Reform in China* (Beijing: Information Office of the State Council, August 1992); and the Forum on Tibet, held in Beijing on 25 September 1992, and organized by the State Commission of Nationalities, to discuss the White Paper, *Tibet—Its Ownership and Human Rights Situation* (Beijing: Information Office of the State Council, September 1992). See *Report of the Second Australian Human Rights Delegation*, i–ii.

12. These included the Centre for the Study of Marxist Science of Man, Beijing University; the Centre for the Study of Human Rights and the Department of Law, Chinese People's University; the Law Institute, Shandong University; the Centre for the Study of the Development of Social Sciences for Higher Education, State Education Commission; the Institute of Social Development, Beijing University; the Law Institute, Chinese Academy of Social Sciences; the Institute of Marxism, Central Party School of the CCP; the International Communication Office of the CCP Central Committee; the State Council; and the Institute for Peace and Development Studies, Shanghai. See *Report of the Second Australian Human Rights Delegation*, Annex 11, v.

13. By 1996, this center had published seven books on human rights and 100 academic papers on human rights. See Gu Chunde, "Theoretical Research on China's Human Rights," *Beijing Review* 39 (4–10 March 1996) 10: 21.

14. See Zhongguo shehui kexueyuan faxue yanjiusuo, bian (ed), *Dangdai renquan* ("Contemporary Human Rights") (Beijing: Zhongguo shehuikexue chubanshe, 1992), 448–468.

15. They included: Dong Yonghu and Liu Wuping, eds., *Shijie renquan yuefa zonglan* ("World Documents of Human Rights") (Chengdu: Sichuan renmin chubanshe, 1990); Ye Lixuan and Li Shizhen, *Renquan lilun* ("Human Rights Theory") (Fuzhou: Fujian Peoples' Press, 1991); Wu Daying and Liu Shu, *Zhengzhi tizhi gaige yu fazhi jianshe* ("Political Reform and the Establishment of the Legal System") (Beijing: Shehui kexue chuban wenxian chubanshe, 1991); "*Zhongguo di renquan zhuangkuang": xuexi ziliao* (" 'Human Rights in China': Study Materials") (Beijing: Hongqi chubanshe, 1991); Pang Sen, *Dangdai renquan ABC* ("Contemporary Human Rights ABC") (Chengdu: Sichuan renmin chubanshe, 1992); Feng Zhuoran, Gu Chunde, eds., *Renquan lunji* ("Collected Essays on Human Rights") (Beijing: Shoudu shifan daxue chuban, 1992); Zhongguo kexueyuan yanjiusuo ed., *Dangdai renquan* ("Con-

temporary Human Rights") (Beijing: Zhongguo kexueyuan chubanshe, 1992); Xu Jianyi, ed., "*Zhongguo di renquan zhuangkuang*": *wenti jieda* ("*Human Rights in China*: Answers to Questions") (Beijing: *Zhonguo qingnian* chubanshe, 1992); Chang Jian, *Renquan di lixiang, beilun, xianshi* ("The Ideal, Paradox and Reality of Human Rights") (Chengdu: Sichuan renmin chubanshe, 1992); Li Long and Wan Exiang, *Renquan lilun yu guoji renquan* ("Human Rights Theory and International Human Rights") (Wuhan: Wuhan daxue chubanshe, 1992); Xia Yong, *Renquan gainian qiyuan* ("Origins of the Human Rights Concept") (Beijing: Zhongguo zhengfa daxue chubanshe, 1992); Sun Guohua, *Renquan: zou xiang ziyou di biaochi* ("Human Rights: Proceeding towards the Rule of Freedom") (Shandong: Shandong renmin chubanshe, 1993); Huang Nansen, Chen Zhixiang, Dong Yunhu, *Dangdai Zhongguo renquan lun* ("On Contemporary Chinese Human Rights") (Beijing: Dangdai Zhongguo chubanshe, 1993); Zhang Xinmin et al., eds., *Zhongguo renquan cishu* ("A Dictionary of China's Human Rights") (Haikou: Nanhai chuban gongsi, 1993); Liu Fuzhi, ed., *Renquan da zidian* ("A Big Dictionary of Human Rights") (Wuhan: Wuhan daxue chubanshe, 1993); Hu Jinguang, Han Dayuan, *Dangdai renquan baozhang zhidu* ("Contemporary Human Rights Guarantees") (Beijing: Zhongguo zhengfa daxue chubanshe, 1993); Chen Chunlong, *Minzhu zhengzhi yu fazhi renquan* ("Democratic Politics and Legal Rights") (Beijing: Shehui kexue wenxian chubanshe, 1993); Bao Zonghao, Jin Chaoxiang, Li Jin, *Quanli lun* ("On Rights") (Shanghai: Sanlian shu-dian, 1993); Teng Wensheng, ed., "*Zhongguo di renquan zhuangkuang*" *baitijie* ("Key to a Hundred Questions on *Human Rights in China*") (Beijing: Huaxia chubanshe, 1992); Xu Chongde, ed., *Xianfa yu minzhu zhengzhi* ("The Constitution and Democratic Politics") (Beijing: Zhongguo jiancha chubanshe, 1994); Hu Yunteng, *Sixing tonglun* ("General Survey of Capital Punishment") (Beijing: Zhonguo zhengfa da-xue chubanshe, 1995); Xia Yong, *Zou xiang quanli di shidai: Zhongguo gongmin quanli fazhan yanjiu* ("Toward the Age of Rights: Research on the Development of Chinese Citizens' Rights") (Beijing: Zhongguo zhengfa daxue chubanshe, 1995). Three other books, without Chinese titles and often without place of publication have been cited in the Report of the Second Australian Human Rights delegation. They are Li Guozhi, *An Outline of Marxist Theory of Human Rights* (Chengdu: Sichuan University Press, 1992): Cheng Jian, *Democracy, Freedom and Human Rights*, 1990; and Shen Guoming, Pu Zengyuan et al, *Human Rights, Fiction and Reality* (Shanghai: Shanghai shehuikexue chubanshe, 1992). However, they have not been located in library catalogues, and their details cannot be confirmed.

16. By 1996, it was estimated that nearly one hundred academic books and over a thousand articles (including newspaper articles) on human rights had been published in China. See *The Progress of Human Rights in China*, 26.

17. For the best and most complete analysis of this literature, see Chen, "Developing Theories of Rights," 123–149. See also "Report of the Second Australian Human Rights Delegation to China," annex 2, vi–xiii; and Zhou Wei, "The Study of Human Rights in the People's Republic of China," in *Human Rights and International Relations in the Asia-Pacific Region*, ed. James T.H. Tang (London: Pinter, 1995), 83–96.

18. The preparedness to cite Western sources seems, as much as any other reason, to be attributable to editorial policy. For instance, contributors to the journal of the Chinese Law Society, *Zhongguo faxue* ("Chinese Legal Science") rarely cite non-Chinese sources: on the other hand, contributors to the Beijing University Law Journal, *Zhongwai faxue* ("Chinese/Foreign Legal Science") liberally cite Western authorities and sources.

19. See Rao Fang, "Renquan yu fazhi," 41–45.

20. See Meng Chunyan, "Jianchi Makesi zhuyi," 17 September 1990; "Yixiang zhongyao di faxue yanjiu keti: 'ru he kaizhan renquan yu fazhi wenti di lilun yanjiu';

zuotanhui zongshu" ("An Important Task for Legal Research: 'How to Develop Theoretical Research into the Question of Human Rights and the Legal System': Summary of a Conference"), 12 March 1991, *Zhongguo faxue* ("Chinese Legal Science") (9 May 1991) 3: 5–7; "Renquan lilun yanjiu zuotanhui zongshu" ("Summary of a Conference on Theoretical Research on Human Rights"), 20 April 1991, *Zhongguo faxue* ("Chinese Legal Science"), (9 July 1991) 4: 46–47; and "Ba renquan lilun yanjiu yin xiang shenru: Zhongguo shehui kexue yanjiusuo renquan lilun taohui zongshu" ("Deepen the Study of Human Rights Theory: Summary of the Symposium of the Human Rights Research Institute of the Chinese Academy of Social Sciences"), 18–21 June 1991, *Zhongguo faxue* ("Chinese Legal Science") (9 September 1991) 5: 121–123.

21. Meng Chunyan, "Jianchi Makesi zhuyi," 5.

22. Tian Jin, "Complexities of Human Rights in Today's World," 14th Conference on the Law of the World, 22–27 April 1990, Beijing, *Beijing Review* 33, 22 (28 May–3 June, 1990): 12.

23. It was, however, useful in summarizing the main topics which interested scholars. They comprised: the concept of human rights; the class nature and universal nature of human rights; the relation between human rights and citizens' rights; the relation between collective and individual rights; the relation between human rights and democracy and the legal system; the relation between human rights protection and social, economic and cultural development; the basic content of the Marxist human rights view; the relation between the Marxist human rights view and a legal view; the historical development of the bourgeois human rights standpoint and its critique; the opposition between the Marxist and bourgeois human rights view; the history and current condition of the protection of Chinese human rights; comparative research on human rights law in China and the major countries of the world; the protection of human rights in Chinese legislation; improvement of the system of legal protection of China's human rights; the relation between human rights protection in international and domestic law; the developing trends in contemporary international human rights theory; the emergence and development of Third World human rights theory; an analysis of democratic socialist human rights theory; research on the legislation of international human rights protection; the history and present condition of the international protection of human rights; the content and national limits of the international protection of human rights; the international protection of human rights and the principle of state sovereignty. See "Yixiang zhongyao di faxue," 12 March 1991, 6.

24. "Renquan shouxian shi renmin shengcun quan guojia duli quan," ("Human Rights are Primarily the People's Right to Subsistence and National Independence"), *Renmin ribao* ("People's Daily"), 15 April 1991, 1.

25. *Beijing Review* 34 (22–28 April 1991) 16: 7.

26. "Renquan lilun," 46–47.

27. "Ba renquan lilun yanjiu," 21 June 1991, 121–123.

28. Zhang Wenxian, "Lun renquan di zhuti yu zhuti di renquan" ("On the Subject of Human Rights and the Human Rights of the Subject"), *Zhongguo faxue* ("Chinese Legal Science") 5 (9 September 1991): 26–34.

29. Li Ming, "'Lianheguo xianzhang' zhong di renquan yu bu ganshe neizheng wenti" ("Human Rights in the UN Charter and the Question of Non-Interference in Internal Affairs") *Zhongguo faxue* ("Chinese Legal Science") 3 (9 May 1993): 43.

30. Pang Sen, *Dangdai renquan ABC*, 215.

31. "Ba renquan lilun yanjiu yin xiang shenru," 21 June 1991, 123.

32. Zhang Liang, "Lunlue zhuquan yu renquan di xianghu guanxi" ("A Discussion of the Interrelationship between Sovereignty and Human Rights"), in Zhongguo shehui kexueyuan faxue yanjiusuo bian, *Dangdai renquan*, 343.

33. Liu Nanlai, "Guoji xin zhixu yu renquan" ("The New International World Order and Human Rights"), in *Dangdai renquan*, 287.

34. Guo Jisi, "China Promotes Civil Rights," *China Daily*, 22 January 1991. This contained excerpts from an article to be published in the *Beijing Review*.

35. See, for instance, Chinese speeches at the UN Human Rights Commission in 1991. Arguments on non-interference included "Wo daibiao zai Lianda renquan hui shang fayan" ("Our Representative Speaks at the UN Human Rights Commission"), *Renmin ribao* 3 February 1991, 6. More constructive statements included "Fazhan-quan shi renquan zhongyao gainian" ("The Right to Development is an Important Concept of Human Rights"), *Renmin ribao* ("People's Daily"), 13 February 1991, 6; and "Zunzhong minzu zijuequan shi xiangshou renquan di qianti" ("Respect for the Right to the Self-determination of Peoples is the Premise for the Enjoyment of Human Rights"), *Renmin ribao* ("People's Daily"), 2 February 1992, 7.

36. See Zhang Yishan, speech at ECOSOC meeting, "Huyu zai renquan lingyu jiaqiang guoji hezuo" ("An Appeal to Strengthen International Cooperation in the Field of Human Rights"), *Renmin ribao* ("People's Daily"), 24 May 1991, 6.

37. Zhonghua renmin gongheguo guowuyuan xinwen bangongshi, *Zhongguo di renquan zhuangkuang* ("Human Rights in China") (Beijing: Zhongyang wenxian chubanshe, October 1991). The following analysis is based on the pagination of the English version, Information Office of the State Council of the People's Republic of China, *Human Rights in China* (Beijing, November 1991). For an analysis of the rights in this paper, see also Ann Kent, *Between Freedom and Subsistence: China and Human Rights* (Hong Kong: Oxford University Press, 1993 and 1995), 222–230.

38. "Weihu renquan, hanwei zhuquan" ("Safeguarding Human Rights, Defending State Sovereignty"), *Renmin ribao*, 2 November 1991, 1, 4.

39. *Human Rights in China*, 1

40. See Henry Shue, *Basic Rights, Subsistence, Affluence and U.S. Foreign Policy* (Princeton, N.J.: Princeton University Press, 1980); and R. J. Vincent, *Human Rights and International Relations* (Cambridge: Cambridge University Press, 1986). For a discussion of the relationship between Vincent's and Shue's theories, see Neil Stammers, "A Critique of Social Approaches to Human Rights," *Human Rights Quarterly* 17 (August 1995) 3: 496–508.

41. See Kent, *Between Freedom and Subsistence*, xiii. This had also used Henry Shue's theories as its conceptual basis, and was thus able to incorporate China's version of the right to subsistence in its theoretical framework before writing was completed in January 1992, three months after the White Paper was published.

42. See Maurice Cranston, *What Are Human Rights?* (London: Bodley Head, 1973), 7; and Jack Donnelly, *Universal Human Rights in Theory and Practice* (Ithaca, N.Y.: Cornell University Press, 1989).

43. Shue, *Basic Rights*, 26.

44. See similar argument in Kent, *Between Freedom and Subsistence*, 223. This mis-translation was subsequently corrected in the 1995 White Paper on human rights, which used the term, "right to existence." See State Council, *The Progress of Human Rights in China*, 4–29.

45. In a discussion between the author and Liu Fenzhi, one of the authors of the first White Paper, Liu insisted that *shengcun quan* embodied both the right to subsistence and the right to physical security. However, like the White Paper itself, he also insisted that for the Chinese people of today, the problems of physical security had been overcome. Interview with Liu Fenzhi, State Council, Beijing, 28 August 1992. A subsequent publication by Liu reiterated the point that the right to subsistence encompassed both aspects of the meaning, the civil rights aspect and the economic and social aspect, but referred only to the economic aspect when discussing its application to post-1949 China. See Liu Fenzhi, "Shengcun quan neihan di fazhan

shi dui renquan lilun di zhongda gongxian" ("The Development of the Right to Subsistence is a Great Contribution to Human Rights"), *Renmin ribao* ("People's Daily"), 31 May 1995, 5; *Beijing Review* 36 (21–27 June 1993) 25: 9–10.

46. Kent, *Between Freedom and Subsistence*, 224.

47. For collation of eight White Papers on human rights published since October 1991, see China Human Rights Research Society, ed., *Human Rights in China: A Collection of White Papers on Human Rights* (Beijing: the Five Continent Media Publishing House, 1997). It contains, "Conditions of Human Rights in China"; "Progress of the Cause of Human Rights in China"; "Progress of the Cause of Human Rights in China in 1996"; "Tibet's Sovereignty Claim and Conditions of Human Rights in Tibet"; "Conditions of Women in China"; "China's Family Planning"; "Conditions of Children in China"; and "Conditions of Criminal Reform in China."

48. *Human Rights in China*, 61, author's emphasis.

49. Xu Jianyi ed., *"Zhongguo di renquan."*

50. Liu Huaqiu, "Proposals for Human Rights Protection and Promotion," Speech by Vice-Foreign Minister Liu Huaqiu, World Conference on Human Rights, Vienna, 15 June 1993, *Beijing Review* 36 (28 June–4 July 1993) 26: 9.

51. Xu Jianyi, ed., *"Zhongguo di renquan,"* 349–54.

52. Although China called the Australian delegations "parliamentary delegations," during their visits the Australians continued to describe themselves as a "human rights delegation." For reports of these delegations, see *Report of the Australian Human Rights Delegation to China, 14–26 July 1991* (Canberra: Australian Department of Foreign Affairs and Trade, September 1991); *Report of the Second Australian Human Rights Delegation to China, 8–20 November 1992*; *Justice Repressive et Droits de l'Homme en République Populaire de Chine: Rapport de la Mission de Juristes Français, Octobre 1991* ("Repressive Justice and Human Rights in the People's Republic of China: Report of the Mission of French Jurists, October 1991") (no publication details); and *Visit to China by the Delegation led by Lord Howe of Aberavon: Report* (London: MMSO, 1993). The Swiss delegation did not release its report, but it has been viewed by the author. Unlike the other delegations, it had placed economic, social and cultural rights on its agenda for discussion with Chinese authorities, but little discussion on these rights eventuated.

53. See Ann Kent, "Australia and China: Monitoring by a Middle Power," 20 July 1995, unpublished paper, 14.

54. See Chen Jie, "Human Rights: ASEAN's New Importance to China," *Pacific Review* 6 (1993) 3: 227–37.

55. Joint Communiqué of the Twenty-Fourth ASEAN Ministerial Meeting, Kuala Lumpur, 19–20 July 1991, 7, 23–4, cited in Chen Jie, "Human Rights," 236.

56. *Renmin ribao* ("People's Daily") 12 January 1992, 1.

57. *Renmin ribao* 12 January 1992, 7.

58. Author's interview of Liu Fenzhi, State Council, Beijing, 28 August 1992.

59. Chen Jie, "Tactical Alliance: Southeast Asia and China's Post-1989 Human Rights Diplomacy," *China Rights Forum* (Fall 1998): 10.

60. The following brief account of the PrepComs for the Vienna Conference is largely based on the detailed articles in *Human Rights Monitor* by Adrien-Claude Zoller, Director of the International Service for Human Rights (ISHR), a central NGO service based in Geneva, which both monitors all developments in the UN which impact on human rights and provides essential advice to NGOs throughout the world on how to work with the UN human rights organs.

61. Interview with UN human rights expert, Canberra, 8 November 1995.

62. Adrien-Claude Zoller, "The Political Context of the World Conference," *Human Rights Monitor* (May 1993) 21: 2–3.

63. Zhonghua renmin gongheguo waijiaobu waijiaoshi bianjishi ("Editorial De-

partment, China's Diplomatic History, Chinese Foreign Ministry"), *Zhongguo waijiao gailan 1992* ("Survey of China's Foreign Relations 1992"), 432.

64. Zoller, "The Political Context," 2–3.

65. Samuel S. Kim, "China in the Post-Cold War World," in *China as a Great Power: Myths, Realities and Challenges in the Asia-Pacific Region*, ed. Stuart Harris and Gary Klintworth (Melbourne: Longman, 1995), 57.

66. Adrien-Claude Zoller, "Third Session of the Preparatory Meeting Ends in Failure," Geneva, 14–18 September 1992, *Human Rights Monitor* (May 1993) 21: 12.

67. Observation by Theo van Boven, citing UNGA resolutions 47/111, 47/125, 47/127, 47/129, 47/131, all adopted in December 1992.

68. Discussion with government delegates and journalists at the UN Human Rights Conference, Vienna, June 1993.

69. Adrien-Claude Zoller, "Saved by the Bell: Fourth Meeting of the Preparatory Committee" (Geneva, 19 April–7 May 1993) *Human Rights Monitor* (May 1993) 21: 23.

70. Khemais Chammari, "The Declaration of Vienna: The Cards Are on the Table," *Human Rights Monitor* (May 1993) 21: 26–27.

71. Discussion with Director of Human Rights Watch/Asia, Sidney Jones, Canberra, 30 July 1995.

72. Sidney Jones, "Culture Clash: Asian Activists Counter their Governments' Restrictive View of Human Rights," *China Rights Forum* (Summer 1993): 8.

73. "The Asia Pacific Regional Meeting (Bangkok, 29 March–April 2, 1993)," *Human Rights Monitor* (May 1993) 21: 20.

74. Jones, "Culture Clash," 8–9, 22.

75. For an excellent analysis of the differences between NGOs and their Asian governments at Bangkok, see Pat Walsh, Australian Council for Overseas Aid (ACFOA), *UN World Conference on Human Rights: Report on the Bangkok Preparatory Meetings*, (Fitzroy: Human Rights Office, ACFOA, 1993), 1–9; see also Jones, "Culture Clash," 8–9, 22.

76. See Jones, "Culture Clash," 22; Gordon Fairclough, "Standing Firm: Asia Sticks to its View of Human Rights," *Far Eastern Economic Review*, 14 April 1993; Mark Baker, "Asia's Struggle for Success and Compassion," *The Age*, 8 April 1993; and "Human Rights and Wrongs," editorial, *Asian Wall Street Journal*, 2 March 1993, contained in Walsh, "UN World Conference."

77. See "Wo daibiao chanshu Zhongguo dui renquan di lichang" ("Our Representative Expounds on China's Human Rights Position"), Speech of Jin Yongjian at Asian Regional Preparatory Meeting for the World Conference on Human Rights, Bangkok, *Renmin ribao* ("People's Daily"), 31 March 1993, 6. This was rendered as, "Asia's Major Human Rights Concerns," in *Beijing Review* 36 (19–25 April 1993) 16: 10–11.

78. Chen Jie, "Tactical Alliance," 10.

79. For text, see Walsh, ACFOA, *UN World Conference*, 10–13.

80. Jones, "Culture Clash," 22.

81. Bangkok Declaration, in Walsh, ACFOA, *UN World Conference*, 11.

82. Fairclough, "Standing Firm."

83. Jin Yongjian, "China's View on the Final Document," *Beijing Review* 36 (31 May–6 June 1993) 22: 8–9.

Chapter 6. The UN World Human Rights Conference at Vienna

1. This account of the UN World Human Rights Conference is based on my first-hand experience attending both the NGO Conference, at the invitation of the Lud-

wig Boltzmann Institute, Vienna, and the formal Conference. It is also based on my attendance at the major press conferences, and on the use of documents and newspapers distributed at the Conference. For text of Declaration, see UN Doc. A/Conf. 157/23, 12 July 1993.

2. See "Analytical Studies on the Six Objectives of the World Conference on Human Rights," UN Doc. A/CONF.157/PC/60, at 1–3.

3. "Pessimists are Dreaming, Says World Conference Coordinator," interview with John Pace, *Human Rights Tribune*, 2 (June 1993) 1: 39.

4. UN Press Conference, Austria Centre, Vienna, 13 June 1993, author's notes.

5. UN Press Conference, Secretary-General Ibrahima Fall, Austria Centre, Vienna, 13 June 1993, author's notes.

6. Helen Trinca, "Whose Rights are They Anyway?," *The Australian*, 19–20 June 1993, 21.

7. These states were cited in press conferences held by Western delegates on the drafting committee, in AP reports and in the press accounts in the Conference newspaper, *Terra Viva*.

8. For an excellent summary from the Conference, see Trinca, "Whose Rights?," 21.

9. For texts of statements by Asian governments, see James T. H. Tang, ed., *Human Rights and International Relations in the Asia-Pacific Region* (London: Pinter, 1995), Appendix 111, 213–249.

10. Liu Baopu and Xiao Qiang, "The Poor Relations Push Their Way in at the Door: NGOs at the Vienna Human Rights Conference," *China Rights Forum* (Fall 1993), 17.

11. Representatives: Liu Huaqiu, Vice-Foreign Minister, Head of Delegation; H. E. Mr. Jin Yongjian, Ambassador and Permanent Representative of China to the United Nations Office at Geneva, Deputy Head of Delegation.

Alternative Representatives: H.E. Mr Chen Shiqiu, Ambassador and Permanent Representative to the United Nations Office at Vienna; H.E. Mr Fan Guoxiang, Ambassador, Chinese Foreign Ministry; Zhang Yishan, Counsellor, Department of International Organisations, Chinese Foreign Ministry; Feng Cui, Counsellor, Permanent Mission of China to the United Nations Office in New York; Du Qiwen, Counsellor, Permanent Mission of China to the United Nations Office at Vienna; and Pang Sen, Counsellor, Permanent Mission of China to the United Nations Office at Geneva; and

Advisers: Tan Songqiu, Senior Research Fellow, Institute of Public Security; Chen Weidan, Director, Department of Discipline, Supreme People's Procuratorate; Fan Hechun, Deputy Director, Department of Policy and Law, State Nationalities Affairs Commission; Wang Lixian, Deputy Director, Department of Foreign Affairs, Ministry of Justice; Zhang Qingfang, Deputy Director, Department of International Affairs, All-China Women's Federation; Guo Chun, Research Fellow, Supreme People's Court; Hu Dingxian, First Secretary, General Office, Foreign Ministry; Huang Yong'an, First Secretary, Permanent Mission of China to the United Nations Office at Vienna; Lin Chonfei, same; Chen Haihua, same; Huang Yu, same; Yin Chengde, Deputy Division Chief, Department of Policy Research, Foreign Ministry; Liu Xinsheng, Deputy Division Chief, Department of International Organisations, Foreign Ministry; Duan Jielong, Deputy Division Chief, Department of International Treaties and Law, Foreign Ministry; Ma Xuesong, Deputy Division Chief, Department of Interpretation and Translation, Foreign Ministry; Shen Yongxiang, Second Secretary, Department of International Organizations, Foreign Ministry; Yang Qiuju, Second Secretary, Permanent Mission of China to the United Nations Office at Vienna; Zhou Jian, same; Wang Min, Second Secretary, Permanent Mission of China to the United Nations Office at Geneva; and Xu Ke, Official, Department of International

Organizations, Foreign Ministry. See Provisional List of Attendance, Vienna, 14–25 June 1993, UN Doc. A/Conf.157/Misc.1

12. "La Chine pour des Droits de l'Homme à la Carte" ("China for Human Rights a la Carte"), AFP report of Liu Huaqiu interview, 10 June 1993 (afp-nc43).

13. Liu Wenzong, "Lun zhuquan yu renquan" ("On Sovereignty and Human Rights"), *Renmin ribao* ('People's Daily'), 13 June 1993, 5.

14. Liu Fenzhi, "Shengcun quan neihan di fazhan shi dui renquan lilun di zhongda gongxian" ("The Development of the Right to Subsistence is a Great Contribution to Human Rights Theory"), *Renmin ribao* ("People's Daily") 31 May, 6.

15. Ramon Isberto, "Dalai Lama: Visit up in the Air," *Terra Viva*, 12 June 1993, 8.

16. Iain Guest, "NGOs Face Exclusion from Crucial Drafting Committee," *Terra Viva*, 12 June 1993, 16.

17. Peter da Costa and Lucy Johnson, "NGO Infighting Gives Way to Patch-Work Compromise," *Terra Viva*, 14 June 1993, 8.

18. Author's observations at NGO plenary session, 12 June 1993, Vienna.

19. Two years after the Conference, in an intervention at the 47th Session of the UN Human Rights Sub-Commission (1995), the expert from France, Louis Joinet, stated that, "it is a secret for nobody that at Vienna, during the World Conference, there were dozens of NGOs obviously established by governments. I remember a similar case of an NGO from China. It was directed by a highly placed civil servant who today is a member of the Chinese delegation sitting just behind me. This is reality. . . ." For full text of his intervention, see "The Rights of NGOs," in *Human Rights Monitor* (September 1995) 29: 40.

20. Lucy Johnson, "False Flags: the 'Other' NGOs that Lurk behind Human Rights," *Terra Viva*, 21 June 1993, 16.

21. Ibid.; and interview with Xiao Qiang, Vienna, 24 June 1993.

22. Publicity brochure on CSHRS (*Zhongguo renquan yanjiuhui*) prepared for the Vienna Human Rights Conference. See also Information Office of the State Council of the People's Republic of China, *The Progress of Human Rights in China*, December 1995, *Beijing Review* 39 (January 1996), 25.

23. "Yi lishi di guandian fazhan di guandian kandai renquan—Zhongguo renquan yanjiuhui huizhang Zhu Muzhi zhi da jizhe wen," ("Considering Human Rights from an Historical and Developmental Perspective—Press Conference of Zhu Muzhi, Chairman of the China Society for Human Rights Studies"), *Renmin ribao* ("People's Daily"), 29 December 1993, 3.

24. The Chairman of CSHRS is Zhu Muzhi; its leading body is its Council and the Steering Committee is in charge of routine matters.

25. Liu Baopu and Xiao Qiang, "The Poor Relations," 16.

26. The author's attempts to interview its members were not successful, as members were not permitted to speak about its activities, but referred would-be interviewers to Li Baodong, who was busy with the official delegation after the NGO conference.

27. Johnson, "False Flags," 16.

28. Author's notes on NGO plenary session, Vienna, 12 June 1993.

29. Liu Baopu and Xiao Qiang, "The Poor Relations," 16–17; and interview with Xiao Qiang, Vienna, 24 June 1993.

30. Author's notes, Vienna, 14 June 1993.

31. Reuters newsclip, Vienna, 14 June 1993.

32. Jonathan Power and Ramon Isberto, "A Dying Emphasis on Human Rights," *Terra Viva*, 14 June 1993, 5.

33. M. Boutros Boutros-Ghali, "Les Droits de l'Homme: Quintessence des Valeurs par Lesquelles Nous Affirmons que Nous Sommes une Seule Communauté Humaine" ("Human Rights: Quintessence of the Values by Which We Affirm that We

Are a Single Human Community"), Communiqué de Presse, 14 June 1993, DH/
VIE/4, 1–16. Fo his subsequent assessment of the Vienna Conference, see Boutros-
Ghali, "Expanding the System: The Vienna World Conference on Human Rights
and Its Follow-up," in *The United Nations and Human Rights, 1945–1995* (New York:
Department of Public Information, United Nations, 1995), Blue Book Series, VII,
92–111.

34. Lucy Johnson and Senthil Ratnasabapathy, "China Hints at Pulling the Plug,"
Terra Viva, 16 June 1993, 1.

35. Author's notes on Dalai Lama's speech, Vienna, 15 June 1993. Text of speech
handed to author.

36. The original document, collected by the author, is the same as that in the
Beijing Review, "Proposals for Human Rights Protection and Promotion," 36 (28
June–4 July 1993), 8–11.

37. Peter da Costa and Lucy Johnson, "NGO Monitors Excluded," *Terra Viva*, 17
June 1993, 1.

38. Author's notes of proceedings, 16 June 1993, Vienna.

39. Lucy Johnson, Peter da Costa and Thalif Deen, "Europe Resorts to Tit-for-Tat
Moves," *Terra Viva*, 18 June 1993, 1.

40. Ramon Isberto and Jim Lobe, "U.S. Slams Chinese-led Go-Slow," *Terra Viva*, 18
June 1993, 1.

41. The original draft of the Vienna Declaration contained brackets around contentious wording or ideas, which then had to be resolved through the deliberations
of the Drafting Committee.

42. Isberto and Lobe, "U.S. Slams."

43. Author's notes at press conference, 17 June 1993, Vienna.

44. Isberto and Lobe, "U.S. Slams."

45. Author's notes from press conference with UN official, Vienna, 18 June 1993.

46. Thalif Deen, Lucy Johnson, Peter da Costa, "Wrangles Continue over Drafting," *Terra Viva*, 19 June 1993, 1.

47. Jim Lobe and Ramon Isberto, "No Shootout at the Vienna Corral," *Terra Viva*,
19 June 1993, 6.

48. The authors of the statement were Human Rights in China (New York Presi-
dent: Liu Qing); China Human Rights Fund (Washington, D.C., Executive Director:
Dimon Liu); Taiwan Association for Human Rights (Taipei, President: Chen Chu);
Chinese Association for Human Rights (Taipei, Executive Secretary: May J.M. Han);
Hongkong Human Rights Commission (President: Ho Hei Wah); International
Coalition for Human Rights in China (Netherlands, Co-ordinator, Josephine Chu);
Inner Mongolian Human Rights Defense League (Germany, President: Xi Hai-
ming); Chinese Students' Human Rights Organization (Australia, President: Yang
Jun); and Alliance of Taiwan Aborigines (Taipei, President: Panu Chapamumu).

49. Press conference with UN officials, Austria Centre, Vienna, 22 June 1993,
author's notes.

50. Press conference with John Shattuck, U.S. Undersecretary of State for Humanitarian Affairs, Vienna, 22 June 1993, author's notes.

51. "A Glass Half Full or Half Empty?" *Terra Viva*, 22 June 1993, 4.

52. "Cujin he baohu yi shou sunhai qunti di renquan," ("Promote and Protect
Fragile Group Rights"), Speech by Zhang Yishan at the Main Committee, *Renmin
ribao* ("People's Daily"), 22 June 1993, 6.

53. "Fazhan, minzhu yu renquan xiangfu xiangcheng" ("Development, Democracy and Human Rights Complement Each Other"), *Renmin ribao* ("People's
Daily"), 18 June 1993, 6.

54. Senthil Ratnasabapathy, "NGOs Defy UN on Tibet," *Terra Viva*, 24 June 1995,
6.

55. Thalif Deen, "Win Some, Lose Some," *Terra Viva*, 25 June 1993, 3.

56. Liu Baopu and Xiao Qiang, "The Poor Relations," 17. For a further critique of NGOs, see "Wo daibiaotuan futuanzhang tan shijie renquan dahui" ("The Deputy Leader of Our Delegation Discusses the World Conference on Human Rights"), *Renmin ribao* ('People's Daily'), 27 June 1993, 6.

57. This analysis, and that of the previous chapter, derives from Ann Kent, "China, the United Nations and the International Human Rights Regime, 1971–1994: The Learning Process" (Ph.D. diss., Australian National University, Canberra, 1996).

58. Liu Huaqiu, "Proposals for Human Rights Protection," 8–11. Liu's speech was published in full in China's English language weekly, *Beijing Review*, but, unlike the coverage of the Chinese White Paper, was given only abbreviated coverage in *Renmin ribao*, the mass circulation Party newspaper. See *Renmin ribao*, 17 June 1993, 6.

59. For text, see UN Doc. A/Conf.157/23, 12 July 1993.

60. Iain Guest, "Winners and a Preliminary Verdict," *Terra Viva*, 25 June 1993, 5.

61. Interview with a member of the UN Committee against Torture, Vienna, 24 June 1993.

62. Liu Baopu and Xiao Qiang, "The Poor Relations," 17.

63. Reed Brody, Donna Sullivan, Iain Guest, "The 1993 World Conference on Human Rights: A Critical Analysis" (Washington, D.C.: International Human Rights Law Group, June 1993), 1. For excellent and more positive assessments, see Boutros-Ghali, "Expanding the System"; and Kevin Boyle, "Stock-taking on Human Rights: The World Conference on Human Rights, Vienna 1993," *Political Studies*, Special Issue, Politics and Human Rights, 43 (1995), 79–95.

64. See Zhonghua renmin gongheguo waijiaobu waijiaoshi bianji shi ("Editorial Department, Diplomatic History, Chinese Foreign Ministry of the People's Republic of China"), ed., *Zhongguo waijiao gailan 1994* "Survey of China's Foreign Relations, 1994" (Beijing: *Shijie zhishi* chubanshe, 1995), 533.

65. See Andrew Clapham, "Creating the High Commissioner for Human Rights: The Outside Story," *European Journal of International Law* 5 (1994) 4: 564; and Boutros-Ghali, "Expanding the System," 109–11.

66. There is no doubt that the U.S. consciously used press conferences to facilitate progress in the drafting committee. At a press conference on 22 June, John Shattuck commented that the major issue was the strengthening of UN human rights mechanisms. He stated that "we will hold fire on how the delays are occurring (but) if the conference takes a turn for the worse, we will say where that comes from." From author's notes at press conference.

67. "Renquan lingyu di zhongyao huiyi" ("An Important Conference in the Field of Human Rights"), *Renmin ribao* ("People's Daily"), 27 June 1993, 6.

68. "Wo daibiaotuan futuanzhang tan shijie renquan dahui," 6.

69. "Jiaqiang guoji renquan lingyu hezuo, cujin renlei gongtong fazhan jinbu," *Renmin ribao, People's Daily* Commentator, 29 June 1993, 1; translated as "International Cooperation Strengthened and Human Development Promoted," *Beijing Review* 36 (12–18 July 1993) 28: 8–9.

70. China later claimed that, "together with other countries, China [had] resolutely resisted and opposed the rude and unreasonable attitudes and actions of a small number of Western countries that provoked confrontation and forced their views on others, trying to hinder the smooth progress of the conference." See State Council, *The Progress of Human Rights in China*, 27.

71. The 1996 White Paper described China's overall contribution to all forums leading up to the Conference similarly: "With an active and constructive attitude China took part in the World Conference on Human Rights held in Vienna in 1993. From beginning to end, China participated in the preparatory work of the conference, attended the four preparatory meetings held by the United Nations and

served as a vice-chairman of the First Preparatory Meeting, the Asian Regional Preparatory Meeting and the World Conference on Human Rights, thus playing an important role in the conference's preparatory success." See State Council, *The Progress of Human Rights in China*, 27.

72. "International Cooperation Strengthened," 9.

73. Author's notes taken at the session, Geneva, 6 August 1993; and UN Communiqué de Presse HR/3474, Geneva, 6 August 1993 (matin), 4.

74. Zhu Muzhi, "Yi lishi di guandian," 3.

Chapter 7. After Vienna

1. Opinion of Philip Alston, 10 November 1997.

2. These obligations are less stringent than those of ILO Convention No. 87, in which Article 2 requires that the workers' and employers' right to establish and join organizations of their own choosing is subject "only to the rules of the organization" and must be "without previous authorization," while Article 3 states that workers' and employers' right to organize their administration obliges public authorities to "refrain from any interference which would restrict this right or impede its lawful exercise." They contain no qualifications in respect of the interests of national security, public order or protection of the rights of others. On the other hand, Convention No. 87 does not include the right to strike. Ratification of the ICESCR by China will inevitably bring it under pressure from the UN Committee on Economic, Social and Cultural Rights to comply with a substantial corpus of industrial rights.

3. Justin Jin, "China Sees Jobless Swelling by 3.5 Million in 1998," Reuters "China" News, 8 March 1998.

4. Xinhua News Agency, "UN Envoy Signs Rights Covenant, Says Parliament Deliberating Ratification," 5 October 1998, BBC Summary of World Broadcasts, Reuters China News, 7 October 1998.

5. International Covenant on Civil and Political Rights, UN Doc. A/RES/2/200 a (XXI), 16 December 1966, in *The United Nations and Human Rights, 1945–1995* ed. United Nations (New York: Department of Public Information, United Nations, 1995), at 235–239.

6. Vivien Pik-Kwan Chan, "Beijing's Qualms on Treaty Confirmed," *South China Morning Post*, 4 October 1998, Reuters China News, 4 October 1998.

7. See United Nations, *Status of and Reservations to the International Covenant on Civil and Political Rights*, UN Doc. ST/LEG/SER.E/15 (1997), at 130. I am grateful to Bruno Simma for bringing U.S. reservations to my attention at a seminar on the United Nations and international law, Helsinki University, Finland, 25 August 1998.

8. See, for instance, "Statement by the Chairperson on Behalf of the Human Rights Committee Relating to the Consideration of the Part of the Fourth Periodic Report of the United Kingdom Relating to Hong Kong," 20 October 1995, in UN Human Rights Committee, "Consideration of Reports Submitted by States Parties Under Article 40 of the Covenant," UN Doc. CCPR/C/79/Add. 57, 9 November 1995, at 6; "State Council Official Questions Overriding Status of Hong Kong's Bill of Rights," Zhongguo xinwenshe, 27 October 1995, in Reuters China News, 3 November 1995; "Hong Kong Government Responds to China's Attack on Bill of Rights," *Ta Kung Pao*, 28 October 1995, in Reuters "China" News, 3 November 1995; and Francisco José Aguilar Urbina, Chairman, Human Rights Committee, "Memorandum on the Report on the Fifty-fifth Session of the Human Rights Committee to the Chairpersons of Each of the United Nations Human Rights Treaty Bodies," 30 November 1995, at 1.

9. For instance, Christine Loh, "One Country: Two Human Rights Reports," *China*

Rights Forum (Winter 1997–8), 14–15; U.S. Department of State, "Hong Kong," in *Country Reports on Human Rights Practices for 1997* (Washington DC: U.S. Government Printing Office, January 1998), 10; and Wang Huiling, "Hongkong Activists Laud Beijing's Move on Human Rights Reports," *Straits Times* 27 December 1997, Reuters "China" News, 27 December 1997.

10. See report in China News Digest (CND), 16 September 1998.

11. See, for instance, Steven Mufson, "Chinese Harassment Angers Women," *The Washington Post*, reprinted in *Guardian Weekly*, 10 September 1995, 18; and Simon Jenkins, "Beijing Shanghais UN Talkfest," *The Times*, reprinted in *The Australian*, 11 September 1995, 11.

12. UN Commission on Human Rights, Report Submitted by the Working Group on Arbitrary Detention, Addendum, *Visit to the People's Republic of China* (hereafter UNCHR, *Visit to the PRC*), UN Doc. E/CN.4/1998/44/Add.2 (Geneva, 22 December 1997), paras. 6–11, at 2–3.

13. See Xinhua News Agency, "China on Reservations to Treaties of Human Rights," 29 October 1998, Reuters China News, 29 October 1998; and Xinhua News Agency, "China on Monitoring Mechanisms of Human Rights Instruments," 29 October 1998, Reuters China News, 29 October 1998.

14. AFP Report in China News Digest, 3 August 1997.

15. Xinhua News Agency, "Foreign Minister and Algerian Counterpart Hold Talks, Agree on Human Rights," 11 January 1998, Reuters "China" News Service, 13 January 1998, 1–2.

16. See, for instance, Xinhua News Agency, "Official Says 'World-Renowned Progress' Achieved in Human Rights," 21 October 1998, Reuters China News, 23 October 1998.

17. See Human Rights in China, *From Principle to Pragmatism: Can Dialogue Improve China's Human Rights Situation?* (New York, 1998), available on http://www.hrichina.org/ ; and "From Principle to Pragmatism," *China Rights Forum* (summer 1998): 12.

18. This law and the Provisional Regulations on the Registration and Management of People-Organized Non-Enterprise Units was drafted by the Chinese Ministry of Civil Affairs with the assistance of the International Center for Not-for-Profit Law (ICNL) in Washington D.C. and the U.S.-based Asia Foundation. See Human Rights in China, *Bound and Gagged: Freedom of Association in China Further Curtailed Under New Regulations* (New York, 13 November 1998), 7.

19. James Pringle, "Tiananmen Taboo Broken by Broadcast," 29 June 1998, *The Times*, Reuters China News, 29 June 1998.

20. UN Commission on Human Rights, *Building a Partnership for Human Rights*, Report of the UN High Commissioner for Human Rights, 24 February 1997, UN Doc. E/CN.4/1997/98, at 7.

21. "Qian Qichen Urges Further Promotion of International Human Rights," 20 October 1998, text in http://www.human rights-china.org.

22. See also Pitman Potter, "Riding the Tiger: Legitimacy and Legal Culture in Post-Mao China," *The China Quarterly* (June 1994) 138: 358; Stanley Lubman, "Introduction: The Future of Chinese Law," Special Issue: China's Legal Reforms, *The China Quarterly* (March 1995) 141: 1–21; and Ann Kent, *Between Freedom and Subsistence: China and Human Rights* (Hong Kong: Oxford University Press, 1993 and 1995), 193.

23. Xinhua News Agency, "Chinese Lawmakers Tighten Supervision of Government," 23 February 1998, Reuters "China" News, 23 February 1998.

24. Jiang Zemin, "Hold High the Great Banner of Deng Xiaoping Theory for an All-Round Advancement of the Cause of Building Socialism with Chinese Characteristics into the 21st Century," Report Delivered at the 15th National Congress of

the Communist Party of China on 12 September 1997, *Beijing Review* 40 (6–12 October 1997), 40: 24. Author's emphasis.

25. See "Jianchi shehuizhuyi chuji jieduan jiben luxian shi women shiye shengli qianjin zui kekao baozheng" ("Promoting the Basic Line of the Primary Stage of Socialism is the Most Reliable Guarantee for the Victorious Advancement of Our Cause"), *Renmin ribao* ("People's Daily"), 13 September 1997, 2.

26. For Western sources, see Donald C. Clarke and James V. Feinerman, "Antagonistic Contradictions: Criminal Law and Human Rights in China," *The China Quarterly* 141 (March 1995): 135–154; Amnesty International, *No One Is Safe: Political Repression and Abuse of Power in the 1990s* (London, March 1996); Human Rights Watch/Asia, "China: The Cost of Putting Business First," 8 (July 1996), 7: 21–23; Lawyers' Committee for Human Rights (Jonathan Hecht), *Opening to Reform? An Analysis of China's Revised Criminal Procedure Law* (New York, October 1996); Amnesty International, *People's Republic of China: Law Reform and Human Rights* (London, March 1997); Human Rights in China, "China: Whose Security? State Security in China's New Criminal Code" 9 (April 1997): 4; Isabelle Thireau and Hua Linshan, "Legal Disputes and the Debate about Legitimate Norms," in *China Review 1997*, eds. Maurice Brosseau, Kuan Hsin-chi and Y.Y. Kueh (Hong Kong: Chinese University of Hong Kong Press, 1987), 349–378; Carol Jones, "The Criminal Justice System of the People's Republic of China," unpublished paper; H. L. Fu, "Criminal Defence in China: The Possible Impact of the 1996 Criminal Procedural Law Reform," *The China Quarterly* 153 (March 1998), 31–48; Human Rights Watch, "China and Tibet," *Human Rights Watch World Report 1998* (New York, 1998), 170–80; U.S. Department of State, "China," in *Country Report on Human Rights Practices for 1997* (Washington, D.C., 30 January 1998), http://www.state.gov/html; and UNCHR, *Visit to the PRC*. For Chinese material see, for example, Fang Chongyi et al., *Xingshi susong faxue yanjiu zongshu yu pingjia* ("Survey and Evaluation of Studies on the Jurisprudence of Criminal Justice") (Beijing: Zhongguo zhengfa daxue chubanshe, 1991); Yu Zhaoyuan, ed., *Zhongguo susong faxue* ("The Jurisprudence of China's Criminal Procedure") (Beijing: Zhongguo fazhi chubanshe, 1994); Cui Min, *Zhongguo xingshi susongfa de xin fazhan* ("The New Development of China's Criminal Procedure Law") (Beijing: Chinese People's Public Security University Press, 1996); Information Office of the State Council of the People's Republic of China, *The Progress of Human Rights in China*, reprinted in *Beijing Review*, Special Issue, 39 (January 1996), 4–29; and Information Office of the State Council, People's Republic of China, *Progress in China's Human Rights Cause in 1996* (31 March 1997), http://www.china-embassy.org/Press/human.htm.

27. For best example of analyses of these laws, see LCHR (Hecht), *Opening to Reform?*; and Amnesty International, *Law Reform and Human Rights*. I have benefited from discussion of these questions with Carol Jones, Carol Heimer and Tom Tyler and from the scholarly exchange at the conference, "Criminal Justice in the People's Republic of China," 28 October 1997, School of Law and Legal Studies, La Trobe University. Particularly useful were Jing Dali, "The Criminal Law Revision in China"; Huang Jinlong, "The Reform of China's Criminal Procedure System"; Ruan Qilin, "Zhongguo xin xingfa zhong di zui yu fei zui wenti" ("Crime and No-Crime in China's New Criminal Law"); and Sarah Biddulph, "The Impact of Legal Refom on Criminal Coercive Powers."

28. Biddulph, "The Impact of Legal Reform." Cf. Amnesty International, which sees these as "two opposite tendencies." See Amnesty International, *Law Reform and Human Rights*, 1.

29. Biddulph, "The Impact of Legal Reform."

30. Thus, the 1997 White Paper stated that: "China has cracked down on serious criminal offences in accordance with the law, and earnestly guaranteed the people's

human rights and safety of lives and property. . . . The severe crackdown on crimes has safeguarded social stability and the human rights of the people all over the country, and won the heartfelt support of the general public." See *Progress in China's Human Rights*, 5. Similarly, the Chief Procurator of the Hunan Provincial People's Procuratorate, Zhang Shuhai, stated that "to mete out punishment for crimes is also to protect the people." See also Xinhua News Agency, "New Criminal Law Enshrines Rule of Law," 14 March 1997, Reuters China News, 19 March 1997, 4.

31. Jones, "The Criminal Justice System," 77.

32. These came into effect on 1 July 1995. For texts, see *BBC Summary of World Broadcasts*, SWB/FE/2259 and SWB/FE/2261.

33. For analysis of the rights implications of this law, see Lawyers Committee for Human Rights, *Lawyers in China: Obstacles to Independence and the Defense of Rights* (New York, March 1998). See excerpts in "Lawyers: No Longer Servants of the State But Not Quite Independent," *China Rights Forum* (summer 1998), 32–37.

34. See analysis of amended Criminal Law below. Interestingly, the UN Working Group on Arbitrary Detention did not mention these three laws in its report.

35. Anthony R. Dicks, "Compartmentalized Law and Judicial Restraint: An Inductive View of Some Jurisdictional Barriers to Reform," *China Quarterly* (March 1995) 141: 84.

36. UNCHR, *Visit to the PRC*, para. 27, at 6.

37. LCHR (Hecht), *Opening to Reform?* 19.

38. Cited in *China Daily*, 27 February 1996, Reuters China News, 1 March 1996.

39. Part 2, Chapter 2, Arts. 92 and 96, Amended PRC Criminal Procedure Law, 17 March 1996, text in Xinhua News Agency, 23 March 1996, Reuters China News, 19 April 1996.

40. Other provisions included Art. 32, which provided that from the day public prosecution had been initiated, the accused had the right to ask defenders to defend him. Art. 203 of the amended law provided that parties and the legal representatives could present petitions regarding judgments that had already become legally effective, and, in certain specified cases, such as proof of untrue or inadequate evidence, new evidence or actual error, that the People's Court should hold a retrial. Under Art. 223, the criminal also had the right to present a petition while punishment was being executed, whereupon the matter should be handled by a People's Procuratorate or People's Court. Under Art. 200, death sentences by an Intermediate Court which were not appealed against were to be reviewed by a higher People's Court. Execution of death sentences should be publicly announced but should not take place in public view: on the other hand, death sentences were now to be executed by injection as well as by shooting (Art. 212).

41. Human Rights Watch/Asia, "The Cost of Putting Business First," 21.

42. UNCHR, *Visit to the PRC*, paras. 54–62, at 10–11.

43. LCHR (Hecht), *Opening to Reform?* 79–80, author's emphasis.

44. AI, *Law Reform and Human Rights*, 5.

45. US Department of State, *China Country Report for 1997*, 7. LCHR (Hecht), *Opening to Reform?* suggests amendments to the CPL which could bridge that gap. On 19 January an implementation rule, "Rules on Several Problems in the Implementation of the CPL" was passed. Consisting of 14 Chapters and 48 Articles, its purpose was to clarify ambiguities, standardize practice and achieve consensus between the relevant bodies. In March 1997, the Vice-President of Beijing Higher People's Court, Chen Chunlong, pointed out that, because it was discovered that trial time had become much longer under the new procedures, to avoid a backlog of cases, a simplified set of rules had been introduced to deal with basic cases. Thus, "if a thief admits his wrongdoing and the amount involved is not large, the prosecutor and defense lawyer could choose not to appear in court." Agatha Ngai, "Judicial System

'Independent of' Communist Party," *South China Morning Post*, 6 March 1997, China "Reuters" News, 8 March 1997.

46. Amnesty International, *No One is Safe*, 79.

47. LCHR (Hecht), *Opening to Reform?*, 63.

48. See Jones, "The Criminal Justice System," 43–44.

49. AI, *Law Reform and Human Rights*, 14.

50. LCHR (Hecht), *Opening to Reform?*, 69.

51. AI, "United Nations Committee against Torture," 3 May 1996, ASA 17/56/96, 9.

52. According to Article 234, whoever intentionally causes a person's serious injury is sentenced to not less than three years and not more than ten years of fixed-term imprisonment; if he "causes a person's death or causes a person's serious deformity by badly injuring him with particularly ruthless means, he is to be sentenced to not less than 10 years of fixed-term imprisonment, life imprisonment, or death." The PRC Criminal Law Amended by the 5th Session, 8th NPC, *FBIS Daily Report*, 14 March 1997. FBIS-CHI-97-056 (17 March 1997).

53. Fang Shirong, "Xingzheng susong shou'an zhong dui gongan jiguan xingshi zhencha xingwei di shibie": ("How to Distinguish An Act of Criminal Investigation by Public Security Organs When Accepting Administrative Lawsuits"), *Faxue* ("Legal Science"), (1994), 8:29, cited in Clarke and Feinerman, "Criminal Law and Human Rights," 146.

54. AI, "The United Nations Committee against Torture," 9.

55. Article 4 (7), "Regulations Governing the Supervision of Public Security Organs," text in Xinhua News Agency, 25 June 1997, Reuters "China" News, 5 July 1997.

56. LCHR (Hecht), *Opening to Reform?*, 61–62.

57. "New Criminal Law Enshrines Rule of Law," 2.

58. UNCHR, *Visit to the PRC*, para. 42, at 9.

59. "Police Geared to Enforce New Criminal Code," *Hong Kong Standard*, 1 October 1997, Reuters "China" News, 1 October 1997.

60. Zhao Bingzhu and Bao Suixian, "Woguo xingfa gaige ruogan redian wenti lunlue" ("Discussion of Several Hot Topics in China's Criminal Law Reforms"), *Hebei faxue* ("Hebei Jurisprudence") (1993), 4, cited in Human Rights in China/Human Rights Watch/Asia, "Whose Security?," 9.

61. "Legislature Official Discusses Defence and Criminal Laws," Zhongguo xinwenshe News Agency, 4 March 1997, Reuters "China" News, 8 March 1997.

62. Human Rights in China/Human Rights Watch, "Whose Security?," 13.

63. UNCHR, *Visit to the PRC*, paras. 43–48, at 9.

64. "Between Crime and Error," *China Labour Bulletin* (September–October 1997) 38:3.

65. Biddulph, "The Impact of Legal Reform."

66. UNCHR, *Visit to the PRC*, para 83, at 16. This report contains an excellent discussion of the administration of this sanction.

67. Revised CPL, Art 60, cited in LCHR (Hecht), *Opening to Reform?*, 26.

68. Jones, "The Criminal Justice System," 9.

69. UNCHR, *Visit to the PRC*, para. 83, at 16.

70. "Re-education through Labor Centres Offer "New Lease of Life'," Xinhua News Agency, 2 August 1997, BBC Monitoring Summary of World Broadcasts, Reuters "China" News, 5 August 1997.

71. Wang Jinfu, "What is the Re-education through Labor System?," Xinhua News Agency, 2 August 1997, Reuters "China" News, 5 August 1997, 2; and "*Laojiao* Camps to Remain in China," CND citing *Legal Daily*, 3 July 1997. The *Legal Daily* stated that "re-education through labor . . . can only be strengthened, not weakened."

72. Clarke and Feinerman, "Criminal Law and Human Rights," 142–143.

73. According to Art. 38 of the Administrative Supervision Law, when handling appeals by units or individuals who do not agree with the administrative punishment made by their administrative units, the supervisory organizations may recommend changes or cancellation of the original decisions if they are found inappropriate after investigation. A further request to re-examine the case may be made within 30 days after receiving notice of the supervisory organization's decision. However, during the period of re-examination and reinvestigation, the implementation of the original decision will not be stayed. The decisions made by the higher supervisory organization after re-examination are final. See The Administrative Supervision Law of the People's Republic of China, adopted on 9 May 1997 at the 25th Session of the Eighth National People's Congress Standing Committee, Xinhua News Agency, 9 May 1997, Reuters "China" News, 16 May 1997.

74. Jones, "The Criminal Justice System," 18–19.

75. Amnesty International figures, cited in "Liberal China Fails to Win Amnesty Approval," *The Australian*, 4 March 1998, Reuters "China News," 4 March 1998.

76. AI, *Law Reform and Human Rights*, 21–24.

77. UNCHR, *Visit to the PRC*, 19–20.

78. Clarke and Feinerman, "Criminal Law and Human Rights," 153.

79. LCHR (Hecht), *Opening to Reform?*, 80 f. 305.

80. Peng Shujie, "Chinese Legal System Gradually Adopts International Practices," *Beijing Review* 39 (3–9 June 1996) 23:15.

81. Helena Kennedy, QC, "China Bows to Legal Evolution," *Sunday Times*, 10 November 1998, www.sunday-times.co.uk/news/pages/, 1.

82. Cited in "New Criminal Law Enshrines Rule of Law," 5.

83. Peng Shujie, "Chinese Legal System," 16.

84. Minxin Pei, "Is China Democratizing?" *Foreign Affairs* 77 (Jan.–Feb. 1998), 1: 76.

85. Xinhua News Agency, "China Plans Comprehensive Reform of Judicial System," 2 December 1998, Reuters "China" News, 2 December 1998.

86. Xinhua News Agency, "Justice Minister Says Foreign Law Firms Promote Reform," 20 February 1998, BBC Summary of World Broadcasts, Reuters "China" News Service, 26 February 1998.

87. Murray Scot Tanner, "How a Bill Becomes a Law in China: Stages and Processes in Lawmaking," *China Quarterly* (March 1995), 141: 60.

88. Kennedy, "China Bows to Legal Evolution," 2.

89. Tom R. Tyler, *Why People Obey the Law* (New Haven: Yale University Press, 1990), 161.

90. Xinhua News Agency, "Chinese Lawmakers." Similarly, an NPC deputy acknowledged that the failure of people to abide by the law, the laxity of law enforcement and the effectiveness of supervision were pressing problems. See "NPC Deputies Hail Progress in Law-making, Supervision," China Business Information Network, Reuters "China" News, 13 March 1998.

91. Tyler, *Why People Obey the Law*, 163–65.

92. Thireau and Hua Linshan, "Legal Disputes." The authors argue that the traditional perception that laws are first of all a government instrument reinforces political reasons to account for the subordinate part played in legal settlements by legal provisions and procedures in China.

93. Xinhua News Agency, "Qiao Shi Speaks at Closing Session of NPC," 14 March 1997, BBC Monitoring Summary of World Broadcasts, Reuters "China" News, 17 March 1997.

94. Hence, the telling comment by a Chinese scholar, after listening to a Western

scholar in Beijing listing important changes in China's criminal codes: "They still can do anything they want." See John Pomfret, "American Justice Goes on Trial in China," *Washington Post* in the *Guardian Weekly*, 15 November 1998, 19.

95. Fu, "Criminal Defence in China," 48.

96. Clarke and Feinerman, "Antagonistic Contradictions," 144.

97. Human Rights Watch/Asia, "The Cost of Putting Business First," 23.

98. "China's Top Judge Calling for Continued Crack-Down on Crimes," Xinhua News Agency, 10 March 1998, Reuters "China" News, 10 March 1998. His position was supported by Zhang Siqing, Procurator-General of the Supreme People's Procuratorate, who stated that procuratorial bodies at all levels had always taken it as a major task to maintain stability and had closely cooperated with public and state security bodies, courts and departments of justice and administration to severely crack down on crimes seriously harming public security. "Chinese Procuratorial Bodies Play Active Role," Xinhua News Agency, 10 March 1998, Reuters "China" News, 10 March 1998. Thus, he said, "In the past five years, procuratorial bodies have examined 2,004,785 arrest warrant applications involving 3,344,709 people submitted by the public and state security departments, and issued 1,799,494 arrest warrants involving 2,893,771 people." They had also put forth 12,806 suggestions for the courts to correct law violations in judicial proceedings and contested judgements in 12,288 cases they believed to be wrong.

99. Kent, *Between Freedom and Subsistence*, 206–7.

100. "China," in U.S. Department of State, *Country Reports on Human Rights Practices for 1995*, Report Submitted to the Committee on Foreign Relations, U.S. Senate and the Committee on International Relations, U.S. House of Representatives (Washington, D.C.: U.S. Government Printing Office, 1996), 2.

101. Amnesty International, *China, No One Is Safe: Political Repression and Abuse of Power in the 1990s* (ASA 17/01/96) (London: Amnesty International, March 1996).

102. U.S. Department of State, "China," 1998, 8.

103. Liu Qing, "Devoted to Democracy and Human Rights: the Development of the Dissident Movement," *China Rights Forum* (Winter 1995), 5. See also positive assessment of personal freedom in Human Rights in China, *Bound and Gagged*, 2.

104. Liz Sly, "China Arrests Reformists as People's Congress Convenes," *Chicago Tribune*, 5 March 1998, Reuters "China" News, 5 March 1998; "Seventeen Chinese Dissidents Send Open Letter to NPC," AFP report, China News Digest, 27 March 1998; and "Dissident Urges MPs to Discuss Closure of Labor Camps," Radio TV Hong Kong, 24 February 1998, BBC Monitoring Summary of World Broadcasts, 26 February 1998.

105. Scott Hillis, "China Dissident Says Free Labour Unions Essential," Reuters News Service, 1 February 1998. Another dissident, Qin Yongmin, also pressed for free labor unions. He was arrested in late March 1998.

106. For details of numerous criticisms of the official line in 1997, including calls for a review of the 1989 suppression of the Democracy Movement, see U.S. Department of State, "China," 12–13.

107. Christopher Lockwood, "Party's Over, Says Beijing Insider," *Daily Telegraph*, 14 March 1998, Reuters "China" News, 14 March 1998.

108. Matt Forney, "Beijing Spring," *Far Eastern Economic Review* 161 (2 April 1998) 14: 20.

109. Andrew Walder, "Does China Face an Unstable Future?" in *China Review 1997*, ed. Brosseau, Kuan, Kueh, 345. For discussion of this political phenomenon, see Wei Jingsheng in "China News Digest Interview with Wei Jingsheng," CND, 15 January 1998–7 February 1998.

110. Peter Seidletz, "Li Peng Clearly Rejects Western Democracy," *Handsblatt*, 1 December 1998, Reuters China News, 2 December 1998.

111. See Conor O'Clery, "Fears of Political Instability Behind Detention of Democracy Activists'," *Irish Times*, 2 November 1998, Reuters China News, 2 November 1998; "Chinese Dissidents' New Bid to Form Party," *The Independent*, 25 October 1998, China Reuters News, 25 October 1998; and "Dissident Detained for Reading Civil Rights Covenant," Central News Agency (Taiwan), 19 October 1998, Reuters China News, 19 October 1998.

112. Mark O'Neill, "200 Monks and Nuns 'Jailed in Tibet'," *South China Morning Post*, 10 September 1997, Reuters "China" News, 10 September 1998. See also Amnesty International, *No One Is Safe*; Tibet Information Network and Human Rights Watch/Asia, *Cutting Off the Serpent's Head: Tightening Control in Tibet, 1994–1995* (New York: Human Rights Watch, March 1996); and Melvyn C. Goldstein, "The Dalai Lama's Dilemma," *Foreign Affairs* 77 (Jan.–Feb. 1998), 1:83–97.

113. Reed Brody, "It's Not Too Late to Save Tibet from Obliteration," *Asian Wall Street Journal*, 6 March 1998.

114. See Jasper Becker, "Police Crackdown in Xinjiang 'Succeeds'," *South China Morning Post*, 13 March 1998, Reuters "China" News, 13 March 1998; and "Beijing Rattled by Separatists," *The Times*, 13 March 1998, Reuters "China" News, 13 March 1998.

115. Thus, immediately after the delinkage, the long-delayed trials of the "Beijing Sixteen," dissidents accused of organizing revolutionary groups, had begun. At least nineteen activists had been arrested for peaceful dissent between March and December 1994, and many of them had subsequently "disappeared." By 1995, all but three of nine signatories of a "Peace Charter" written by democracy advocates in 1993 were in jail or exile. Two leaders from the 1989 movement, Chen Ziming and Wang Dan, earlier released from prison, were back in detention, while other critics lived under virtual house arrest. See *Human Rights Watch World Report 1995: Events of 1994* (New York, Human Rights Watch, 1995), 142–143.

116. These broadened the basis for restricting peaceful political dissent and freedom of religion, expression, association and assembly, by heavily penalizing the "cooperation" of Chinese activists with "hostile" non-governmental organizations outside China. Speech, including rumors, or writing harmful to state security, were defined as "sabotage." See ibid. 143–44. See also Steven Mufson, "Chinese Dissident Gets Harsh Jail Sentence," *Washington Post*, reprinted in *Guardian Weekly*, 24 December 1996, 11.

117. See reports in Jonathan Mirsky, "Lawyers Race to Defend Wei," *The Australian*, 12 December 1995, 11; Benjamin Kang Lim, "China Dissident Wei's Brother to Dispute Evidence," Reuters China News, 17 December 1995; Jasper Becker, "Wei Was 'Ready for Verdict'," *South China Morning Post*, 15 December 1995, Reuters China News, 17 December 1995; and "Dissident Wei Jingsheng's Brother Describes Trial," *Ming Pao*, in Chinese, 14 December 1995, Reuters China News, 17 December 1995.

118. HRIC and HRW/Asia, "Whose Security?" 27.

119. Simon Beck and Jasper Becker, "Wei Term Forces Clinton to Act Against China at UN," *South China Morning Post*, 15 December 1995, Reuters China News, 17 December 1995.

120. Apart from the *quid pro quo* described above, China had suspended bilateral human rights dialogues for the remainder of 1995 as a result of its pique at some governments' support for the China resolution at the 1995 session of the UN Commission on Human Rights. See Department of State, "China," 26. The White Paper, which focused equally on economic-social rights and civil-political rights, was a more sophisticated, substantial, and credible document than the first. Like the first, it emphasized *shengcun quan* (now more accurately translated as "the right to existence") and related economic and social rights, but this time failed to identify it as a

"basic" or prior right. It also placed emphasis on China's progress in legislation for the protection of citizens' and workers' rights, its progress in the promotion of human rights education, and its extensive international human rights activities. It was divided into ten sections: the right to existence and development; civil and political rights; judicial work safeguarding human rights; the right to work and workers' rights; the right to education; the rights of women and children; the rights of ethnic minorities; the rights of the disabled; the study and popularization of human rights; and the promotion of international human rights activities. China also claimed success in its activities in the UN Human Rights Commission, the Sub-Commission, in its activities in the UN Commission on the Elimination of Discrimination against Women and its attendance at UN conferences on human rights: "In the aforementioned bodies and sessions, China always conscientiously performs its duty, actively participates in the examination and discussion of subjects on human rights, and elaborates its views, making contributions to constantly enriching the connotation of human rights and promoting universal respect for human rights." See Information Office of the State Council of the People's Republic of China, *The Progress of Human Rights in China*, December 1995, *Beijing Review*, Special Issue 39 (January 1996), 27. Attached to the Special Issue was an article: Chen Hanchang and Yin Qingyan, "Historical Jump of Tibetans' Human Rights," 30–32.

121. See Huang Wei, "Continued Improvement in Chinese Legislation," *Beijing Review* 39 (8–14 January 1996) 2: 22–24; "On the Issue of Human Rights: an Interview with Prof. Liu Wenzong," *Beijing Review* 39 (4–10 March 1996), 18–20; Gu Chunde, "Theoretical Research on China's Human Rights," in ibid. 20–21; "Status of China's Economic and Social Development in the World," ibid. 22–23; Jiang Wandi, "Grass Roots Democracy" 39 (March 11–17 1996) 11: 11–14; and Ren Yanshi, "A Comparison of Human Rights in China with Those in the United States," *Beijing Review* 39 (April 1–7, 1996) 14: 10–15.

122. Amnesty International, Media Briefing on "China: United Nations Committee against Torture" ASA 17/56/96 (3 May 1996), 1. Human Rights in China has stated that "torture is still a systemic problem and is often instigated by the authorities," in Human Rights in China, *Words Without Substance*, 1; and in 1998 Human Rights Watch reported "consistent reports of torture" in China's prisons. See *Human Rights Watch World Report 1998*, 171.

123. Information Office, *The Progress of Human Rights*, 14.

124. AI, *No One Is Safe*, 81. For details of torture in China and its victims, see 31–97.

125. See James D. Seymour and Richard Anderson, *New Ghosts, Old Ghosts: Prisons and Labor Reform Camps in China* (Armonk, N.Y.: M. E. Sharpe, 1998), 177–80. See also Harry Wu, *Laogai — The Chinese Gulag* (Boulder, Colo.: Westview Press, 1992).

126. Brody, "It's Not Too Late," 1.

127. "World Leader in Executions," *The Economist*, 30 August 1997, Reuters "China" News, 2 September 1997. Statistics compiled from official Chinese news media by Amnesty International had recorded 1,313 executions and more than 500 suspended death sentences in the first half of 1995, as compared with the figures of 2,050 executions and some 700 suspended death sentences in 1994. Francis Deron, "Executions on the Rise Again in China," *Le Monde* in *The Guardian Weekly*, 21 January 1996, 20.

128. "World Leader in Executions."

129. U.S. Department of State, "China," 10.

130. Deron, "Executions, 20."

131. "World Leader in Executions," 1. Those targeted included two men executed for stealing badminton racquets; a Sichuan farmer who sold the head of a stone Buddha he found for 300 yuan ($36); and a man accused of hooliganism for sticking thorns and pointed sticks into the backsides of passing female cyclists.

132. "Justice Minister, Legal Chief Comment on Death Penalty, Rights," Zhong-guo xinwenshe News Agency, 16 September 1997, Reuters "China" News, 18 September 1997.

133. "World Leader in Executions," 1.

134. For figures see Daniel Kwan, "Economist Predicts 28% Jobless Figure by 2000," *South China Morning Post*, 16 March 1998, Reuters "China" News, 16 March 1998; and Matt Frei, "Beijing Braces for Jobs Catastrophe," *Sunday Telegraph*, 1 February 1998, Reuters "China" News, 1 February 1998.

135. Xinhua News Agency, "Labour Disputes in Guangdong Affecting Social Stability," 14 October 1998, Reuters China News, 17 October 1998.

136. ICFTU Press Release, 9 April 1997, reprinted in *China Labour Bulletin* (March–April 1997) 35:9. See also edited extracts in "Search and Destroy," *China Labour Bulletin* (May–June 1997) 36:15–16.

137. "China Premier Says Reforms Will Help Workers," citing *China Daily* of 28 March 1998, Reuters "China" News, 28 March 1998.

138. "China Hit by Soaring Number of Labour Disputes," Reuters "China" News, 29 August 1997, citing *China Market Economic News*, 26 August 1997. According to the Labor Ministry, the annual growth rate of reported disputes had been increasing continuously since 1992, with the annual growth at around 50 percent, except for 1995 when disputes increased by 73%. Collective disputes were up 42 percent in the same period and the number of people involved in disputes rose by 35 percent. On top of the 44,704 cases seen by arbitrators, a further 100,000 had not been settled.

139. "Workers' Grievances Aired as Lay-offs Become Hot Topic," *South China Morning Post*, 8 March 1998, Reuters "China" News, 8 March 1998.

140. "Organizing — Against All Odds," *China Labour Bulletin* (January–February 1998), 40:2.

141. For statistic, see International Labour Office, *World Labour Report: Industrial Relations, Democracy and Social Stability, 1997–1998* (Geneva, 1998), 248. For national workers' survey, see *Workers Daily* abstracted in *Sinofile*, 8 August 1998, Reuters China News, 11 August 1998.

142. Han Dongfang, "Letter to Qiao Shi," *China Labour Bulletin* (January–February 1998) 40: 11–12.

143. "Unions Announce Initiative to Help Unemployed," Xinhua News Agency, 6 November 1997, Reuters "China" News, 13 November 1997.

144. Yang Xingfu, Vice-President of the ACFTU, added that "if more than 50% of the enterprise workers congress representatives decide that an official is unfit for his job, he should be removed from his post." See "Trade Unions Urged to Rely Entirely on Workers," Xinhua News Agency, 31 August 1997, Reuters "China" News, 3 September 1997; and *China Daily*, cited in China News Digest, 25 December 1997.

145. Xinhua News Agency, "President Hopes Unions Will Play Greater Role in Uniting Party and Workers," 26 October 1998, Reuters China News, 27 October 1998.

146. At his first Press Conference as Premier, Zhu Rongji noted that workers have their democratic rights to elect the heads of enterprises and that democratic elections have been carried out in both basic rural areas and in industrial enterprises. See "Chinese Premier on Democratic Election," Xinhua News Agency 19 March 1998, Reuters "China" News, 19 March 1998.

147. Felix Chan, "Employers Defended over Labour Law Compliance," *South China Morning Post*, 4 November 1997, Reuters "China" News, 4 November 1997.

148. Sharon Cheung, "Repeal of Laws Backed," *South China Morning Post*, 2 November 1997, Reuters "China" News, 2 November 1997.

149. Translated excerpts of *70 Years of the All-China Federation of Trade Unions* (China's Workers Press, July 1995), *China Labour Bulletin* (May–June 1997) 36: 2–16.

150. For best evaluation, see Minxin Pei, "Is China Democratizing?"

151. Seidlitz, "Li Peng Clearly Rejects Western Democracy."

152. Judy Polumbaum, "In the Name of Stability: Restrictions on the Rights of Assembly in the People's Republic of China," *The Australian Journal of Chinese Affairs*, (July 1991), 26:43–64.

153. "Hong Kong Legislature Amends Bill of Rights," Reuters "China" News, 25 February 1998. For different views of the extent to which China has honored its pledge to preserve Hong Kong's political and legal system a year after reversion, see Chris Yeung, ed., *Hong Kong China: The Red Dawn* (Sydney: Prentice Hall, 1998). See also former Governor Chris Patten's praise cited in Chris Yeung, "Last Governor's Credit to Beijing; I Sympathise with Tung, Says Patten," *South China Morning Post*, 10 October 1998, Reuters China News, 29 October 1998.

154. Human Rights Watch, "Rights Group Condemns Move to Put Government above the Law," 7 April 1998, citing Sidney Jones.

155. Kent, *Between Freedom and Subsistence*, 209.

156. Cited in Joseph Fewsmith, "Chinese Politics on the Eve of the 15th Party Congress," in *China Review 1997*, ed. Brosseau, Kuan and Kueh, 8. These views drew from a similar perspective in Deng Xiaoping, "On Reform of Party and State Leadership System" in August 1980.

157. Minxin Pei, "Is China Democratizing?," 69.

158. For details of these reforms, see Minxin Pei, 70–77. See also Kenneth Lieberthal, *Governing China: From Revolution through Reform* (New York: W.W. Norton and Co., 1995); and Tong Yanqi, "Political Development in Reforming China"; and Lam Tao-chiu and Cheung Kai-chee, "The Rise and Challenge of Administrative Reform in China: Post-Mao and Beyond," both in *China in the Post-Deng Era*, ed. Joseph Y.S. Cheng (Hong Kong: Chinese University Press, 1998), 81–109; and 137–170.

159. "'Heated Debate' at National People's Congress on Administrative Reform," *Hsin Pao*, 10 March 1998, Reuters "China" News, 13 March 1998; and "Party Urged to Set 'Rule of Law' Example," *South China Morning Post*, 13 March 1998, Reuters "China" News, 13 March 1998. Members of the Chinese People's Political Consultative Conference called for efficient law enforcement, a fair judiciary and improved general awareness of legal rights. They said that without government support there would be no guarantee of success for the rule of law.

160. Lorien Holland, "Zhu Wins a Free Rein to Modernise Bureaucracy," *The Australian*, 18 March 1998, 10.

161. "Top Posts to be Filled in One-Candidate Elections," AFP citing Xinhua News Agency, 10 March 1998, China News Digest, 11 March 1998. On the other hand, two "hotly contested" categories of vice-Premiers and state councillors reportedly had four candidates each. Willy W.-L. Lam, "Cabinet 'Surprise' Still on the Cards," *South China Morning Post* 13 March 1998, Reuters "China" News, 13 March 1998.

162. He said: "[In 1997] the situation of national unity and social stability was further consolidated. Governments at all levels subjected themselves to supervision by the people's congresses at corresponding levels and their standing committees and placed great stress on soliciting opinions concerning their work from democratic parties, people without party affiliations, experts, scholars and the masses of the people. Grassroots democracy was further developed." See Li Peng, "Work Report," 4.

163. These Parties are: the Revolutionary Committee of the Chinese Kuomintang; the Chinese Democratic League; the China Association for Promoting Democracy; the Chinese Peasants and Workers Democratic Party; the China Democratic National Construction Association; the China Zhi Gong Party ; the Jiu San Society; and the Taiwan Democratic Self-Government League. Under the principle of "democratic centralism," they have merely a subordinate, consultative role. See "Demo-

cratic Parties," *Yearbook of the People's Republic of China* (*Zhongguo nianjian*) 1996–97 (Beijing: PRC Yearbook Ltd., 1997), 108–12.

164. "Chinese Premier on Democratic Election."

165. Min Xinpei, "Is China Democratizing?" 69.

166. For details of this process, see Bai Gang, *Cunmin zizhi: Zhongguo nongmin di zhengzhi canyu* ("Villagers' Autonomy: Political Participation of Chinese Peasants") (Beijing: Research Center for Public Policy, Chinese Academy of Social Sciences), Working Paper No. 960201, 12–18.

167. He stated that the goal was to "enable villagers to enjoy more freedom, such as the right to select heads of their villages through election, to supervise the villages' heads and have more say in villages' affairs." See "Democracy Experiment to Defuse Rural Anger," *Sunday Morning Post* (Hong Kong), 8 May 1994. This instrumental purpose is also identified in Daniel Kelliher, "The Chinese Debate over Village Self-Government," *The China Journal* (January 1997), 37:63–86; and it is discussed in Bai Gang, *Villagers' Autonomy.*

168. See Xinhua News Agency, "China's Jiang Chunyun Says Village Committee Law Boosts Party's Link with Masses, 5 November 1998, Reuters China News, 11 November 1998.

Conclusion

1. Cf. Abram and Antonia Handler Chayes, "On Compliance," *International Organization* 47 (Spring 1993) 2: 176.

2. Marc A. Levy, Oran R. Young, and Michael Zurn, "The Study of International Regimes," *European Journal of International Relations* 1 (September 1995), 3: 294, citing Donald Campbell and Julian Stanley, *Experimental and Quasi-Experimental Designs for Research* (Chicago: Rand McNally, 1966).

3. See Samuel S. Kim, "China's Pacific Policy: Reconciling the Irreconcilable," *International Journal* 50 (Summer 1995), 475.

4. See also Ann Kent, "China and the Universal Declaration: Breaker or Shaper of Norms?" in Australian and New Zealand Society of International Law, *Proceedings of the Sixth Annual Conference 1998*, (Canberra: Australian National University, 1998), 15–19.

5. Advice from Philip Alston, 10 November 1997. The U.S. has signed, but not yet ratified, the ICESCR.

6. Jack S. Levy, "Learning and Foreign Policy: Sweeping a Conceptual Minefield," *International Organization* 48 (Spring 1994) 2: 289. See also Introduction.

7. See Sandra L. Gubin, "Between Regimes and Realism — Transnational Agenda Setting: Soviet Compliance with CSCE Human Rights Norms," *Human Rights Quarterly* 17 (May 1995) 2: 289.

8. Charles E. Ziegler, *Foreign Policy and East Asia: Learning and Adaptation in the Gorbachev Era* (Cambridge: Cambridge University Press, 1993), 167.

9. Paul H. Kreisberg, "China's Negotiating Behaviour," in *Chinese Foreign Policy: Theory and Practice*, ed. Thomas W. Robinson and David Shambaugh (Oxford: Clarendon Press, 1994), 477.

10. Philip Tetlock, "Learning in U.S. and Soviet Foreign Policy: In Search of an Elusive Concept," in *Learning in U.S. and Soviet Foreign Policy*, ed. George W. Breslauer and Philip E. Tetlock (Boulder: Westview Press, 1991), 28. See also Introduction.

11. Benjamin I. Schwartz, "The Chinese Perception of World Order, Past and Present," in *The Chinese World Order: Traditional China's Foreign Relations*, ed. John King Fairbank (Cambridge: Harvard University Press, 1968), 288.

12. Robert Gilpin, *War and Change in World Politics* (Cambridge: Cambridge University Press, 1981), 227. See also Chapter 1.

13. At this session, under Agenda Item 10, the no-action motion on the draft resolution (L.90) on China was adopted by 27 votes to 20 with 6 abstentions. In the 1996 Commission vote, for the first time both the Russian Federation and the Philippines abstained.

14. For instance, China succeeded in blocking BBC websites, including Internet sites, and blocked access to BBC's Mandarin-language broadcasts. See Teresa Poole, "Peking Censors BBC's Websites," *The Independent*, 14 October 1998, Reuters China News, 14 October 1998.

15. Hong Kong's Chief Justice, Andrew Li, has indicated his determination to defend the rule of law in Hong Kong against the rule from the north, and to abide by the separation of powers. Insisting that "there is no place in a free society for a supine judiciary," he has asserted that "the judiciary has a vital constitutional role to ensure that the acts of the executive and the legislature comply fully with the law." See Robin Fitzsimons, "Keeper of the Common Law," *The Canberra Times*, 19 January 1998, Reuters "China" News, 19 January 1998. See also Human Rights Watch, "Rights Group Condemns Move to Put Government above the Law," Press release, 7 April 1998. However, the recent death sentence handed down in a PRC court for crimes committed in Hong Kong by triad leader Cheng Tze-keung has raised fears for Hong Kong's legal autonomy.

16. Chayes and Chayes, "On Compliance," 197.

17. See Levy, Young, Zürn, "The Study of International Regimes," 291.

18. Thus, for instance, Wei's alleged involvement with foreign interests formed a large component of the charges against him. See Zhou Cai, "Evidence for Wei Jingsheng's Crime Authentic," *Beijing Review* 39 (15–21 January 1996) 3: 14–16.

19. Maxime Tardu, *The Effectiveness of United Nations Methods and Mechanisms in the Field of Human Rights: A Critical Overview*, UN Doc. A/CONF.157/PC/60/Add.5, 1 April 1993, at 37.

20. It thus meets a number of the criteria of regime effectiveness as set out in Levy, Young, and Zürn, "The Study of International Regimes," 287.

Index